CONTROL *of* MICROSTRUCTURES *and* PROPERTIES *in* STEEL ARC WELDS

Materials Science and Technology

Series Editor
Brian Ralph
Brunel University
Uxbridge, U.K.

Control of Microstructures and Properties in Steel Arc Welds
Lars-Erik Svensson, *The Esab Group, Gothenburg, Sweden*

The Extraction and Refining of Metals
Colin Bodsworth, *Brunel University, Uxbridge, U.K.*

Quantitative Description of the Microstructure of Materials
K. J. Kurzydlowski, *Warsaw University of Technology, Warsaw, Poland*

Grain Boundary Properties and the Evolution of Microstructure and Texture
G. Gottstein, *Institute of Metallurgy and Metal Science, RWTH Aachen, Germany*
L. S. Shvindlerman, *Institute of Solid State Physics, Russian Academy of Sciences, Moscow, Russia*

CONTROL *of* MICROSTRUCTURES *and* PROPERTIES *in* STEEL ARC WELDS

Lars-Erik Svensson

The Esab Group
Esab AB, Gothenburg, Sweden

CRC Press
Taylor & Francis Group
Boca Raton London New York

CRC Press is an imprint of the
Taylor & Francis Group, an **informa** business

CRC Press
Taylor & Francis Group
6000 Broken Sound Parkway NW, Suite 300
Boca Raton, FL 33487-2742

First issued in paperback 2019

ISBN-13: 978-0-367-44963-6 (pbk)
ISBN-13: 978-0-8493-8221-5 (hbk)

Visit the Taylor & Francis Web site at
http://www.taylorandfrancis.com

and the CRC Press Web site at
http://www.crcpress.com

Library of Congress Cataloging-in-Publication Data

Svensson, Lars-Erik.
Control of microstructures and properties in steel arc welds / Lars-Erik Svensson.
p. cm. — (Materials science and technology)
Includes bibliographical references and index.
ISBN 0-8493-8221-1
1. Steel—Welding. 2. Gas and metal arc welding. 3. Microstructure—Mathematical models. 4. Steel—Mechanical properties. I. Title. II. Series: Materials science and technology (Boca Raton, Fla.)
TS227.2.S96 1994
672.5′.212—dc20

94-1203
CIP

Library of Congress Card Number 94-1203

PREFACE

Welding is a fascinating subject, involving knowledge from many disciplines such as physics, chemistry, metallurgy, electronics, and mechanical engineering. However, welding is still in many respects regarded as a craftsmanship, with the welder having a large influence on the final properties of the welded joint. Thus, the possibility of predicting and controlling the properties of a welded joint is limited.

The intention of this book is to show that the properties of a weld in steel can be predicted and controlled through control of the microstructures that appear. There has been a rapid development in this field during the 1980s, mainly through the development of models for the microstructure of steels subjected to welding. These models are quantitative to a certain degree, with calculations carried out on mainframe computers or PCs. However, it must be realized that these models are still far from mature and certainly much more development is needed to say that we can completely control the microstructure and properties of a welded joint.

The book begins with a chapter on the welding processes and the defects that are commonly associated with welds, i.e., what is commonly described as the weldability of steels. The chemistry and processing of the base material is described in Chapter 2, and the microstructural changes that occur under the influence of welding are presented in Chapter 3. In Chapter 4 the microstructure of the fused weld metal is thoroughly reviewed. This complex area is often treated more superficially in other textbooks. In Chapter 5 the relation between the properties and the microstructure of the welded joint is described. The book ends with a chapter in which some specific cases of welding of steels are discussed.

The book is intended to be used by undergraduate and graduate students specializing in welding. It is also aimed at practicing welding engineers, who may find that it improves their understanding of the factors that control the properties of welds, a subject which I believe occupies much of their time today.

Lars-Erik Svensson
Gothenburg
February 1993

LIST OF SYMBOLS

a — a_1, a_2, a_3: constants
edge size of weld metal austenite grains
crack length
a_N: activity of nitrogen

b — $y^2 + z^2$

c — specific heat

d — d_p: plate thickness
d_{pc}: critical plate thickness
d_γ, $d_{\gamma 0}$: austenite grain size
d_1, d_2: primary and secondary arm spacing of dendrites

e — natural logarithm base
e_i: Wagner interaction parameter

f — f_s: volume fraction of solid material

k — partition coefficient

l — carbide thickness

m — constant

n — strain rate exponent
n_1: exponent for austenite grain growth

p — Péclet number
p_{N2}: nitrogen partial pressure

q — heat input rate
q': heat input

r — two-dimensional radial coordinate
r_p: distance between isotherms
r_r: side plate tip radius
r_c: critical side plate tip radius
r: particle radius
r_0: initial particle radius

t — time

u — thickness of allotriomorphic ferrite

v — welding speed

x — coordinate
exponent in Equation 3.12

y — coordinate
exponent in Equation 3.12

z — coordinate
a length in CTOD measurement

A — constant in Equation 3.12
A_5: ductility
A_0: initial cross-section area
A_f: final cross-section area

B — Basicity index
constant in Equation 3.12
specimen thickness (CTOD measurements)

C — carbon concentration
C_1, …: C constants
C_s*: actual concentration
C_0: average concentration
C_1 and C_2: constants in Equation 1.18

D — diffusivity

E — Young's modulus
E_w: carbon equivalent

F — Weibull distribution function

G — G_α: allotriomorphic ferrite growth rate
G_W: side plate growth rate
thermal gradient

H — H_{JIS}: hydrogen content according to JIS
HV: hardness according to Vickers

I — welding current

J_c — critical J-integral value

K — $=YP/BW^{1/2}$
K_{Ic}: fracture toughness
$K_0(\ )$: modified Bessel function of the first kind, zero order
K_0: constant in grain growth

L — L_l: austenite grain size, measured on longitudinal section
L_0: initial gauge length
L_f: final gauge length

M — concentration of metallic elements

P — load
P_{cm}: carbon equivalent according to Ito and Bessey

Q — activation energy

R — three-dimensional radial coordinate
gas constant
solidification rate
R_{eL}, R_{eH}, $R_{p0.2}$: yield strength
R_m: ultimate tensile strength
R_F: amount of restraint

S — constant in Equation 4.7
S_2: Trivedi function

T — temperature
T_0: preheat/interpass temperature
T_p: peak temperature

U — welding voltage
potential energy (J-integral method)

V — V_f: volume fraction
V_v: volume fraction
$V_{v(cal)}$: calculated volume fraction
V_p: clip gauge deflection

W — specimen width

Y — compliance function

α — integration constant
ferrite
shape parameter

α_1 parabolic rate constant
β a ratio
scale parameter
γ austenite
η thermal efficiency
ρ density
τ integration constant
σ σ_y: yield stress
σ_F: fracture stress
δ COD value
δ-ferrite
δ_a: shift parameter
υ Poisson's ratio
λ thermal conductivity
$\Delta t_{8/5}$ cooling time from 800 to 500°C
Ω_0 carbon supersaturation
γ_p plastic work energy
γ surface energy
κ thermal diffusivity
Θ ratio between SiO_2 and MnO

ACKNOWLEDGMENTS

During the writing of the book I have had a lot of help from many people. First of all, I would like to express my deep gratitude to Dr. Harry Bhadeshia, University of Cambridge, U.K. We have been cooperating on the subjects dealt with in this book since 1982, developing the model for calculating the microstructure and properties of weld metals. Without his cooperation, this book would never had been written. During the course of writing, Harry also read numerous drafts of the text and made a lot of sensible comments, improving the quality of the content substantially.

I have also received a lot of very helpful comments from several other people. In particular, I would like to thank Dr. Peter Hart of TWI, Cambridge, U.K.; Dr. Anders Samuelson and Mr. Jan Steninger of Swedish Steel AB in Oxelösund, Sweden (who also kindly provided Figure 2.3); Dr. Tad Siwecki of the Institute of Metals Research in Stockholm, Sweden; Dr. Graham Thewlis of British Steel in Rotherham, U.K.; Drs. Ron Smith and Stan Ferree of Alloy Rods Inc., Hanover, PA; Dr. David Widgery of Esab Group (U.K.), Waltham Cross, U.K.; Messr. Nils Thalberg and Johan Elvander and Dr. Lennart Wittung of Esab Group, Gothenburg, Sweden; and Mr. Klas Weman, Esab Arc Equipment in Laxå Sweden.

I am very grateful to my employer, Esab AB, for their permission to write the book and use so many illustrations and examples from the work carried out in the Esab laboratories. In particular, I would like to mention Dr. Anders Backman, Vice President, Consumables, and Mr. Bertil Pekkari, Technical Director, for their interest and encouragement.

Many illustrations have been produced by the staff in the Esab Group Central Laboratory in Gothenburg. Also, the many hours of discussions during investigations have been an invaluable source of knowledge and inspiration. My sincere thanks are devoted to my colleagues Mr. Bengt Utterberg, Ms. Berit Gretoft, Ms. Susan Pak, Ms. Ann-Charlotte Gustavsson, and Dr. Leif Karlsson.

The book was written during many evenings, weekends, and holidays. In spite of this, I have always felt support and encouragement from my wife, Carina, and our sons, Markus and Niklas, for which I am deeply grateful.

TABLE OF CONTENTS

Chapter 1

ARC WELDING PROCESSES

1.1. GENERAL

The purpose of this chapter is to describe the most common arc welding processes, concentrating mainly on aspects important for metallurgical behavior. Broadly speaking, there are three different groups of arc welding processes:

- Shielded metal arc welding (SMAW), often also called manual metal arc welding (MMA)
- Gas-shielded arc welding, including gas-metal arc welding (GMAW) using both solid and cored wires as well as gas-tungsten arc welding (GTAW)
- Submerged arc welding (SAW)

There are a large number of other welding processes not dealt with in this book. However, for the sake of completeness, these are listed in Table 1.1. Some of these processes may be of very significant industrial interest, such as spot welding for the automotive industry, while others have a very limited use, such as electron beam welding, e.g., for aerospace applications.

The description of the three groups of processes above consists of a brief review of the engineering aspects followed by an explanation of how consumables for the various processes are designed. We begin, however, with a review of the fundamental concepts to set the scene.

1.2. GENERAL CONCEPTS

All arc welding systems have the same general configuration: a *power source,* necessary for generating the *arc* between the *electrode* and the *workpiece.* To protect the molten weld metal from the air, a *shielding system* is used, which can vary in complexity and activity.

An *arc* is created in the gap between the electrode and the workpiece. A *plasma,* consisting of ionized atoms and free electrons, is formed by the arc. The arc is extremely hot, with temperatures around 10,000°C in the core. The electrode is heated by resistance heating from the current passing through it and by the arc. The heat generated is carried in the plasma to the workpiece, causing parts of the workpiece to melt. The forces in the plasma also provide possibilities for melted drops from the electrode to be transported to the workpiece. Welding must be made in many positions, such as horizontal, vertical, or overhead, so the plasma forces can even overcome the force of gravity.

A *weld pool* is thus created, in which molten material from the workpiece is mixed with the liquid drops from the filler material. The degree of mixing

TABLE 1.1
Common Welding Processes

Fusion welding processes	Pressure welding processes
Arc welding	Resistance welding
Shielded metal arc welding	Spot welding
Gas-metal arc welding	Seam welding
Gas-tungsten arc welding	Projection welding
Plasma arc welding	Resistance butt welding
Submerged arc welding	Flash welding
Carbon arc welding	High-frequency resistance welding
Stud welding	Forge Welding
Gas welding	Blacksmith welding
Electro-slag welding	Hammer welding
Electro-gas welding	Roll welding
Electron beam welding	Pressure gas welding
Laser welding	High-frequency pressure welding
Thermit welding	Cold-pressure welding
	Friction welding
	Explosive welding
	Ultrasonic welding
	Precussion welding
	Diffusion welding
	Thermit pressure welding

between the electrode material and the base metal is called *dilution.* The electric current flows through the workpiece to earth and back into the power source, completing the closed circuit. The heat generated is dissipated, both through radiation to the surrounding air and by heat diffusion through the workpiece, the latter being the main heat flow path. This general description does not apply to gas-tungsten arc (GTA) welding because the electrode is made of tungsten or a tungsten alloy and does not reach its melting point and, consequently, does not enter the weld pool. GTA welds can, thus, take two forms:

- Autogenous, in which the weld pool is formed by simply melting a part of the workpiece
- A weld in which filler material is added separately

A more precise description of the nomenclature is as follows (see Figure 1.1). The *electrode* is the current-carrying part of the setup. The material added to the weld pool is called a *consumable* or a *filler metal.* The two workpieces to be joined constitute the *base material.* After the welding is finished, the two base materials are in fact so well bonded by the *weld metal* that they are regarded as one structural unit. In the zone of the base material closest to the

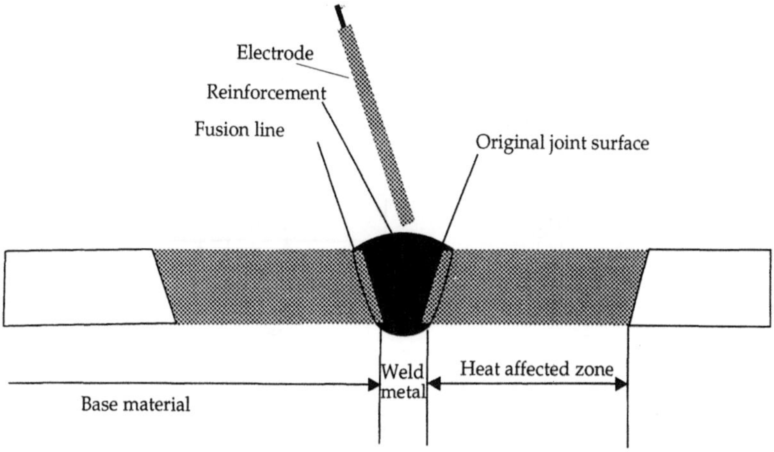

FIGURE 1.1. Definition of the most common terms for the description of welded joints.

weld metal, the heat from the fusion process can cause transformations. This zone is of significant importance from metallurgical, mechanical, and corrosion properties points of view and it is commonly called the *heat-affected zone (HAZ).*

The edge surfaces of the two pieces of material to be joined together are prepared in a manner suitable for welding. Some common types of joint preparations for steels are shown in Figure 1.2. Naturally, there is an almost unlimited number of such preparations and only the principal configurations are shown. The most common welds are *butt welds,* where the plates to be joined are approximately in same plane, and *fillet welds,* where the surfaces of the plates are approximately at right angles to each other. However, fillet welds are usually made without edge preparation, while if plates in T-joints are made with edge-prepared plates, these are also called butt joints (see Figure 1.2).

The voltages used for these types of arc processes are usually fairly low (13 to 40 V, with the lower voltages typical for self-shielded cored wires). The currents can vary greatly, typically from 100 A for a small-diameter stick electrode to approximately 1000 A for a coarse, submerged arc wire. It is actually better to compare *current densities* of different processes because the effect of the size of the electrode is then eliminated.

The product

$$q' = (U \times I) \tag{1.1}$$

where U is the voltage and I the current is defined as the *heat input.* The most common parameter used is the heat input rate, q'/v, where v is the welding speed. As will be seen later, in most equations of heat flow, the quantity q'/v appears. The heat input rate is given in kilojoules per millimeter (kilojoules

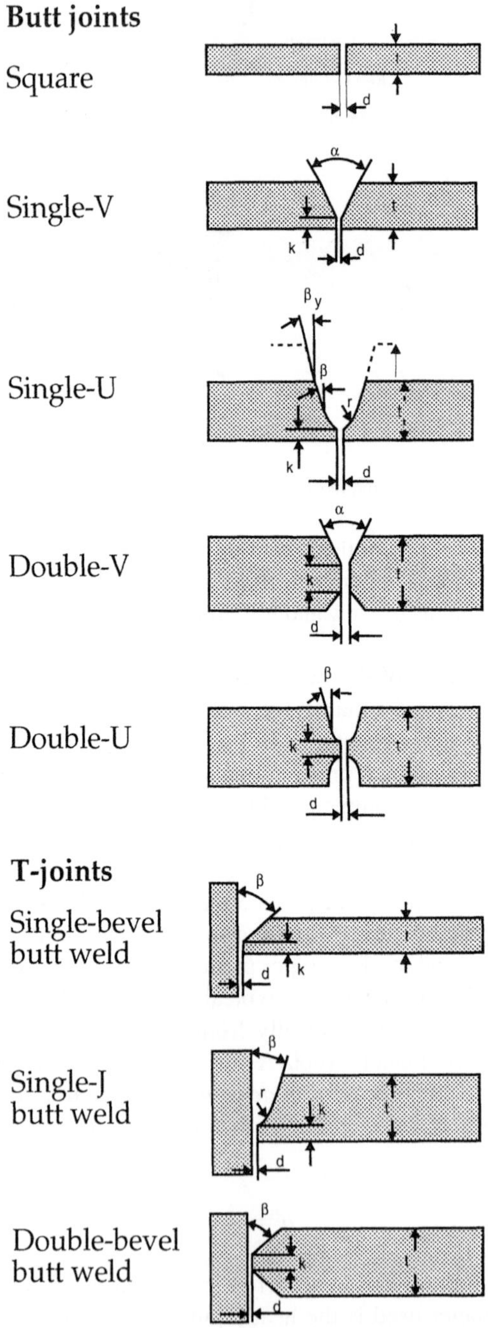

FIGURE 1.2. Common types of joint preparations for steels. (From Lundquist, B., *Sandviken Welding Handbook*, Sandvik Steel AB, Sandviken, Sweden, 1977. With permission.)

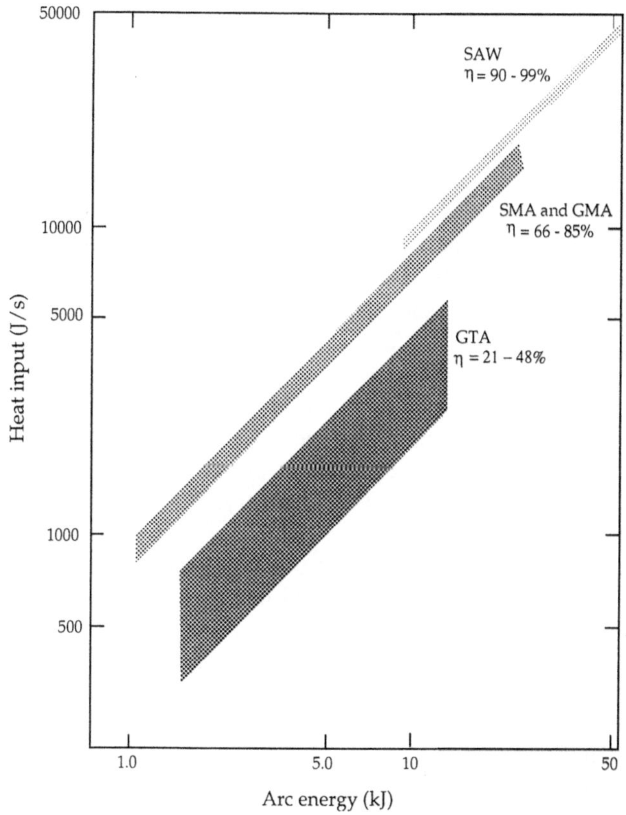

FIGURE 1.3. The arc efficiency of different processes. (From Christensen, N., v de Davies, L., and Gjermundsen, K., *Br. Weld. J.*, 12, 54, 1965. With permission.)

per inch) and typically varies from 1 kJ/mm (25 kJ/in.) up to 8 kJ/mm (150 kJ/in.).

Proper treatment of this concept must also, however, take into account the so-called "thermal efficiency" (η) of each process. This describes the fraction of the energy generated that actually goes into the weld pool. The rest of the energy is lost, for example, in radiation or heating of the shielding gas. During so-called "short-arc welding" (which will be explained further later) hardly any energy is generated during the short-circuiting period of the current. This leads to a reduction of the total heat input by a few percent. The arc efficiency has been investigated in detail by Christensen et al.[1] and their findings have been supported by later investigations. The data are shown in Figure 1.3. The thermal efficiency of the submerged arc method is close to unity over a range of heat inputs, while for GTAW it is much lower (0.2 to 0.5), and for GMAW and SMAW it is in between (0.7 to 0.9). In practice, the thermal efficiency is often assumed to be unity, e.g., when the heat input is calculated. When comparing different processes, it is necessary to include the thermal efficiency.

The corrected expression for the heat input is then given by

$$q' = (\eta) \times (U \times I) \tag{1.2}$$

Preheating the base material prior to welding is sometimes necessary in order to reduce the cooling rate and hence avoid cracking after welding. Preheating is usually carried out by gas burners directed at the workpiece, although electrical heating is also common. The preheat temperatures are in the range 50 to 200°C for structural steels.

After a welding run has been deposited, the bead cools down to a predetermined *interpass* temperature before the next bead is deposited. From a more fundamental viewpoint, the *thermal cycle* of the weld is the most important parameter, because this, together with the chemical composition, controls the microstructure of the weld and by this means the mechanical properties. The thermal cycle is determined by the heat input, plate thickness, preheat/interpass temperature, welding process, and weld geometry. This will be treated in more detail in Section 1.7.

The way the weld is fabricated, i.e., process used, welding conditions (current, voltage, travel speed, preheat and interpass temperatures, polarity), number of runs to fill the joint, and sequence of runs, constitutes the *welding procedure specification (WPS).* The WPS is an extremely important concept because it serves as a specification for the whole joint and is a means of communicating the fabrication process.

As shown in Figure 1.4, the joint can be completed in several ways, e.g., by the use of one *single run* (giving one *single bead*), by *two runs,* or by a *multirun* technique. The particular technique used is dictated by several factors, such as thickness and constitution of base material, demands of productivity, quality of the joint, etc. The way the welds are made also affects the dilution of the weld metal with the base plate. The dilution is expressed as

$$D = \frac{\text{weight of parent material melted}}{\text{total weight of fused metal}} \times 100 \tag{1.3}$$

The choice of welding method is dictated by two factors: demands on productivity and mechanical properties. Of course, there are several boundary conditions such as the availability of process and applicability (not all methods can be used in all situations), but the drive for increased productivity controls much of the development work in this area.

Productivity is commonly measured as the amount of weld metal deposited per unit time. This would give a zero deposition rate for processes such as laser and electron beam welding. A better measure may be the length of joint completed per unit time. High productivity can then be obtained, for example, by choosing a process in which a narrower joint can be used, reducing weld metal volume.

1.3. THE SHIELDED METAL ARC WELDING PROCESS

The shielded metal arc welding (SMAW) method is also commonly called manual metal arc welding (MMA), referring to the fact that in the majority of cases it is carried out by a welder guiding the stick electrode. This method was the first fusion welding method developed and dominated the welding industry for many decades. Its usage has gradually decreased in favor of more productive processes, but it will certainly continue to be a major process due to the quality, flexibility, and versatility that can be achieved.

The principle of the SMAW process is shown in Figure 1.5. The electrode consists of a metallic core and a complex coating. The current passes through the metal rod and the tip of the electrode is heated by resistance heating and the action of the arc. In the original electric arc welding process, welding was carried out with a bare steel rod, which not surprisingly gave poor results. Difficulties occurred with both arc stability and the quality of the weld metal. The invention of the covered electrode in 1904 by the Swedish engineer Oscar Kjellberg led to a major breakthrough in the use of electric arc welding. The coating has several tasks:

- To provide arc stability
- To protect the molten metal from the surrounding air by generation of shielding gas
- To allow addition of alloying elements
- To provide a suitable cover slag
- To increase productivity by the addition of iron powder (increased *efficiency*)

Efficiency of an electrode is defined as the ratio between the weight of the weld metal and the weight of the core wire, expressed in percent. If no iron powder is added to the coating, the efficiency is around 85%. With some iron powder, normal efficiency electrodes have an efficiency of about 120 to 150%. High-efficiency electrodes have an efficiency of about 250%.

Many different kinds of coatings exist, each giving the electrode welding characteristics and mechanical properties typical to the type. The coating types can be divided into acid, cellulosic, rutile, and basic. The essential components in different electrode coatings and the role they play are presented in Table 1.2. There are by no means sharp limits between these different kinds of coatings. Many hybrids exist, such as the rutile-basic electrode. However, the most popular coatings are predominantly rutile or basic in character and these will be described in more detail later. Before discussing these types, a few words about the other types may be appropriate.

The acidic coatings, having high contents of MnO and SiO_2, have almost become completely redundant, replaced mainly by rutile types, as the latter have better operating characteristics for positional welding.

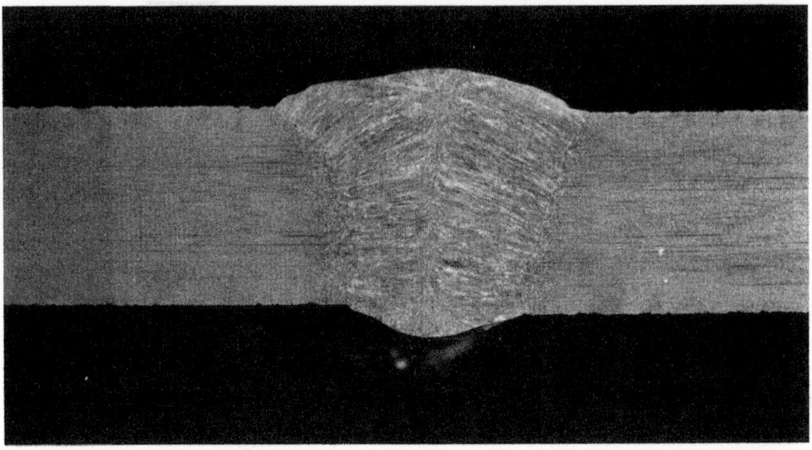

a

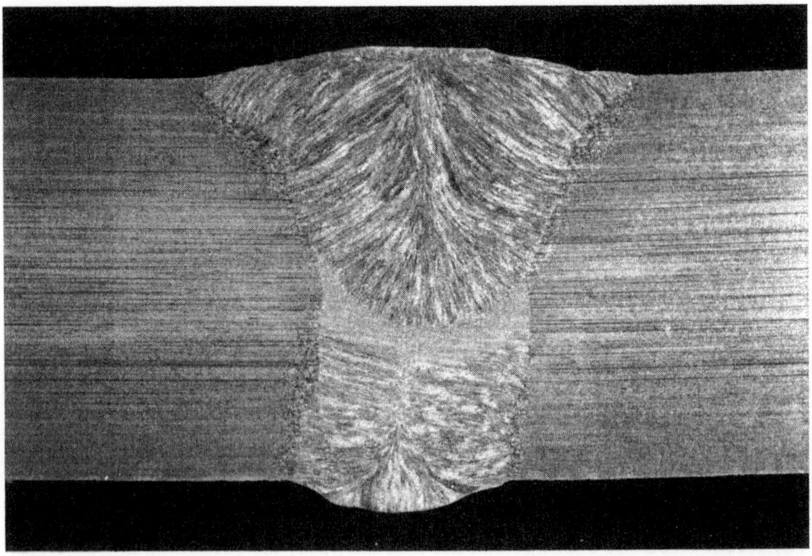

b

FIGURE 1.4. The joint can be completed in several ways: (a) as one single run (giving one single bead) (plate thickness 10 mm), (b) by two runs from one side (plate thickness 20 mm), (c) by two runs, one from each side (plate thickness 20 mm), or (d) by a multirun technique (plate thickness 50 mm).

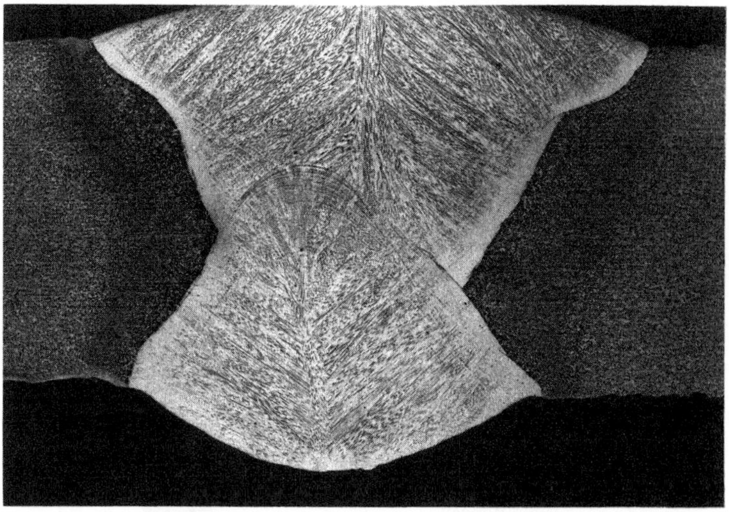

FIGURE 1.4.c

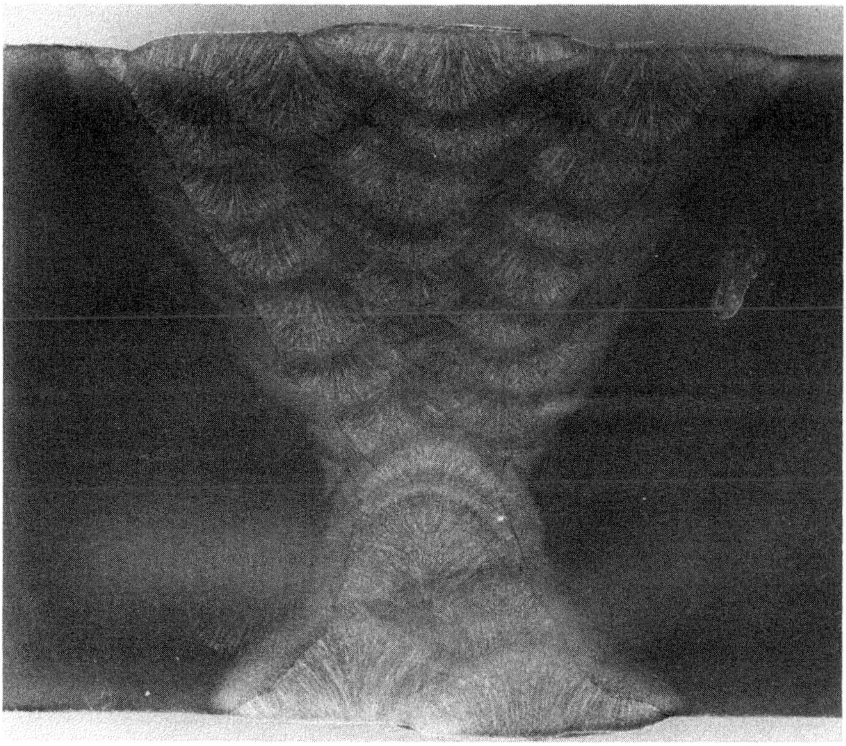

FIGURE 1.4.d

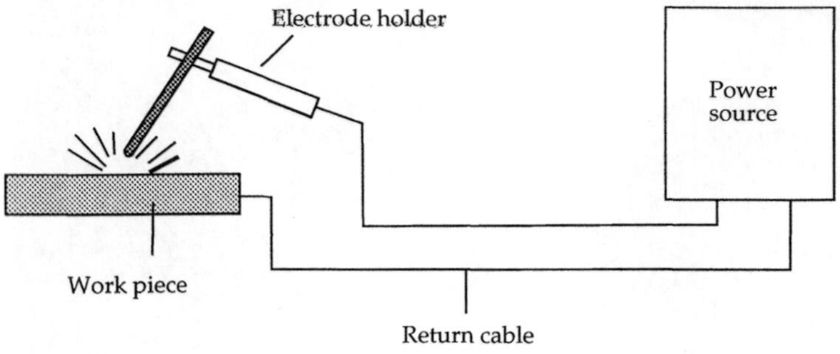

a

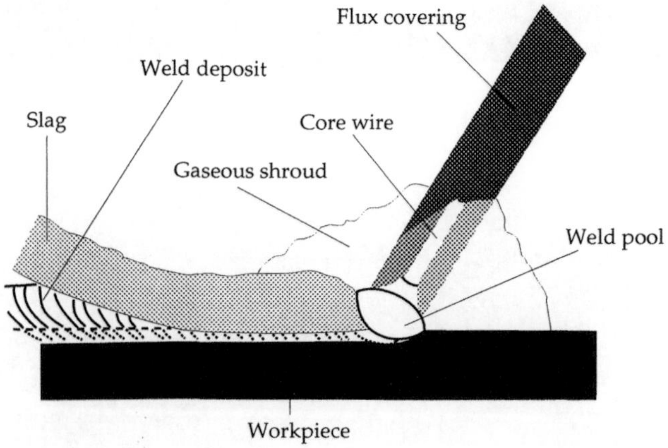

b

FIGURE 1.5. (a) The principle of the SMAW process. (b) The components of a covered electrode and the associated weld. (From Houldcroft, P. and John, R., *Welding and Cutting*, Woodhead-Faulkner, Cambridge, U.K., 1988. With permission.)

Some normal efficiency acid electrodes are still on the market, used because they give a smooth weld in the flat position, with a weld metal of adequate toughness, normally acceptable at –20°C (–4°F). However, the acid electrodes are used mostly as high-efficiency electrodes, because high welding speeds can be achieved.

Another type of coating is one that is rich in cellulose. The cellulose develops an atmosphere of hydrogen, resulting in a fierce arc, which gives deeper penetration. The electrodes have very good operating characteristics, especially when welding downward, due to a fast-freezing slag. Thus, the welding can be carried out very rapidly and efficiently. The drawbacks of these

TABLE 1.2A
Typical Composition of the Coating of Covered Electrodes

Basic	Cellulosic
Ca carbonate, 20–50%	Rutile, 20–60%
Fluorspar, 20–40%	Cellulose, 10–20%
Rutile, 0–10%	Quartz, 15–30%
Quartz, 0–5%	Carbonates, 0–15%
Ferroalloys 5–10%	Ferromanganese, 5–10%
Rutile	Acid
Rutile, 40–60%	Manganese oxide
Quartz, 15–20%	Quartz
Carbonates, 0–15%	Carbonates
Ferromanganese, 10–14%	
Organic compounds, 0–5%	

TABLE 1.2B
Role of Different Compounds in Consumables

Weld metal alloying elements	Gas-shield-forming elements
Iron powder	Limestone
Ferrosilicon	Magnesite
Ferromanganese	Dolomite
Ferroalloys	Cellulose
Slag-forming elements	Extrusion aids
Rutile	Glue, CMC, algenates
Zirconium dioxide	Potassium silicates
Quartz	Sodium silicates
Feldspar	
Caolin	
Fluorspar	

types of electrodes are that the fume emission and the hydrogen content are high. The high fume emission generally presents no problem because the electrodes are used outdoors. The high moisture content (3 to 6%), which results in the high hydrogen content, is however essential for the running characteristics of the electrode. They are used mainly during field circumferential welding of pipelines. For thin-walled, low-strength steel pipes, the resulting high hydrogen is not enough to cause cracking, and for higher strength steels, a special welding technique is used to avoid cracking. This technique involves deposition of subsequent beads before the previous bead has cooled down to a temperature where there is a risk of cracking. The root bead is especially sensitive in this respect.

The rutile type of coating consists of approximately 50% rutile (TiO_2), a natural mineral which has the desirable property of being a semiconductor, in contrast to most other minerals, which are very poor conductors. The relatively good electrical properties give rutile-coated electrodes very nice operating characteristics, with an even detachment of a spray of drops and a "soft" feeling with very low spatter. The remaining 50% of the coating consists of organic matter (such as wood flour) and $CaCO_3$ (calcium carbonate) to generate a gas shield, metal oxides (to improve arc stability), and alloying elements such as FeSi and FeMn (also used as deoxidizing elements). The production of electrodes demands that sodium and potassium silicates are used as binders and extrusion aids. These will of course also be present in the final electrode. The $CaCO_3$ dissociates to CaO + CO_2. However, CaO is not found in the slag. Instead, CaF_2 or CaSi are found and the oxygen then reacts with metallic elements such as manganese, silicon, aluminum, etc. Calcium can also react with sulfur, removing it from the melt. However, the most essential function of the carbonate is the generation of the CO_2 gas, which, together with the gas generated from the organic material, provides a protective atmosphere around the arc. The gas volume generated by rutile coatings is comparatively small. The weld metals from rutile-coated electrodes thus usually contain relatively large amounts of oxygen.

The other main group of coating is the basic type. This type has in general less than 10% TiO_2, about 50% $CaCO_3$, and the remainder is usually in the form of minerals which are classified as basic. By this composition good gas protection is developed around the arc. The main reason for the high quality of the weld metal is that the cover slag is of a metallurgically basic type, giving good deoxidation and cleaning of the melt. The running characteristics of the electrode during welding are, however, not as good as for rutile-coated electrodes and higher demands on the skill of the welder are required. One particular thing that happens to an electrode is the "cavity" that develops at the electrode tip during welding. The cavity arises as drop formation leaves a part of the coating sticking out in front of the electrode core. If the welding is interrupted and then started again, restriking the arc must be made on the coating. Restriking a basic electrode is more difficult than with a rutile electrode due to different semiconducting properties.

Another important function of the coating is the formation of the cover slag. The cover slag protects the hot metal from the surrounding atmosphere when the electrode with its gas shield has moved away. It supports the hot weld metal, for example, in positional welding, and helps to shape the weld metal surface in order to obtain a nice appearance with a smooth transition to the base metal. Finally, when the weld has cooled down, the slag should be easy to remove from the weld metal. The physical requirements this puts on the slag can be expressed as solidification temperature range, viscosity, and thermal expansion coefficient. These properties should then be combined with the chemical characteristics of the slag, which determine how effective the slag is in removing elements such as oxygen, sulfur, and phosphorus from the weld metal. The chemical characteristic is usually divided as acid or basic. An acid coating gives higher contents of impurity elements left in the melt, while basic coatings can clean the weld metal considerably.

There is also a difference between the coating types when it comes to mechanical properties. The impact toughness is especially dependent upon the oxygen content of the weld metal. Rutile types (having more acid-type coatings) having higher oxygen contents (600 to 1000 ppm by weight) generally give lower impact toughness. They are usually tested at 0°C (32°F). As a consequence of the high oxygen content, rutile-type electrodes have quite a low manganese content (around 0.5 wt%), because this gives a lower strain hardening and thus provides a better possibility for "accepting" a high impurity content. With variants that are slightly more basic (i.e., rutile-basic), acceptable impact toughness at –20°C (–4°F) can be achieved. Basic electrodes (oxygen content around 300 to 400 ppm) usually have good impact toughness at least down to –40°C (–40°F) and sometimes to even lower temperatures. In these types higher manganese contents can be used.

The hydrogen content in weld metals from rutile electrodes is usually quite high, on the order of 20 to 30 ml/100 g weld metal. The high hydrogen content limits the use of these electrodes to steels with low yield strength. The hydrogen content in weld metals from basic electrodes is much lower, around 5 ml/100 g weld metal. Rapid development of low-hydrogen basic electrodes has taken place during the last few years and it is now possible to have as low as 3 ml hydrogen per 100 g weld metal in special types. These electrodes are usually packed in special, diffusion-tight boxes so that the moisture content can be kept low for a very long time.

The hydrogen in the weld metal is mainly due to the moisture of the coating. This has two sources. The first one is crystalline water found in some minerals and the second comes when silicates and other extrusion aids are added. The coating is extruded onto the core wire and the coating paste must therefore possess good rheological properties. The moisture can be removed by drying at elevated temperatures. However, the maximum temperature admissible is different for different types of coatings. Rutile coatings must be dried at relatively low temperatures (around 100 to 150°C, 220 to 300°F). Drying at higher temperatures destroys the organic compounds in the coating, leading to reduced protection of the molten metal. Basic coatings can be dried at considerably higher temperatures (400 to 450°C, 750 to 835°F), leading to less moisture (0.15 to 0.30%, measured at 1000°C, 1800°F) in the basic coatings. The moisture content can be affected further by choosing minerals that are nonhygroscopic and by optimizing the binder silicate mixture (see Figure 1.6). By very careful optimization of the coating formulation and baking procedure, extremely low moisture contents have been achieved, which in turn produce very low hydrogen concentrations in the weld metal mentioned above.

A widely used way of classifying electrodes is the AWS (American Welding Society) system. This gives a simple but imprecise classification. It is built

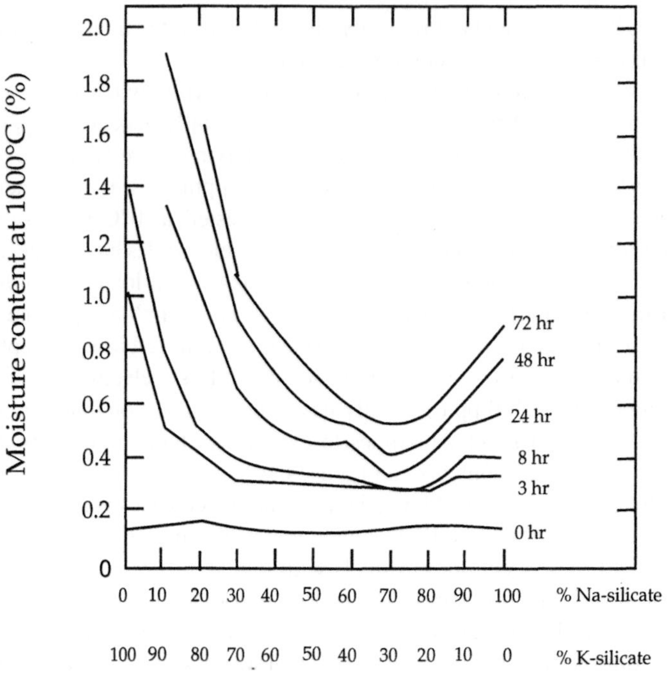

FIGURE 1.6. The effect of different ratios of sodium and potassium silicates on the moisture pickup properties of covered basic electrodes. The curves show the moisture pickup at different exposure times at a climate of 32°C (90°F) and 70% relative humidity. The baking temperature in this case was 450°C (835°F). (From Almquist, G., Budgifvars, S., Lindström, L., Magnusson, B., and Wittung, L., *Proc. 2nd Int. Conf. on Offshore Welded Structures,* The Welding Institute, London, 1982, Paper 41. With permission.)

up by four numbers with an "E" in front to indicate that it is an electrode classification. The first two numbers indicate the tensile strength in 1000 psi (approximately 6.9 times the first two digits gives the tensile strength in MPa). The third number is used to identify the recommended welding position and the fourth digit gives the coating type. Table 1.3 shows some of the more commonly used numbers. Examples of well-known designations according to this system would be E6013 and E7018.

The denomination of electrode sizes is governed by the diameter of the core wire. For mild steel, the common electrode dimensions range from 1.6 to 6.0 mm (1/16 to 1/4 in.). The size of the coating can vary considerably, depending on the specific use of the electrode. To describe the thickness of the coating, a coating factor, defined as the outer diameter of the electrode divided by the diameter of the core wire, is sometimes given.

The SMAW method is difficult to mechanize. With gravity welding, it is however possible to obtain a kind of mechanization for fillet welding. In gravity welding, special 700-mm-long rutile-coated electrodes are used. They

TABLE 1.3
Meaning of the Numbers in Positions 3 and 4 in the AWS Denomination System

Position 3		Position 4	
"1"	All-positional welding	"3"	Rutile type
"2"	Down-hand welding	"4"	Rutile type with addition of iron powder
"4"	Suitable for vertical-down welding	"6"	Basic type
		"8"	Basic type with addition of iron powder

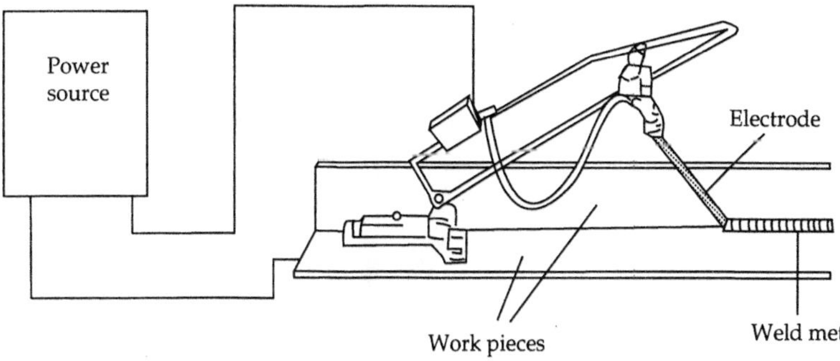

FIGURE 1.7. The principal layout of the gravity welding process.

are attached to holders, which can be moved along the joint. The tip of the electrode touches the welding area and an arc is established. The electrode is gradually moved toward the weld as it melts. The process is shown in Figure 1.7. With this, one welder can handle several welds simultaneously, increasing productivity.

1.4. GAS-SHIELDED ARC WELDING

Looking at the trends in market development of welding methods, gas-shielded arc welding is the most widely used welding method in all developed countries. If only C-Mn types of steels are considered, GMAW using solid wires accounts for more than 50% of the amount of weld metal deposited in Europe. Welding with tubular wire (either metal cored or flux cored) is on a much lower level, but is rapidly increasing in Europe. In the U.S. and Japan, the use of cored wires is much more frequent than in Europe and accounts for about 15% of the amount of consumables sold in these countries. GTAW is used on a much lower level. The main use of this method is found in welding of other alloys, for example, stainless steels, copper alloys, or aluminum. For C-Mn steel applications GTAW is used for root passes of pipes or for welding of very thin material.

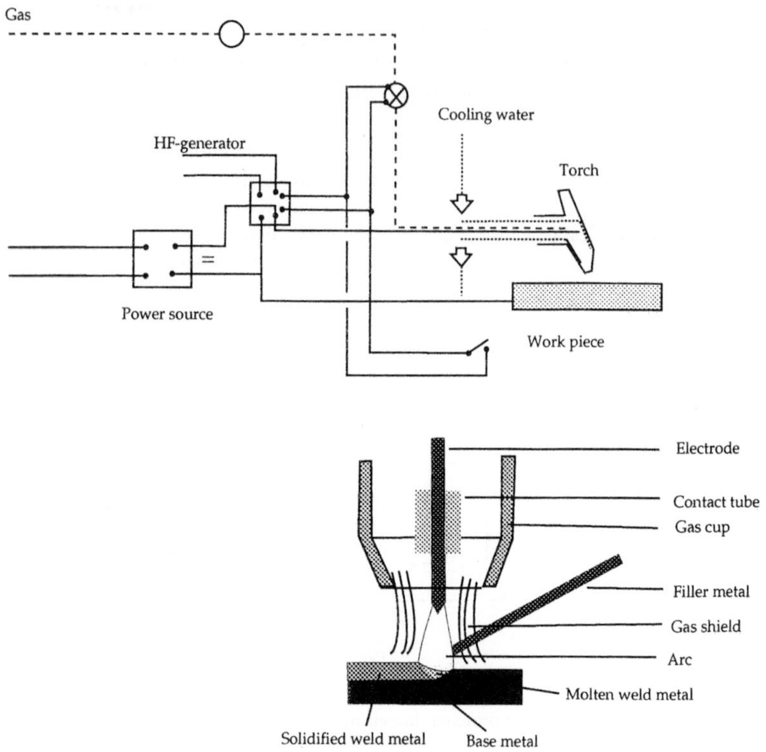

FIGURE 1.8. The GTAW process, showing both the engineering design and a closeup of the arc area. (From Lundquist, B., *Sandviken Welding Handbook,* Sandvik Steel AB, Sandviken, Sweden, 1977. With permission.)

1.4.1. GAS-TUNGSTEN ARC WELDING

This method was invented during the 1930s. The nonmelting electrode, made from tungsten or tungsten-thorium alloy, usually has a negative polarity versus the workpiece when welding steels. A gas shield from an inert gas protects the arc and the weld pool. Figure 1.8 shows the principal layout. The arc is usually initiated by applying a high-frequency field in the gap between the electrode and the workpiece. In robot applications this may be unsuitable and the arc can instead be initiated by a slight touch to the weld metal. This may lead to tungsten inclusions in the weld metal. The arc melts the base material, so that a fused zone is established. This requires a relatively close fit of the two parts to be joined. Autogenous welds involving no filler material are often made. A more conventional joint preparation is possible if a filler rod is used.

GTAW has a low thermal efficiency (0.2 to 0.5), consistent with high losses of energy by thermal radiation from the electrode tip. The main factor

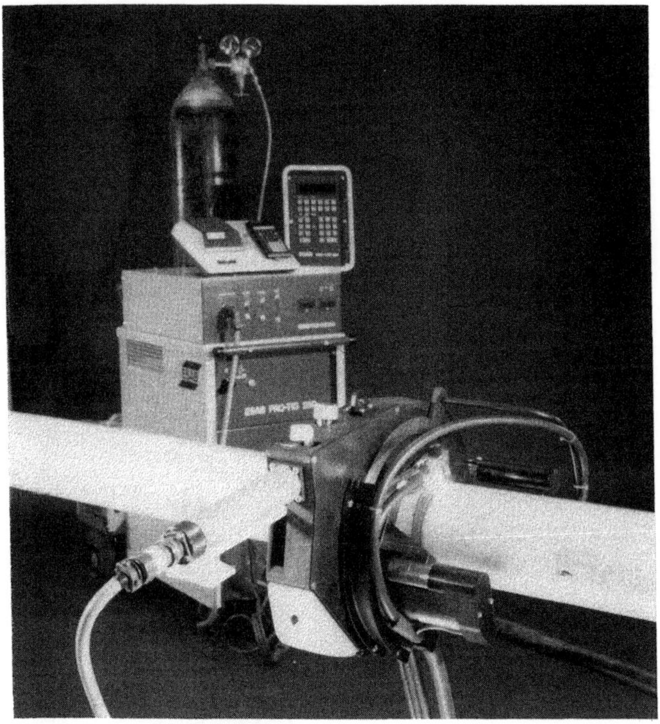

FIGURE 1.9. Mechanized circumferential welding of tubes using GTAW.

contributing to the low thermal efficiency is however that there is no transfer of melted drops from the electrode to the weld pool. If it is roughly assumed that in GMAW 50% of the energy developed is used for melting the base material and the other 50% for melting the tip of the electrode, then it is easily seen why GTAW has such a low thermal efficiency. The heat generated at the electrode tip in GTAW must be cooled to avoid overheating the tungsten electrode.

This method is often called TIG (tungsten-inert gas). The shielding gases used are mainly argon or helium. With the use of inert gases, the weld metal becomes very clean and of high quality. The method is usually applied manually, but is capable of easily lending itself for mechanization. One typical application in the mechanized form is tube welding (Figure 1.9).

Consumables for the GTA process generally have a composition that matches the base material to be welded, although with some additional deoxidants (mainly silicon) to take care of oxygen from surface oxides or from air entrapment. Often, wires intended for GMAW can be used. For unusual alloys, where no standard wires are accessible, small strips from the base material can be used as filler material.

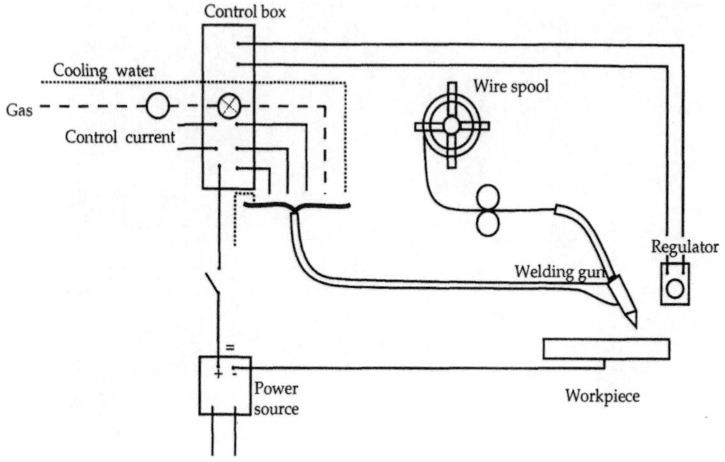

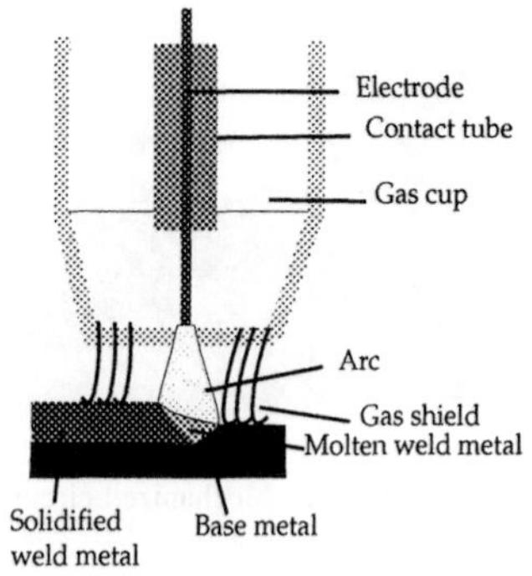

FIGURE 1.10. The GMAW process. This differs from the GTAW shown in Figure 1.8 in that a consumable electrode is used. (From Lundquist, B., *Sandviken Welding Handbook,* Sandvik Steel AB, Sandviken, Sweden, 1977. With permission.)

1.4.2. GAS-METAL ARC WELDING

This method was first presented in 1948, using argon as the shielding gas. However, because argon is an expensive gas, extensive exploration was delayed until four years later, when it was shown that the much less expensive CO_2 gas could also be used for shielding. Figure 1.10 shows the different pieces of equipment. GMAW has now developed into a well-established technique. It is used for a broad range of applications, from very simple joining of objects, where very low demands are put on the welded joint, to joining of medium-thickness plates and even to some extent for welding of plates of heavier gauge. The process has the drawback that lack of fusion occurs more easily than with other techniques due to the lower heat inputs used.

GMAW is usually semi-automatic, with the welder manually steering the welding gun, while the wire is fed automatically. With the increasing usage of welding robots, fully automatic GMAW is employed. The introduction of very

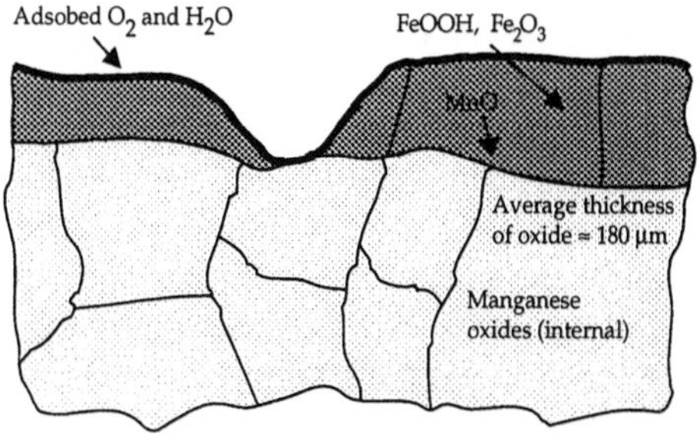

FIGURE 1.11. The oxide layers on a steel wire surface. Ferrous oxides and hydroxides form as the outermost layer, while manganese oxides form below. These oxides can disturb the current transfer during welding and can also cause flaking of copper layers. (From Blickwede, D. J., *Metal Prog.*, 77, 1969. With permission).

large drums with wires, containing about 200 kg, has improved the use of welding robots with GMAW.

The wires are alloyed so as to approximately match the base materials. However, they must possess some additional requirements. They must be able to travel through the feeding unit smoothly, they must give good contact in the contact tips, and they must provide good deoxidation and weld pool behavior.

The wires are produced by drawing or by a combination of rolling and drawing of hot rolled wires, often starting from a diameter of about 6 mm (1/4 in.). The drawing operation leads to an increased hardness and stiffness of the wire. An annealing operation to reduce the wire hardness is sometimes necessary, especially when fine-diameter wires are required.

An essential factor for good contact properties is the surface condition of the wire. Some wires are delivered in "bare" condition, i.e., as drawn and, possibly, heat treated. There always exists an oxide layer on the steel surface, usually built up by layers of different oxides (Figure 1.11). Because the oxides are insulating, they lead to a high resistance against current transfer from the contact nozzle to the wire. This problem can be counteracted by deposition of some suitable element on the pickled wire surface. The most common element is copper, deposited in a thickness of approximately 0.5 μm. For some wires, very thin copper films have been deposited (about 0.1 μm), but this still leads to a disturbance of the current transfer properties. Other elements that have been used are tin, nickel, and phosphorus. Measurements of surface resistance characteristics have shown that the steepest characteristic is obtained with copper coating, indicating that this provides the least resistance to current transfer. However, these measurements were made in a very low current and voltage range, much lower than the values used for actual welding. It can of course be questioned whether these measurements can be regarded as representative of a real welding situation. In the current/voltage range used for welding, it is difficult to make similar measurements. Instead, disturbances in the current transfer are noted as irregular arc behavior and bad drop transfer, which are difficult to quantify.

Finally, the design of the alloy used in the manufacturing of the wire should provide adequate deoxidation and give suitable viscous properties of the melt, so that the welder can easily control the weld pool. The most important elements in this respect are silicon and manganese. Silicon both strongly deoxidizes the melt and favorably affects the fluidity of the melt. Manganese mainly contributes to the deoxidation. Excessive spatter may occur with too high a level of oxygen present in the wire. Oxygen is tied up in slag particles, often appearing as a band of slag particles in the center of the wire. When these particles are rapidly heated during drop formation, the particles decompose and give off the gas, which make the droplet "explode" (see Figure 1.12 from a high-speed recording sequence).

The shielding gases used for arc welding of steels are pure argon, mixtures of argon and CO_2, mixtures of argon and oxygen, and pure CO_2. The role of the gases is both to protect the drops, the weld pool, and the HAZ from the surrounding air and to improve the arc behavior. The choice of gas also can affect the penetration of the arc.

Because no flux is involved in the process, the only possible source of hydrogen is the wire. If good cleanliness is maintained, with as little feeding agents as possible on the wire surface, very low hydrogen values (about 1 to 2 ml/100 g weld metal) can in principle be achieved.

To describe the influence of the gas on the loss of elements and on oxygen content of the weld metal, the concept "oxygen potential" (OP) of a gas is used. The oxygen potential of CO_2 has been found to obey the following relation:

$$\mathrm{OP} = K\left(\mathrm{CO_2}\right)^n \tag{1.4}$$

where K is a constant. It has been shown that n is often close to 0.5. When comparing several different gases, being mixtures of argon with both O_2 and CO_2, a relatively good fit was found between alloy element losses (Figure 1.13) and weld metal oxygen content (Figure 1.14) with the oxygen potential parameter

$$\mathrm{OP} = \mathrm{O_2} + K\sqrt{\mathrm{CO_2}} \tag{1.5}$$

1.4.3. GAS-METAL ARC WELDING WITH CORED WIRES

Cored wires are made from a metallic tube, filled with metal or flux powder (Figure 1.15). The metal tube is usually made from a mild steel strip and alloying is facilitated through the use of powder mixtures. This is a convenient way to change the composition of GMAW metals. The alternative would be to change composition through the solid wire, which is likely to be much more expensive. The cored wires may have an advantage over solid wires when it

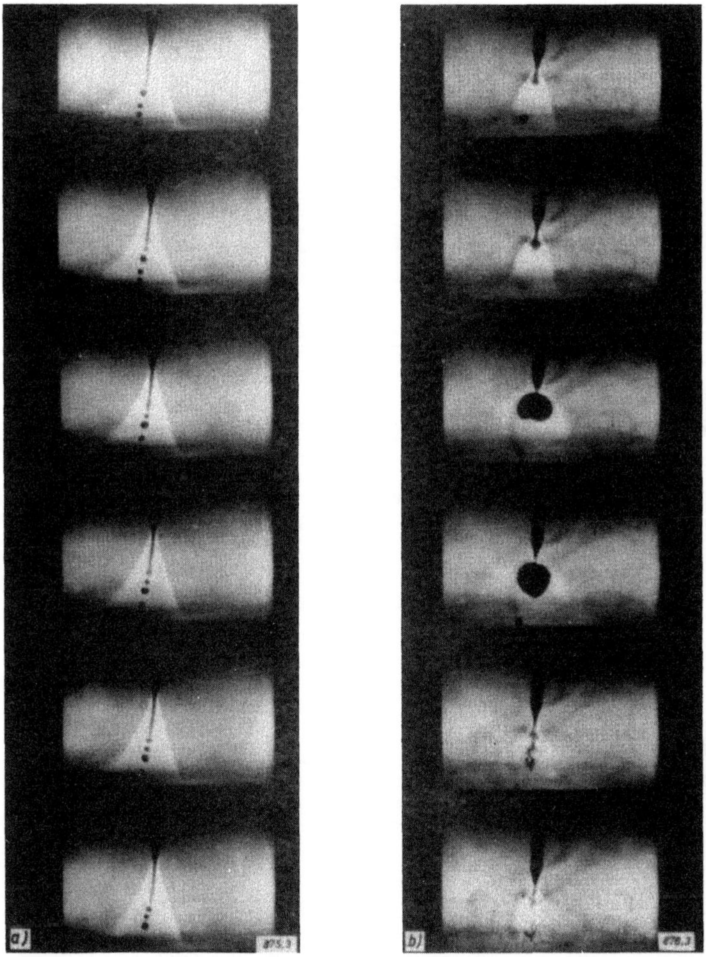

FIGURE 1.12. High-speed recording of the welding sequence in GMAW, showing a spray of drops (left) and exploding drops (right). The drops explode from internal gas generation due to the decomposition of oxide inclusions in the wire. (From Hutt, G. A. and Lucas, W., Res. Rep. 173, The Welding Institute, London, 1982. With permission.)

comes to productivity, penetration, and weld metal quality. Sometimes spatter may also be less when flux-cored wires are used, but it is mainly a function of shielding gas and the particle transfer mode.

The better productivity achieved with cored wires, when compared to solid wires, is intimately connected to the design of the consumable. The current density is naturally much higher in a cored wire than in a solid wire, because the current is conducted through a much smaller cross-sectional area. It is also possible to have a longer distance between the contact nozzle and the plate (a

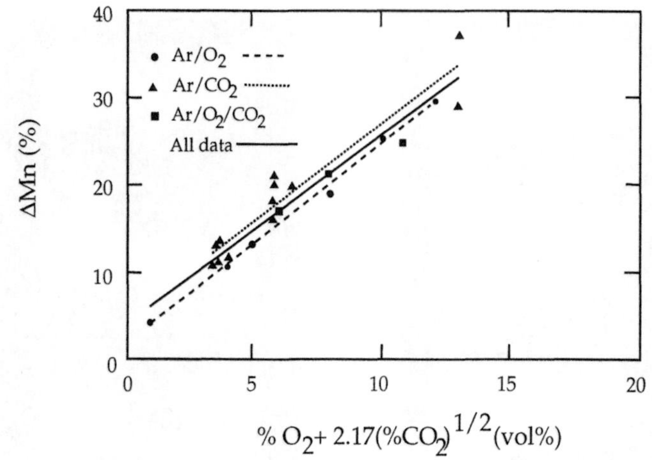

FIGURE 1.13. Manganese loss as a function of the oxygen potential parameter. (From Runnerstam, O., Rep. GW-88044, Aga AB, Lidingö, Sweden, 1988. With permission.)

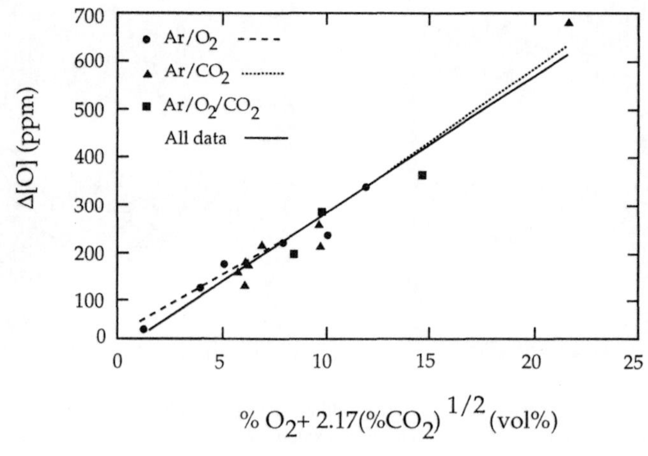

FIGURE 1.14. Weld metal oxygen content as a function of the oxygen potential parameter. (From Runnerstam, O., Rep. GW-88044, Aga AB, Lidingö, Sweden, 1988. With permission.)

longer *stick-out*). This increases the Joule heating of the wire. With some wires a slag is deposited, which helps to control the weld pool and allows higher currents to be used. All these factors contribute to higher melting rates and thus higher productivity. The deposition rate for two cored wires is shown in Figure 1.16 and is compared to welding with solid wires and SMAW electrodes.

The penetration of the arc is better with a cored wire than a solid wire due to the higher currents used. A contributing factor to this is that the shape of the

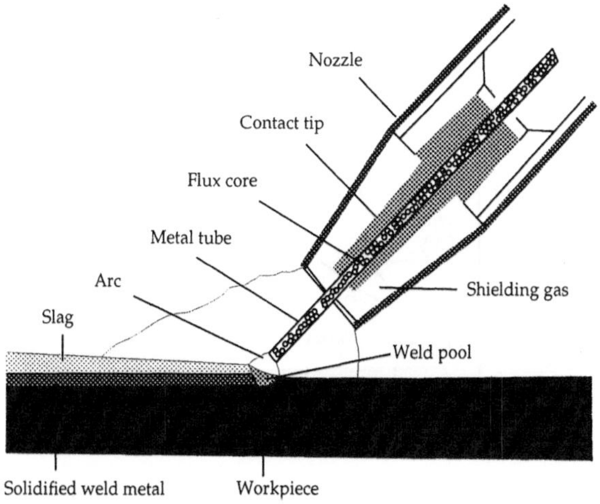

a

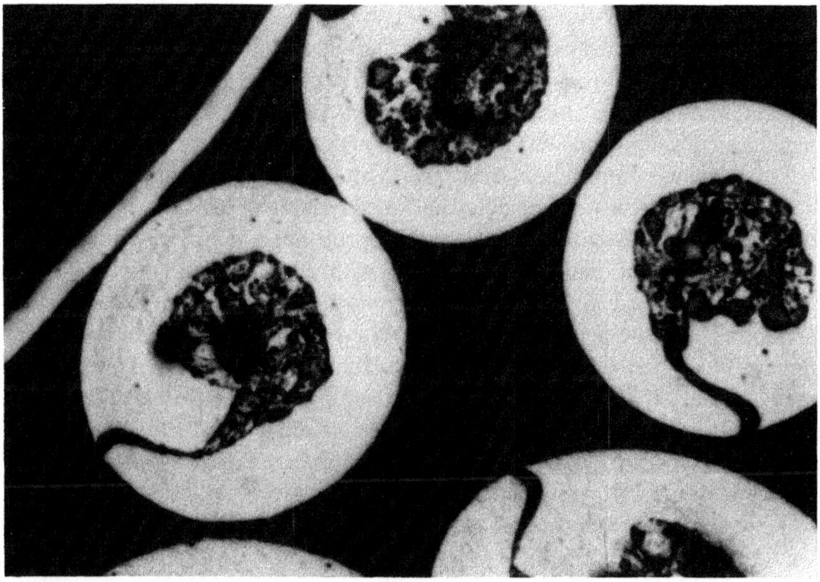

b

FIGURE 1.15. (a) The GMAW process, using cored wire. The principle are very similar to solid wire GMAW. (From Houldcroft, P. and John, R., *Welding and Cutting,* Woodhead-Faulkner, Cambridge, U.K., 1988. With permission.) (b) Cross-sections of a cored wire in which the metal tube and the mineral filling can be identified. The heavy reduction in diameter of the wire during drawing makes the grains of the filling stick together. They also stick to the metal tube side.

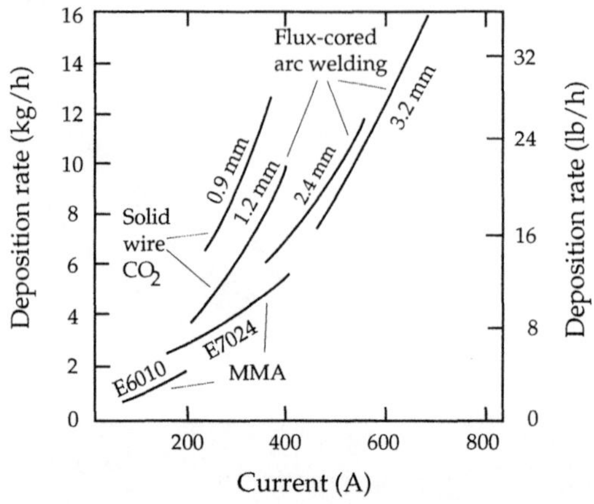

FIGURE 1.16. The deposition rate as a function of welding current for GMAW with both solid and cored wires. The wires are not directly comparable because the diameters are different. For comparison, the deposition rates for two different covered electrodes are also shown. (From Houldcroft P. and John, R., *Welding and Cutting,* Woodhead-Faulkner, Cambridge, U.K., 1988. With permission.)

arc is more widespread with cored wires, giving better side wall fusion. The wires are manufactured by forming a band into a tube, filled with a powder mix, and drawing the tube to the correct size. After the drawing operation, the band has reduced in thickness and at the same time the diameter of the wire has decreased, due to compaction of the powder inside the tube. The particles in the compacted powder stick together and to the sides of the tube rather well, preventing the powder mixture from falling out of the tube. The filling in the core can either be mainly iron powder, with alloying elements and some deoxidants, giving a *metal cored wire,* or minerals similar to those used for the coating of covered electrodes, giving a *flux-cored wire.* There are two main types of flux-cored wires: rutile and basic. They behave much the same as their equivalent covered electrodes. One important difference is that no silicates are needed for binding the grains together in the cored wires. Thus, the moisture content is much less and cored wires usually give very low hydrogen. However, some minerals are hygroscopic. Hydrogen levels less than 5 ml/100 g weld metal can thus be expected for basic cored wires and less than 10 ml/100 g weld metal for rutile types.

Self-shielded wires can be welded without any gas shield. They are either of rutile type (for high-speed welding of thin plates) or of a type similar to basic (for heavy plate thickness welding). They contain extra deoxidants (often aluminum), denitriding elements, and gas-forming compounds. The wires are used during field fabrication, where drafts may destroy the conventional gas shield. Self-shielded wires generate much more fume than gas-shielded wires and are therefore not often used indoors. Despite the unusual weld metal composition that is achieved with these wires (aluminum contents around 1 wt% and about 400 ppm nitrogen), acceptable impact toughness values at –40°C (–40°F) have been reported.

1.5. SUBMERGED ARC WELDING

This process was developed during the 1930s and was a natural consequence of the combination of a better understanding of the manual metal arc process and the wish to increase the productivity and automation of the welding process. Essentially, the coating and the core wire of a covered electrode were separated and fed to the place of welding by two different feeding systems.

The avoidance of manual handling means that much higher currents can safely pass through the wire, giving higher melting rates. By using a continuous wire (either solid or cored), the process can easily be automated. The drawback of the method is that it can only be used in the flat and horizontal position.

The method is in principle very similar to GMAW, i.e., the wire in the form of a coil is fed through an appropriate unit toward the workpiece. Current is transferred in a contact nozzle, and to provide good current transfer the wire is usually copper coated. The flux is fed separately, as shown in Figure 1.17. The wire is submerged in a bed of flux and the arc is ignited between the wire and the workpiece. The arc is not visible and very little fume is generated during welding, making the method attractive from an environmental point of view. The arc operates in a "cavity" inside the flux bed, arising due to the arc melting the flux and the wire. The drops are transferred via a flux wall-guided mechanism. The molten flux covers the weld metal and protects it from the air during solidification.

The process has found many applications, both for relatively thin and for thick plates. A typical application for thin materials is in the spiral welding of tubes, where very high welding speeds can be attained, or for welding of gas bottles. For thin materials, smaller wires naturally are used. The size of the wires used for SAW normally ranges from 2.0 mm (5/65 in.) diameter up to 6.0 mm (1/4 in.) diameter, the most popular being between 2.4 mm (3/32 in.) and 4.0 mm (5/32 in.). For thick materials, the advantages of SAW in terms of productivity are more obvious. Typical applications here are in shipbuilding, pressure vessels, and in offshore constructions.

The productivity of the SAW method can be increased in several ways. The parallel wire method uses two wires, fed through the same contact nozzle and connected to the same power source. The wires are small in diameter (usually 2.0 or 2.4 mm, 5/65 or 3/32 in.), but due to the higher current density achieved in each wire, the total melting rate is higher than if a single wire was used. Tandem welding, where two wires are placed one after another and each wire

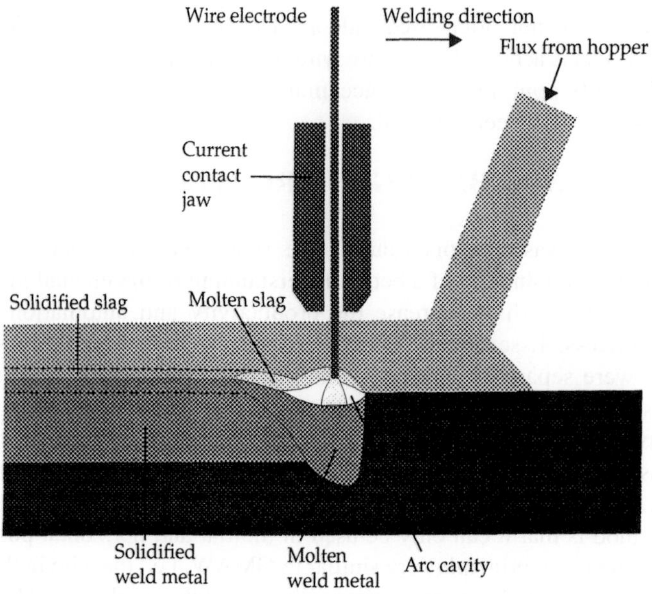

FIGURE 1.17. The principles of the SAW process. (From Houldcroft, P. and John, R., *Welding and Cutting,* Woodhead-Faulkner, Cambridge, U.K., 1988. With permission.)

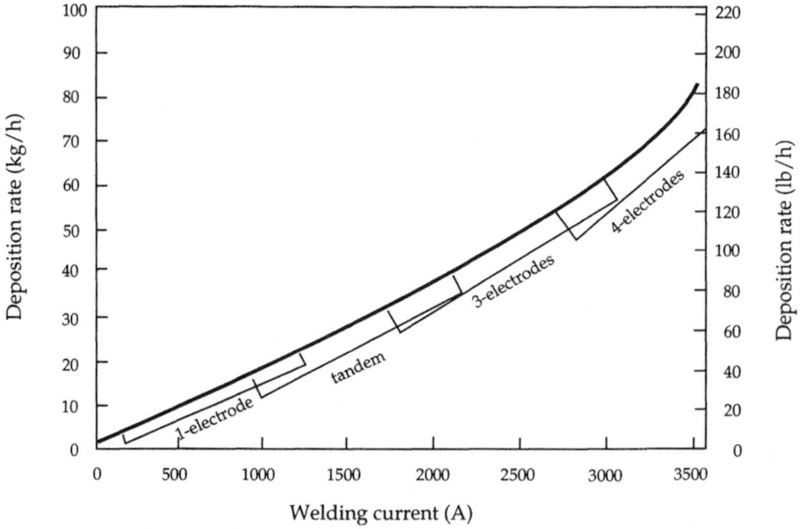

FIGURE 1.18. The deposition rate as a function of the welding current obtained with different SAW wire systems.

is connected to a separate power source, is another method to increase productivity. This can then be expanded to three or four wire systems. Figure 1.18 shows the productivity obtained with different numbers of wires. A further step, which has found increasing use, is to add iron powder, fed through a separate unit (Figure 1.19a). The productivity of this method, compared to some other modes of SAW, is shown in Figure 1.19b.

These methods have slightly different effects and each has its own advantages and disadvantages. The parallel wire technique is fairly simple to operate, because only one power source has to be adjusted. However, the gain in productivity is limited, because only smaller diameter wires can be used. With the multiwire technique, there are several considerations. The wires should all melt down in the same weld pool (i.e., the weld metal should not solidify in the distance between the successive wires). The distance between the wires can have a pronounced effect on penetration and the height of reinforcement. It is also important to choose the polarity of the voltage correctly, so as to avoid arc blow effects. Normally, direct current (DC), with the electrode positive, is used on the first wire and alternating current (AC) is used on the second. When magnetic arc blow is a pronounced problem, AC is used on both the leading and the trailing wires.

With iron powder additions, a cold nonmelted material is added to the weld pool. Some energy is required to heat and melt the iron powder and, thus, the thermal cycle of the process is changed. This in turn will affect microstructure and properties of both the weld metal and the HAZ.

The narrow-gap process was developed as an alternative to the use of higher energies (Figure 1.20). In thick materials this technique has special advantages because the weld metal volume that has to be deposited can be significantly reduced, compared with the use of standard V-joint. This is due to the narrow joints that are used in narrow-gap welding. The heat input is fairly small (~2 kJ/mm, 50 kJ/in.). Possible problems with the method are lack of side wall fusion and slag pockets from entrapped slag. However, these problems seem to have been largely overcome. An example of a weld metal from a narrow-gap joint is shown in Figure 1.21. The regular buildup of the weld shows the excellent reproducibility of the process.

There are two main kinds of fluxes: agglomerated and fused. The agglomerated fluxes are the most common. They are made by adding silicates to a dry blend of fine-grained mineral powder. Agglomerates of the powder are then formed. These are dried by heating to approximately 600 to 900°C (1100 to 1600°F), depending on flux type. The flux grains consist of relatively round "balls" (Figure 1.22a) and in cross-section (Figure 1.22b) it is possible to see some of the separate components of the flux. Fused fluxes are made by melting the powder mix and then cooling rapidly, so that a glassy phase is formed. The flux is then crushed and ground down to fine particles. The appearance of fused fluxes is very different from that of agglomerated fluxes (Figure 1.23). The

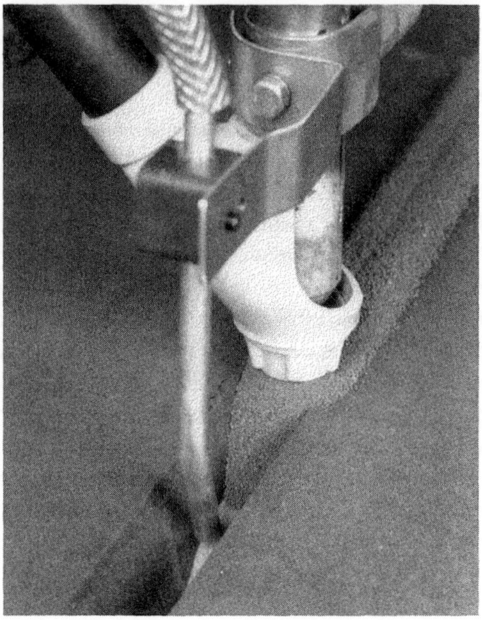

a

FIGURE 1.19. (a) The deposition rate in SAW can be increased significantly by separate feeding of iron powder. The cold iron powder has the further advantage of cooling down the melt so that a smaller heating of the weld takes place. (b) The deposition rate as a function of the welding current obtained with single wire, using either AC or DC+, with parallel wire or with metal powder addition.

fused fluxes have some advantages over agglomerated fluxes. The main advantage is that they are nonhygroscopic, i.e., the moisture content of the flux is very low, resulting in very low hydrogen values in the weld metal. However, it should be noted that the modern agglomerated fluxes also have excellent properties with respect to initial moisture and moisture pickup. The fused fluxes are also chemically homogenous. The disadvantage is that the fused flux cannot contain elements that affect the operational characteristics or the deoxidation ability. These elements are destroyed in the production process by the high temperatures used. Agglomerated fluxes are designed after much the same principles as the coating of covered electrodes, with one basic difference. For covered electrodes, much of the coating is used to generate gas protection. In SAW this is not necessary, because the flux protects the weld area. The mineral systems used are based on, for example, SiO_2-TiO_2-Al_2O_3, which gives a fairly fluid slag and good welding properties, or $CaCO_3$-Al_2O_3-MgO, which gives a high basic flux, with good cleaning of the weld metal but does not have very good operating characteristics.

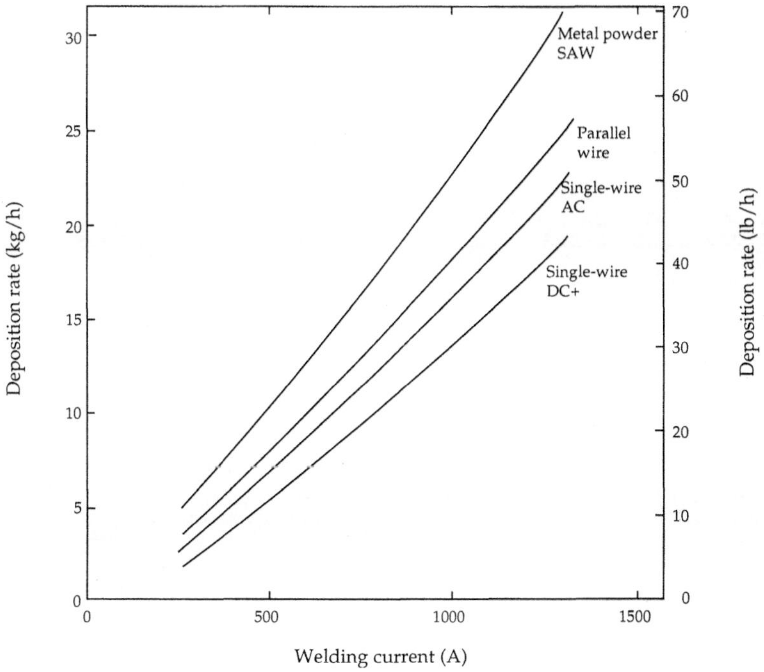

FIGURE 1.19.b

The basicity index concept was developed by Tuliani et al.[2] to describe the role of different minerals for weld metal composition. The basicity index is given by

$$B = [CaO + MgO + BaO + SiO + K_2O + Li_2O + CaF_2 + 1/2(MnO + FeO)]/[SiO_2 + 1/2(Al_2O_3 + TiO_2 + ZrO_2)] \quad (1.6)$$

where the oxides (and the salt CaF_2) in the numerator are of basic type and those in the denominator are of acid or amphoteric type. Fluxes with $B = 1$ are called acid, with $1 < B < 1.5$ semibasic, $1.5 < B < 2.5$ basic, and $B > 2.5$ highly basic. A basic flux gives a basic slag, which cleans the weld metal from oxygen and impurities such as sulfur. Acid fluxes give slags which do not clean the weld metal. The slag-metal reactions are relatively complicated and will be dealt with further in a separate chapter.

The hydrogen content of weld metals from SAW is generally at a low level, around 5 ml/100 g weld metal. This is independent of the slag system in the flux because all fluxes are dried at a relatively high temperature. However, there are some older types of fluxes which contain minerals that are avoided in modern fluxes, and these fluxes tend to give higher hydrogen contents.

FIGURE 1.20. The narrow-gap equipment. A very narrow joint is used so that less weld metal is needed. This of course means that the demands on mechanical stability are very high and that properties such as slag detachability are crucial. The method is most economical for thicker plates because the difference in weld metal volume between a conventional joint configuration and a "narrow joint" increases rapidly with plate thickness.

A further way to classify fluxes is to describe the alloying ability. Normally, three groups are considered:

- Neutral fluxes, where no alloying takes place
- Active fluxes, alloying silicon and manganese
- Alloying fluxes, which alloy more elements, such as chromium

The composition of the flux very significantly affects the arc properties (arc stability, heat, etc.) as well as the fluid properties of the molten slag. Both these factors are crucial to the operation of the consumables. The wire seldom has any particular effect on the welding properties.

1.6. WELDING DEFECTS

There will always be inhomogeneities in a welded joint. If these inhomogeneities are above a certain size, they cannot be tolerated and are called defects. There are a number of defects that may arise during welding, either due to unsuitable materials or due to the way the welding is made. There are both external defects (i.e., mainly arising in connection with the plate

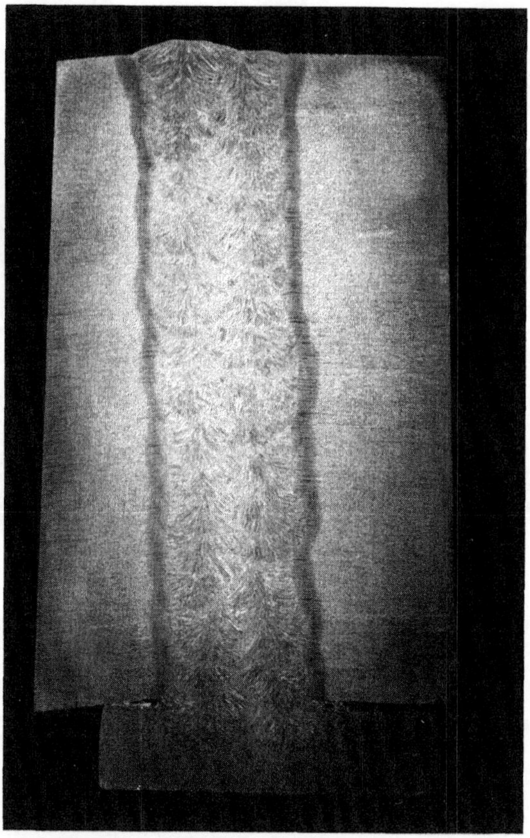

FIGURE 1.21. An example of a weld metal from a narrow-gap joint. When correctly employed, a very regular pattern of weld beads is obtained.

surface) and internal defects. Defects are detected using nondestructive examination methods, such as X-raying, ultrasonic testing, dye penetrants, or magnetic particles. Depending on the demands on the weld, some defects can be accepted during production welding. Defects that can be accepted include pores, which mainly give a reduction of the load-carrying cross-sectional area. Significant cracks can never be accepted, because they cause stress concentrations, which ultimately can lead to brittle fracture. In this section the most common crack types will be described in some detail and then a briefer description of other defects will be provided.

1.6.1. SOLIDIFICATION CRACKING

Solidification cracking occurs at high temperatures, typically 200 to 300°C below the solidus temperature. They are easily recognized, because they usually follow the weld centerline, although in SAW metals, a special kind of

a

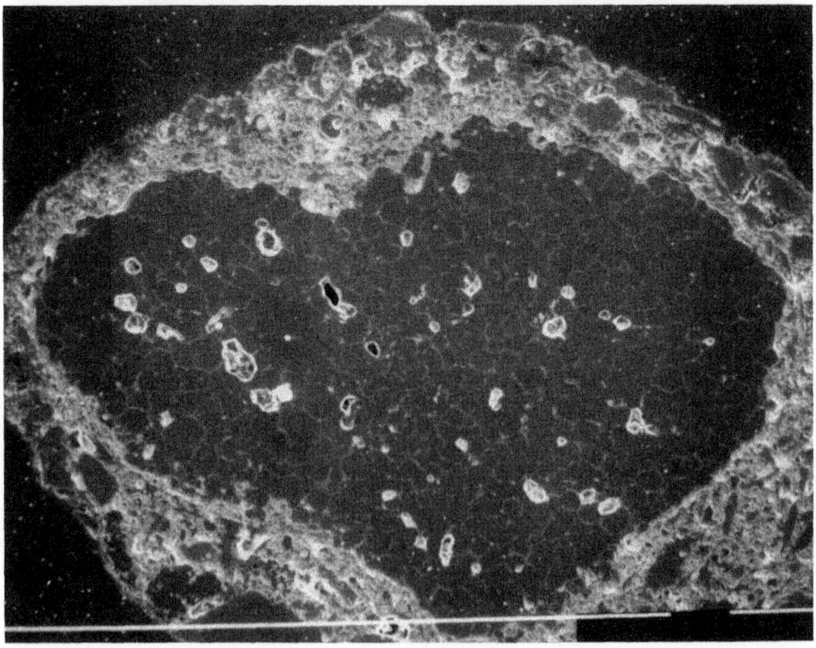

b

FIGURE 1.22. The appearance of agglomerated flux grains: (a) surface of grains and (b) cross-section of grains. (Scanning electron micrographs, with gold evaporated on the grain surfaces.)

FIGURE 1.23. The appearance of the grains in a fused flux. (Scanning electron micrograph, with gold evaporated on the grain surfaces.)

solidification crack, called "dove-wings," can appear. The typical appearance of solidification cracks is shown in Figure 1.24. The cracks often appear toward the end of the welds, due to stresses arising from the thermal field. The crack surfaces can be heavily oxidized if the crack has been exposed to air at high temperatures, and in a scanning electron microscope, the dendrite tips from the solidification process are readily seen. Solidification cracks arise due to the formation of low melting point compounds in between the dendrites (Figure 1.25). When the temperature has fallen sufficiently below the solidus, stresses start to build up across the weld, due to shrinkage of the weld pool. The compounds are still molten and cannot take up stresses, and consequently a crack is formed. The conditions controlling the extent of the formation of these cracks are the *amount of impurities* and the *shape of the weld.*

Solidification cracks in conjunction with low dilution methods such as SMAW are very rare, while in high dilution methods, such as SAW, solidification cracking can be more frequent. In general, the amount of impurities from the consumables is very low. The main source of impurities is the base plate. High-quality base material with particularly low sulfur is required to ensure the avoidance of cracking. The allowable quantities of impurities in many wrought steel specifications are still too high. Solidification cracking has been noticed

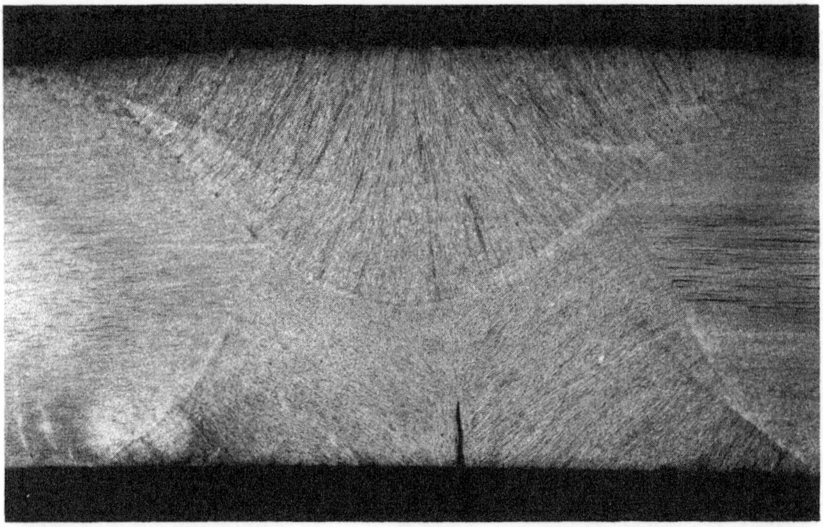

a

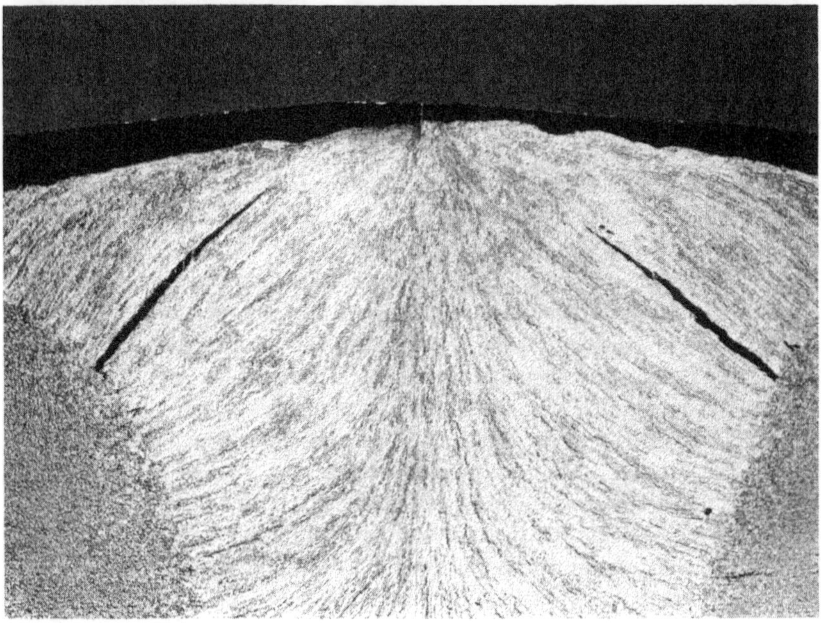

b

FIGURE 1.24. Examples of solidification cracks. (a) Typical centerline crack in a two-pass SAW weld. (b) "Dove-wing" cracking in a SAW weld.

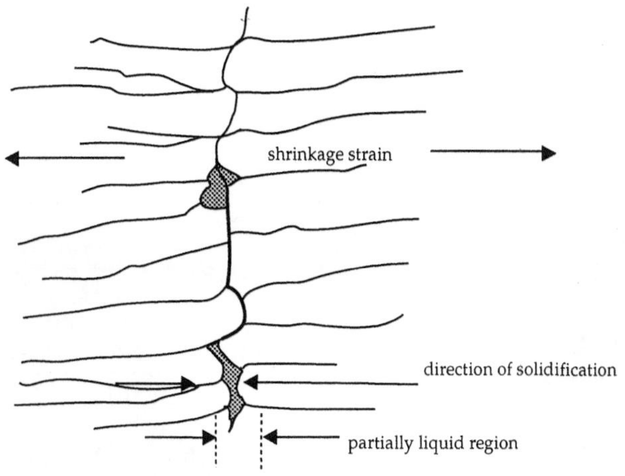

FIGURE 1.25. Mechanism of solidification crack formation. (After Baker, R. G., in *Rosenhain Centenary Conf. Proc.*, Baker, R. G. and Kelly, A., Eds., The Royal Society London, 1975, 129. With permission.)

several times during the manufacture of relatively simple objects, where the quality of the base material has been low. A further factor that may contribute to the occurrence of cracks in SAW metals is the larger size of the weld pool, which creates larger deformations or higher stresses. High welding speeds also increase the risk of solidification cracking.

Solidification cracks are sometimes found in GMAW, although this process generally gives lower dilution than SAW. The explanation for this is that the shape of the weld bead was unsuitable (Figure 1.26a). The weld should solidify in such a way that the impurities are transported toward the top surface and not toward the center of the weld. When the depth-to-width ratio is larger than unity, there is an increased possibility that the dendrites grow toward the center of the bead, causing solute enrichment in the remaining melt. There are many examples where such unsuitable solidification microstructures may arise, both from GMAW (when excessive currents have been used, causing exaggerated penetration) and from SAW one-sided welding (where the straight joint edges formed easily promote an unsuitable solidification profile).

A special kind of solidification cracking occurs when solidification is delayed in a certain area. This happens when there is a lack of material on which the melt may nucleate, e.g., when there is too wide a gap between the plates (see Figure 1.26b). This may also happen in one-sided welding if the backing flux used for some reason does not work efficiently as a nucleating agent.

Testing of susceptibility to solidification cracking is not easily done. Wilken and Kleistner[3] recently reviewed the test methods used. The most common is the Varestraint test. In this test and the similar Transvarestraint test the specimen

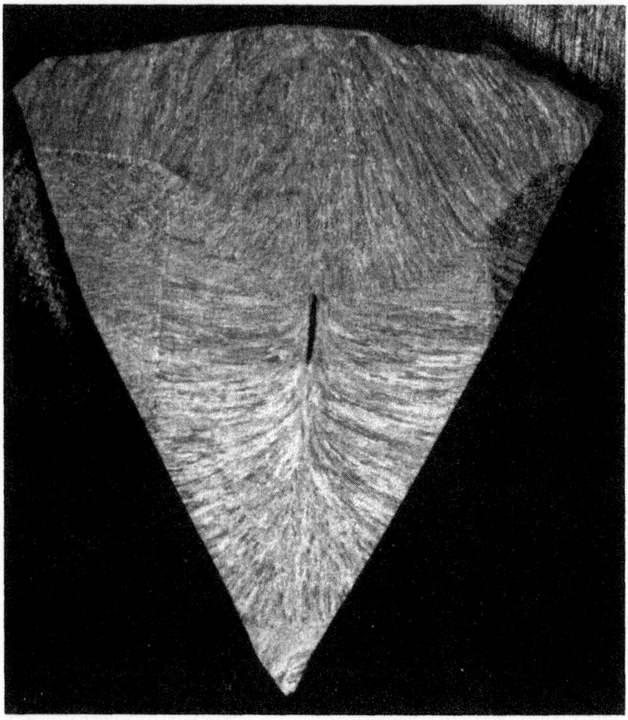

a

FIGURE 1.26. Further examples of solidification cracks. (a) Too-high currents in a GMAW has caused an unsuitable depth-to-width ratio, the weld being deeper than the width. Solidification will then occur from the sides toward the center of the weld, creating a high risk for the accumulation of impurity elements there. (b) The gap between the workpieces has been too large. Thus, in the gap the weld will experience a lack of nucleating agents, leading to delayed solidification in this area. Once again, this is likely to lead to a concentration of impurity elements in the last solidified area and consequent cracking.

is subjected to a controlled deformation during cooling. Other tests are the T-crack test and the circular groove test, which are self-restraint tests. All these tests rank different materials with respect to solidification cracking susceptibility, but do not predict whether an actual joint in a construction will crack.

Regression analysis of cracking in Transvarestraint tests led Bailey and Jones[4] to develop an equation relating crack susceptibility to chemical composition in the diluted weld metal, as (all concentrations in weight percent):

$$UCS = 230C + 190S + 75P + 45Nb - 12Si - 5.4Mn - 1 \qquad (1.7)$$

where UCS means Unit of Crack Susceptibility. When UCS is larger than 30, the risk of cracking is great, and when UCS is lower than 10 the risk is small.

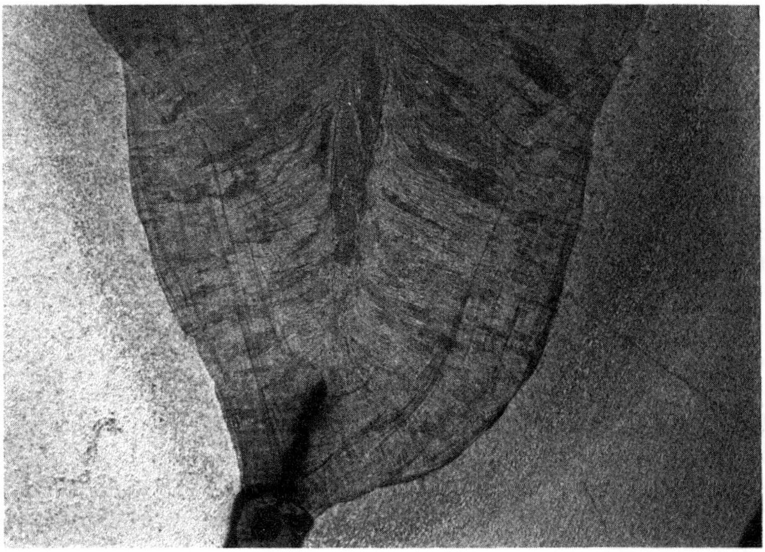

FIGURE 1.26.b

1.6.2. LIQUATION CRACKING

Liquation cracking occurs in the grain boundaries of the base material or in underlying beads in the weld metal, adjacent to the fusion line. It is due to the formation of low melting point compounds, just as for solidification cracks. However, the origin of segregation is different, in one case as a result of different solubilities in the melt and solid material, and in the other case as a solid-state enrichment at the grain boundaries. The impurity segregation takes place in the high-temperature parts of the HAZ, where sulfides present in the material dissolve into the austenite and subsequently migrate to the grain boundaries. Some additional impurity elements may come from the remelting of inclusions in the partially melted zone, just beside the fusion line.

The best way to cure problems with liquation cracking is to change the material to a higher purity grade. Because rupture of the grain boundaries occurs under the influence of tensile stresses building up as the weld cools, welding with small size electrodes that give smaller weld pools may help. Another way to try and cure the problem is to butter the joint surfaces (i.e., clad them with one or two layers of weld metal), avoiding tensile stresses across the melted grain boundaries. When the plates are subsequently joined together, the zone that has been subjected to high temperatures now lies in the buttered layer, which is less susceptible to liquation cracking. However, this technique is only a first attempt to avoid further cracking. Often this procedure does not help, unfortunately.

1.6.3. HYDROGEN-INDUCED CRACKING

Hydrogen-induced cracking takes place in the temperature range below about 200°C (400°F). The cracking is often delayed, i.e., it can occur several days after welding is finished. Nondestructive examination (NDE) of welds should for this reason not be made too soon after welding. A common requirement is to wait 48 h before making an NDE. Cracks of this type are most common in the HAZ, close to the fusion line, but can also occur in the weld metal itself. In the HAZ, cracking can be both intergranular, following the prior austenite grain boundaries, and transgranular. The cracks often nucleate at points of high stress intensity, such as the weld toe (the transition between the weld reinforcement and the base plate) or in the root. Examples of cracks are shown in Figure 1.27. When occurring in the weld metal, the cracks generally follow the allotriomorphic ferrite, decorating the prior austenite grain boundaries, as shown in Figure 1.28. Macroscopically, the cracks appear in a 45° angle to the welding direction. This appearance is called Chevron cracking.

There are three requirements that must be fulfilled for cold cracking to occur:

1. Presence of hydrogen
2. Presence of stresses
3. A "susceptible" (brittle) microstructure (martensite)

The stresses are in practice always present as residual stresses, of the order of the yield stress. However, what might be of critical importance is the stress concentrations that occur near discontinuities, such as the weld root or at the transition between the weld bead and the base plate. The average stress levels also vary, depending, for example, on the restraint of joint and local joint geometry. However, in a given joint the only variables that can be affected are the hydrogen content and the microstructure. Both these variables are the focus of research by manufacturers of consumables and base material.

The exact mechanism as to how hydrogen acts in conjunction with stress in order to induce cracking is not clear. The original theory suggested that hydrogen atoms diffuse to sites such as micropores, interfaces between inclusions and matrix, or other discontinuities where they combine to H_2. The molecule cannot diffuse in the lattice and the hydrogen is therefore trapped, unless the molecule is dissociated at the trap surface. High pressure is built up, which leads to a local "burst" of the surrounding matrix. Although this theory does not explain all features of hydrogen-induced cracking, it serves as a good qualitative model.

Other theories have explained the influence of hydrogen as lowering the surface energy by adsorption of hydrogen, thereby promoting brittle fracture, or that hydrogen interacts with dislocations, so that local plastic fractures appear.

The solubility of hydrogen is much larger in austenite than in ferrite. When the welded joint is cooled down, the weld metal normally transforms first to

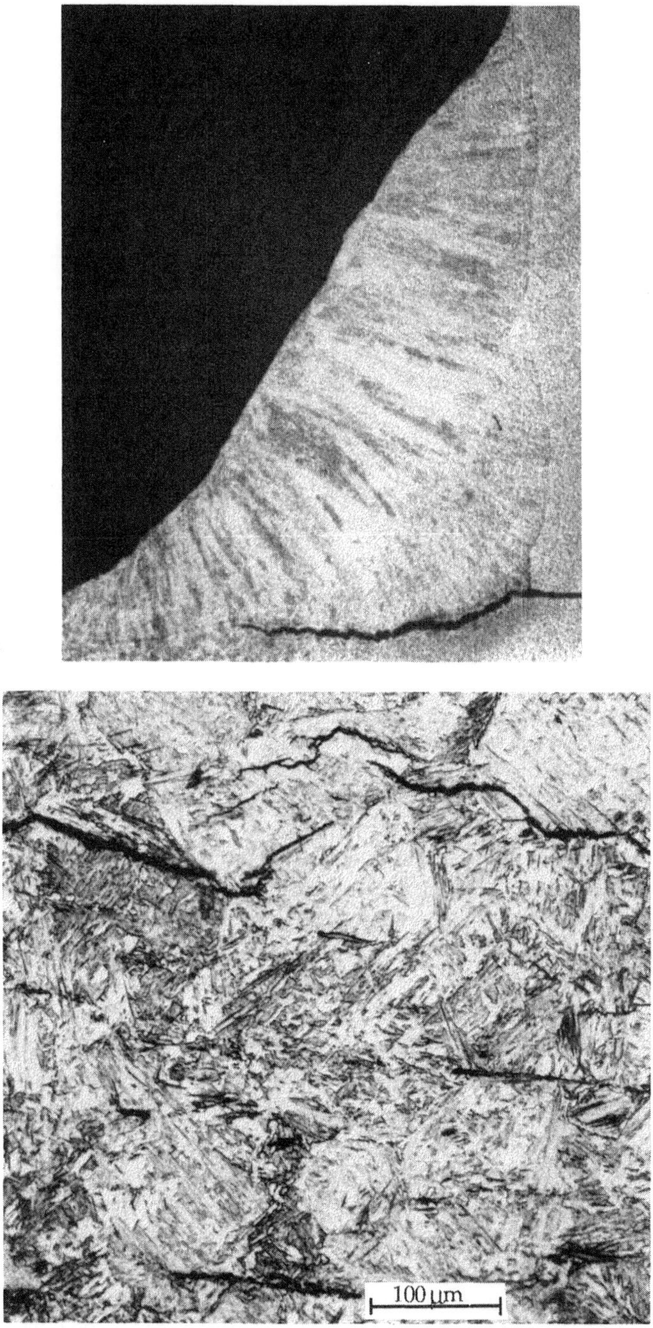

a

b

FIGURE 1.27. Examples of hydrogen-induced cracks in the HAZ. (a) Crack in a fillet weld. (b) The cracks appear in HAZs that are martensitic and where the hydrogen content has been too high. They also often appear at points of stress concentrations, such as weld toes or in the root region.

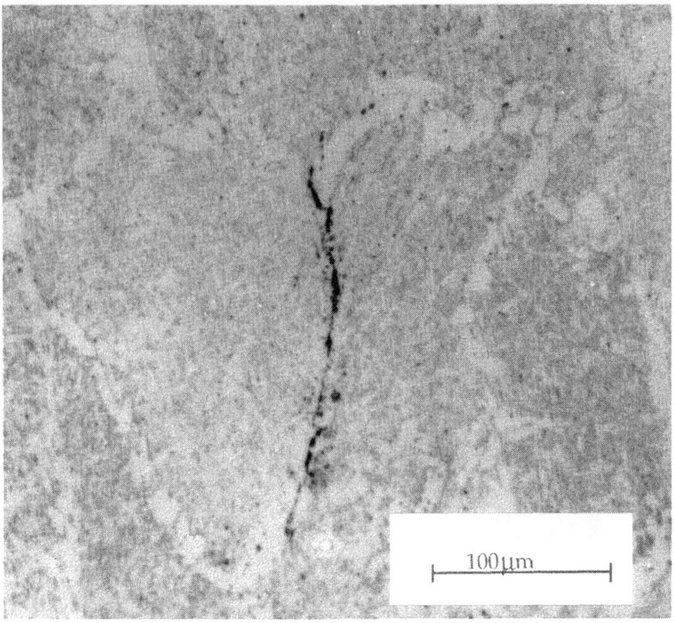

a

FIGURE 1.28. (a) Hydrogen cracking in weld metals, showing how the cracks follow the prior austenite grain boundaries. Weld metal hydrogen cracking differs from HAZ cracking in that weld metal cracking can occur without martensite being present. (b) Longitudinal section through a weld metal, showing how the cracks lie at approximately 45° to the welding direction.

ferrite, while the base material is still austenitic due to the differences in chemical composition. This acts as a driving force for the diffusion of hydrogen from the weld metal to the HAZ. However, the main driving force for the diffusion of hydrogen into the HAZ is the difference in concentration (Figure 1.29).

Hydrogen diffuses relatively rapidly in α-Fe. At temperatures above 200°C (400°F), the scatter in the published values for the diffusivity is relatively small, but for lower temperatures the scatter is very large, as shown by Coe.[5] The large scatter makes quantitative predictions at the lower temperatures difficult.

The most common way to avoid cold cracking is to preheat the workpiece or at least a sufficiently large area around the joint. Preheating has two functions: it reduces the risk of martensite formation and it speeds up hydrogen diffusion, so that when the joint finally reaches room temperature, the hydrogen level is below that which causes fracture. The preheat temperature is determined from codes, such as British Standard (BS) 5135:1984. The parameters used for determining the preheat temperature are carbon equivalent, plate

FIGURE 1.28.b

thickness, hydrogen content, and heat input. The carbon equivalent is a hardening index, developed by regression analysis of relationships between chemical composition and maximum hardness in the HAZ of a welded joint. The carbon equivalent most commonly used is that developed within the International Institute of Welding (IIW). The preheat necessary to avoid cold cracking is then experimentally determined for a range of the parameters. The result is given in graphs, an example of which is shown in Figure 1.30. The applicability of these graphs is for carbon equivalents from approximately 0.4 to 0.56. It should be noted that the carbon equivalent formula used

$$E_w = C + Mn/6 + (Cr + Mo + V)/5 + (Ni + Cu)/15 \quad (1.8)$$

(all elements in wt%) was developed for steels having small amounts of chromium, molybdenum, vanadium, nickel, and copper. The sum of these elements should not exceed about 1 wt%. When other kinds of steel, with compositions falling outside this range, require welding, the steel supplier should be contacted for advice on appropriate preheat conditions.

The other common carbon equivalent formula used is the Ito–Bessey formula, P_{cm} (all elements in wt%)

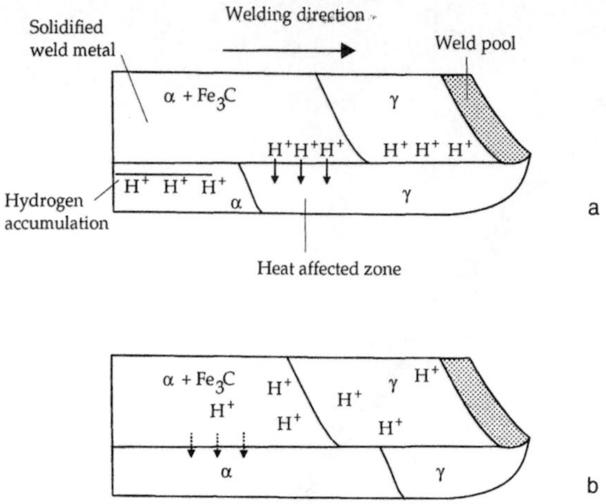

FIGURE 1.29. (a) Flow of hydrogen atoms from the weld metal into the HAZ due to differences in concentration and solubility. This situation relates to a conventional normalized steel, in which the transformation from austenite to ferrite takes place at a lower temperature in the steel than in the weld metal. As the weld metal transforms to ferrite, there is a driving force for hydrogen diffusion to the austenitic HAZ. (b) In modern TMCP (thermomechanical controlled processing) steels, the alloying content is lower, giving a higher transformation temperature. Thus, the hydrogen atoms remain in the austenitic weld metal. When the weld metal subsequently transforms to ferrite, the driving force to diffuse the hydrogen atoms into the HAZ is relatively small, and the hydrogen to a large extent remains in the weld metal.

$$P_{cm} = \mathrm{C} + (\mathrm{Mn} + \mathrm{Cr} + \mathrm{Cu})/20 + \mathrm{Si}/30 + \mathrm{V}/10 + \mathrm{Mo}/15 + \mathrm{Ni}/60 + 5\mathrm{B} \quad (1.9)$$

Several investigations have suggested that the IIW formula E_w gives a better correlation with maximum hardness for steels having a carbon content above 0.18 wt%, while the P_{cm} formula is better for steels with a lower carbon content.

In Japanese codes, the degree of preheat is determined graphically by calculating an index, *WI,* comprised of the carbon equivalent P_{cm}, the hydrogen number (determined according to Japanese standard H_{JIS}, which differs considerably from European and American standards), and the restraint R_F, as:

$$WI = P_{cm} + R_F/40{,}000 + H_{\mathrm{JIS}}/60 \quad (1.10)$$

Using Tekken testing (see below), empirical formulas and nomograms have been developed relating the index *WI* and the preheating temperature.

The restraint is not specified in BS 5135:1984. The restraint in Japanese codes is assumed to be proportional to thickness. In the BS code the thickness is taken into consideration by having different curves in the diagrams for different values of the combined thickness. However, it should be realized that the thickness correction is not due to restraint per se, but may equally well be thought of as influencing the cooling rate of the weld.

Hydrogen scales		
Diffusible hydrogen content		
ml/100 g weld metal		
Over	Up to and including	Scale
15	-	A
10	15	B
5	10	C
-	5	D

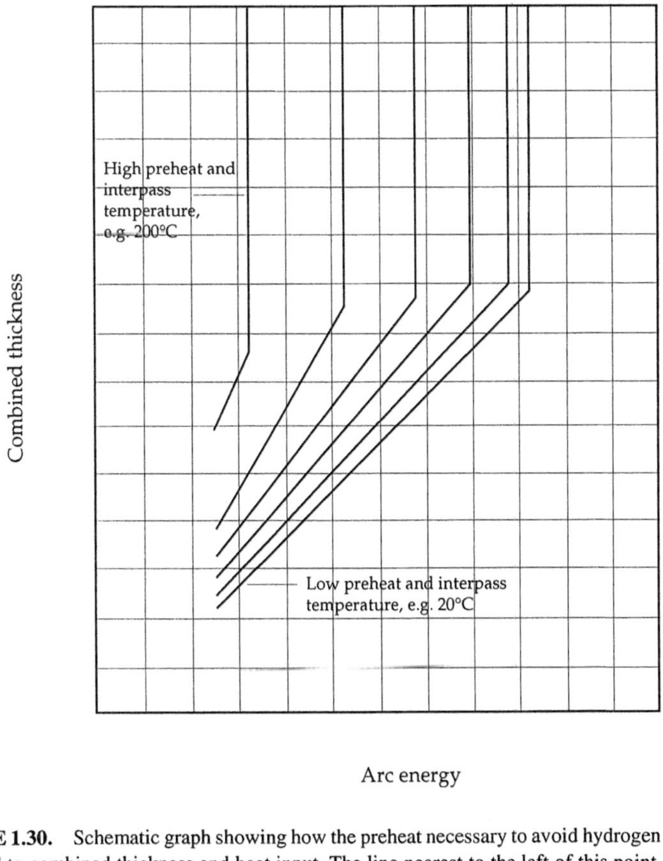

FIGURE 1.30. Schematic graph showing how the preheat necessary to avoid hydrogen cracking is related to combined thickness and heat input. The line nearest to the left of this point gives the preheat temperature necessary. The diagram is constructed for normalized steels and may be very conservative for modern low-carbon steels.

These different preheat formulas are widely used for selection of base materials and for erecting welding procedure specifications. However, it must be realized that they are rather coarse, have limitations in terms of applicable chemical compositions, and are mostly overly conservative, leading to extra construction costs. To more exactly evaluate a base material for cold cracking resistance, there are several cold cracking tests. These tests can be divided into two groups: *self-restrained tests,* where the stress is set up by the shrinkage of the weld as it cools down, and *externally loaded tests.* Examples of the first type are the Tekken test, the IRC (instrumented restraint cracking) test, the CTS (controlled thermal severity) test, and the cruciform cracking test. Examples of the second type are implant testing and the TRC (tensile restraint cracking) test.

1.6.4. OTHER CRACKS

Two other crack types will be briefly described: lamellar tearing and reheat cracking. Lamellar tearing is a kind of cracking that is relatively uncommon today. It arises when tensile stresses act in the thickness direction of a plate. If the plate contains slag inclusions, mainly of MnS, which are elongated in the rolling direction of the plate, these inclusions may serve as initiation sites for cracks. A characteristic step-like cracking pattern is found. This mode of cracking was common when heavier thickness plates were first used in offshore structures. The occurrence of cracks led to the development of methods to obtain rounded rather than elongated sulfides, and today most steel suppliers can produce steel that is not susceptible to lamellar tearing.

Reheat cracking is a cracking mode that is encountered in creep-resistant steels. These steels draw their creep strength from precipitated carbides inside the grains. To relax stresses, the creep strain concentrates at the grain boundaries, which are less creep resistant than the interior of the grains. This occurs when the steels are heat treated after welding. Large creep strains eventually lead to cracking. Reheat cracking is promoted by the presence of impurity elements and the common way to cure this type of cracking is to select a base material with a low impurity element content.

1.6.5. OTHER DEFECTS

Although solidification cracks and cold cracks are regarded as the most important defects in a welded joint, there are a number of other defects that should be considered and will be briefly described here: pores, undercuts, lack of fusion, and root defects.

Pores arise due to the presence of dissolved gases. They have either a spherical shape, where the gas has been completely locked into the weld metal, or a more elongated shape, often extending to the surface of the weld. The latter shape is due to pore formation between the growing dendrites during solidification. The pores grow with the same speed as the solidification front. They are often called *worm holes* (see Figure 1.31). The gases that cause pore formation are hydrogen, nitrogen, or carbon monoxide. Hydrogen enters the weld pool from moisture that comes from the consumables or from the joint surfaces. The moisture content of the consumables in the delivery condition is too low to cause porosity. However, during exposure to air, the moisture content can increase. The increase is dependent upon the temperature and relative humidity of the air. To avoid problems, the consumables should be stored under conditions

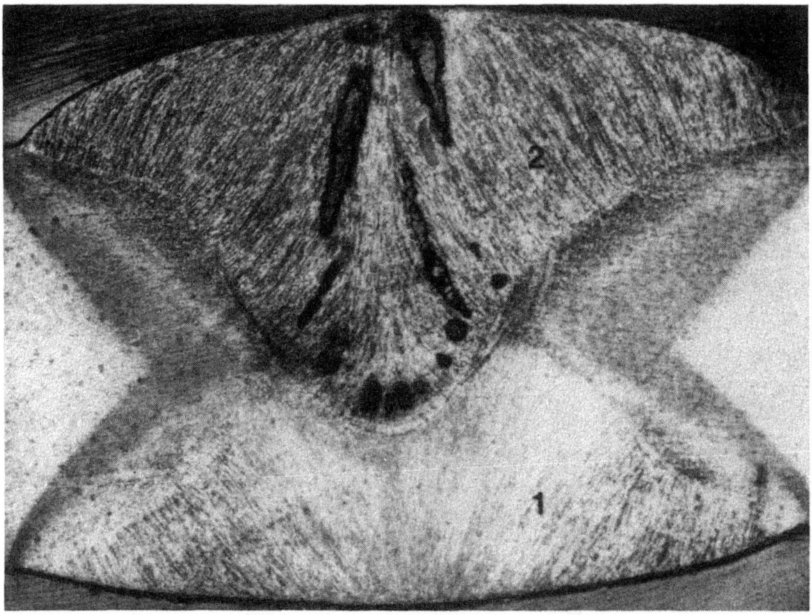

FIGURE 1.31. Cross-section of a SAW weld metal showing a large amount of worm holes formed by the presence of unescaped gas.

specified by the suppliers and redried at temperatures and times appropriate to the particular consumable.

Nitrogen can enter the weld metal from the surrounding air, for example if too long an arc length is used. Welding speeds that arc too high can also cause nitrogen uptake. Carbon dioxide can cause porosity when welding on nonkilled steels. However, most consumables contain enough silicon to avoid porosity from this cause. Pores can be observed around the starting area when welding with basic types of electrodes. This is due to an insufficient gas shield immediately at the start of welding, as it takes some time to develop a complete gas shield when the arc is ignited. By moving the electrode over the starting area for a short time these pores will vanish.

In GMAW, pores can arise due to both too high and too low a flow of gas. Using too low a gas flow will permit the air to enter the weld pool, while too high a gas flow will cause a turbulent flow of the shielding gas, once again making room for air to enter. Turbulent gas flow can also be caused by spatter that has stuck to the gas nozzle. The inclination of the welding gun can be important. If the inclination is too large, especially in forehand welding, the gas shield can be blown from the weld metal. One additional factor is worth mentioning, namely the high nitrogen content present in the joint surfaces

FIGURE 1.32. Crater crack, arising from stop porosities in the crater.

when air plasma cutting has been used for joint preparation. In a thin layer at the surfaces, a high nitrogen content can occur due to cutting without any shielding. It is recommended practice to grind away the layer before welding. A special kind of defect appears in the crater where the welding is finished. In the crater, a lack of material can be seen if the welding is finished erroneously.

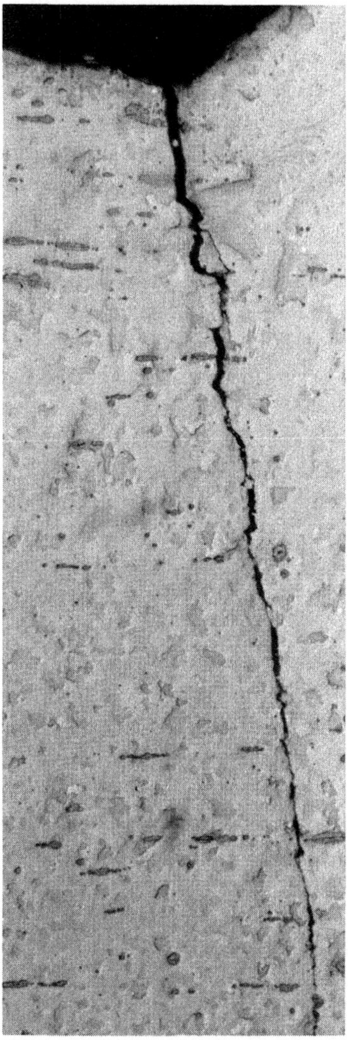

FIGURE 1.33. Fatigue crack, propagated from an undercut.

Small porosities *(pipes)* arise, which due to stress concentrations can give rise to crater cracking (see Figure 1.32). Crater cracks can easily be avoided by a backward motion of the consumable, filling in the pipe.

Undercuts and *root defects* are probably the most dangerous defects in a welded joint, because fatigue cracks often develop from such defects when the joint is subjected to a dynamic load (see Figure 1.33). Undercuts arise due to too high of a welding current, too long an arc, or careless movement of the electrode. A typical case when undercuts appear is when one is trying to get too large a throat thickness in a fillet weld, using only one bead. In butt welding it is especially important to completely fill with weld metal to the edges. In GMAW, undercuts occur as a consequence of improper balance between voltage and current; too much voltage in relation to the current favors undercuts. Undercuts should be removed as much as possible before construction is begun. This can be accomplished by grinding or remelting the transition area, using GTAW.

There are three kinds of root defects: nonpenetrating weld (i.e., the back part of the plate has not been melted), lack of fusion, and slag in the root area. The cause of this defect is often that a too large a diameter electrode has been used, so that it cannot be placed deep enough in the joint. Other common problems are that the root gap is too small or that the unbevelled edge is too large. Too low a current or too high a welding speed also cause root defects.

Lack of fusion occurs either between the weld metal and the base metal or between beads. It is due to an inadequate heat supply to melt the underlying material. Often the welding current is too low or the welding speed is too high. The inclination of the electrode also has a large influence and it is important to adjust the inclination so that the arc may melt the base material. Especially when welding plates of different thicknesses, lack of fusion easily appears in the thicker material, because this has a higher cooling efficiency. Lack of fusion can be caused by the presence of molten slag or gas, prohibiting the fusion of the materials. This appears most often when the melt is flowing in front of the arc, making penetration of the arc to the base material more difficult. The risk for this is highest in GMAW, with the welding gun inclined away from the solidified weld.

Slag inclusions appear when parts of the cover slag have "frozen" into the metal melt. With high alloyed electrodes, parts of the coating can fall off the electrode and form nonmelted areas in the weld metal. This is more likely when the coating contains compounds having high melting temperatures. In ordinary steel electrodes the risk is insignificant. To avoid slag inclusions in general, careful deslagging of the beads is paramount. In difficult cases, even grinding is necessary. Slag pockets often appear at the transition between beads or between beads and base material, mostly when exaggerated convex beads are made. These slag pockets can be covered by subsequent beads and give rise to stringers of slags, detected by, for example, X-raying. Even in GMAW, where no slag system is used, surface oxides, lying like "islands" on the weld metal surfaces, can give rise to slag inclusion problems.

1.7. HEAT FLOW IN WELDING

Heat flow during welding determines the thermal condition to which the material will be subjected. For the deposited weld metal, there is only a cooling phase of the thermal cycle, while for reheated weld metal and the HAZ of the base metal, both a heating and a cooling phase appear.

Heat generated by the arc is lost both through radiation and convection, in addition to heat flow through the material. However, the contribution from radiation and convection is very small and is usually neglected when heat flow problems are analyzed. Heat flow can be analyzed in two different ways: by analytical solutions of the heat flow differential equations and by finite element methods (FEM).

Analytical solutions to the problem of a moving heat source over a solid material have been presented in the classical works of Rosenthal[6] and Rykalin,[7] who obviously developed the theory independently. To be able to solve the differential equation, a number of assumptions must be made:

- The base material is isotropic and homogenous at all temperatures and no phase changes occur on heating.
- The source is either point shaped (for thick plates) or line shaped (for thin plates).
- Thermal conductivity, specific heat, and density are temperature-independent constants.
- Heat flow through the surface is neglected.
- A quasistationary temperature distribution is obtained, i.e., there is no temperature variation with time for a point with a fixed position relative to the arc.
- Nonmelting electrodes are used.

Using FEM, the differential equations are solved in a number of nodes in a mesh, taking appropriate boundary conditions into account. The advantage is that the physical constants are allowed to vary with temperature. The size of the mesh can be varied so that in principle very exact solutions can be obtained. However, due to the high costs of extensive calculations, it is necessary to find a reasonable balance between accuracy and computational time.

It is customary to divide the solutions into two regimes: thick plate and thin plate. The solution to the thick plate heat flow problem is

$$T - T_0 = q'/(2\pi\lambda R)\ \exp(-(v(x + R)/2\kappa)) \tag{1.11}$$

In this equation T is the temperature, T_0 is the preheat (or interpass) temperature, q' is the supplied power ($q' = \eta\ UI$), v is the welding speed, λ is the thermal conductivity, ρ is the density of the alloy, c is the specific heat, κ is the thermal diffusivity ($\kappa = \lambda/\rho c$), and R is the radius $R = \sqrt{x^2 + y^2 + z^2}$. Typical values of the physical constants λ, ρ, c, and κ are given in Table 1.4.

For thin plates the solution is

$$T - T_0 = q'/(2\pi\lambda d)\ \exp(-vx/2\kappa)K_0(vr/2\kappa) \tag{1.12}$$

TABLE 1.4
Values of Thermal Diffusivity (κ), Specific Heat (c), Heat Conductivity (λ), and Density (ρ) for Different Steel Types

Alloy	κ (mm²/s)	c (J/°C g)	λ (W/mm (°C))	ρ (g/mm³)
Ordinary carbon steel	8	6.1×10^{-7}	0.038	7800
C-Mn steel	4.6	7.2×10^{-7}	0.026	7800
Low-alloy steel	3	8.1×10^{-7}	0.019	7800

where d is the plate thickness, $r = \sqrt{x^2 + y^2}$, and K_0 is the Bessel function of the first kind, zero order.

The shape of the temperature distribution in space is shown in Figure 1.34. Note the very steep rise in temperature as the arc is approaching, while the decrease in temperature is slower. The loci of constant temperatures are called *isotherms*. The distance between the isotherms becomes progressively longer as the temperature decreases.

To simplify the analysis of heat flow on the metallurgical reactions in the HAZ, limiting cases are usually considered. In most welding situations, the velocity of the arc is much faster than the rate of the thermal diffusion, meaning that the heat flow in the direction of travel can be neglected, compared to heat flow in the perpendicular direction. By substituting $t = x/v$, the simplified form of Equation 1.11 then becomes

$$T - T_0 = (q'/v)/(2\pi\lambda t)\ \exp(-b/4\kappa t) \tag{1.13}$$

where b now is $y^2 + z^2$.

Similarly, Equation 1.12 becomes

$$T - T_0 = (q'/v)/(d(4\pi\lambda\rho c t)^{1/2})\ \exp(-y^2/4\kappa t) \tag{1.14}$$

The locus of the *peak temperature* is obtained by letting $\partial T/\partial t = 0$. This gives $t = r^2/4\kappa$, which gives

$$r_p = (2/\pi e)^{1/2}\ [(q'/v)/\rho c(T_p - T_0)]^{1/2}\ \text{(thick plates)} \tag{1.15}$$

$$r_p = (1/\pi)^{1/2}\ (q'/v)/(2de\rho c(T_p - T_0))\ \text{(thin plates)} \tag{1.16}$$

where e is the base of the natural logarithms (= 2.718).

Calculation of the *cooling time between 800 and 500°C* ($\Delta t_{8/5}$), which is one of the most important concepts, due to the austenite to ferrite transformation occurring in this temperature regime, is easily done using the simplified Formulas 1.13 and 1.14:

$$\Delta t_{8/5} = (q'/v)/(2\pi\lambda)[1/(500 - T_0) - 1/(800 - T_0)]\ \text{(thick plates)} \tag{1.17}$$

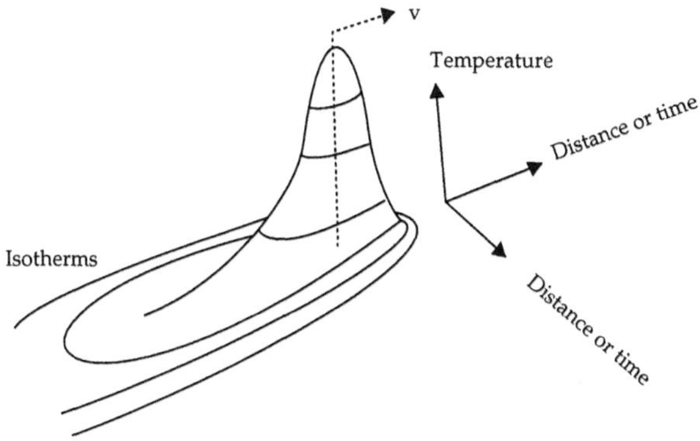

FIGURE 1.34. The shape of the temperature distribution in space around a moving heat source. The rapid rise in front of the source and the slower drop at the rear can be seen. The isotherms connect points of equal temperature.

$$\Delta t_{8/5} = (q'/vd)^2\ 1/(4\pi\lambda\rho c)[1/(500 - T_0)^2 - 1/(800 - T_0)^2] \text{ (thin plates)} \quad (1.18)$$

It should be noted that by choosing the point $y = z = 0$, it is in fact the cooling rate of the weld metal (at the rear of the weld pool) that is calculated.

By equating the equations for the thin and thick plate solutions (1.13 and 1.14), a critical plate thickness d_c is found where the applicability of one of the solutions changes over to the other:

$$d_c = \{(q'/v)/(2\rho c)[(1/500 - T_0) - 1/(800 - T_0)]\}^{1/2} \quad (1.19)$$

Measurements of the thermal cycle can be made by placing thermocouples in predrilled holes at various distances from the fusion boundary. Traces from such measurements are shown in Figure 1.35. In general, the agreement between measured and calculated values is quite good. The experimental problem with thermocouples is quite large, as it is difficult to place the hole exactly relative to the fusion line. The repeatability of the location of the fusion line is not very good, due to the "workshop" nature of the welding process. The thermocouple measurements thus are on a much cruder level with respect to the influence of the position than the predictive power of the equations.

The equations given are not applicable to the fused metal. Measurements of the cooling behavior, made by harpooning thermocouples into the weld pool, have shown that the cooling rate can be modeled on the functional form

$$dT/dt = C_1(T - T_0)^{C_2} \quad (1.20)$$

However, the constants C_1 and C_2, which are mutally dependent, have no values corresponding to either thin or thick plate solutions, but fall between these two cases. Values of the constants are given in Table 1.5.

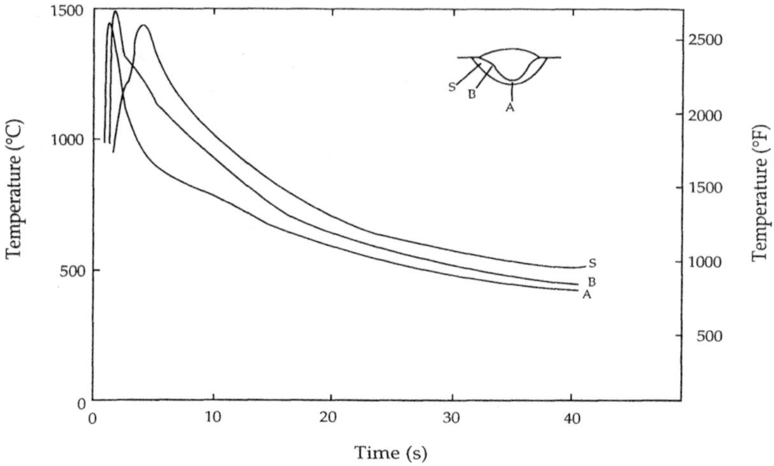

FIGURE 1.35. Traces from measurements of the thermal cycle in different positions in the HAZ in a SAW weld. (From Kohno, R. and Jones, S. B., Welding Institute Res. Rep. 81/1978/PE, The Welding Institute, London, 1978. With permission.)

TABLE 1.5
Constants for Calculation of Heat Flow in Weld Metals

Process	C_1	C_2
SMAW	1325	1.6
FCAW	4.45	2.41
FCAW/Ar-CO_2	28.54	2.06
SAW	4359	1.51
SAW, tandem	1.08	2.68

To simplify the evaluation of the thermal cycle, dimensionless parameters of temperature, coordinates, etc. can be used. By this, data from different materials can be used. Maps for heat flow analysis can also be conveniently constructed using this approach. The major heat flow model used to construct the maps was the medium thickness plate solution, which is more complex than Equations 1.11 and 1.12. The thin and thick plate solutions then are special limiting cases. The same assumptions as those made for the analytical solutions apply for the maps. With the help of the maps, the dominant heat flow mechanism can easily be determined. An example of a heat flow map is shown in Figure 1.36.

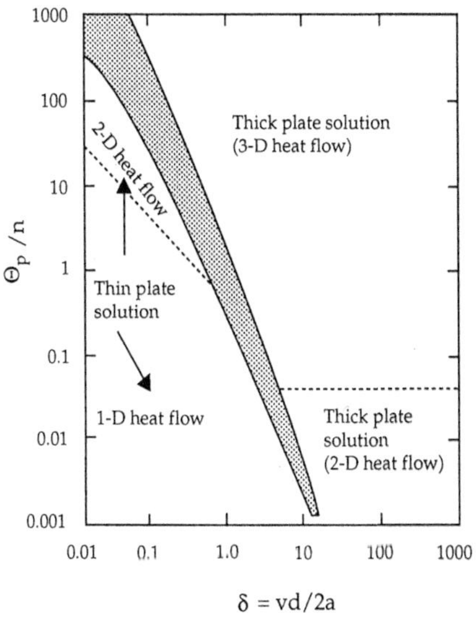

FIGURE 1.36. An example of a heat flow map, showing the dominant modes of heat flow. The dimensionless thickness is plotted on the horizontal axis and a dimensionless parameter related to the temperature on the vertical axis. (Reprinted from Myhr, O. R. and Grong, Ø., *Acta Metall. Mater.*, 38(3), 449, 1990. With permission from Pergamon Press Ltd., Oxford, U.K.)

REFERENCES

1. **Christensen, N., v de Davies, L., and Gjermundsen, K.,** Distribution of temperatures in arc welding, *Br. Weld. J.*, 12, 54, 1958.
2. **Tuliani, S. S., Boniszewski, T., and Eaton, N. F.,** Notch toughness of commercial submerged arc weld metal, *Weld. Metal Fabr.*, 37(8), 327, 1969.
3. **Wilken, K. and Kleistner, H.,** The Classification and Evaluation of Hot Cracking Tests for Weldments, IIW Doc. IX-1379-85, International Institute of Welding, London, 1985.
4. **Bailey, N. and Jones, S. B.,** The solidification cracking of ferritic steel during submerged arc welding, *Weld. J.*, 57(August), 217-s, 1978.
5. **Coe, F. R.,** *Welding Steels without Hydrogen Cracking,* The Welding Institute, London, 1973.
6. **Rosenthal, D.,** The theory of moving sources of heat and its application to metal treatments, *Trans. ASME,* 68, 849, 1946.
7. **Rykalin, N. N.,** *Berechnung der Wärmevorgänge beim Schweissen,* Verlag Technik, Berlin, 1957.

Chapter 2

METALLURGY OF THE BASE MATERIAL

2.1. INTRODUCTION

The key properties required from structural steels are strength, toughness, and weldability. From the steelmakers' point of view, economy is a fourth requirement, which undoubtedly has stimulated many of the developments in steel metallurgy that have resulted in modern alloys and their associated technologies.

The main degrees of freedom in the design of rolled steels can be divided into:

- Steel cleanliness
- Content of alloying elements
- Rolling schedule
- Cooling conditions
- Heat treatments after the mechanical processing is completed

Of these, the rolling schedule is the most complex, having several interrelated effects that involve both cooling and deformation.

The physical metallurgy variables, influenced by the parameters listed above, are

- Inclusion and impurity chemistry and distribution
- Solid solution hardening
- Precipitation hardening
- Phase transformations
- Grain size
- Dislocation hardening

The general effect of these variables on the strength and toughness properties is shown schematically in Figure 2.1. From this it can be seen that a fine ferrite grain size increases both the strength and toughness and thus easily can be identified as the key factor. Both alloying and rolling technologies have evolved on a grand scale over the past 40 years, with the objective of decreasing the grain size.

The strength levels (measured as yield strength or as a 0.2% proof stress) attainable with the weldable steels under discussion here range from about 200 MPa (mild steels) to about 1000 MPa (high-strength quenched and tempered steels). Some alloys can be treated to have yield strengths of the order of 1500 MPa, but these are fully martensitic, with high carbon contents, not designed

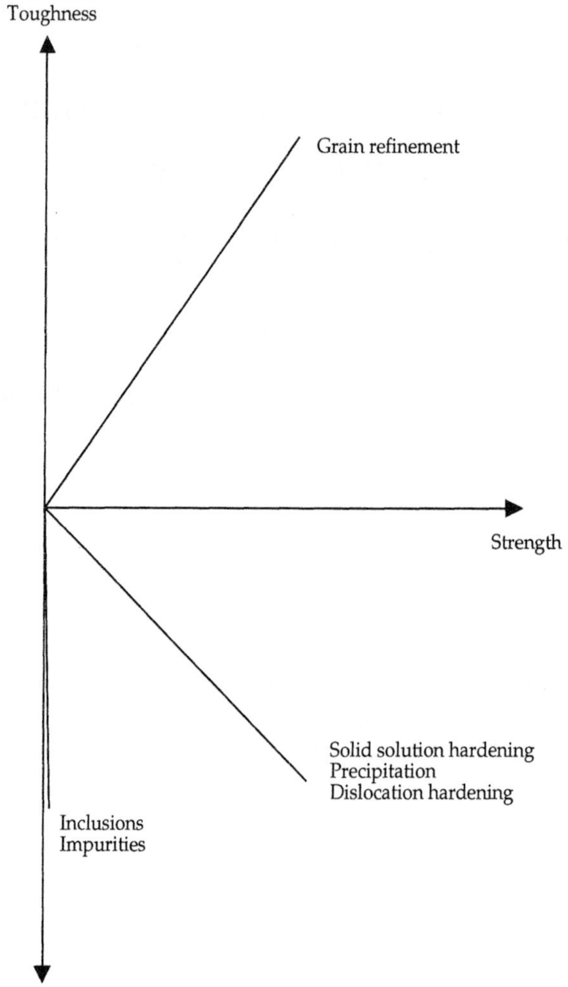

FIGURE 2.1. The influence of metallurgical factors on the strength and toughness of steels. Strengthening mechanisms other than a refined grain size are detrimental to toughness.

for fabrication by welding. Other types of steels are designed for high-temperature creep-resistant use, alloyed with chromium, molybdenum, and sometimes vanadium. These steels are not discussed in this book.

For many applications, the mild steel strength levels are quite adequate. For large structures, there is a clear incentive to use higher strength alloys, to be able to make slimmer constructions and thus reduce weight and weld metal volume. For offshore structures and bridges, steels with a yield strength of 350 MPa have been used for many years (Figures 2.2 and 2.3). To a relatively large extent, use has been made in offshore applications of 420 and 450 MPa yield

FIGURE 2.2. The substructure of an oil production platform. The substructure consists of a lattice of tubes that connect three giant storage tanks. The tanks are also a part of the support for the platform deck. Most of the steel used was conventional carbon-manganese steel. For some heavy thicknesses, a modified ASTM A533B quench and tempered steel was used. The steels were welded with shielded metal arc welding, gas–metal arc welding, using flux–cored wires and submerged arc welding. (Courtesy of Alloy Rods, Inc., Hanover, PA.)

strength steels, mainly in the topside area. Steels with very high yield strength (around 700 MPa and above) are used, for example, in transportation vehicles, cranes, submarines, and buildings (Figure 2.4). An important application, in which high demands are put on the construction, is pressure vessels. Steels for pressure vessels normally have yield strengths in the lower range, but also as much as 690 MPa has been used.

Strength itself is of little use without adequate toughness. Toughness is most commonly expressed as impact toughness and there are generally some well-defined levels of toughness that must be met, especially in quality control or in ranking tests. Examples of requirements commonly found are 47 J (35 ft-lb) at –20°C (–4°F) (typical for shipbuilding) or 40 J (30 ft-lb) at –40°C (–40°F) (typical for offshore constructions). The original requirement of 27 J (20 ft-lb) is now mainly found in the American Welding Society (AWS) classifications for consumables. The level required is often connected to the strength of the steel (higher strength demands higher toughness), and the temperature requirement is often specified as (at least) 30°C lower than the expected service temperature. Weldability (in terms of freedom of defects) was briefly discussed in Section 1.6. All construction steels must be weldable, but

a

FIGURE 2.3. (a) The "Tjörnbridge" on the Swedish west coast. This bridge was designed and built in 18 months, substituting an older bridge that was destroyed in January 1980, when it was hit by a ship. The new bridge is constructed in a titanium-vanadium microalloyed steel, with 355-MPa yield strength and impact requirements at –20°C. Due to a reduced carbon content and the presence of titanium nitrides, the weldability is very good. (b) Details of a section of the bridge. (Courtesy of Svenskt Stål AB, Oxelösund, Sweden.)

weldability can conflict with strength requirements because it is impaired by extensive alloying. The reduced weldability has been met by preheating the steel prior to welding, but this is a costly operation that fabricators would want to avoid.

To be able to decrease the alloying content (especially the carbon content) but still maintain the yield strength, significant developments have been made in the rolling processing stage, so that yield strength is kept up using deformation hardening and refined grain size. Also, the toughness can be kept on an acceptable level and weldability is improved significantly.

The purpose of this chapter is to describe the steps in the steelmaking process from a metallurgical point of view and the method by which steelmakers can design alloys of the desired quality. The steps considered are the treatment of the melted steel, the effect of alloying additions, and the rolling practice. The chapter concludes with a description of some of the classification systems that are most frequently used.

FIGURE 2.3.b

2.2. TREATMENT OF THE MELTED STEEL AND SOLIDIFICATION

Steels are produced either from minerals extracted from ores or from the recycling of scrap (Figure 2.5). Production from minerals takes place in a blast furnace or by a direct reduction process. From a blast furnace the resulting melt, often called "pig iron," is then transferred to a steelmaking furnace for further treatment. The minerals used are either Fe_2O_3 (hematite) or Fe_3O_4 (magnetite). These minerals are loaded together with coke and limestone in the blast furnace and hot air (blast) is blown through the heated material. The oxides are then reduced by reactions such as:

$$Fe_2O_3 + 3CO \Leftrightarrow 2Fe + 3CO_2$$

Elements such as manganese, silicon, and phosphorus can be reduced by similar reactions. When the process is finished, hot metal is trapped at the bottom of the furnace. This cast iron has a high carbon content, around 3 to 4 wt%.

Many blast furnaces were closed down during the 1980s, partly because of the implementation of much larger scale furnaces, but also because of the increased use of scrap as source material.

FIGURE 2.4. "Big Muskie," one of the largest machines on earth. It is used for removing overburden such as dirt and rock from atop coal seams at a large surface mine. The machine was provided with a new base in 1983. The dragline base was made from ASTM A537 Class 1 and A633 Grades C and D steels, having a thickness of 1 to 11/4 in. (25 to 32 mm), with some heavier sections being 2 in. (50 mm) and 6 in. (150 mm). Welding was made using FCAW, with a preheat of 250°F (170°C). (Courtesy of Alloy Rods, Inc., Hanover, PA.)

In direct reduction processes the oxygen is removed from the ore at temperatures between 650°C (1200°F) and 1200°C (2200°F), i.e., below the melting temperature. The reactions taking place are the same as those found in the blast furnace.

The most common steelmaking furnaces are electric, either acid or basic, and the basic oxygen furnace. The difference between acid and basic processes comes from the nature of the furnace lining and the flux used. A basic character is usually preferred, because cleaner steels and consequently higher quality can then be obtained.

Electric furnaces exist in several types, but the most common is the electric-arc furnace. The heat is generated by high currents flowing between three carbon electrodes in contact with the metal. The furnace is charged with various proportions of pig iron, scrap, and ferroalloys. Normally basic linings are used, but for castings acid linings are common.

The basic oxygen process uses a tiltable vessel, which is charged with molten pig iron. No further heating is required. The molten metal is blown by a large amount of oxygen, through an oxygen lance. Oxygen reacts with carbon and impurities in the steel.

The next step in steel processing takes place in the ladle, into which the molten steel has been poured from the previous step. In the ladle the steels are refined with respect to nonmetallic inclusions, including oxides and sulfides. Ladle treatment can generally be divided into five categories:

- Synthetic slag systems
- Gas stirring or purging
- Direct immersion of reactants, such as rare earth elements
- Lance injection of reactants
- Wire feeding of reactants

Combinations of these processes are often used to obtain synergic effects.

Synthetic slag systems are used to prevent heat losses by radiation from the molten metal. By choosing a suitable composition of the slag, e.g., based on calcia-alumina with an addition of fluorspar and reducing elements such as carbon, aluminum, and calcium silicide, further reduction in sulfur content is possible. As little slag as possible from the furnace should be allowed to follow the steel into the ladle, because sulfur then may revert into the steel.

Gas stirring is achieved by bubbling of gases such as nitrogen or argon through the melt. This helps to separate inclusions from the steel. Local metal currents are also created, flowing vertically downward, aiding the more effective mixing of the additions made.

Enhanced desulfurization or control of sulfide shape are the two means to improve the through thickness properties of steel plates. The desulfurization process takes place by lance injection of elements such as magnesium or calcium silicides ($CaSi_2$). Addition of calcium silicide wires is a growing alternative to lance injection. Better reproducibility is obtained and several alloying elements can be added simultaneously. Sulfide shape control is achieved by the addition of rare earth metals or calcium. Lance injection systems can also be used for the injection of microalloying elements. Reactants for sulfide level control can also be fed into the ladle in wire form or as a wire core.

After the ladle treatment, the molten steel is poured into a tundish and subsequently into a mold. To avoid oxygen pickup during pouring, the stream of metal must be protected by some shrouding system. A further refining step is promotion of flotation in the tundish and mold.

Vacuum treatment to decrease the amount of soluble gases is a further refinement of the steel. In principle the same effect can be achieved by very strict control of the process. In critical applications, there can be demands from the steel purchaser that vacuum degassing be used.

Utilizing the possibilities outlined above, the impurity levels that can be achieved routinely are

$$P < 100 \text{ ppm}, S < 50 \text{ ppm}, H < 2 \text{ ppm}, N < 40 \text{ ppm and } O < 40 \text{ ppm}$$

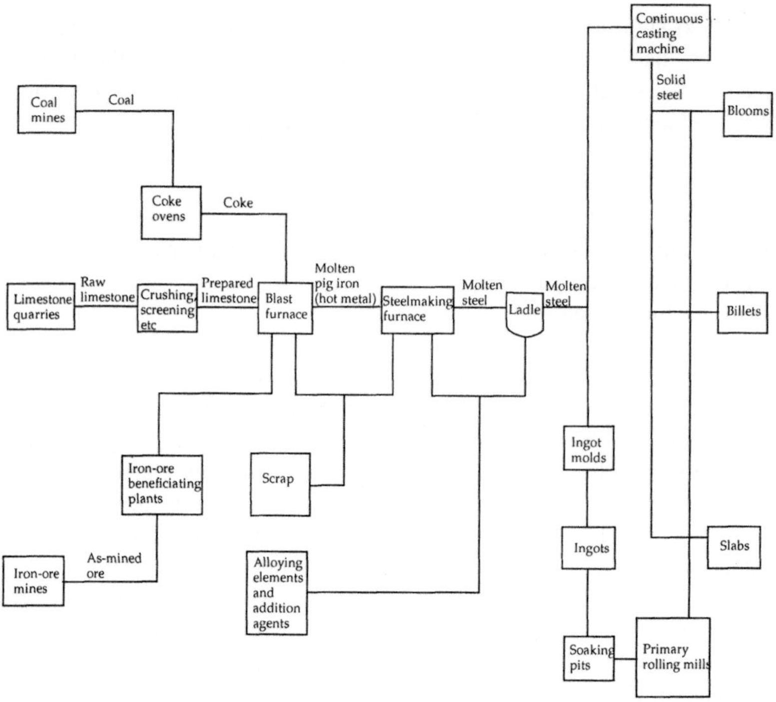

FIGURE 2.5. Scheme illustrating the steps in the production of steels, from ore to casting. (From Pehlke, R. D., *Metals Handbook, Desk Edition,* Boyer, H. E. and Gall, T. L., Eds., American Society for Metals, Metals Park, OH, 1985, chap. 22. With permission.)

Steels are cast either into ingots or continuously cast for further processing by rolling or forging for example. If the steel is cast into its final shape, it is called a true casting. Ingot casting, long the predominant method, has largely been replaced by continuous casting. Today, only extremely thick plates and special high-alloyed steels are ingot cast.

Ingot casts can be divided into four types, depending on the degree of killing of the steel: fully killed, semikilled, capped, and rimmed. For most applications, fully killed steels are required and these steels have a relatively low process yield, due to the cavity formed as a result of shrinkage during solidification. In the other types of ingot cast steels, pipe formation is compensated for by gas evolution, which makes blow holes in the cast. These blow holes are later welded shut during rolling.

The continuous casting process (Figure 2.6) has greater metal yield than ingot casting, resulting in lower fuel cost and higher productivity. The equipment is also relatively inexpensive and can be applied in a small-scale production plant. A further advantage is that special cross-sectional shapes can be cast, which can be rolled into structural sections. The technological

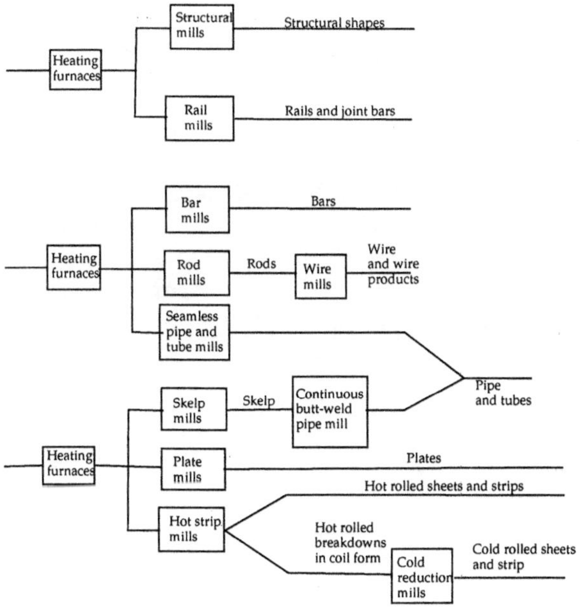

FIGURE 2.5 (continued).

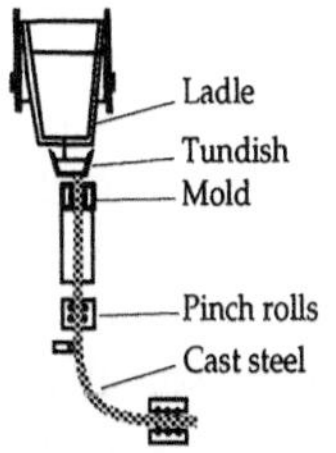

FIGURE 2.6. Schematic drawing of a curved continuous casting machine, which is the most common type. (From Pehlke, R. D., *Metals Handbook, Desk Edition,* Boyer, H. E. and Gall, T. L., Eds., American Society for Metals, Metals Park, OH, 1985, chap. 22. With permission.)

problems with the method are related to surface defects of the slabs, reduction in the quantity of nonmetallic inclusions, and centerline segregation. Surface cracking of slabs is related to the reduction of ductility over a certain temperature range (often 900 to 700°C). Embrittlement is found to be excessive when niobium is present in the steel, while the presence of titanium is generally beneficial. Nitrogen content is very important and there is a complicated interplay between these elements. If the slab is subjected to stresses from rolling or unbending, for example, cracks may occur.

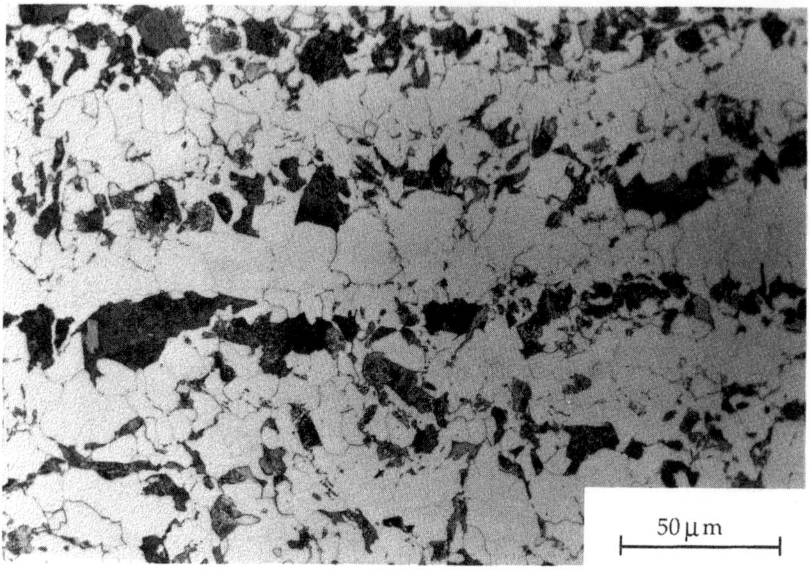

FIGURE 2.7. Banded structure of a steel, due to fine-scale segregation of manganese. In manganese-rich areas, the transformation is delayed, so that the partitioning of carbon from the ferrite forming in the manganese-depleted region leads to a higher fraction of pearlite.

Centerline segregation can be very pronounced in continuously cast steels. The segregation is caused by the combined action of two factors. The solidification starts from the walls of the slab and progresses toward the center, giving an enriched melt to solidify last. Due to shrinkage of the metal as it solidifies, it is necessary to feed in extra liquid at the end of the process to avoid cavity formation. This gives rise to so-called V-segregation. To avoid V-segregation, a soft (small mechanical) reduction is employed to squeeze the solidification fronts together. Electromagnetic stirring has also been used successfully to widen the segregation zone and thus reduce the negative effects. Certain elements (manganese, niobium) segregate more than others. By controlling the contents of these elements, the segregation problem can be reduced. However, the process parameters are the most important factors in reducing segregation. Segregation of manganese can also occur on a finer scale, leading to the characteristic banding of steels (Figure 2.7).

2.3. ALLOYING ELEMENTS

The state of individual elements in common low-alloy steels can be categorized as follows, although each element in general can have several different effects:

Substitutional elements	Microalloying elements	Carbide formers	Impurities
Manganese	Aluminum	Molybdenum	Sulfur
Silicon	Vanadium	Chromium	Phosphorus
Nickel	Niobium	Vanadium	Tin
Copper	Titanium	Niobium	Arsenic
Molybdenum	Boron	Titanium	Antimony
Chromium		Tungsten	Calcium
			Zirconium
			Rare earth elements

Sulfide shape control elements	Gases	Nonmetallic inclusions
Calcium silicates	Nitrogen	Oxides
Rare earth elements	Oxygen	Sulfides
	Hydrogen	Silicates

The presence of carbon is perhaps not necessary to mention, because by definition a steel is an alloy of iron and carbon. The carbon content of construction steels is at most 0.25 wt% (0.20 wt% in certain specifications). In many modern steels (both plates and line pipes) for use in offshore construction the carbon content is around 0.1 wt%. Steels under development now have ultra-low carbon contents (about 0.02 wt%) and are alloyed considerably with manganese, chromium, molybdenum, and nickel to achieve very high strengths (of the order of 900 MPa). The low carbon content greatly improves the weldability so that even these very high-strength steels can be welded without preheating if the weld metal does not need it.

The iron-carbon phase diagram (Figure 2.8) shows the different phases that appear in plain carbon steels as a function of temperature and carbon content. At highest temperatures either body-centered cubic (BCC) δ-ferrite or face-centered cubic (FCC) austenite appears during equilibrium cooling from the liquid state. Which phase is formed depends on the carbon content of the steel. If δ-ferrite forms, it is replaced by austenite as the temperature is lowered. On further cooling, the austenite transforms into BCC α-ferrite, the BCC phase being stabilized due to magnetic effects. Although the BCC lattice is less densely packed than the FCC lattice, it has a smaller solubility for carbon. Consequently, during the austenite to ferrite transformation, carbon must precipitate as another phase. Normally, the Fe_3C-phase cementite is formed. If the transformation occurs rather slowly, ferrite and cementite form together to generate a microstructure called pearlite, which is a eutectoid transformation product, with a typically lamellar appearance.

The phase diagram only shows the equilibrium phases. However, the transformations quite often proceed so rapidly that nonequilibrium phases are formed. The kinetics of the phase transformation are described by TTT

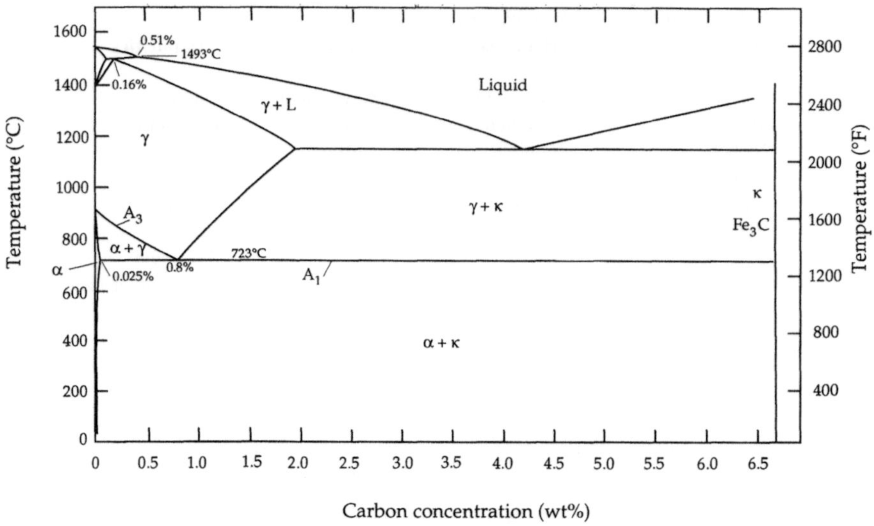

FIGURE 2.8. The iron-carbon phase diagram.

(time-temperature transformation) diagrams or CCT (continuous cooling transformation) diagrams. TTT diagrams are used when transformation takes place isothermally, while CCT diagrams describe transformations during continuous cooling from the austenite phase field. The typical appearance of these diagrams is shown in Figure 2.9. The TTT diagrams consist essentially of two C-curves. The upper C-curve describes diffusion-controlled transformations (diffusional transformation) to ferrite and pearlite. The lower C-curve describes displacement reactions to Widmanstätten ferrite and bainite. At higher temperatures within the lower C-curve, upper bainite is formed where cementite precipitates are found between the ferrite platelets. At lower temperatures, lower bainite is formed where cementite precipitates are found within the bainitic ferrite. If the transformation occurs at temperatures below the lower C-curve, then the austenite transforms without any diffusion to martensite. A more detailed description of the phase transformations will be given in Chapter 3.

The TTT diagram is affected by the alloying elements. Ferrite-stabilizing elements such as silicon and molybdenum move the transformation start temperatures to higher values, so that ferrite and pearlite form more easily. However, at the same time the curves may be displaced to the right, because the transformation may be more sluggish, thus delaying the transformation. Austenite stabilizers such as manganese and nickel both lower the transformation start temperature and displace the curves to the right. Thus, by alloying additions, it is possible to prevent the formation of ferrite and pearlite and instead obtain bainite or martensite. The ability of a steel to form martensite during quenching is called the hardenability of the steel. Bainite and martensite

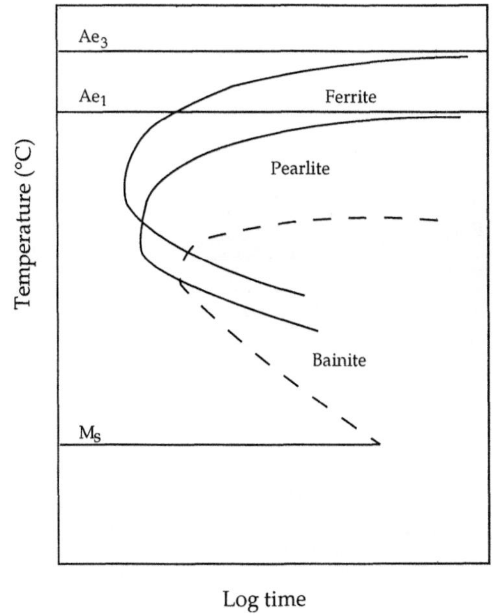

a

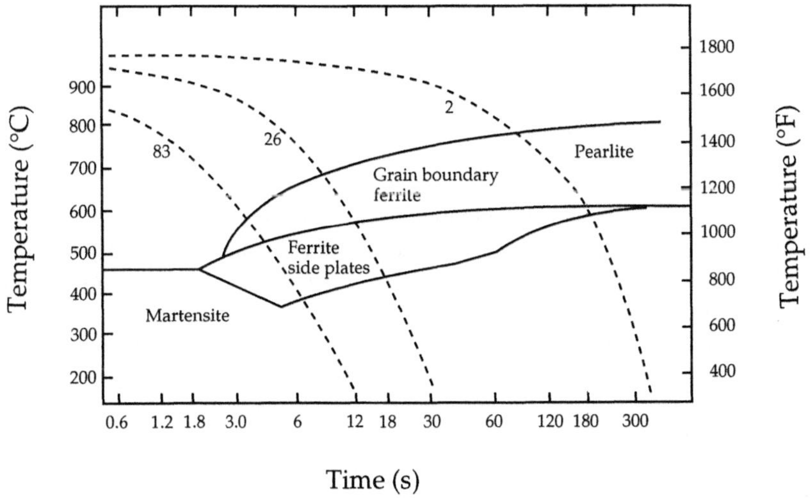

b

FIGURE 2.9. (a) A TTT diagram. (b) A CCT diagram. In (b), three different cooling curves have been superimposed, with the cooling rates given in °C/s.

FIGURE 2.10. Transmission electron micrograph of platelets of bainite. These platelets are separated only by low-angle grain boundaries and the effective unit from the strength and toughness point of view is a package of many platelets. (Courtesy of H. Bhadeshia, University of Cambridge, Cambridge, U.K.)

have higher hardness and strength than ferrite, but are often more brittle. Low-carbon martensite can, however, be relatively ductile, due to the fine grain size and relatively low hardness of the matrix. This fact is now being exploited in the design of both wrought alloys and high-strength weld deposits.

It is often desirable to have a fine grain size, because this can increase both strength and toughness. Although the lower temperature phases may have finer grains, this can be offset by the higher hardness. Bainite can be especially brittle because platelets of identical crystallographic orientation grow in packets, leading to the effective grain size of bainite being almost the same as the ferrite grain size (see Figure 2.10). The most efficient way to decrease the effective grain size is to have many nucleation sites where the transformation can begin. The most effective nucleation sites are grain boundaries, but impurity particles may also act as nucleants, as well as deformation bands. To achieve a fine ferrite grain size, it is thus necessary to have a fine austenite grain structure. A deformed austenite grain structure further enhances the possibilities of obtaining a fine ferrite grain size.

Other than carbon, manganese is the most common alloying element. It is present in most steels, with at least 0.5 wt%. For a steel to be called manganese-alloyed, the manganese content is usually larger than 1 wt%. The manganese content is seldom above 2 wt%, except for the ultra-low carbon bainitic steels. Manganese strengthens the steel by solid solution hardening, but it also has a strong effect on the austenite to ferrite transformation so that a finer ferrite grain size is achieved.

Nickel works in much the same way as manganese, but has a smaller solid solution effect. On the other hand, nickel is believed to improve toughness at low temperatures by influencing the stacking fault energy of the ferrite in such a way that plastic deformation at low temperatures is facilitated. Depending upon application, varying amounts of nickel alloying are used. For steels to be used at moderately low temperatures (below –60°C, e.g., for liquid petrol gas (LPG) purposes) about 1 wt% nickel is added. For lower temperatures (below –100°C, e.g., for liquid natural gas (LNG) purposes) 1 to 3 wt% nickel is added, and for extremely low temperatures (–196°C) 9 wt% nickel steels are used.

Copper influences the microstructure in a manner similar to manganese and nickel. However, the content of copper is kept fairly low in construction steels (<0.5 wt%). Higher amounts of copper may lead to precipitation of copper particles (ε-Cu). A special steel containing copper is the so-called "weathering steel," used for corrosion and oxidation protection. In these steels, higher amounts of copper are used.

Silicon has a powerful solid solution hardening effect, but the basic reason for adding silicon is to kill the steel, i.e., to react with the dissolved oxygen in order to avoid porosity. For some years aluminum was used instead of silicon for killing the steel, but this trend has been reversed. For high-quality steels silicon killing is used more and more. A positive factor with silicon killing is that lower nitrogen content is achieved.

Microalloying elements (aluminum, niobium, titanium, and vanadium) are used primarily to control austenite grain size, either during normalizing or during thermomechanical rolling. Aluminum sometimes has a dual role. It is used to kill the steel, both in conjunction with and as a replacement for silicon. Aluminum also reacts with nitrogen to form AlN. This reaction is relatively sluggish and does not take place during cooling in connection with rolling. Instead, AlN precipitates during normalizing heat treatment and helps to restrict grain growth. The fine austenite grain size thus formed leads to a fine ferrite grain size.

Vanadium and niobium are used in several types of steels: normalized, controlled rolled, and quench and tempered. In normalized steels the dispersion of particles prevents grain growth during the heat treatment. The yield strength is thus increased by a refined grain size. The particle distribution in itself also increases the yield strength, although the particles are relatively coarse. For thermomechanically rolled steels the MX-particle dispersion helps prevent recrystallization, if rolling is made in the non-recrystallizing temperature regime. Here, M stands for the metal (either vanadium or niobium) and X stands for the metalloid (either carbon or nitrogen). The precipitates can also be mixed carbonitrides. Both vanadium and niobium precipitate further during the austenite to ferrite transformation and increase the strength by precipitation hardening. In quench and tempered steels, the elements as in the other types of steel decrease the austenite grain size and increase hardenability. Carbonitrides are also precipitated during the tempering process.

Titanium is also used for austenite grain size control during hot rolling, but a more common application is in connection with welding. Titanium reacts with nitrogen to form TiN, which is stable up to high temperatures and retards austenite grain growth in the heat-affected zone during welding.

The carbide-forming elements chromium, molybdenum, and tungsten are mainly used in low-alloyed heat-resisting steels, where the carbides formed prevent dislocation movement. In these steels the content of molybdenum and tungsten is around 1 wt%, while the content of chromium varies from 1 up to 12 wt%. These steels have relatively low toughness at room temperature and below, so that their use at these temperatures is relatively limited. To achieve some moderate toughness properties the steels must be heat treated (normalized and tempered). Strength advantages are thus lost and the steels do not have strength levels much above ordinary controlled rolled steels. In small quantities (<0.5 wt%) these elements are used in ordinary construction steels in order to increase hardenability. This occurs by shifting the C-curves in the CCT diagram to the right, as for most of the other alloying elements. Molybdeneum is particularly useful in this sense.

The impurity elements mainly cause decreased toughness. The mechanisms for this vary, depending on the specific element. Oxygen forms slag particles together with elements such as silicon and manganese. These may serve as initiation points for cleavage fracture. The slag particle content also affects the ductile fracture energy, in that higher amounts lead to decreased toughness. Manganese also forms sulfides by reacting with sulfur. These inclusions are often soft and become elongated in the rolling direction. During welding, cracks may form at the interface between the elongated sulfides and the steel matrix. This problem can be cured by the addition of calcium silicide. The sulfides then become much harder and keep their rounded shapes, even after rolling. Rare earth elements, such as cerium, can also be used for this, but in offshore applications, for example, this so-called REM treatment is often not allowed.

Oxygen often coprecipitates with sulfur to form oxysulfides. It is important to prevent sulfur from combining with iron, to form FeS, because this compound has a low melting point and may wet the grain boundaries, leading to liquid phase embrittlement.

Hydrogen in large quantities may give rise to porosity. Smaller amounts may also give rise to problems because it causes low toughness. The exact mechanism for this is not clear but a popular theory is the accumulation of hydrogen at interfaces. Hydrogen is an interstitial and diffuses rapidly in the iron lattice. Accumulation of hydrogen may occur at interfaces such as between the matrix and inclusions, where a small crack may initiate due to the high pressure built up. Any drop in toughness is not noted by impact toughness testing however, because the hydrogen does not affect the high strain rate deformation and cracking. Instead, it is more common to find reduced ductility in tensile testing or as a low toughness in fracture mechanics testing.

The elements phosphorus, antimony, tin, and arsenic decrease toughness by segregating to the grain boundaries and decrease the bonding between the atoms there. Preferential segregation occurs to the prior austenite grain boundaries and the fracture surface of a specimen embrittled by these elements has a typical intergranular appearance.

2.4. ROLLING OF THE STEEL

Rolling of steels naturally has the aim of obtaining the correct dimensions (thickness, width, and length) of the product for a certain application. However, it has long been realized that rolling is a thermomechanical treatment of the steels which can be utilized to improve the properties. The rolling techniques have developed since the mid-1960s to ever-higher degrees of sophistication. The different rolling procedures used today are listed below. However, it should be realized that the rolling procedures used are connected intimately to the chemistry of the steel.

All plates are hot rolled as a first stage to use the facility of easy rolling to reduce the thickness of the plates. The slabs that come out from the continuous casting usually have a thickness of 200 to 250 mm. A considerable reduction in thickness must be made, because the final thickness of the steel is seldom more than 100 mm and very often much lower.

Somewhat different production schemes may be used, depending on the final thickness of the plates. Thin plates are usually defined as being in the range 2 to 16 mm. They are hot rolled in a continuous hot rolling unit. Some of the thin plates (e.g., for the automotive industry) are cold rolled, after being hot rolled down to a thickness of 2 to 6 mm. Cold rolling is carried out in a continuous cold rolling unit, down to a thickness of around 0.5 to 2 mm. After the rolling process, the plates are heat treated to achieve properties for pressability. Such thin plates as mentioned above are seldom used for construction purposes. The weldability problems are also different from those in the construction industry. For thin plates the problems are mostly concerned with surface protective layers, e.g., of zinc or aluminum, which may cause problems such as porosity during welding.

Thick plates are defined as those in the thickness range above 6 mm. The hot rolling usually takes place in a reversible rolling unit, followed by further deformation in some of the above-mentioned schemes. The hot rolling procedures used can be subdivided as:

- Conventional rolling with high finish rolling temperatures (in the interval 1000 to 1100°C, followed by air cooling)
- Normalizing rolling
- Thermomechanical rolling (TM) (also called thermomechanical controlled processing, TMCP); for some types of steel this can be followed by accelerated cooling
- Quenching and tempering (QT) steels or direct quenching and tempering (DQ + T)

Conventional rolling with high finish rolling temperatures requires only moderate-strength rolling equipment. The steels will get a fairly coarse ferritic grain size because the austenite grains easily recrystallize and become fairly coarse, leading to few nucleation points for ferrite during transformation. The structure of the steels will be ferritic/pearlitic.

To improve the properties of hot rolled steels, a normalizing heat treatment at around 900°C can be performed. The steels will be reaustenitized but the austenite grain size will be finer than in the hot rolled condition. This then gives a finer ferrite grain size. By using AlN, the size of the austenite grains during the heat treatment can be controlled even further. Niobium additions give steels with even higher strengths with no deterioration in toughness, because the austenite grain size is decreased even more than in AlN-treated steels. Also, these steels have a microstructure consisting of a mixture of ferrite and pearlite.

Thus, hot rolled and normalized steels basically obtain their properties from the alloying content, by solid solution hardening, and to some extent from grain size control.

Normalizing rolling can be seen as an alternative to normalizing heat treatment of hot rolled plates. The purpose is to obtain the same properties as in normalized steels. Also, the properties should remain even if the steel is subjected to a heat treatment at temperatures around 900°C. Other steel types, described below, will lose their mechanical properties if they are subjected to a high-temperature heat treatment. Final reduction during normalizing rolling takes place between 900 to 1000°C. The austenite grains are deformed, but the rolling is made at such a high temperature that the structure can recrystallize (although not completely) and thus form new austenite grains. However, these grains are considerably smaller than the original ones, leading also to the formation of small ferrite grains. The steels can often be microalloyed with small amounts of the carbide-forming elements such as vanadium and niobium. Quite often they are also microalloyed with titanium. Microaddition of vanadium and/or niobium results in precipitation of V(C,N) or Nb(C,N) during the austenite to ferrite transformation or in the ferrite. This precipitation further increases the yield strength of the steel, which otherwise is due to solution hardening and fine grains.

There is one significant difference between conventionally normalized steels and normalizing rolled steels, if the steels are aluminum treated. During furnace normalizing, aluminum combines with nitrogen to form AlN. However, this reaction is sluggish and will not occur during normalizing rolling, meaning that such steels may contain significant content of free nitrogen. This in turn can lead to a higher risk for strain aging. Addition of titanium is to some extent used to tie up the surplus of nitrogen in the form of very fine (<20 nm) "TiN" particles which inhibit grain growth of austenite during reheating and hot rolling.

Thermomechanical rolling (TM) is used for rolling of niobium or niobium, vanadium, and titanium microalloyed steels. Rolling takes place with a strictly controlled deformation and temperature program and the finish rolling temperature is quite low. Rolling takes place at temperatures where the austenite can recrystallize (around 950°C), in the nonrecrystallization temperature region (around 900°C), and in the dual-phase (austenite + ferrite) temperature region. This type of process requires that microalloying elements are used to control the grain size of the austenite during rolling by precipitation of carbonitrides. By rolling just above 900°C, a deformed austenitic structure is obtained which recrystallizes very slowly. By using microalloying elements, especially niobium, recrystallization is slowed down even further. The deformed austenite grains will have a pancake shape, with many internal defects. Some recovery may take place, building up low-angle boundaries in the austenite grains. During transformation, ferrite nucleates on both ordinary grain boundaries and low-angle boundaries, leading to a small ferrite grain size. Simultaneously, further precipitation of microalloying carbides during transformation can occur. The basic structure is still a mixture of ferrite and pearlite, but with very fine ferrite grains. The rolling in the two-phase region gives a deformation of the ferrite.

Thus, the mechanisms contributing to the increased strength in this class of steel are finer grain size and dislocation hardening. Alternatively, the alloying content (mainly carbon) is reduced and the strength level is kept as for the normalized steels. However, this process does not always give steels with acceptable strength and toughness for many applications. Also, weldability is limited for heavier thickness and higher strength steels because preheat normally is required. Thus, further refinement of the microstructure is necessary. This has been achieved by faster cooling through the transformation temperature regime by water spraying of the steel surface.

If the water spraying is interrupted at a temperature that is between the start and finish temperatures of the transformation, then the process is called accelerated cooling. The start and finish temperatures as well as the cooling rate during water spraying are process variables that have been studied in detail during the development of the process. To optimize the properties of the steels, these variables must be carefully controlled. The microstructure of these steels is no longer ferrite and pearlite, but a fine-grained bainite, at least for thinner plates, where the cooling rates have been sufficient. Using this approach it is possible to further reduce the carbon content, improving weldability significantly, and still have high yield strength.

The increased strength is achieved by still finer grain size and by the higher dislocation content of the lower transformation products (bainite) that may appear. The yield strengths that are possible with either of the processes described above depend to some extent on thickness (larger thickness giving lower yield strength), but in general 360 MPa yield strength is obtained. With the TM process 500-MPa yield strength steels are made in thicknesses up to 50 mm. TM steels processed without accelerated cooling can be made with yield strengths of 420 MPa in thin dimensions. Figure 2.11 shows the rolling procedures and the resulting microstructures.

QT steels are made by a fundamentally different process than those described above. The steels are rolled at temperatures above 900°C and then quenched using water to ambient temperature (Figure 2.12). The cooling rates employed can vary from a few to around 30°C/s. By keeping a relatively high alloying content (e.g., of manganese), the austenite transforms to martensite, with a very fine grain size. However, the martensite is too brittle to be used directly. After quenching, the steels are therefore tempered at around 600°C. The martensite then decays into very fine-

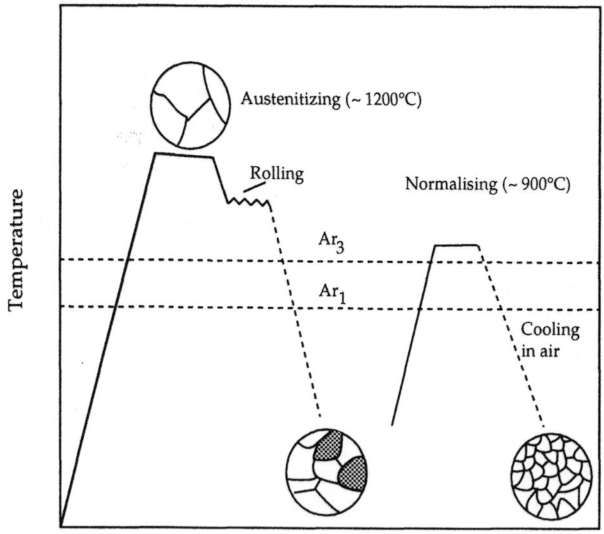

a

FIGURE 2.11. (a) Schematic drawing of the conventional hot rolling process, followed by normalizing heat treatment. (b) Microstructure of a normalized steel. (c) The thermomechanical rolling process, followed either by air cooling or water spraying. The rolling is made at a lower temperature as compared to hot rolling. If rolling is made above the recrystallization temperature, an equiaxed austenite is formed, giving an equiaxed ferrite. If rolling takes place below the recrystallization temperature, the austenite grains will have a pancake shape, with a high defect content. The ferrite grains can then nucleate at many sites, giving a fine ferrite grain size. (d) Microstructures of a thermomechanical rolled steel. (e) Microstructure of a steel produced by thermomechanical rolling followed by accelerated cooling. (b, d, and e from Siwecki, T., Res. Rep. IM-1582 and IM-2515, Institute of Metals Research, Stockholm, 1990. With permission.)

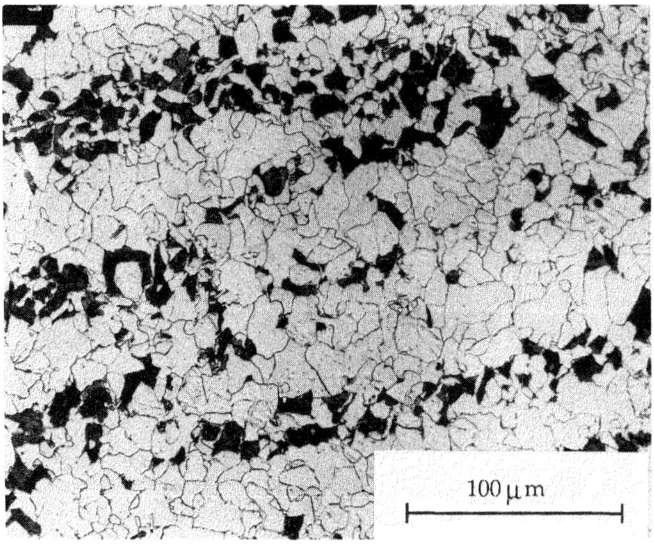

FIGURE 2.11b

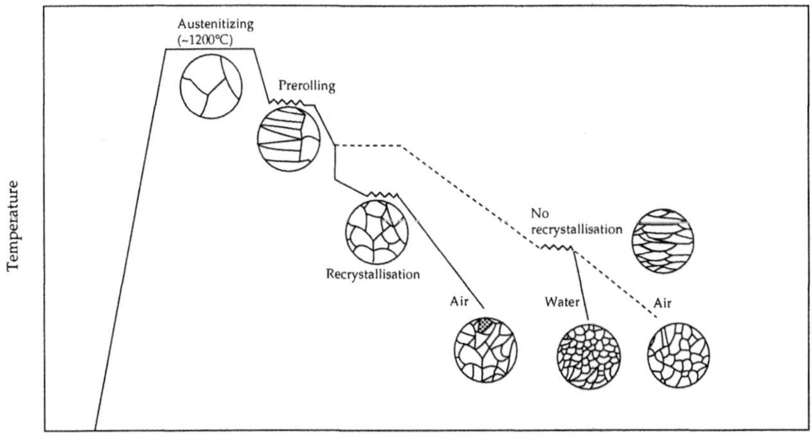

FIGURE 2.11c

grained ferrite and carbides. Weldable QT steels have yield strengths ranging from 450 to 1000 MPa. Variations in yield strengths are achieved by modifications of chemical composition. For the lower range of yield strengths, typical contents of alloying elements are (wt%) 0.10 to 0.15 carbon and 1.0 to 1.7 manganese. A common class of structural steels, for example, for marine applications, are those having a yield strength of 700 MPa (100,000 psi). The

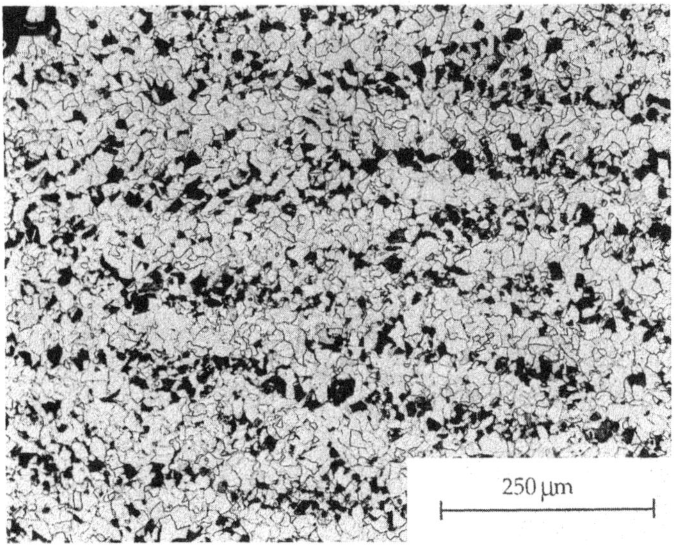

FIGURE 2.11d

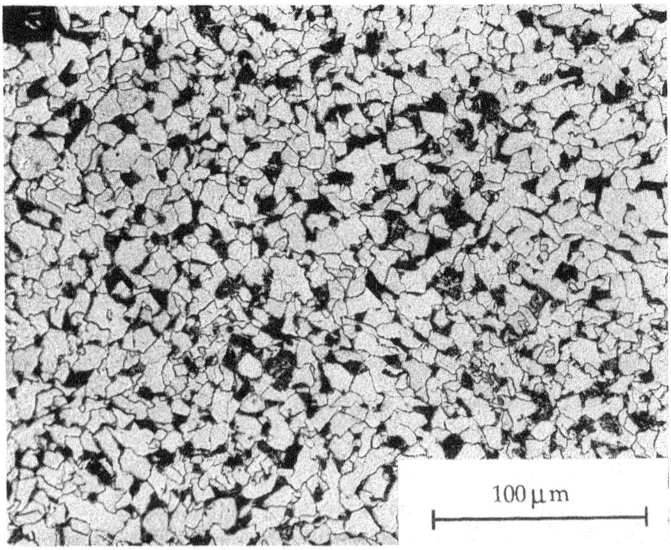

FIGURE 2.11e

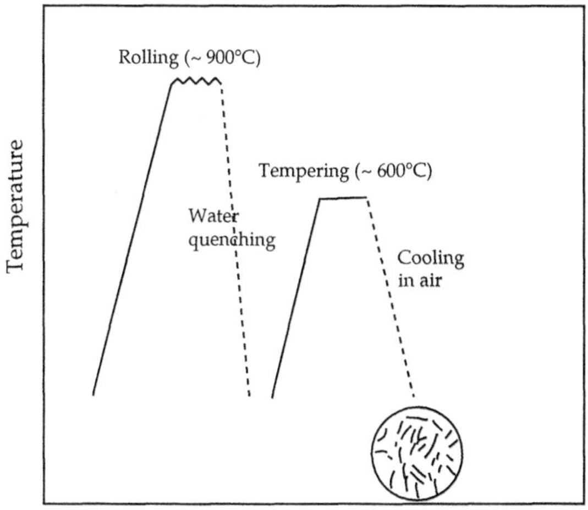

a

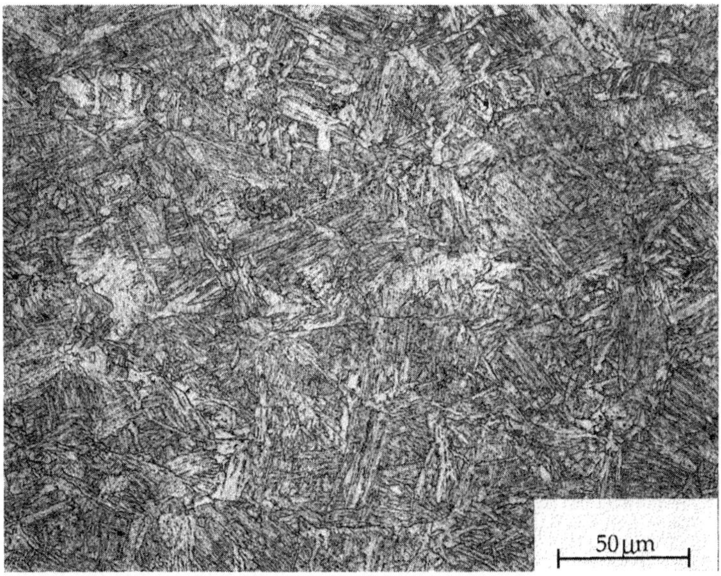

b

FIGURE 2.12. (a) Rolling schedule for the QT process. (b) Microstructure of a high-strength QT steel. (Courtesy of T. Siwecki, Institute of Metals Research, Stockholm.)

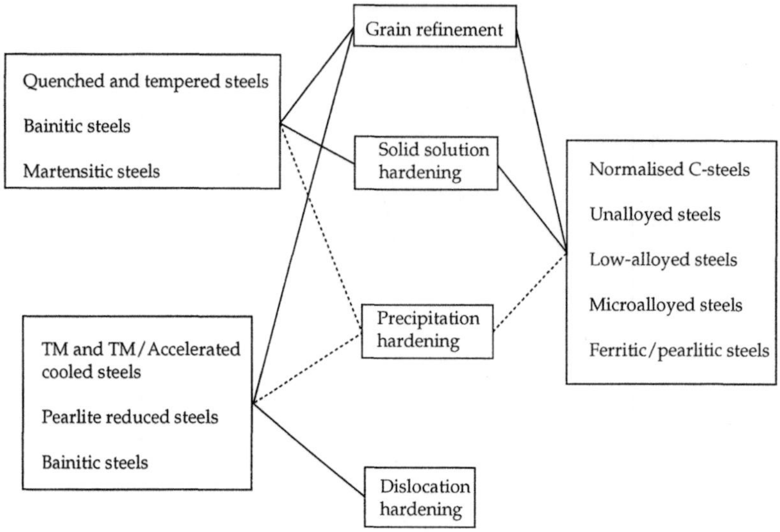

FIGURE 2.13. Diagram illustrating how the strengthening processes are utilized in different kinds of steel.

higher yield strength is achieved by modifying the composition by addition of about 0.3 wt% chromium, 0.5 wt% molybdenum, and sometimes 1 wt% nickel. Further enhancement of the yield strength requires addition of more alloying elements and sometimes use of elements such as boron in small quantities.

The DQ process is obtained by applying water spraying in a manner similar to TM steels, but continuing the spraying down to temperatures much lower than the austenite to ferrite transformation finish temperature. This can be regarded as a variant of the QT process. The steels are either rolled with a high finish rolling temperature, giving a recrystallized austenite, or with a lower finish rolling temperature, giving a nonrecrystallized austenite.

Figure 2.13 summarizes the different metallurgical mechanisms that are used to affect the strength of steels.

Table 2.1 summarizes the connection between process and chemical composition. It should be noted that the exact composition of a steel is dependent upon the details of the steelworks equipment, so that deviations from Table 2.1 may occur. The mechanical properties and the weldability obtained from the different rolling processes are shown in Table 2.2. Once again, these values are quite general and exceptions may be found.

2.5. CLASSIFICATION, DESIGNATION, AND SPECIFICATION

The classification and designation of steels usually follow national codes and thus there is a large variety of steel designations. However, some codes are

TABLE 2.1
Schematic Presentation of the Chemical Composition of Steels from Various Rolling Processes

	Chemical composition					
Process	**C**	**Si**	**Mn**	**V**	**Nb**	**Ti**
Normal rolling, high finish rolling temperature	0.20	0.3	0.5 — 1.8	—	—	—
Thermomechanical rolling	0.15	0.3	1.0 — 1.7	0.05	0.030	0.01
Thermomechanical rolling with accelerated cooling	0.07 — 0.15	0.3	1.0 — 1.7	0.05	0.03	0.01
Quenched and tempered	0.07 — 0.15	0.3	1.0 — 1.7	0.05	0.03	0.01 — 0.03

Note: Large variations may exist between different steel works and the values in the table should be regarded only as guidelines.

internationally used more frequently than others, such as the German DIN, the British BS, and the U.S. ASTM standards. A common standard for most of the countries in Europe (European Norm, EN) has been in effect since September 1990 and will replace national standards for most of the European countries. The aim of this section is to briefly describe the designation system of some of the most frequently used codes and also to briefly introduce the EN system.

2.5.1. CLASSIFICATION AND DESIGNATION

Steels are often *classified* with respect to four major concepts: intended use, chemical composition, finishing method (e.g., hot rolled), and product form (e.g., pipes). Furthermore, a subdivision can be made within these concepts. Steels are often denoted after the main alloying elements (e.g., carbon steels, carbon-manganese steels, chromium steels, etc). In U.S. practice these are often called "grades" of steels, while in EN "grade" denotes the strength level within the standard. The classification after intended use provides names such as ship plate, line pipe steels, construction steels, pressure vessel steels, etc. Quality classification often refers to the Bonhomme system, adopted by the International Institute of Welding (IIW). The steels are classified in groups A to E, where group A has the lowest demands. The evaluation of a steel depends on the level of impurities and on the impact toughness requirements.

The principal basis for the *designation* of steels (i.e., identification of a certain steel using numbers and/or letters or other symbols) is chemical composition or intended use and strength level. In the U.S., the AISI (American

TABLE 2.2
Rough Summary of the Properties that Can Be Obtained with Different Rolling Practices

Process	Strength (MPa)	Toughness (J)	Weldability
Normal rolling, high finish rolling temperature	200–360	27 J/0°C	Good–moderate
Normalized steels	200–360	27 J/–40°C	Good–moderate
Thermomechanical rolling	300–420	27 J/–20°C	Good
Thermomechanical rolling with accelerated cooling	300–500	40 J/–40°C	Very good
Quenched and tempered	450–1000	40 J/–40°C	Very good–moderate (dependent on thickness)

Note: A range of properties for the same rolling practice can be obtained due to variation in alloying content.

Iron and Steel Institute) designation system is the most well known. This system is almost identical to that of the SAE (Society of Automotive Engineers). This system uses a four-digit notation to describe the type of steel. For example, plain carbon steels, with a maximum manganese content of 1.00 wt%, are designated 10*xx*. For the "*xx*" the carbon content, in hundredths of a percent, is to be inserted. The ASTM (American Society for Testing and Materials) and the ASME (American Society of Mechanical Engineers) have a designation system for their specifications, consisting of the letter A (for ferrous materials), followed by three digits, in serial order. A steel can be identified by referring to the ASTM specification that it fulfills. However, this is not always enough to completely specify a steel.

A unified numbering system (UNS) has been developed by ASTM, SAE, and other bodies. This designation system consists of one letter and five numerals. The letter indicates the broad class of steels and the numerals define the specific alloy within the class.

One group of steels commonly referred to are HSLA (high-strength low-alloy steels). These steels have been developed with special reference to mechanical properties. The steels can be divided into two groups of compositions:

1. Vanadium and/or niobium steels, with a manganese content generally not exceeding 1.35 wt%, with the addition of 0.2 wt% copper when specified
2. High-strength intermediate-manganese steels, with a manganese content in the range of 1.10 to 1.65 wt%, with the addition of a minimum of 0.2 wt% copper when specified

The strength levels attainable with HSLA steels match those of the older HY steels, which were QT steels.

In Germany structural steels are described by a DIN W (Werkstoff) number, e.g., 1.0037, which refers to the number of the standard. The steels are often simply denoted by a symbol name, such as St 37. This approximately describes the ultimate tensile strength of the steel in kilograms per square millimeter.

In the U.K. weldable structural steels are described in British Standard (BS) 4360; they are denoted as 50D, where 50 stands for the ultimate tensile strength in kilograms per square millimeter and D stands for the quality level, represented by the impact toughness requirement.

The European Norms (EN) for the steels under consideration here are EN 10025, 10028, 10113, and 10184. The EN standards are directed toward a group of applications and a number of steels can then fall within this specification. The designation of the steels will be made with an alphanumerical system. This looks like EN 10025 Fe 510 C, where 510 stands for the minimum specified tensile strength in MPa and C is the quality designation. This classification is different from the Bonhomme classification. A comparison between the Bonhomme system and the EN system is shown in Table 2.3. There may in certain cases be additional letter combinations following the quality description, which describe the deoxidation method, particular applications, and delivery conditions.

An eventual result of the work to harmonize the standards in the European countries is that national standards will gradually disappear.

2.5.2. SPECIFICATIONS

Specification of steels means a written document describing the attributes the product must possess in order to be used for a certain application. The difference between classification and specification should be noted.

There are standard material specifications issued by organizations such as ASTM, ECISS (European Committee for Iron and Steel Standardization), BSI (British Standard Institution), DIN, AFNOR (Association Francaise de Normalization), and others. Most constructions are designed with a reference to international or national materials standards, such as ISO, EN, BSI, DIN, and ASTM. Likewise, classification societies, such as Det Norske Veritas, Lloyd's Register of Shipping, American Bureau of Shipping, ASME, and others, have their own standard specifications. Many oil companies also have their own specifications for steels to be used in offshore operations.

The specifications contain information about chemical composition, either by detailing the allowed quantities or by referring to a standard. Further, there is a quality description which uses a defined set of quality descriptors to identify the type of product. The steelmaking process allowed is also given. This is then followed by quantitative requirements, such as allowable range of compositions, mechanical properties requirements, etc. The test methods used to measure the properties are also given. Information about tolerances of dimensions, surface condition, and general delivery conditions is also found.

TABLE 2.3
Comparison between the Bonhomme Quality System and the EN System

		Impact testing requirement	
Bonhomme	EN 10025	Testing temp (°C)	Impact toughness (J)
–0	—	—	—
A	—	—	—
B	B	(+20)	27
C	C	0	27
D	D	–20	27
—	DD	–20	40
E	—	–40	27

TABLE 2.4
The American Petroleum Institute Specification for Weldable Pipe Steels

Specification	Product
2B	Welded steel plate pipe for construction of offshore drilling platforms
5A	Welded or seamless steel pipe for oil or gas well casing, tubing, or drill pipe
5AC	Welded or seamless steel pipe with restricted yield strength range for oil or gas well casing or tubing
5AX	High-strength seamless steel pipe for oil or gas well casing, tubing, or drill pipe
5L	All-welded or seamless steel line pipe for oil or gas transmission

For pipes there are two sets of specifications: ASTM and API (American Petroleum Institute). The API specification system is shown in Table 2.4.

The steels are generally denoted according to their tensile strength, e.g., X65 indicates a steel with 65,000 psi in yield strength. To translate this into SI units, it should be multiplied approximately by a factor 6.9, so that a X80 steel has a yield strength of approximately 560 MPa.

Another type of specification is an *object norm* which includes requirements for the construction and design stresses. The material standard is included in the object norm. Examples of such norms are ASME pressure vessel codes, TÜV codes, Eurocode 3, etc. These codes provide the requirements for heat-affected zone properties, welding procedure specifications, and similar properties.

Chapter 3

THE HEAT-AFFECTED ZONE

3.1. INTRODUCTION

During welding, parts of the base metal lying adjacent to the fused zone will be subjected to one or more severe thermal cycles. In this *heat-affected zone* (HAZ) significant changes in the microstructure and properties take place due to the transformations induced by the thermal cycles. In this chapter the metallurgical processes that take place will be described in detail, while the consequences to properties will be discussed in Chapter 5.

The HAZ can be divided into several subzones, depending on the peak temperature that the material has experienced. Closest to the fusion line the steel reverts first to austenite and then possibly to δ-ferrite, if the carbon content is low. However, this zone, which reaches temperatures in excess of 1500°C (2700°F), is very narrow and is seldom noticed. One effect that can occur in this zone is that it becomes partially molten only to resolidify without significant mixing with the rest of the weld metal. There can even be a very thin layer which is completely molten, but has not mixed with the rest of the weld pool. An *unmixed zone* is created, but in most steels considered here, this zone is of little consequence and will not be dealt with further. The austenite grain size is often smaller in this zone than in the coarse-grained zone lying next to it. This is thought to be due to the austenite to δ-ferrite transformation, followed rapidly by a transformation back to austenite.

For regions of the HAZ that achieve peak temperatures between 1100 to 1500°C (2000 to 2700°F), the steels transform to austenite, the grains of which can grow significantly during the high-temperature part of the thermal cycle. This part is called the "coarse-grained zone." The grain growth just described is one of the main problems in welding metallurgy and a large part of this chapter is devoted to the examination of the grain growth, its consequences, and how the problem can be tackled.

Areas that are heated to temperatures in the range 900 to 1100°C (1600 to 2000°F) usually achieve a relatively fine and uniform grain size, as if the steel has been normalized. This area is called the fine-grained zone and is usually considered to possess relatively good mechanical properties.

Below the fully reaustenitized regions, where the temperature range is somewhere between approximately 700 to 900°C (1300 to 1600°F), the steel transforms only partially to austenite, while some ferrite is retained. In certain circumstances this can lead to deterioration of the properties. This zone is called the "intercritically heated zone." Finally, the steel in the subcritically heated zone does not transform at all to austenite, but is tempered. The peak temperature remains below the Ae_1 temperature, i.e., below ca. 700°C (1300°F). (For definition of A_1 and A_3 temperatures, see the phase diagram in Figure 2.8.)

There are no phase changes, but several reactions can occur in the ferrite phase. In the higher temperature range, the ferrite can recover or recrystallize. Carbides and nitrides from microalloying elements may precipitate and cause an increase in hardness. Cementite particles can spherodize or precipitate during the tempering of martensite. Significant effects are found even in the regions tempered at temperatures below 200°C (400°F). Strain aging due to the diffusion of the interstitial elements to dislocation cores can make plastic flow more difficult and hence lead to embrittlement.

In Figure 3.1 a low-magnification micrograph is shown illustrating the complete HAZ, together with more detailed micrographs of the different zones. In this case the combination of plate thickness, heat input, preheat, and steel chemistry has been such that martensite has formed in the coarse-grained zone. The color micrographs in Plate 1* show the microstructure obtained with very slow cooling, where a coarse lath type of ferrite is formed.

Of course, the HAZs can also be generated in the weld metal during multirun welding. Many regions experience multiple thermal cycles of differing magnitudes. In total, this creates a complicated pattern with a variety of different zones of varying microstructure, each zone being perhaps only of the order of a millimeter and bearing its unique mechanical properties.

The details are discussed here in terms of the various ferritic constituents which grow from the austenite, followed by an examination of the austenite grain growth behavior. The chapter concludes with a discussion of some qualities of steel that are especially pertinent to the HAZ.

3.2. PHASE TRANSFORMATIONS

The first phase transformation to consider is that which occurs as the ferrite is heated into the austenite phase field. The characteristics of such reactions are not well established. Knowledge about reaustenitization is obviously less advanced when compared with the transformation of austenite during cooling. It is worth bearing in mind that there are some fundamental differences between the two kinds of transformation. For example, whereas the diffusivity decreases and the driving force increases during cooling of austenite, both diffusivity and driving force increase during the superheating of ferrite into regimes where only austenite is stable. Thus, it is well established that the austenite to ferrite transformation shows "C"-curve behavior in time-temperature transformation (TTT) diagrams because at high temperatures the driving force is small but diffusivity is large, while at low temperatures the opposite is true. In contrast, the rate of reaustenitization must increase indefinitely with temperature so that the relevant TTT diagrams must show an ever-decreasing time period to achieve a specified degree of transformation as the superheat is increased. Recent work by Yang and Bhadeshia[1] on the reaustenization of weld

* Plate 1 appears following page 84.

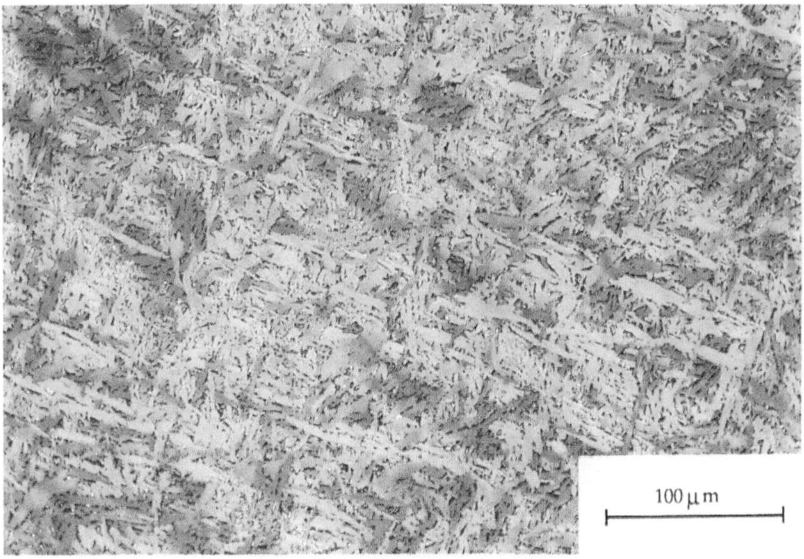

PLATE 1a.

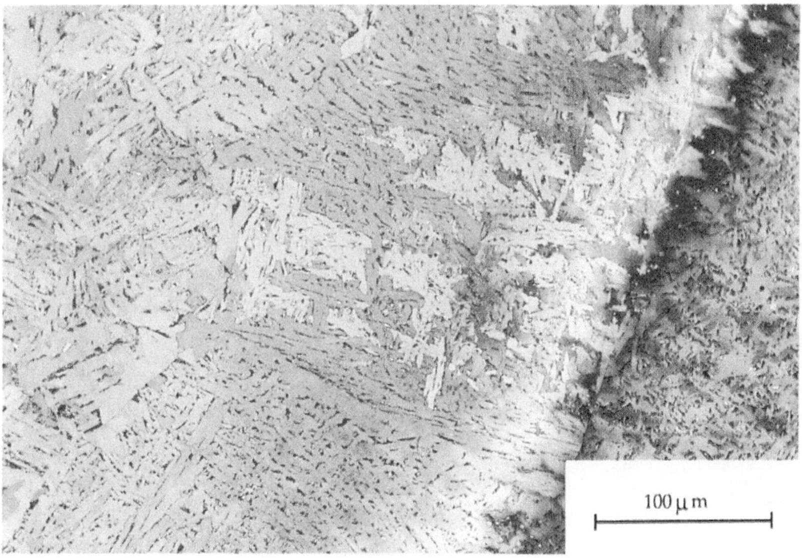

PLATE 1b.

PLATE 1. The microstructure of the HAZ in a 25-mm welded joint, welded with two-pass SAW, giving a heat input of about 3 kJ/mm. (a) The weld metal structure. (b) Transition between weld metal and HAZ. (c) Lath ferrite in the coarse-grained zone. (d) The fine-grained zone. (e) The intercritically heated zone. (f) The unaffected base metal.

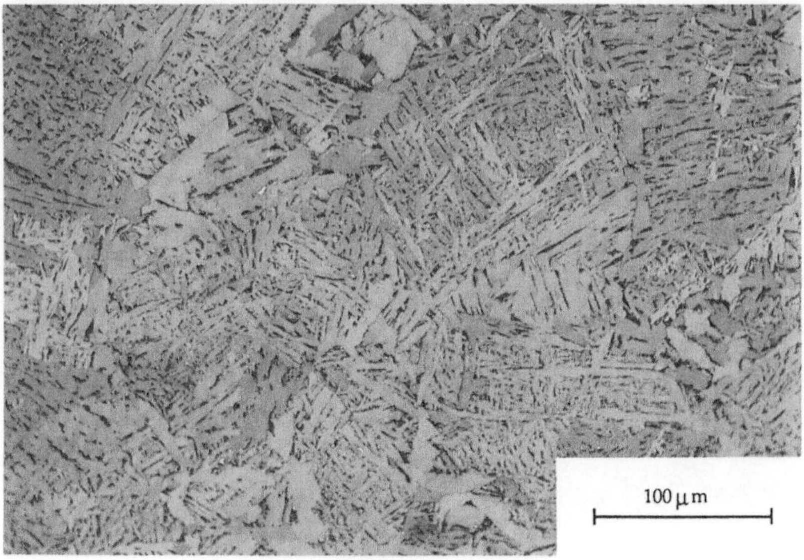

PLATE 1c.

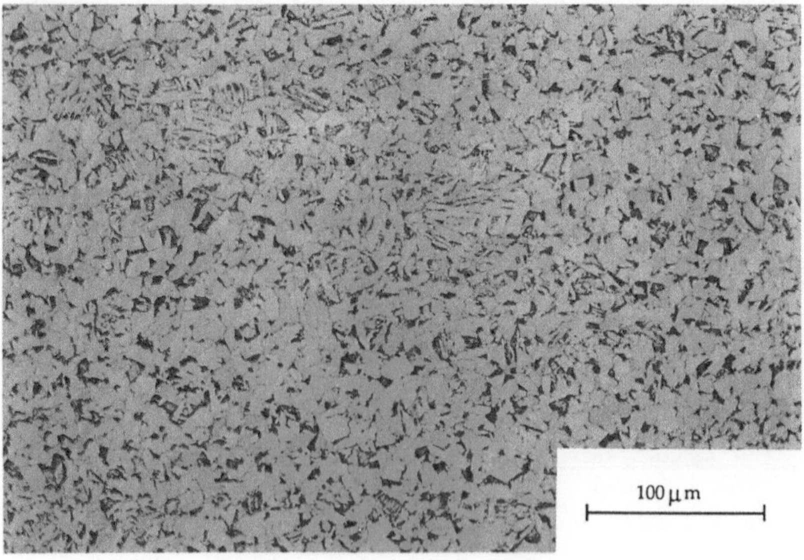

PLATE 1d.

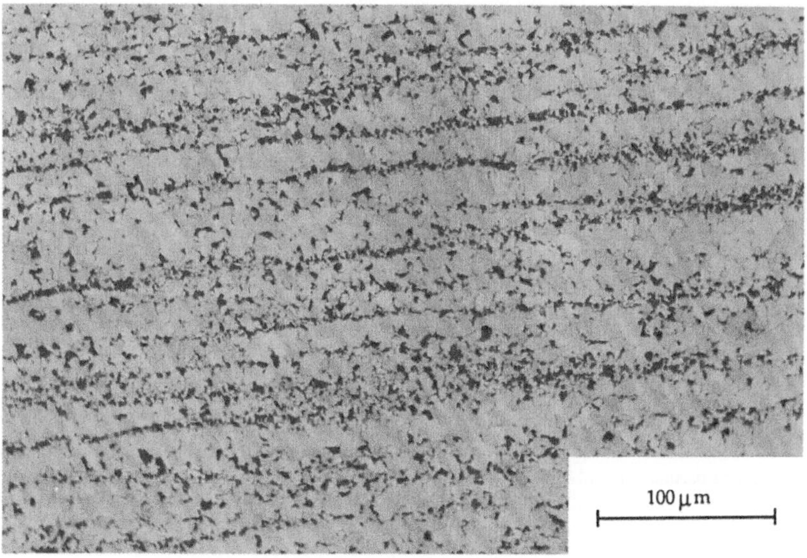

PLATE 1e.

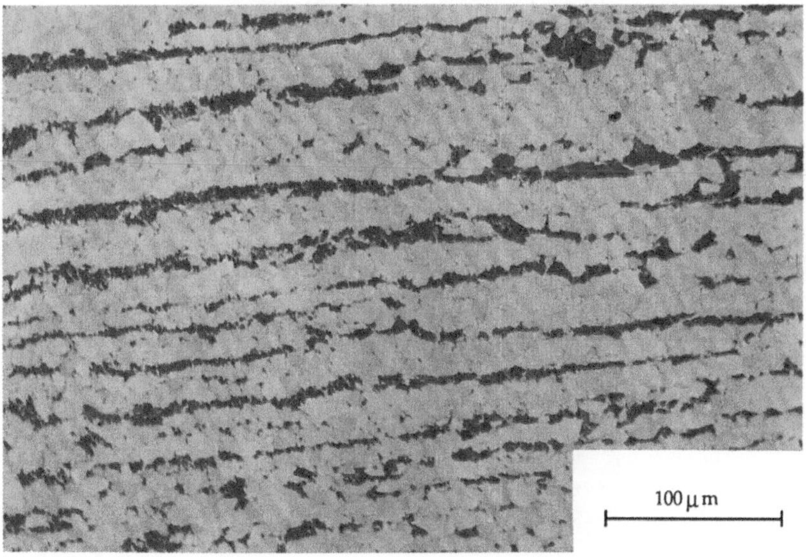

PLATE 1f.

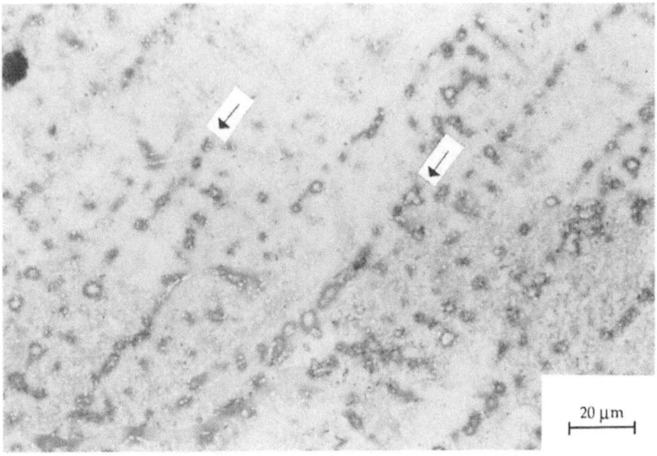

PLATE 2. Color etching, using Klemm's reagent to reveal the solidification pattern, showing segregated particles, mainly phosphides and sulfides, which appear white (arrows). The ferritic microstructure can be seen simultaneously from pre-etching with a nital-type etchant.

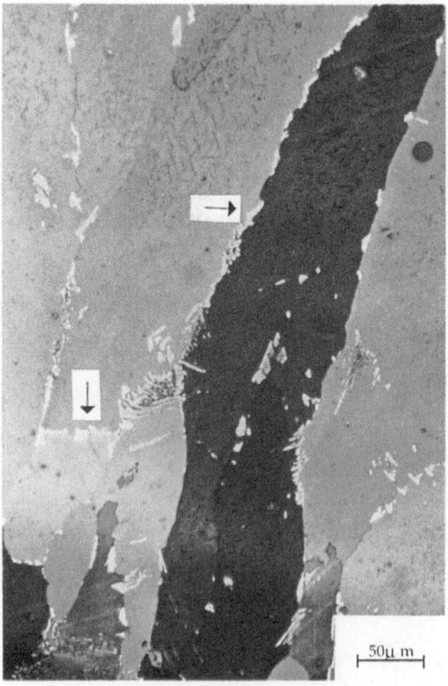

PLATE 3. A plain C-Mn weld metal, in which the austenite loop has been closed by the addition of aluminum. The δ-ferrite to austenite transformation has thus occurred to a very limited extent. The nucleation of austenite (white) in the δ-ferrite grain boundaries can be seen (arrows). This austenite subsequently transformed to martensite.

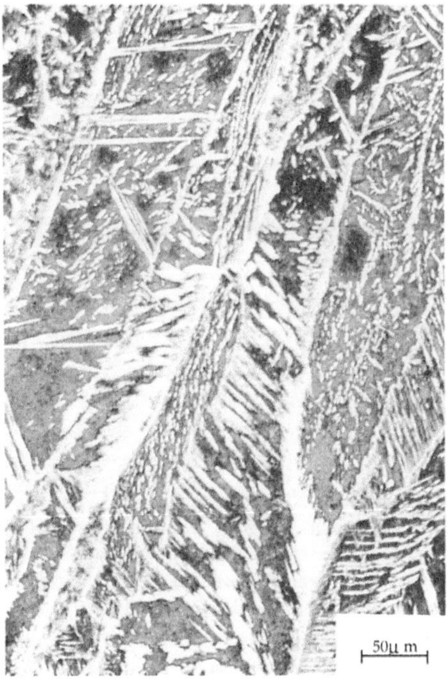

PLATE 4. Micrograph of a duplex stainless steel weld metal. The microstructure consists of two phases (austenite and ferrite) in approximately equal amounts. There are some similarities between this microstructure and the microstructure in Plate 3. The austenite grows from the ferrite grain boundaries in a side plate manner.

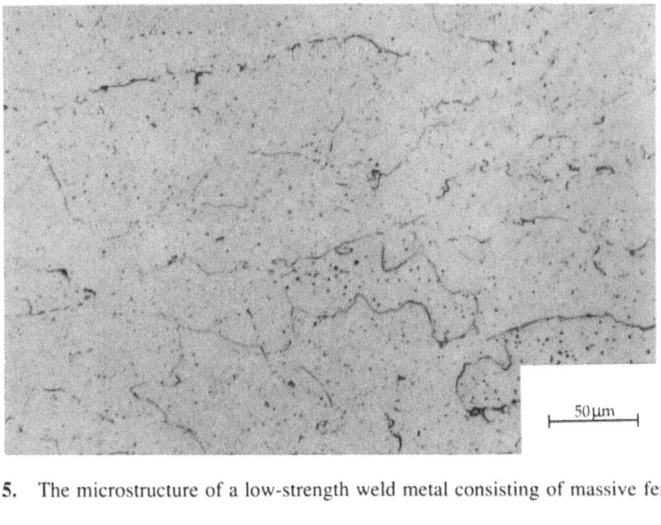

PLATE 5. The microstructure of a low-strength weld metal consisting of massive ferrite.

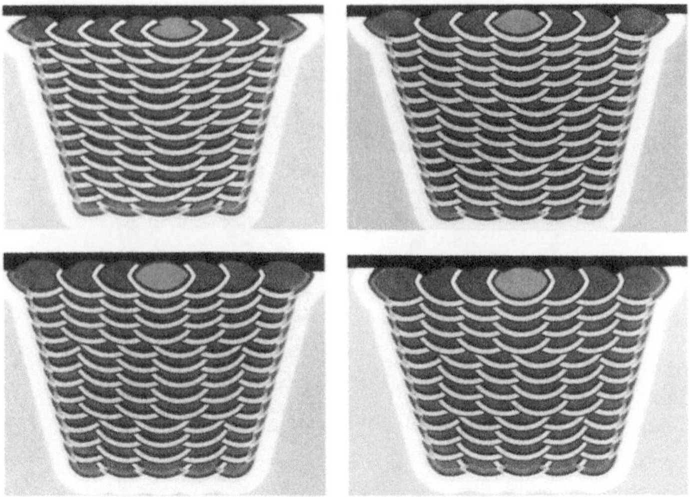

PLATE 6. Graphical output from a computer program, illustrating how a joint is filled with a number of beads. The different colors represent various degrees of "heat treatments" that the material has received due to the deposition of subsequent beads. The effect of increasing the electrode diameter *d* from 3.25 to 6 mm, but keeping the current constant, is shown. A larger diameter electrode means that fewer beads need to be deposited to fill the joint. A slight reduction in the fraction of unreaustenitized (columnar) weld metal is also obtained. (Top left) 3.25 mm diameter, (top right) 4 mm, (bottom left) 5 mm, (bottom right) 6 mm. (Courtesy of R. Reed, Imperial College, London, U.K.)

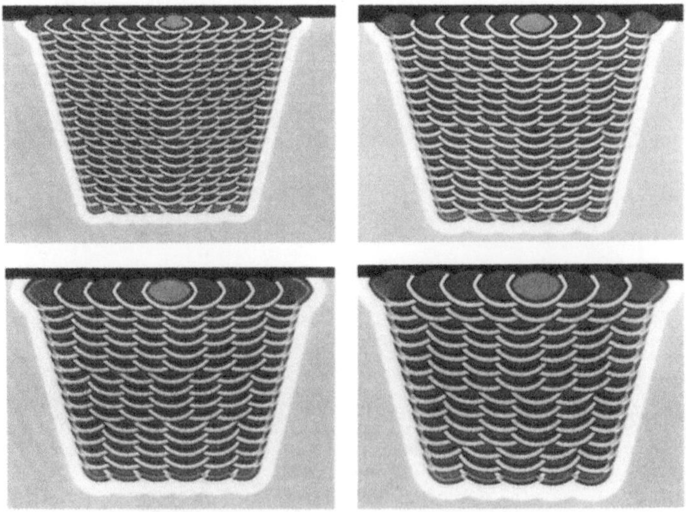

PLATE 7. The effect of welding current for a constant electrode diameter (3.25 mm). Increasing the current leads to fewer beads deposited. The volume fraction of columnar weld metal increases with increasing current. (Top left) 100 A, (top right) 150 A, (bottom left) 200 A, (bottom right) 250 A. (Courtesy of R. Reed, Imperial College, London, U.K.)

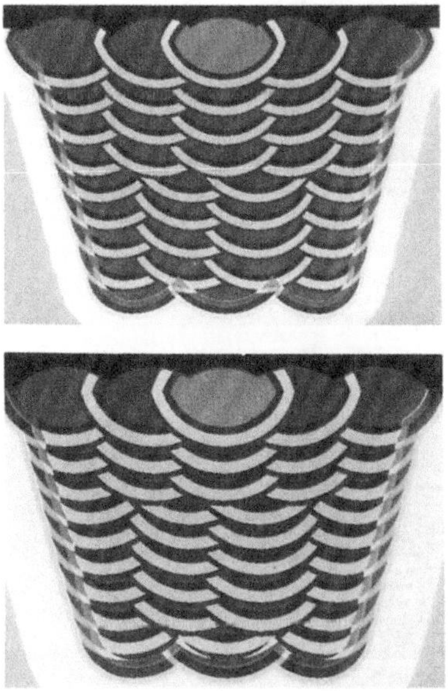

PLATE 8. The effect of variations in interpass temperature. The volume fraction of columnar weld metal is decreased with increasing interpass temperature. (Top) 20°C, (bottom) 250°C. (Courtesy of R. Reed, Imperial College, London, U.K.)

PLATE 9. The effect of variations in Ac_3 temperature. (Top) Ac_3 = 817°C, (middle) $Ac3$ = 917°C, (bottom) Ac_3 = 1017°C. A very significant decrease in the volume fraction of columnar weld metal is obtained with a decreasing Ac_3 temperature. (Courtesy of R. Reed, Imperial College, London, U.K.)

PLATE 10. The effect of the feed speed. (Top) 3.60 mm/s, (bottom) 2.06 mm/s. Low feed speeds give a large volume fraction of reaustenitized material and very little columnar grain structure. (Courtesy of R. Reed, Imperial College, London, U.K.)

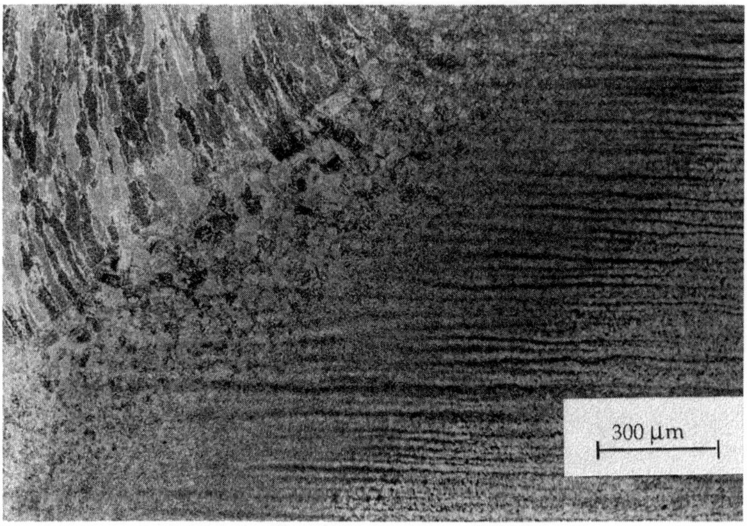

a

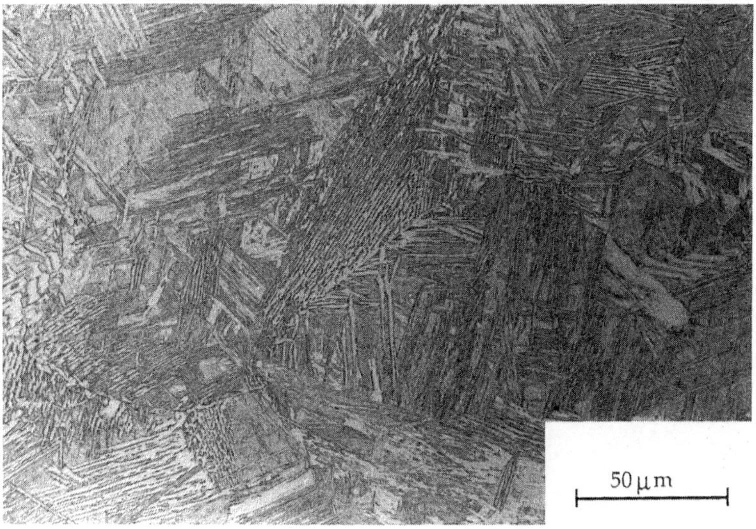

b

FIGURE 3.1. The microstructure of the HAZ in a welded joint. The weld was made in a 50-mm-thick plate. The plate was a 0.17C-1.3Mn (wt%) normalized steel. The welding was made vertically, with a heat input of approximately 2 kJ/mm, without preheat. (a) Low magnification, showing the extent of the HAZ. (b) The coarse-grained zone, consisting mainly of martensite. (c) The lower part of the coarse-grained zone where the peak temperature was approximately 1150°C. (d) The fine-grained zone. (e) The intercritically heated zone, where the pearlite has dissolved and the carbon-rich austenite has retransformed to martensite.

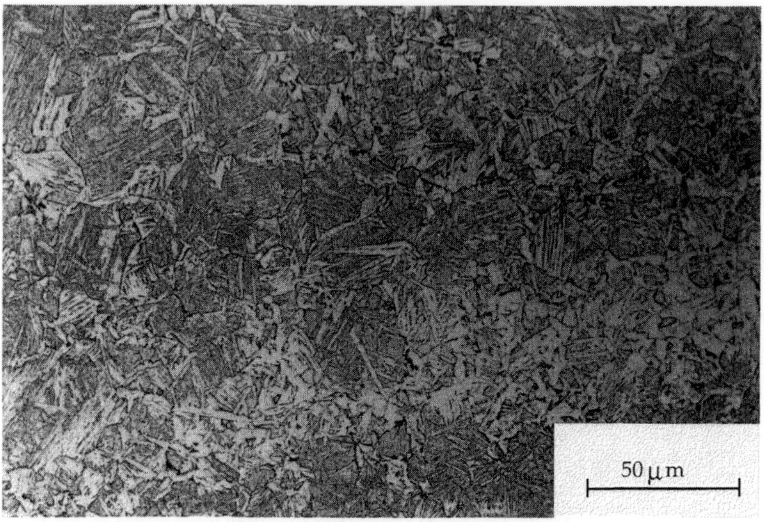

FIGURE 3.1.c

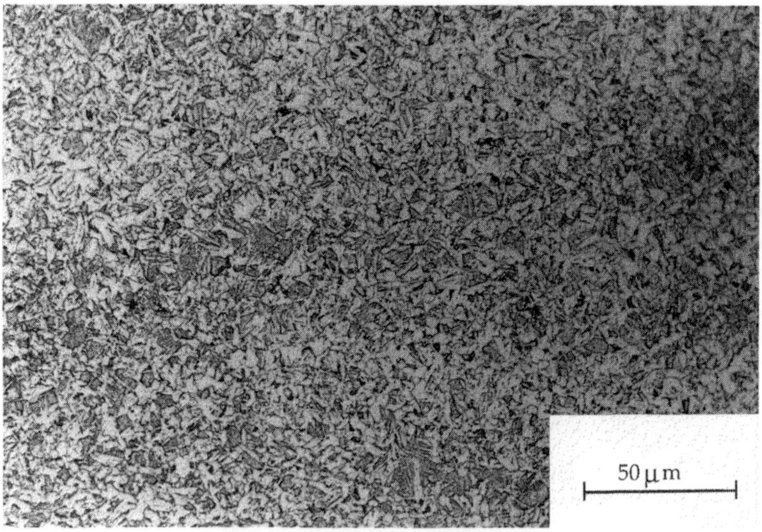

FIGURE 3.1.d

metals showed that considerable superheating may be necessary to induce the transformation to occur. Nucleation of austenite generally takes place at cementite/ferrite interfaces. If retained austenite is dispersed in the structure, as in bainitic steels, for example, then the nucleation of austenite is not necessary, and the transformation may proceed more easily.

Turning now to the transformation of austenite during the cooling part of the thermal cycle, the microstructures that appear in the HAZ are often

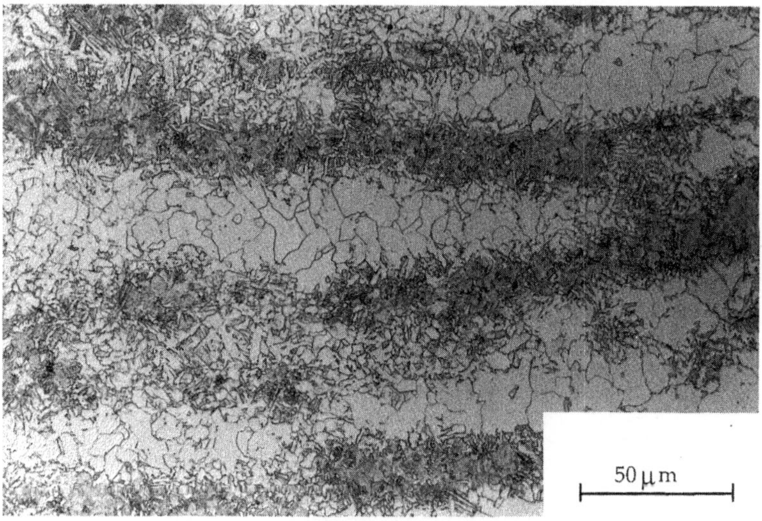

FIGURE 3.1.e

non-equilibrium products, such as bainite and martensite, due to the rapid cooling rates. This is in contrast to the unaffected base material. As described in Chapter 2, many steels have a microstructure which is a mixture of ferrite and pearlite, both of which are closer to equilibrium.

In the HAZ, the microstructure must obviously vary with the distance from the fusion line in correspondence with the fact that both the austenite grain size and the cooling rate are a function of this distance. To be able to understand which microstructures appear, it is necessary to briefly consider their formation mechanisms. In areas that have been heated to such high temperatures that austenite has formed, there will be a transformation back to ferrite on cooling. The most likely sites to nucleate new products during a phase transformation are grain corners, grain edges, grain boundaries, and inclusions, in that order of prominence.

If the cooling rate is low, as would be the case during high heat input welding or if the plate thickness is small, then *allotriomorphic ferrite* nucleates heterogeneously at the austenite grain boundaries. It grows progressively by a diffusional process during further cooling. As the temperature falls, the growth rate of allotriomorphic ferrite eventually begins to decreases, and it gives way to products that are able to grow faster at lower temperatures. First, *Widmanstätten side plates* appear. These plates nucleate either at austenite/austenite grain boundaries or at austenite/ferrite grain boundaries and grow by a combination of carbon diffusion and shear of the substitutional lattice. At even lower temperatures *bainite* forms. Bainite also nucleates at the grain boundaries and grows by a shear mechanism. If carbon is rejected rapidly into the austenite between the growing sheaves of bainite, then upper bainite is

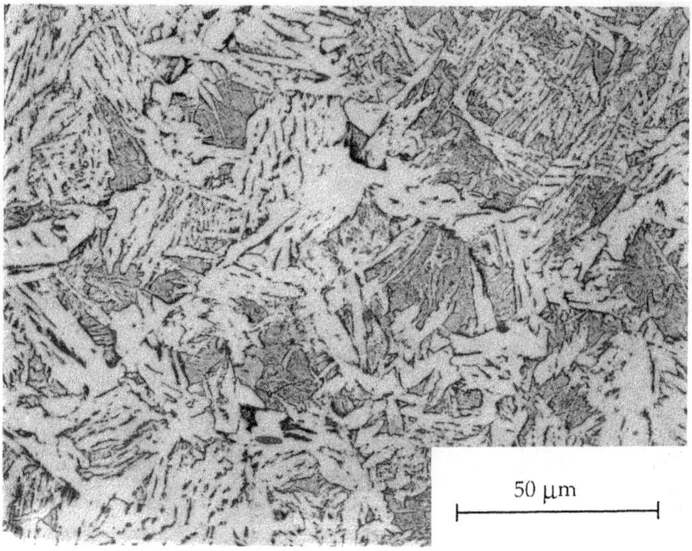

FIGURE 3.2. Allotriomorphic ferrite, forming a rim of ferrite along the prior austenite grain boundaries.

formed because this carbon eventually precipitates as carbides from the austenite. If, on the other hand, the carbides have an opportunity to precipitate from supersaturated ferrite, then lower bainite is formed. The carbon supersaturation in the ferrite is therefore relieved largely by formation of carbides inside the bainitic sheaves. Finally, if the transformation is completely diffusionless, then *martensite* is said to form. The term "grain boundary ferrite" is commonly used to denote the allotriomorphic ferrite that forms along the austenite grain boundaries. However, this is inappropriate, because most of the constituents described above are nucleated at grain boundaries. To describe what is commonly called grain boundary ferrite the term allotriomorphic ferrite will be used here, in agreement with the classical Dubé classification of ferrite morphologies.

As stated earlier, allotriomorphic ferrite nucleates at various places along the austenite grain boundaries. Its growth along the boundaries occurs rather rapidly, so that a fairly uniform rim of ferrite is formed along the grain boundary (see Figure 3.2). Growth then occurs in a direction perpendicular to the grain boundary by a diffusion process. The kinetics of the transformation can be described by a parabolic rate equation, which under isothermal conditions takes the form

$$u = \beta t^{1/2} \tag{3.1}$$

where u is the half-thickness of the ferrite layer, β is the parabolic rate constant, and t is time. The rate constant β is dependent upon the alloying content, diffusion rate, and temperature. Thus under continuous cooling conditions the following integral must be solved:

$$u = 1/2\int\beta(T)\ t^{-1/2}\ \mathrm{d}t \tag{3.2}$$

The equation can be transformed into an integral over temperatures if the cooling cycle is known. The limits of the integral then become the transformation start and stop temperatures. The start temperature is determined by the chemistry of the steel and the rate of cooling below the Ae_3 temperature. The austenite grain size has relatively little influence on the transformation start temperature. The transformation stop temperature is more difficult to define. Bhadeshia et al.[2] suggested in their work on weld metals that the transformation stop temperature could be approximated as the temperature where other phases become kinetically more favorable, i.e., where the respective C-curves in the TTT diagrams cross.

The volume fraction (V_f) of allotriomorphic ferrite is given by

$$V_f/V_{eq} = 1 - \exp(-2\chi G_\alpha t) \tag{3.3}$$

where V_{eq} is the equilibrium volume fraction, χ is the grain boundary surface area per unit volume, and G_α is the growth rate of allotriomorphic ferrite.

Widmanstätten side plates become kinetically favored with decreasing temperature, because the substitutional atom diffusion becomes too slow; the transformation mechanism changes to one involving displacement rather than diffusion. Consequently, the shape of the ferrite changes to one consistent with the minimization of strain energy, i.e., the ferrite adopts a thin plate shape. The carbon is then rejected to the sides of the growing plates, giving much shorter diffusion distances. The side plates nucleate either on austenite/austenite grain boundaries (primary side plates) or on ferrite/austenite boundaries (secondary side plates) (Figure 3.3). They grow with a Kurdjumov–Sachs-type orientation relationship between austenite and ferrite, i.e., close-packed planes and close-packed directions are parallel:

$$\{111\}_\gamma\ //\ \{110\}_\alpha$$

$$\langle 1\bar{1}0\rangle_\gamma\ //\ \langle 11\bar{1}\rangle_\alpha$$

As emphasized earlier, the plate shape arises as a consequence of the displasive mechanism, in which the shape consistent with minimum strain energy is a thin plate. In fact, the strain energy is further minimized by the simultaneous growth of pairs of self-accommodating plates. The strain energy thus amounts to only 50 J/mol. Thus, the side plates can grow with a relatively small undercooling

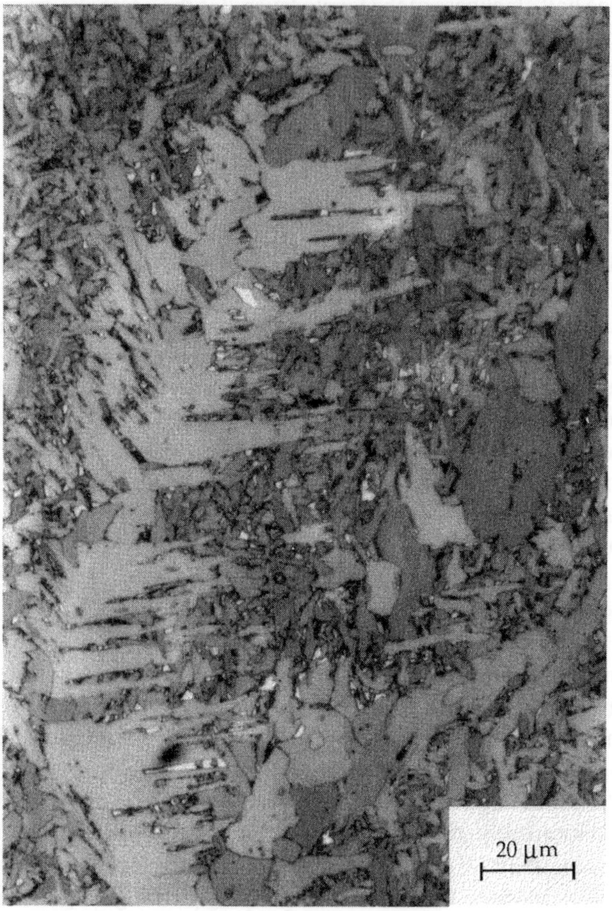

FIGURE 3.3. Widmanstätten side plates, nucleating on ferrite/austenite boundaries (secondary side plates).

below the Ae_3 temperature. The growth rate of the plates can be calculated by solving the equation

$$\Omega_0 = (\pi p)^{0.5} \exp(p)\ \mathrm{erfc}(p^{0.5})[1 + (r_c/r)\ \Omega_0 S_2] \tag{3.4}$$

In this equation $\Omega_0 = (x - x^{\gamma\alpha})/(x^{\alpha\gamma} - x^{\gamma\alpha})$ is a measure of the supersaturation; p is the Péclet number = $Gr/2D$, where G is the growth rate, r is the plate tip radius, and D is the weighted average diffusivity of carbon in austenite; and S_2 is a function of p. $x^{\gamma\alpha}$ and $x^{\alpha\gamma}$ are the paraequilibrium carbon contents in the austenite and ferrite, respectively. The growth rate for Widmanstätten side plates in steel weld metals, as calculated by Bhadeshia,[3] is shown in Figure 3.4. The strong influence of carbon content on the growth rate can be noted.

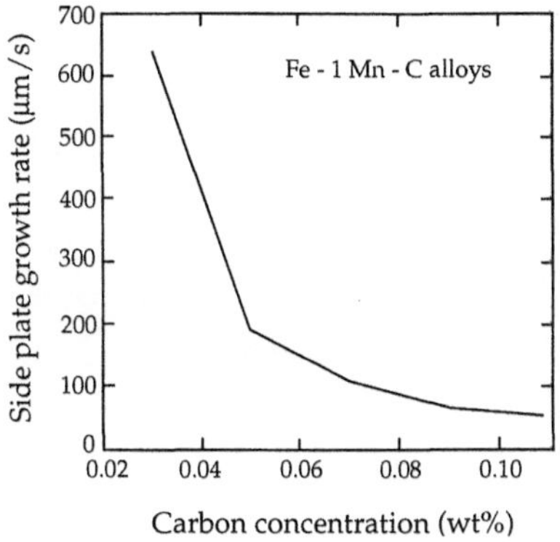

FIGURE 3.4. The calculated growth rate for Widmanstätten side plates in steel weld metals. (Courtesy of H. K. D. H. Bhadeshia, University of Cambridge, Cambridge, U.K.)

Bainite takes two forms, upper and lower. Bainite forms in the temperature range between allotriomorphic ferrite and martensite. There is a difficulty in deducing the growth mechanism of bainite. Both shear and diffusive mechanisms have been suggested. However, most evidence now points toward growth by a shear mechanism. This is associated with a relatively large strain energy amounting typically to 400 J/mol.

Bainite starts to grow below a certain temperature, the bainite start temperature B_s. However, the growth process is both temperature and time dependent. The reaction is not completed even if the steel is held for very long periods of time below B_s. This is called "the incomplete reaction phenomenon." It arises because the reaction stops when the carbon concentration in the austenite reaches the T_0'-curve in the phase diagram. The T_0'-curve is the locus of all points where the free energies of austenite and ferrite (with a certain amount of stored energy) of the same composition are equal. This phenomenon is useful when trying to characterize the mechanism of a transformation. Upper bainite resembles Widmanstätten side plates, although the latter have a rather coarser microstructure. Under an optical microscope, bainite seems to consist of sheaves which are separated by high-angle grain boundaries (Figure 3.5). With higher resolution, the sheaves can be seen to consist of subunits separated from each other by low-angle grain boundaries. The carbon atoms are rejected into the adjacent austenite. There will then be a layer of carbon-rich phases, such as carbides, martensite, or retained austenite, between the bainitic ferrite platelets.

Lower bainite has a plate-like morphology, with the plates being much finer than for upper bainite. Lower bainite more closely resembles a tempered martensitic transformation. In lower bainite, the carbon is not rejected as rapidly as in upper bainite because of the reduced transformation temperature. Thus, small carbides can form inside the bainitic plates. The carbides usually have an angle of 55 to 60° to the major axes of the bainitic plate (Figure 3.6).

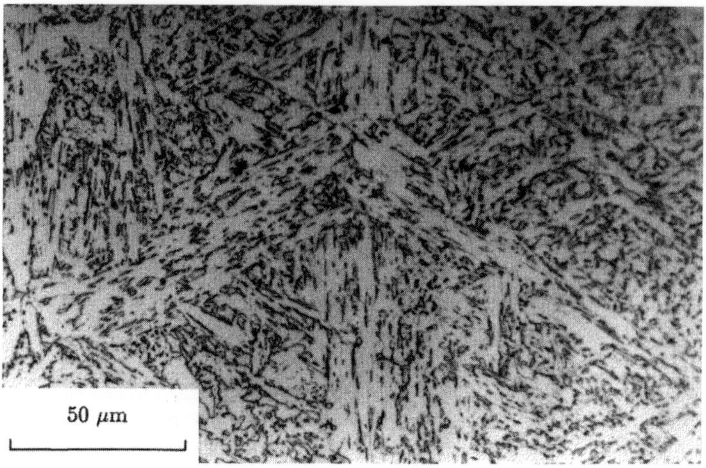

FIGURE 3.5. Optical micrograph, showing the typical sheaves of bainite. These sheaves in turn consist of smaller units, which are difficult to resolve with optical microscopy. (Courtesy of H. K. D. H. Bhadeshia, University of Cambridge, Cambridge, U.K.)

It is very difficult to calculate the volume fraction of bainite as a function of time at a certain transformation temperature. If the steel is held at a certain temperature for a very long time, then the volume fraction of bainite can be derived from the T_0' temperature.

The austenite which has not decomposed to any of the above transformation products eventually undergoes partial martensitic transformation at a sufficiently low temperature. Nucleation occurs heterogeneously but is not confined to grain boundaries. Because the transformation occurs without diffusion and with a highly crystallographic character, the martensite has a typical lath-like structure in low-alloy steels (Figure 3.7). The reaction starts below a certain temperature M_s, the martensite start temperature. M_s can be as high as 500°C for steels with a low solute content. When the alloying concentration is increased, M_s decreases. During continuous cooling, the martensite transformation begins as the temperature reaches M_s for the residual austenite. The reaction ceases at the martensite finish temperature M_f, although this is less well defined because some austenite may be retained at all temperatures. M_f can in some steels be significantly below room temperature and then large amounts of retained austenite can be found.

Because martensite can contain significant amounts of carbon in solid solution, its crystal structure can deviate from that of ferrite. The structure is body-centered tetragonal, the degree of tetragonality increasing with dissolved carbon content. Martensite is observed in two main variants: laths and twinned plates. The lath type appears in steels with low carbon content (below <0.5 wt% carbon) and the twinned type in higher carbon steels. For construction steels then, only the lath type is of importance. However, the twin morphology may occur in small amounts when the residual austenite is carbon-

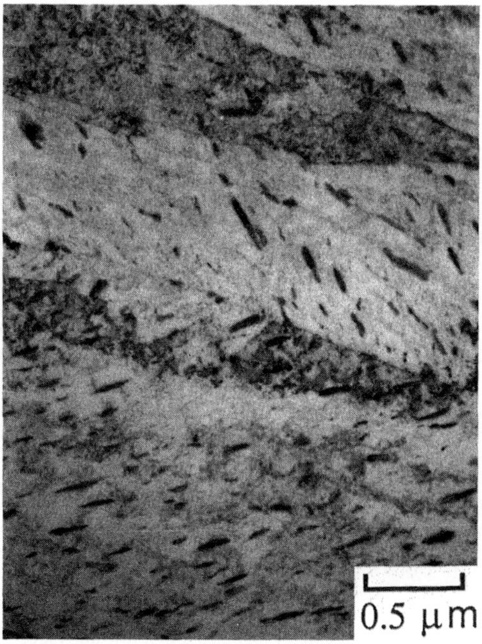

FIGURE 3.6. The carbides in lower bainite will usually have an angle of 55 to 60° to the major axes of the bainitic plate. (Courtesy of H. K. D. H. Bhadeshia, University of Cambridge, Cambridge, U.K.)

enriched due to prior transformations. If the M_s temperature for this austenite is above the operating temperature, then twinned plates of martensite can appear.

3.3. AUSTENITE GRAIN GROWTH DURING WELDING

Two kinds of grain growth can be considered in conjunction with welding: free grain growth (i.e., no particles interacting) and particle-controlled grain growth. Grain growth during isothermal conditions can be described by the relation:

$$d_\gamma^{1/n_1} = d_{\gamma 0}^{1/n_1} + K_0 \exp(-Q/RT)t \tag{3.5}$$

where d_γ is the time-dependent grain size, $d_{\gamma 0}$ is the initial grain size, n_1 is an exponent, and Q is the activation energy for grain growth. n_1 is usually on the order of 0.1 to 0.3 for steels.

During nonisothermal conditions, as in welding, the time-dependent part of the equation must be integrated over the time spent in the grain growth regime. The integration can be complicated to be carried out analytically and numerical procedures are often used. Simplified analytical integration procedures were

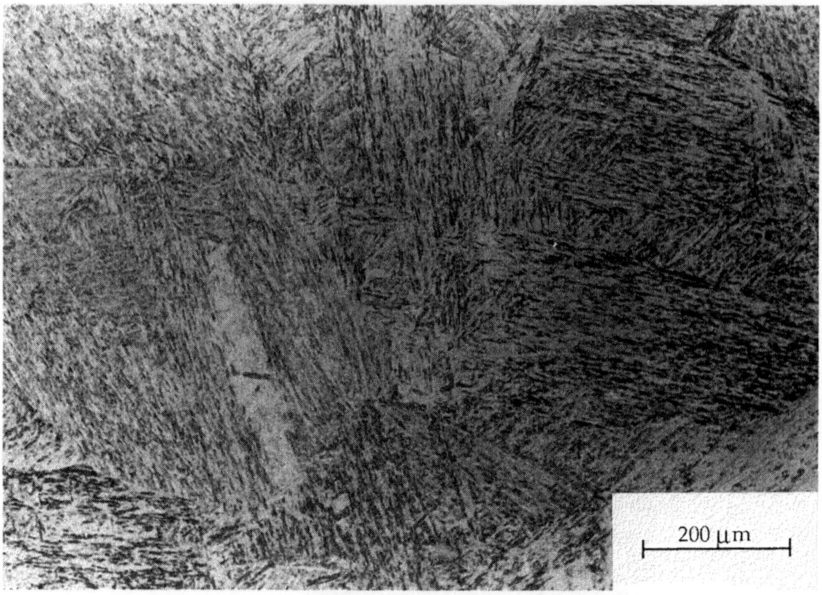

FIGURE 3.7. Typical lath-like structure of martensite in a low-alloy steel. (Courtesy of H. K. D. H. Bhadeshia, University of Cambridge, Cambridge, U.K.)

developed by Ion.[4] Assuming that the high-temperature part of the heating and cooling curve can be described by a parabola (see Figure 3.8), the integral can be solved as

$$\int \exp(-Q/RT)dt = \alpha\tau \exp(-Q/RT_p) \tag{3.6}$$

where T_p is the peak temperature. α and τ are given by (for definition of symbols, see Section 1.7)

$$\alpha = \sqrt{2\pi RT_p/Q} \tag{3.7}$$

$$\tau = (q'/v)/[2\pi\lambda e\,(T_p - T_0)] \tag{3.8}$$

for welding on thick plates and by

$$\alpha = 2\sqrt{\pi RT_p/Q} \tag{3.9}$$

$$\tau = (q'/vd)^2/[4\pi\lambda\rho e\,(T_p - T_0)^2] \tag{3.10}$$

for welding on thin plates.

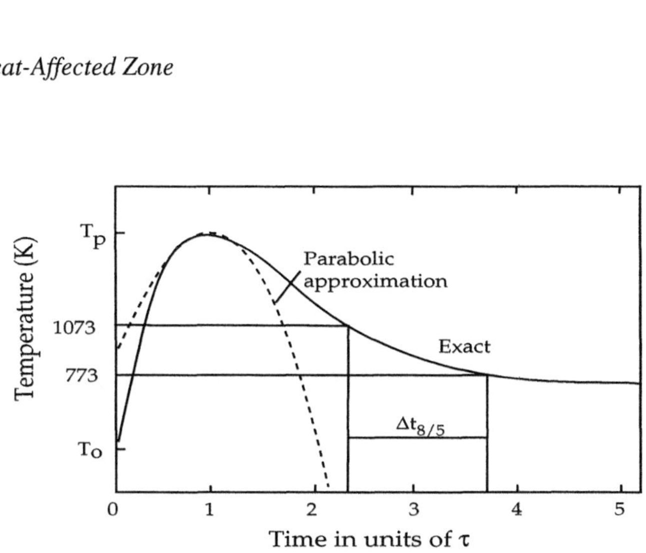

FIGURE 3.8. The high temperature part of the thermal cycle curve can be described by a parabola. (Reprinted from Ion, J. C., Easterling, K. E., and Ashby, M. F., *Acta Metall.*, 32, 1949, 1984. With permission from Pergamon Press, Ltd., Oxford, U.K.)

To achieve these solutions, the limiting case of rapid welding with a high-energy source, as discussed in Section 1.7, has been used. These expressions involve approximations and calculations of grain sizes will be accordingly uncertain. However, the values of the parameters K, Q, and n_1 are also uncertain and relatively large errors can be expected, so it is normal practice to calibrate the calculation using a single measurement in the HAZ. The main variables in the expressions are the peak temperature and the heat input. A two-dimensional map can thus be constructed, showing the austenite grain size as a function of the peak temperature and the heat input (Figure 3.9).

The austenite grain growth does not occur completely freely, but is restrained by two mechanisms. The first mechanism, occurring more or less in all steels, is called thermal pinning. This has been found by comparing the maximum grain size in a real HAZ with that found in simulated samples. In a real HAZ the grains are normally smaller. The effect is most pronounced in steels welded with a medium heat input. The exact mechanism is not understood and it is difficult to quantify the effect. It is believed that the smaller grains, which have not been subjected to a very high peak temperature, pin the neighboring grains, which experience a high peak temperature. The second mechanism is due to the influence of particles, which may be deliberately added. When a dispersion of particles is present in the steel, with a volume fraction V_v, a maximum grain size limited by particles can be defined as shown in Figure 3.10. According to Zener, the maximum grain size is given by

$$D_{max} = 4r'/3V_v \tag{3.11}$$

where r' is the radius of the particles. The pinning force of the particles is then large enough to completely oppose the driving force for grain growth.

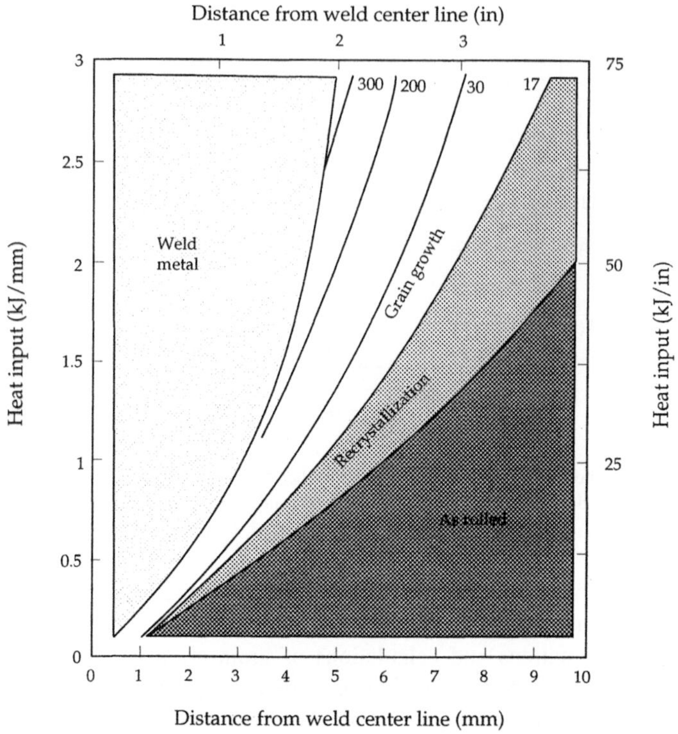

FIGURE 3.9. A two-dimensional map showing the calculated austenite grain size as a function of the peak temperature and the heat input. It was assumed in the calculations that three-dimensional cooling occurred. The calculations were made for a niobium microalloyed steel. (From Easterling, K. E., *Introduction to the Physical Metallurgy of Welding*, Butterworth-Heinemann Ltd., Oxford, U.K., 1983. With permission.)

From Equation 3.11 it is seen that the optimum particle dispersion needed to achieve a fine grain size is one with a high volume fraction of very small particles. The microalloyed steels thus should give the smallest austenite grains. However, most of the particles formed by the microalloying elements dissolve at relatively low temperatures and cannot prevent grain growth in the HAZ. The solubility product for typical microalloying-induced particles, such as Nb(CN), is given by a relation of the form

$$\log\,[\%M]^x[\%C]^y = A - B/T \qquad (3.12)$$

where $\%M$ is the content of the metallic element and $\%C$ is the carbon content in wt%. A similar relation can be made for nitrides. The exponents x and y result from the stoichiometry of the reaction

$$M_xC_y = xM + yC \qquad (3.13)$$

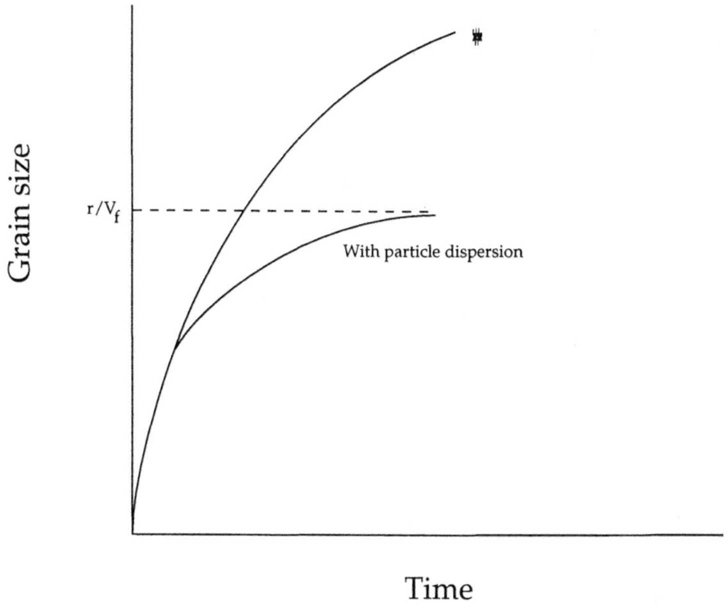

FIGURE 3.10. Maximum grain size achieved when a dispersion of particles, with a volume fraction V_v, is present in the steel. (From Porter, D. A. and Easterling, K. E., *Phase Transformations in Metals and Alloys,* Chapman & Hall, London, 1981. With permission.)

It is assumed that the concentrations of M and C are low so that the activity of the elements can be substituted with the actual concentration.

The solubility products of some of the most common microalloying element carbides and nitrides are shown in Figure 3.11 and the dissolution temperatures are shown in Figure 3.12. As can be seen, titanium nitride is stable up to much higher temperatures than the other compounds, making it a good candidate for restricting austenite grain growth.

During welding, where rapid heating takes place, the particles dissolve at higher temperatures than shown in Figure 3.12, because the dissolution process is controlled by the diffusion of the elements. If a very rapid thermal cycle is imposed, there is not enough time to diffuse the elements away and the particle does not dissolve fully. The size of the particles also influences the rate of solution, with larger particles dissolving more slowly.

Although titanium nitride will dissolve much more slowly during the high-temperature cycle, the particles will coarsen and thus be less effective in preventing grain growth. The particle coarsening (Ostwald ripening) taking place during isothermal conditions can be expressed by the Wagner equation:

$$r^3 - r_0^3 = (kt/T) \exp(-Q/RT) \quad (3.14)$$

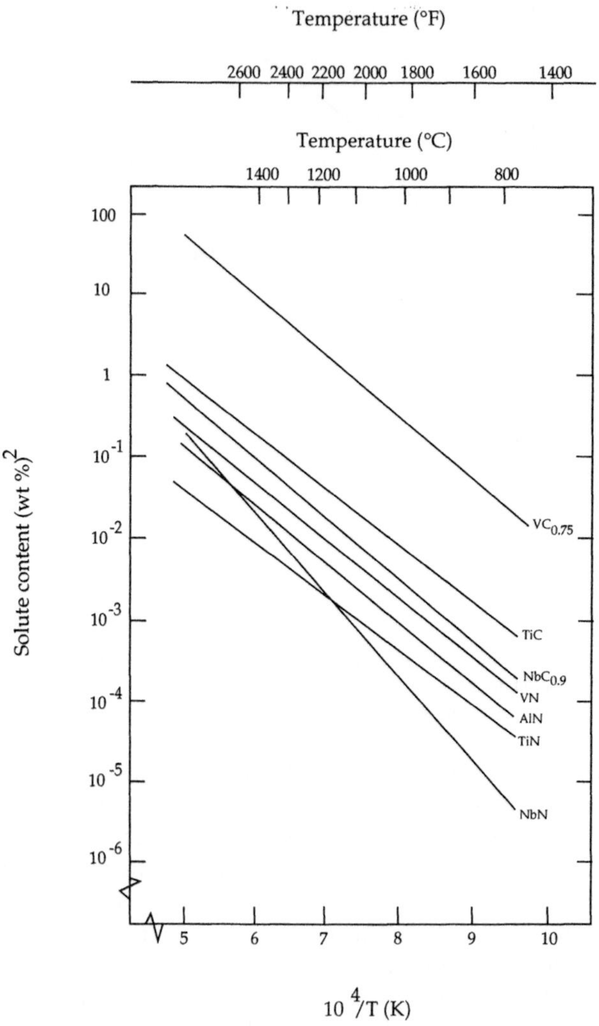

FIGURE 3.11. The solubility products of some of the most common microalloying elements, carbides and nitrides. As can be seen, it is only titanium nitride that is stable up to the melting temperature of the steel. (From Easterling, K. E., *Introduction to the Physical Metallurgy of Welding*, Butterworth-Heinemann Ltd., Oxford, U.K., 1983. With permission.)

where r_0 is the original particle radius, k is an experimentally determined constant, and Q is the activation energy for particle growth. For a welding thermal cycle, this expression must be integrated over the time spent in the high-temperature regime. This can be done in the same way as given above for the unrestricted grain growth. The result is

$$r^3 - r_0^3 = k\,(\alpha\tau/T_p)\,\exp(-Q/RT_p) \qquad (3.15)$$

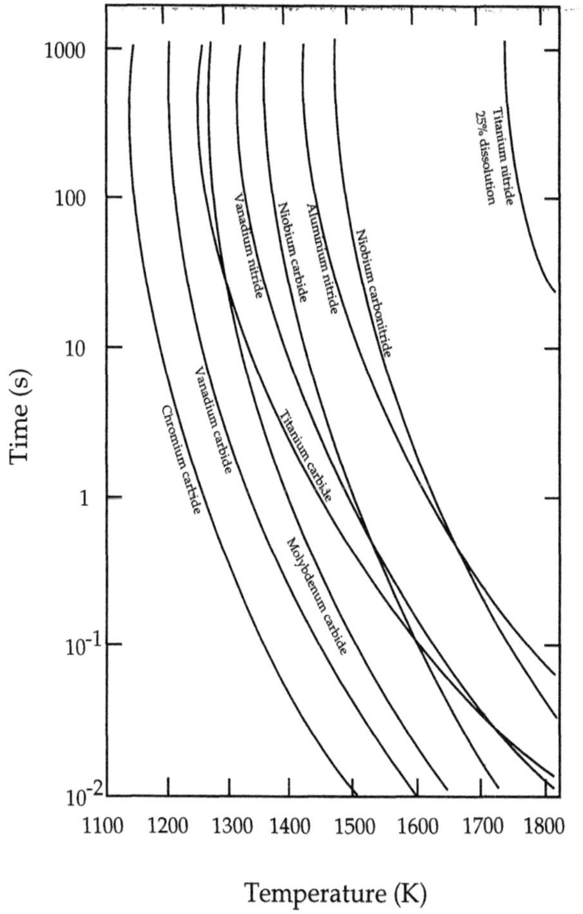

FIGURE 3.12. The calculated times for complete dissolution of some carbides and nitrides in austenite, as a function of temperature. The calculations are based on a model by Ashby and Easterling. (From Easterling, K. E., *Introduction to the Physical Metallurgy of Welding*, Butterworth-Heinemann Ltd., Oxford, U.K., 1983. With permission.)

α, τ and T_p have the same meaning as in Equations 3.9 and 3.10. Calculation of particle coarsening is shown in Figure 3.13.

The Wagner equation assumes that the volume fraction of the particles is constant. By combining Equations 3.15 (to find the particle size) and 3.11, the grain size can be found. A grain growth diagram for a titanium microalloyed steel is shown in Figure 3.14. Comparing this figure to Figure 3.10, it can be seen that the austenite grain size will be about half that in a steel without any particle constrained growth.

In weld metals, there is a high-volume fraction of oxides which neither dissolve nor grow during the thermal cycle. The grain size in heat-affected weld metals can be calculated from Equation 3.11 to be of the order of 100 μm.

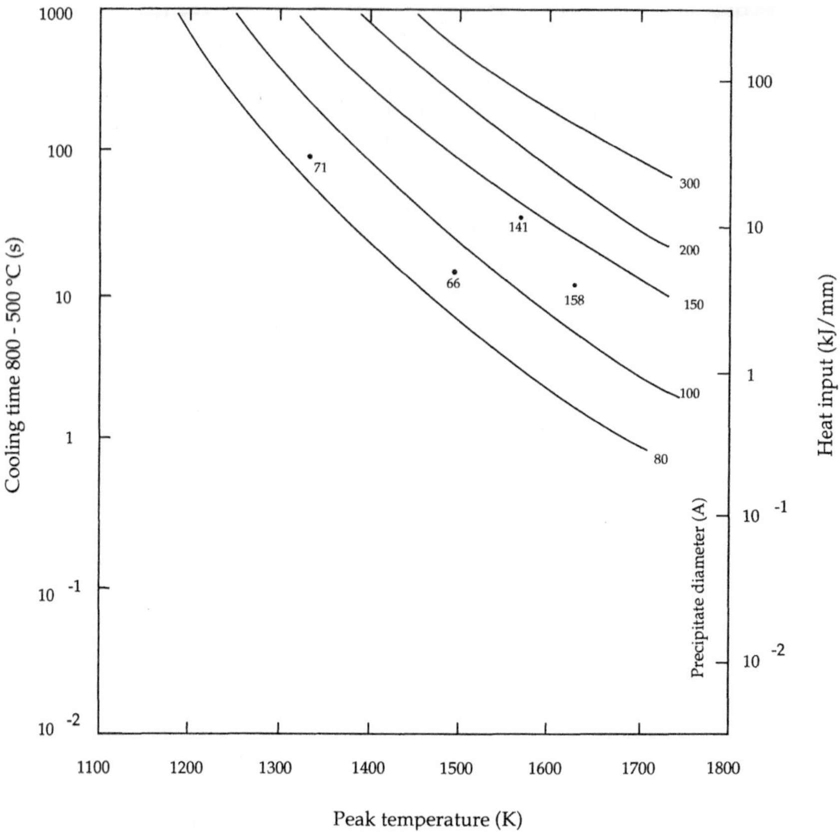

FIGURE 3.13. Calculation of titanium nitride particle coarsening as a function of heat input and peak temperature. The points given refer to experimental measurements. (From Easterling, K. E., *Introduction to the Physical Metallurgy of Welding,* Butterworth-Heinemann Ltd., Oxford, U.K., 1983. With permission.)

This has also been confirmed by measurements. For steel subjected to high-energy welding, oxides should be preferable over nitrides as grain growth inhibitors, because they are more insensitive to the thermal cycle. Japanese steels have recently been developed that utilize titanium oxide particles as grain growth inhibitors. However, the most important function of the particles is as nucleating agents for intragranular ferrite products. The practical problem with this type of steel is to achieve a particle dispersion which is fine enough, because particles that are too coarse will be easy nucleation sites for brittle fracture. The particles tend to have an average size of 1 to 2 μm, which with a volume fraction of around 3×10^{-3} gives an austenite grain size of almost 1 mm. Thus the grain growth for these steels occurs virtually unconstricted.

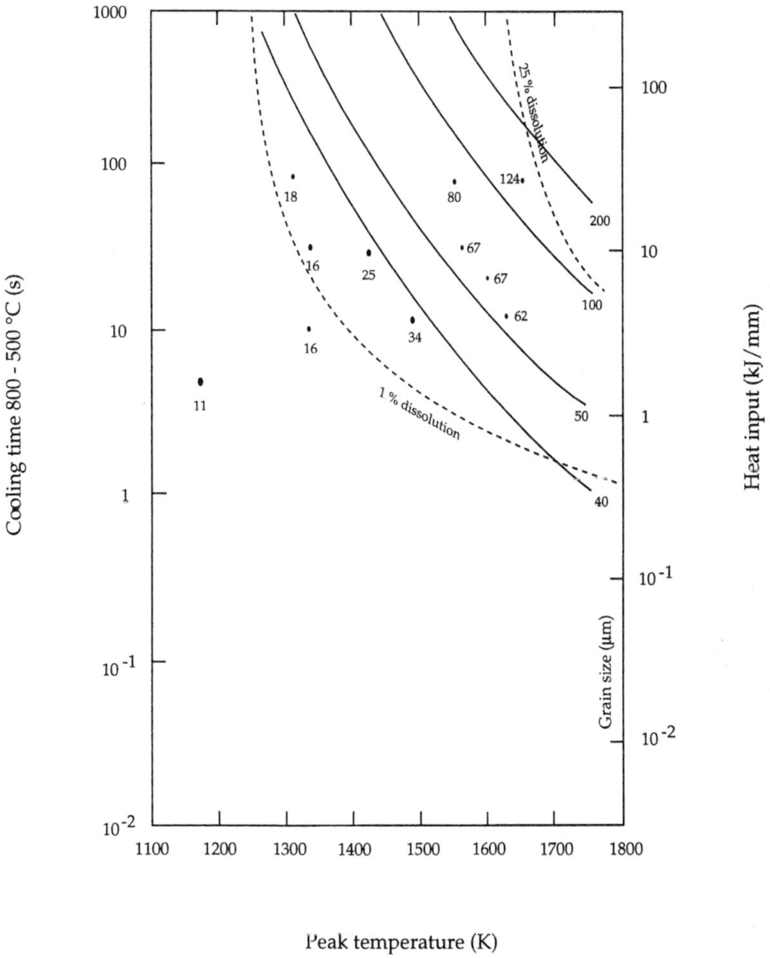

FIGURE 3.14. The calculated austenite grain growth in a titanium microalloyed steel. The calculations were performed using the model in which the particles inhibit grain growth. However, this model is not straightforward because the volume fraction of particles is difficult to estimate. In this case it was assumed that at a certain time the Gladman equation $d \approx 0.5\ (r/V_f)$ holds, and from measurements of the grain size and particle radius the volume fraction was estimated. (From Easterling, K. E., *Introduction to the Physical Metallurgy of Welding,* Butterworth-Heinemann Ltd., Oxford, U.K., 1983. With permission.)

3.4. MICROSTRUCTURE DEVELOPMENT IN THE HEAT-AFFECTED ZONE

The microstructure that develops in the different parts of the HAZ depends upon the chemical composition (hardenability) of the steel, the thermal cycle, and the austenite grain size. These variables are to some extent interrelated, because the grain size depends upon both the chemical composition and the thermal cycle. The two zones of main concern are the coarse-grained zone and the intercritically heated zone. The microstructures that appear are now examined by looking at variations in the thermal cycle for some different kinds of steel.

In the coarse-grained zone, grain growth is the main problem. With a low heat input, the thermal cycle will be such that only a comparatively short time is spent above the temperature for grain growth. This has two effects. First, the austenite grain size will not be excessively large. Second, the coarse-grained growth zone will be narrower, because the peak temperature is reached above the grain growth temperature only very close to the fusion line. The drawback associated with a low heat input is that it gives a higher cooling rate during the austenite to ferrite transformation. With a high hardenability of the steel, the likelihood of forming bainite or martensite is thus great. However, this tendency is partly counteracted by the small austenite grain size, because the amount of grain boundary surface area is larger, increasing the chance for nucleation of allotriomorphic ferrite.

A high heat input gives a wider coarse-grained zone, with a larger mean grain size, but the cooling rate through the transformation temperatures is slower. Slow cooling decreases the risk of formation of bainite or martensite, while the coarse austenite grains will promote the formation of these constituents. However, martensite formation as a consequence of coarse austenite grains has not been observed in welded steels. Instead, lath-like structures, being either upper bainite or Widmanstätten ferrite, are commonly observed. With increasing heat input, the coarseness of these components increases.

For conventional normalized steels, with a fairly high carbon content (typically 0.18 wt%), brittle and highly deleterious martensite is formed when rapid cooling takes place. According to the continuous cooling transformation (CCT) diagram in Figure 3.15, nothing but martensite is formed when the 800 to 500°C cooling time is shorter than about 10 seconds. Such cooling times are typically found when using a heat input of 1 kJ/mm when welding plates thicker than 20 mm. If longer cooling times are used, lath-like structures appear. Figure 3.16 shows a diagram over microstructures in the coarse-grained zone as a function of heat input, illustrating the sensitivity to martensite formation for rapid cooling.[5]

These relatively short cooling times are difficult to avoid, using shielded metal arc welding (SMAW) or even gas-metal arc welding (GMAW), especially when welding large structures. The traditional way to cope with this problem is to use higher heat inputs or preheat, because this slows down the cooling rate. Use of preheat is usually connected to avoidance of hydrogen cracking and not to improvement of mechanical properties. Avoiding cracking is also partly related to the absence of martensite, but the main effect of preheating is to reduce the hydrogen content. The most efficient way to control hardness is by adjusting the heat input.

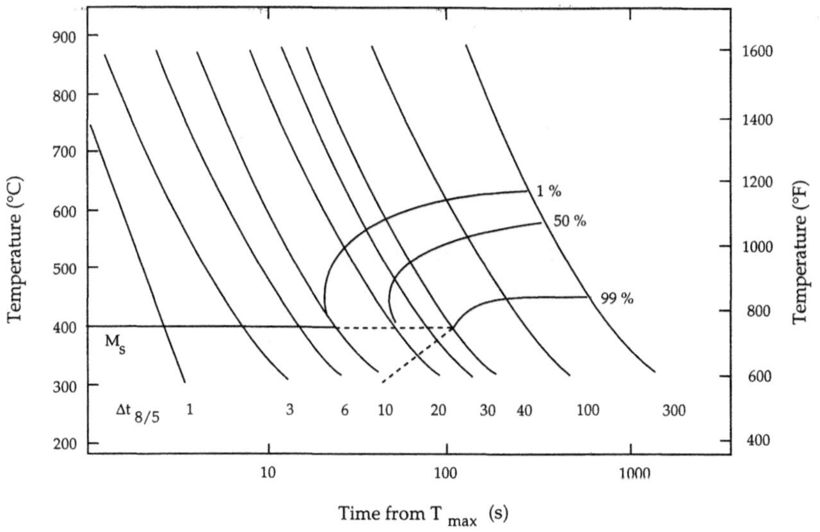

FIGURE 3.15. A CCT diagram showing that only martensite is formed when the 800 to 500°C cooling time is shorter than 10 seconds. Such cooling times are typically found when using a heat input of 1 kJ/mm when welding plates thicker than 20 mm. If longer cooling times are used, lath-like structures appear. (From Hansson, P., Res. Rep. IM-2388, Institute of Metals Research, Stockholm, 1988. With permission.)

The newly developed steels have lower carbon concentrations than the older steels, typically 0.1 wt%. When welded with relatively low heat input (below 1 kJ/mm, 25 kJ/in.), these steels will have an autotempered martensitic structure in the coarse-grained HAZ. The M_s temperature will increase with decreasing carbon content, leading to martensite formation starting at a relatively high temperature. During cooling this martensite is tempered. The grain size of the martensite is extremely fine, so this autotempered martensite will tend to have very good toughness. With higher heat inputs, the microstructure will be coarse bainite or side plates, similar to the microstructure of the higher carbon content steels, and will therefore be of lower toughness.

As discussed earlier, the growth of the austenite grains is regarded as the main problem, because this leads to a coarse structure in general. This grain growth is counteracted by a dispersion of TiN particles. The limitation of the grain size is most important for medium-heat input welds (about 3 kJ/mm, 75 kJ/in.). For higher heat inputs the TiN also will either coarsen extensively or even dissolve and thus grain growth will occur unrestricted. It has also been suggested that it is not the restriction of the austenite grain size that is the most important role of the TiN particles, but that they serve as nucleants for intragranular ferrite during the austenite to ferrite transformation, thus giving a fine grain size for ferrite. However, this subject has not been investigated in detail.

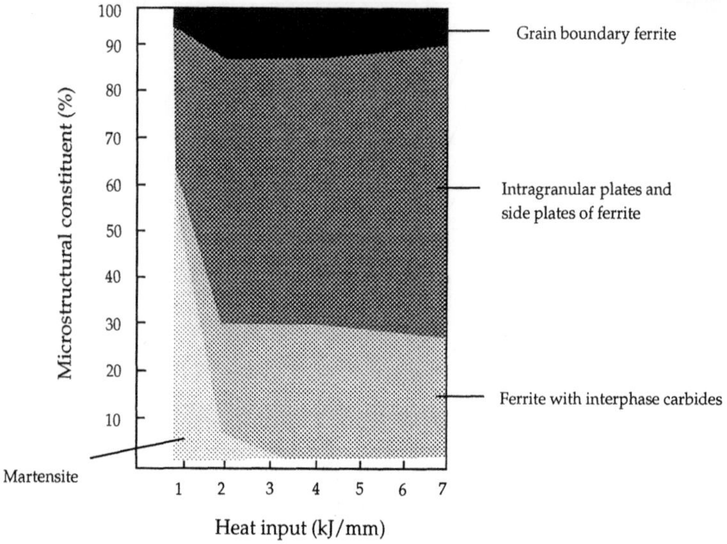

FIGURE 3.16. Diagram over microstructures in the coarse-grained zone as a function of heat input, illustrating the sensitivity to martensite formation for rapid cooling. (From Dolby, R. E., *Weld. J.*, 58(8), 225, 1979. With permission.)

The reduction of carbon content is the main factor in improving weldability and toughness of the coarse-grained HAZ. There are also other important effects. Microalloyed steels, with either niobium or vanadium, can show a drastic reduction in toughness in the coarse-grained zone. During the heating sequence of the thermal cycle the niobium or vanadium carbonitrides dissolve more or less completely. During cooling they may reprecipitate, preferably then as an interphase precipitation during the austenite to ferrite transformation. This is more likely to occur with high heat input (i.e., slower cooling). With lower heat input these elements remain in solid solution, where the effect on toughness is not as large. They affect the austenite to ferrite transformation, but in different ways. Niobium promotes Widmanstätten side plate structures, while vanadium favors a transformation to fine-grained intragranular ferrite. Thus, addition of vanadium may even be beneficial for toughness. Even if the effect on toughness is not that large in the as-welded condition, the toughness properties usually significantly deteriorate if the structure is subjected to a stress-relieving heat treatment.

The quench and tempered steels behave much the same as steels of equivalent composition, processed by other routes. The starting structure is of no importance when the steels are reaustenitized, as in the coarse-grained zone.

The best properties are achieved in the fine-grained zone. Because no problems are associated with this zone, very few investigations have been carried out. The fine austenite grains grow in the temperature regime 900 to

1100°C (1600 to 2000°F) and during cooling transform to fine ferrite grains. The extent of the fine-grained zone can be larger in microalloyed steels, because the precipitates can pin the austenite grain boundaries, preventing grain growth. Otherwise, the same behavior is reported for all types of construction steels.

In the intercritically heated zone, it is common to find that carbon-rich areas such as pearlite rapidly become austenitic, while ferritic areas can remain as ferrite, depending on the exact temperature. The parts that become austenitic are still carbon-rich during the transformation back to ferrite. The risk is therefore high that martensite can form. A mixture of martensite and retained austenite, called MA constituent, is usually found. These MA constituents appear as small islands (Figure 3.17)[6] and can initiate brittle fracture. The exact conditions under which MA constituents form are not clear. Steels very similar in chemical composition, subjected to simulated thermal cycles, have been shown to give MA constituents for one composition, while very fine pearlitic structures were found in the other steel.

The above discussion is related to the zones in a single-pass weld. During multirun welding, reheating of zones in a HAZ can lead to further complications. What has attracted special interest is the reheating of a formerly coarse-grained zone into the intercritical temperature regime, thus creating an *intercritically reheated coarse-grained zone* (ICGCZ). Local brittle areas can also be created in this zone.

Toughness can be a problem under certain conditions in the subcritical zone. The most common embrittling process is strain aging. This occurs if the steel has been deformed plastically. The amount of strain needed is very low. Typically 5% plastic strain is quoted, but strain aging can occur at even lower strains. The new dislocations created are easily mobile for further deformation, but can be locked by an atmosphere of interstitial atoms (carbon or nitrogen) at the cores of the dislocations. This of course requires that these elements are free and not tied up in any second-phase particles. The formation of the atmosphere takes place at temperatures from ambient up to around 250°C (500°F). This means that this embrittlement appears fairly far away from the weld. The usual cure for strain aging is to add aluminum to form AlN. The formation of AlN is relatively sluggish and only takes place during normalization of the steel. Thus, strain aging may be a problem with thermomechanically rolled steels because there is no time to form AlN.

Other processes that take place in the subcritical zone occur at temperatures just below the A_1 temperature. In microalloyed steels precipitation of carbonitrides of, for example, niobium, vanadium, or titanium may occur. This is especially so in multipass welding, if an area which was a coarse-grained zone has been subcritically reheated. During the first cycle, the microalloying carbonitrides dissolve and are then precipitated again during the second thermal cycle. However, this can also have a positive effect, because it may reduce

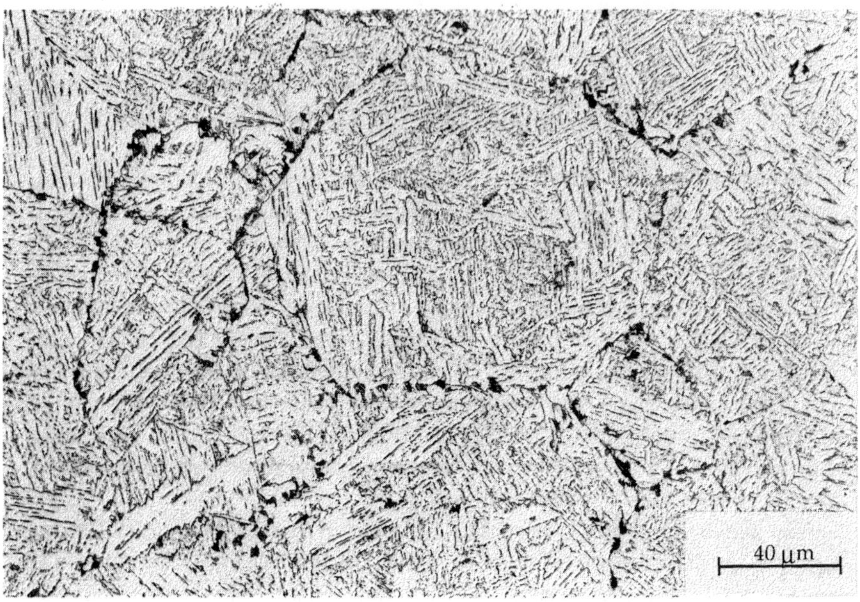

FIGURE 3.17. MA constituents appearing as small islands in intercritically reheated zones. (From Barnes, A., *Weld. Inst. Res. Rep. 402*, The Welding Institute, Cambridge, U.K., 1989. With permission.)

the amount of free nitrogen. Free nitrogen is known to severely embrittle ferritic steels.

Carbide precipitation from a martensitic matrix may of course occur during subcritical heating of a coarse-grained zone and generally this is positive for toughness. Similarly, already precipitated grain boundary cementite spherodizes, which also is beneficial.

The recovery that takes place at temperatures around 600°C (1100°F) can result in a structure that is softer than the rest of the steel. This is especially so for quench and tempered steels, where further tempering of the tempered martensite reduces the strength. These steels must not be welded at too high a heat input in order to prevent overtempering of the structure. In addition, thermomechanically rolled steels can suffer from reduced strength in the subcritical zone, due to the recovery of the deformed ferritic structure, which is responsible for some of the strength of the steel.

REFERENCES

1. **Yang, J.-R. and Bhadeshia, H. K. D. H.,** *Proc. Int. Conf. Welding Metallurgy of Structural Steels,* TMS-AIME, Warrendale, PA, 1987, 549.
2. **Bhadeshia, H. K. D. H., Svensson, L.-E., and Gretoft, B.,** A model for the development of microstructure in low-alloy steel (Fe-Mn-Si-C) weld deposits, *Acta Metall.,* 33(7), 1271, 1985.

3. **Bhadeshia, H. K. D. H.,** Modelling of steel welds, *Mater. Sci. Technol.*, 8(February), 123, 1992.
4. **Ion, J. C.,** Modelling the Microstructural Changes in Steel due to Fusion Welding, Ph.D. thesis, Luleå University of Technology, Luleå, Sweden, 1984.
5. **Dolby, R. E.,** HAZ toughness of structural and pressure vessel steels — improvement and prediction, *Weld. Res. Suppl.*, 58(August), 225-s, 1979.
6. **Barnes, A. M.,** The Effect of Intercritical Thermal Cycles on HAZ Microstructure and Toughness in C-Mn-Al-Nb Steel, *Weld. Inst. Res. Rep. 402,* The Welding Institute, Cambridge, U.K., 1989.

Chapter 4

THE WELD METAL

4.1. INTRODUCTION

Although there are many similarities between the physical metallurgy processes occurring in the heat-affected zone (HAZ) of the base material and in the fused weld metal, there are also several important differences. The specific features of the weld metal that will be treated here are

- The drop transfer stage
- The deoxidation of the molten weld pool
- Gas absorption
- Solidification
- Phase transformations

Although these subjects will be discussed separately, it is emphasized that they interact to generate the final structure of the weld metal. Traces of each of the processes can be found in the microstructure and often have a direct influence on the properties of the welded joint. The phase transformations that occur are to a large extent similar to those in the HAZ. Only the differences in the phase transformations will be highlighted here.

4.2. DROP TRANSFER

Three important items are described below: the *drop transfer* mode, the *maximum temperature* that the metal reaches, and the *formation of fume* during welding. The drop transfer modes differ among the welding processes. In shielded metal arc welding (SMAW) the drops usually are transferred by contact between the tip of the electrode and the workpiece (bridging transfer), while in gas-metal arc welding (GMAW) both bridging transfer and free-flight transfer can be found. Free-flight transfer is most often used because this provides better penetration. A higher current is used for this transfer mode, which could give a higher heat input, but this can be counteracted by a higher welding speed. Use of pulsed welding may then be beneficial. Irregular drop transfer may give rise to excessive spatter, which is undesirable. In submerged arc welding (SAW) free-flight transfer always occurs.

The maximum temperature that the liquid metal reaches is estimated to be around 2400°C. This is of interest because both the deoxidation reactions that occur in the molten state and the subsequent cooling of the weld can be understood better if this temperature is known.

During drop transfer, some elements are evaporated, i.e., fume is created. The fume is important both from the point of view of health and from the

TABLE 4.1
IIW Classification of Metal Transfer

Designation of transfer type	Welding process (examples)
1 Free-flight transfer	
1.1 Globular	
1.1.1 Drop	Low-current GMAW
1.1.2 Repelled	CO_2-shielded GMAW
1.2 Spray	
1.2.1 Projected	Intermediate-current GMAW
1.2.2 Streaming	Medium-current GMA
1.2.3 Rotating	Rotating high-current GMAW
1.3 Explosive	SMA (coated electrodes)
2 Bridging transfer	
2.1 Short-circuiting	Short-arc GMAW, SMAW
2.2 Bridging without interruption	Welding with filler wire addition
3 Slag-protected transfer	
3.1 Flux-wall guided	SAW
3.2 Other modes	SMAW, cored wire, electro-slag

information it may reveal about the mechanism of elemental loss. It is the latter aspect that will be discussed here.

4.2.1. DROP TRANSFER MODES

The different kinds of drop transfer modes have been classified by the International Institute of Welding (IIW), shown in Table 4.1. The main technique used for studying the mechanisms of drop transfer is high-speed photography. For open arc processes this is a powerful technique, but it obviously cannot be used for SAW. High-speed X-ray recording is used instead. Drop transfer modes have long been studied. A recent review was presented by Lancaster.[1] The first studies in this area were concerned with the SMAW process and the early work was reviewed by Sparagen and Lengberg in 1943. Later work on this welding process was reported by Becken in 1969.[2] Except for the work of Becken, most recent research has concentrated on drop transfer in GMAW, mainly using solid wires. Some work has been carried out on cored wires as well, and on SAW.

In SMAW the drop is thought to form as a consequence of pressure from emitted vapor at the cathode spot (the point on the electrode tip where the arc base is located). The pressure causes a depression of the liquid metal at the cathode spot, consequently causing a corresponding rise of the metal at some other point. The cathode point is shifted to this new peak, which will then become depressed. This wave-like motion eventually builds up a drop large enough for either a bridging transfer or a detachment of the drop. Bridging transfer means that an undetached drop touches the weld pool and is forced into the weld pool by capillarity.

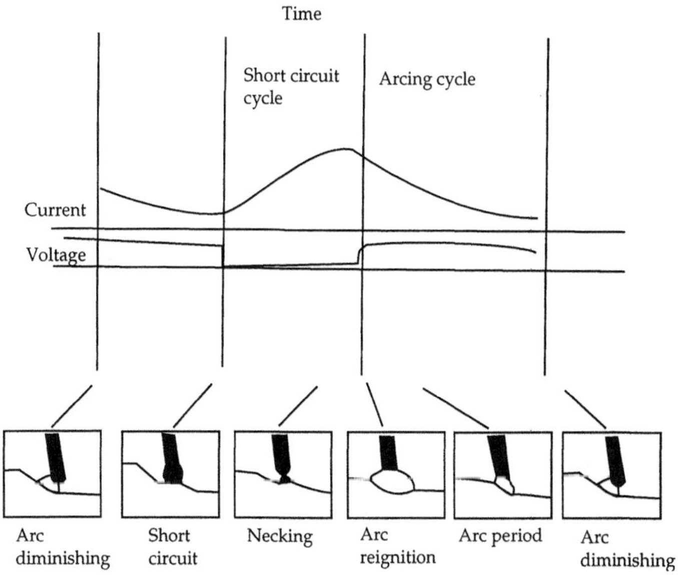

FIGURE 4.1. Voltage and current variations during dip transfer. (From Houldcroft, P. and John, R., *Welding and Cutting,* Woodhead-Faulkner, Cambridge, U.K., 1988. With permission.)

For GMAW the material transport in the arc can occur in two principally different ways: bridging and free-flight transfer. In bridging transfer, just as in SMAW, there is a short-circuiting between the electrode and the workpiece, when the molten drop touches the weld pool (Figure 4.1). This is the most common mode of operation and occurs at relatively low voltages. If the voltage is lowered, there will be an irregular arc which occasionally extinguishes. If the voltage is increased above the value for convenient bridging transfer, the drops will be pinched off before short-circuiting occurs. If the current is also increased, larger magnetic forces will arise, which will lead to more spatter.

Free-flight transfer can occur as a globular transfer or as a spray of drops. The spray mode may be further subdivided into projected or streaming transfer. The transition from one mode to another occurs with increasing levels of the current at relatively high voltages. The exact value of the current when the transition takes place is dependent upon the wire diameter. This mode of operation only occurs in shielding gases that contain significant amounts of either argon or oxygen. The spray mode has many advantages from the drop transfer point of view, but can be inconvenient for the welder because it is hotter to work with. On the other hand, spatter is less and many welders prefer to work in the spray mode. The spray mode means that a higher heat input is used. The weld pool then becomes difficult to control in welding positions other than horizontal.

The different modes are illustrated in Figure 4.2. With very high currents, instabilities in the drop transfer may occur, such as kink and flute instabilities.

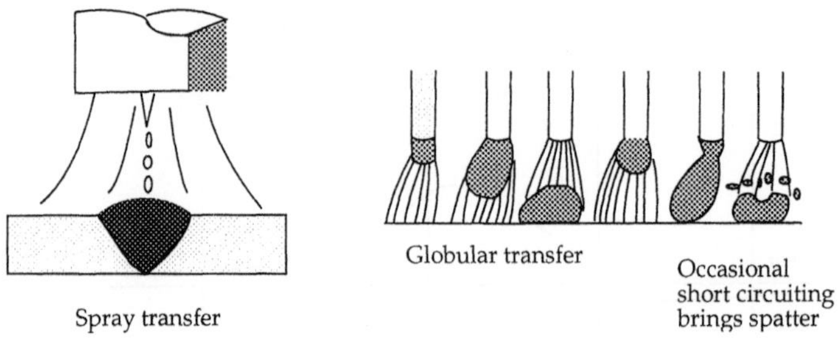

FIGURE 4.2. Free-flight transfer, either as globular drops or as a spray of drops. (From Houldcroft, P. and John, R., *Welding and Cutting,* Woodhead-Faulkner, Cambridge, U.K., 1988. With permission.)

In these cases, the wire behaves as one (kink) or two (flute) rotating spirals, creating a rotating transfer mode.

It should also be noted that with solid wires the spray arc can only be achieved with positive polarity of the electrode. If the electrode has negative polarity, a repelled transfer mode arises. The resultant forces that develop are directed upward and sideways and the drops will follow a rotating spiral trajectory toward the weld pool. Naturally, this transfer mode is unsuitable for welding, as it gives rise to much spatter.

Other sources of instabilities may arise from exploding drops, due to gas emission from within the drop. The gas pressure can arise from the dissociation of oxide inclusions in the metal rod or from the use of gas-forming minerals in cored gas-shielded wires.

The shielding gas can also affect the transfer properties. For example, pure CO_2 creates large, irregular drops that cause splashes as they are propelled into the weld pool. Pulsed spray welding is a special kind of spray mode, induced by a pulsed current that is superimposed on a small background current. One drop is normally detached by each pulse. The advantage of this mode of operation is that welding in all positions can be made using higher energy levels than for the short-circuiting transfer mode. Consequently, thinner materials can be welded than is possible for the normal spray mode because the heat input is smaller.

Studies of SAW metal transfer show that the tip is conical and the tip of the cone is moving in a circle around the electrode axis. The drops are either projected along the arc or move sideways into the molten flux surrounding the arc.

4.2.2. TEMPERATURE OF THE LIQUID

The temperature that the liquid metal reaches during the transfer stage has been the subject of many investigations. The problems associated with making correct measurements are numerous. Pyrometric and calorimetric methods have been used, but may be subject to considerable errors. With pyrometers, only the surface temperature is measured and the results may be influenced by arc radiation. Calorimetric techniques measure the average temperature of the drops, but, depending on how far from the point of detachment the drops are collected, the arc heat may influence the result. Other experiments have involved the collection of drops on cross wires which form a thermocouple, with the droplets welding the junction of the thermocouple. This method seems to produce consistent results which are frequently cited in the literature.[3]

By correcting the recorded temperature for the cooling action of the mass of the thermocouple, the "true" drop temperature can in principle be calculated. The important result is that the drops from steel welds can reach temperatures up to about 2400°C. This value is regarded as the starting value for the cooling sequence that ultimately leads to the formation of the weld metal.

Calculations of the droplet temperature,[4] using measured heat per unit volume at the tip of the electrode, have also been carried out. The heat was calculated in an indirect manner, by establishing a relationship between the wire feed rate, the electrode stick-out, and the current density. It was concluded that the heat content of the melted tip corresponded to an average temperature of the drop just above the melting temperature, i.e., some 1600°C. The surface temperature is, however, likely to be much higher. As long as the drop is in contact with the wire, this may seem a realistic temperature, provided the convection within the molten drop is sufficient to maintain a uniform temperature.

Indeed, this result apparently is at variance with the measurements of the drop temperature using thermocouples. However, there are more facts which indicate that relatively high temperatures are achieved in the drops. Grong and Christensen[5] found that the oxygen content of the weld correlated well with equilibrium data for the silicon-oxygen and the manganese-oxygen reactions at temperatures around 1900 to 1800°C, indicating that the drops should have at least achieved this temperature. One possible way to reconcile these different results is to assume that the drops are heated by the much hotter arc surrounding the drops during transfer. Although the drop transfer time is very short (0.01 to 0.1 s), the plasma temperature is somewhere between 6000 to 30,000 K, so it is feasible for the plasma to heat the drop during its flight to the pool.

4.2.3. FUME FORMATION

An important event that occurs during drop transfer is the formation of fume. Fume particles are in the micrometer-size range and generally consist of oxides of the compounds found in the coating of covered electrodes or in cored wires. SAW fluxes produce insignificant amounts of fume. A large part of the fume particles consists of FeO. In GMAW, the fumes contain FeO, SiO_2, and MnO. The relative amounts of these compounds depend upon both the shielding gas used and the welding parameters.

The fume is largely generated during the drop transfer stage and only insignificant amounts originate from the weld pool. The fume arises as the vapor pressure increases, because of the rise in temperature, but boiling at the surface of the drops with elemental evaporation and the formation of gaseous oxides also occurs. From the metallurgical point of view, the most important factor in fume generation is the loss of alloying elements it causes. It is an important function of the mineral system used in slag shielding processes to compensate for the loss of elements, in order to achieve the desired weld composition. The risk of loss increases with the tendency of the elements to form oxides. The elements thus most likely to be lost are manganese, silicon, and chromium. Loss also occurs when oxides of the elements are formed in the melt and incorporated into the cover slag.

The composition of the fume particles also may give a hint as to how the drops are transferred. It is commonly believed that in slag shielded processes, the drops are transferred with a slag coating. This has generally been assumed by examination of high-speed film recordings, although the results are not completely convincing. The existence of large amounts of FeO in the fume indicates that there is at least a very turbulent situation in the drop during transfer and fresh metal is frequently exposed at the drop/arc plasma interface. From this it seems rather unlikely that the drops are completely covered by slag. High temperature and turbulent internal motion in the drops seem to be more consistent with a mixing of metal and slag.

4.3. REACTIONS IN THE MOLTEN WELD POOL

During the short time that the weld pool is molten, a separation of the metal and the slag takes place. The phase separation takes place via the fluid flow. As the temperature falls, the molten bath becomes more stagnant and the phase separation process ceases. A certain proportion of the deoxidation products will then remain in the weld metal. The size, number density, crystallography, and chemical composition of these particles are important parameters because they influence the further transformations that occur in the weld metal as it cools. At the same time they can influence the mechanical properties. This section describes the reactions that occur and the nature of the particles that remain in the weld metal.

4.3.1. FORCES

The weld pool is usually created by mixing the metal drops from the consumable electrode with melted parent material. The size of the weld pool varies substantially with the welding process and welding parameters. The smallest pool is formed with GTAW, where no consumable electrode is used, and the largest pool is formed with the high-energy SAW process.

The weld pool exists in its melted state for some 1 to 10 s, depending on the size of the pool. Large pools can only be handled in the horizontal position. For positional welding (e.g., vertical up or overhead) lower current and voltages must be used, so that the weld pool can be controlled. The heat input, however, at least in welding vertical up, can be relatively high, because a weaving technique is used, resulting in a slower forward motion. To control the weld pool in positional welding using slag shielding welding techniques, the formulation of the mineral coating is such as to give a quick-freezing slag. This helps to contain the weld pool.

The molten weld pool is a fluid which is subject to electromagnetic forces, surface tension, and buoyancy force. The fluid flow field set up by the electromagnetic forces, created by the electric current passing through the weld metal to the base plate, is illustrated in Figure 4.3. This effect is by far the most dominant of the three mentioned above. Theoretical calculations of the flow pattern in the cross-section of a weld are shown in Figure 4.4. Apart from the effects of the flow on weld metal deoxidation (described below), the flow field also has a considerable effect on the shape of the weld bead. A flow directed outward will create a wide, shallow pool, while a flow pattern that is directed downward and then from the edges toward the center will give a deep, narrow pool.

4.3.2. INCLUSION FORMATION

The presentation made here for the chemical reactions that occur largely follows the work of Grong and Christensen[5] from the early 1980s, later continued by Grong et al.[6] Their work was carried out on gas-metal arc (GMA) welds without considering any slag/metal reactions.

The weld pool is thought to consist of two regions: the "hot" part, close to the arc root, and the "cold" part, well away from the arc root. The temperature in the "hot" part is very high, the flow rate of the fluid is also high, and the possibilities for the formation and transport of deoxidation products are very good. In the "cold" part of the weld pool, the driving force for formation of deoxidation products is higher than in the "hot" part, but the flow rate of the fluid is much smaller, giving insignificant phase separation. This is illustrated in Figure 4.5.

The basic understanding of the deoxidation process stems from theory developed for steelmaking. The influence of the combined effect of silicon and manganese is shown in Figure 4.6. If for a specific temperature, the Mn/Si combination is below the curve, then molten manganese silicates are formed. This leads to a low activity of SiO_2, making deoxidation more effective. However, it should also be noted that the *total* concentration of deoxidizing elements is of critical importance, not just the Mn/Si ratio.

If the same concept is applied to a weld metal containing only manganese and silicon as deoxidizing elements, the deoxidation products will be molten SiO_2 and MnO in the form of manganese silicate, containing only small amounts of FeO. This is the simplest system to analyze and can be obtained by GMA welding a "plain" C-Mn steel using an argon-rich shielding gas. The melt will invariably contain oxygen and the following reaction between oxygen, manganese, and silicon will take place:

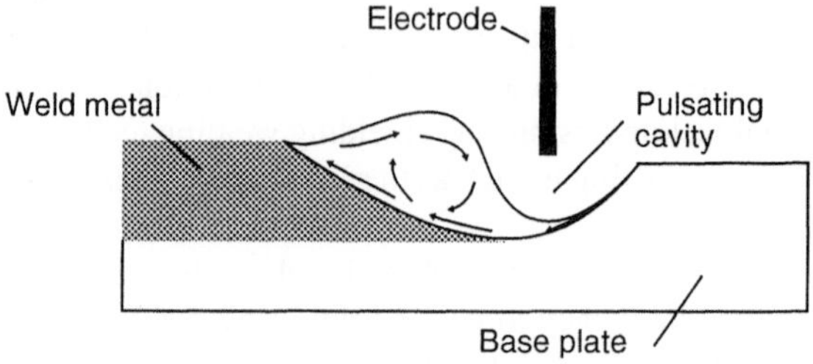

FIGURE 4.3. Flow field in a SAW weld pool, due to electromagnetic forces. (From Lancaster, J. F., *Metallurgy of Welding,* 3rd ed., Chapman & Hall, London, 1980. With permission.)

$$Si + 2MnO \Leftrightarrow 2Mn + SiO_2$$

The Mn/Si ratio should be adjusted in accordance with Figure 4.6 so that nonsaturated manganese silicates are formed, giving the best possible deoxidation. The oxygen content as a function of silicon and manganese contents is shown in Figure 4.7; and in Figure 4.8, the oxygen content as a function of the Mn/Si ratio is plotted. A substantial decrease is found with increasing contents of silicon and manganese and also with an increased Mn/Si ratio. The decrease in oxygen content in Figure 4.8 seems much lower than that in Figure 4.7 but this is due to differences in the range of silicon and manganese contents studied. The two investigations, in fact, give approximately comparable oxygen contents. An increased Mn/Si ratio leads to decreased activity of silica. This results in better deoxidation, which is in line with Figure 4.6. However, beyond a certain threshold value there is no further decrease in oxygen content, so there will always remain a significant amount of oxygen in the weld metal.

The oxygen that remains in the weld pool is assumed to be equal to the oxygen concentration marking the boundary between the "hot" and the "cold" parts of the weld pool (Figure 4.5). This boundary temperature can be found by calculating the temperature for the measured oxygen content in equilibrium with manganese or silicon. The results of such calculations are shown as solid lines in Figure 4.7. The boundary temperature is estimated to be around 1800 to 1900°C. It has been shown that for a system using only silicon and manganese for deoxidation the oxygen concentration can be related to the deoxidation parameter $([Mn][Si])^{-0.25}$. This relation is illustrated in Figure 4.9. For comparison, data in the literature for SMAW are also included in Figure 4.9. As can be seen, the equilibrium temperature is lower for SMAW than for GMAW. Thus, a slag shielded system does not work exactly as a gas shielded system, but it seems that the same fundamental concepts can be used. This simple relationship is obtained only when silicon and manganese are used for deoxidation. When other elements such as aluminum are used, no such simple relationship can be found.

The details of slag/metal reactions are not understood, but some understanding can be gained from reactions that take place during steelmaking. However, the time scales are very different, so that the reactions in the weld pool probably

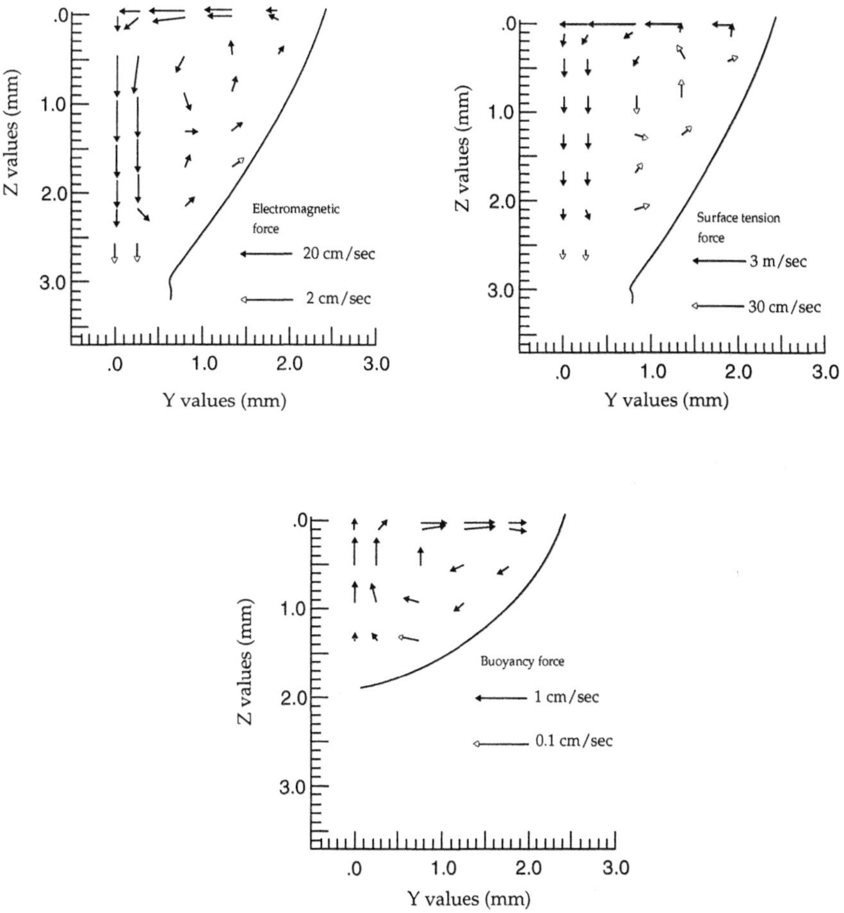

FIGURE 4.4. Theoretical calculation of flow field in the weld pool, due to electromagnetic forces, surface tension, and buoyancy force. (From Wang, Y. H. and Kou, S., *Advances in Welding Science and Technology,* David, S. A., Ed., ASM International, Metals Park, OH, 1986. With permission.)

deviate significantly from equilibrium. This deviation is largest for SMAW, while SAW welds are closer to equilibrium.

The concept of the basicity index was introduced in Equation 1.4. The basicity index consists of the sum (in mole percent) of the basic components divided by the sum of the acid and amphoteric components. This concept is in general only used for submerged arc fluxes, but in principle it works for all slag shielded processes. The basicity index is a semiquantitative factor, which correlates reasonably well with the cleanliness of the weld metal. The decrease in the sulfur content correlates especially well with increased basicity. The phosphorus content, on the other hand, is more or less insensitive to the basicity of the slag.

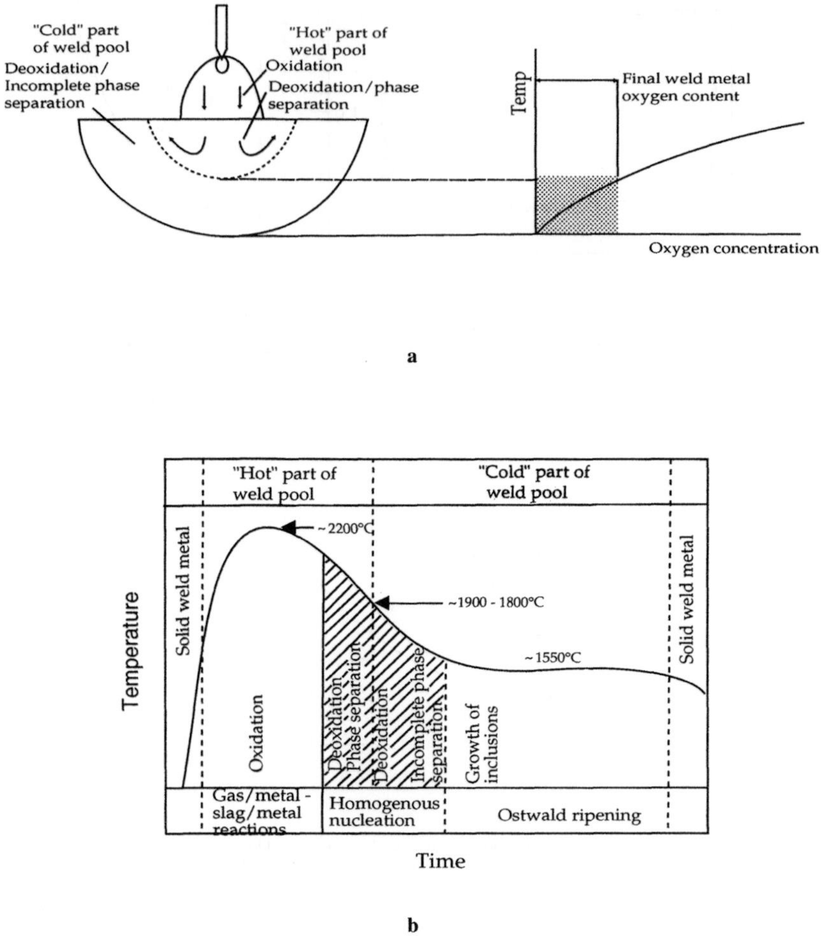

FIGURE 4.5. Illustration of the "hot" and "cold" part of the weld pool. (a) Schematic drawing of the weld pool, with the hot and cold parts indicated. (b) Proposed sequence of reactions in the hot and cold parts of the weld pool. (From Grong, Ø., Siewert, T. A., Martins, G. P., and Olson, D. L., *Metall. Trans. A,* 17A(October), 1797, 1986. With permission.)

The oxygen content decreases with an increased basicity index and this is of the utmost importance, because this creates the possibility of improving the toughness of weld metals. An approximate equation, which at least qualitatively shows some of the likely mechanisms that control the oxygen content of the weld metal, was given by Palm:

$$K_{Mn}\ ([MnO]/[Mn]) = K_{Si}\ ([SiO_2]/[Si])^{1/2} = K_{Fe}\ [FeO] \tag{4.1}$$

This is achieved by assuming that there is a balance:

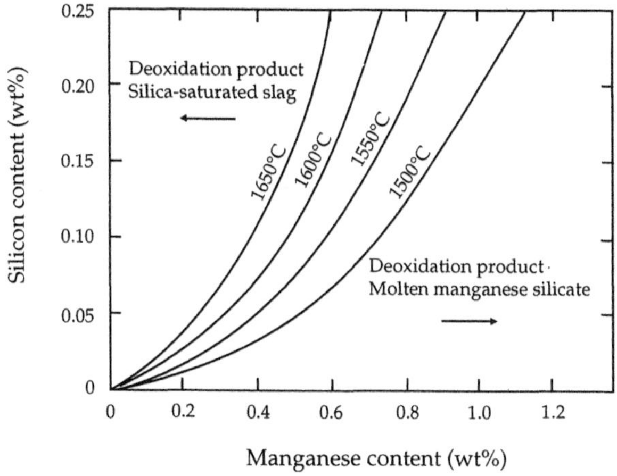

FIGURE 4.6. The influence of the combined action of silicon and manganese on the deoxidation of steels. (From Turkdogan, E. T., *Proc. Int. Conf. Chem. Metall. Iron and Steel*, The Iron and Steel Institute, Sheffield, U.K., 1973. With permission.)

$$M_xO_y + y\mathrm{Fe} \Leftrightarrow x\mathrm{M} + y\mathrm{FeO}$$

i.e., the oxides (of manganese and silicon) in the melt are in equilibrium with FeO (in the slag). This ignores the fact that the slag is ionic in character and that many other oxides are used in the flux to form the slag. With increasing basicity (i.e., with higher contents of minerals having a "basic" character, meaning that they can provide oxygen anions, O^{2-}), there is a greater chance that a silicate ion is produced by the reaction

$$SiO_2 + 2O^{2-} \Leftrightarrow SiO_4^{4-}$$

This silicate ion does not provide oxygen to the melt and the oxygen content is decreased. Thus, as basicity increases (e.g., by addition of lime, CaO) the oxygen content decreases. However, this only occurs up to a certain value of the basicity index, as shown in Figure 4.10. It is assumed that this value corresponds to all silica being used and hence no further decrease in oxygen is possible.

A somewhat different view is held by Lancaster. The oxygen content will be lower with increasing basicity, but that is due to basic oxides not easily dissociating and giving off oxygen at the weld metal surface, rather than a better cleaning action of the slag. However, the decrease in sulfur content of the weld metal is due to the refining action of the slag.

It must be kept in mind that the reactions that occur during slag shielded welding are highly dynamic, with many reactions taking place near the metal/slag interface. Reaction products from this interface are stirred into the weld pool, affecting any further reactions. The models presented above give a very simplified picture of the physical processes that actually occur.

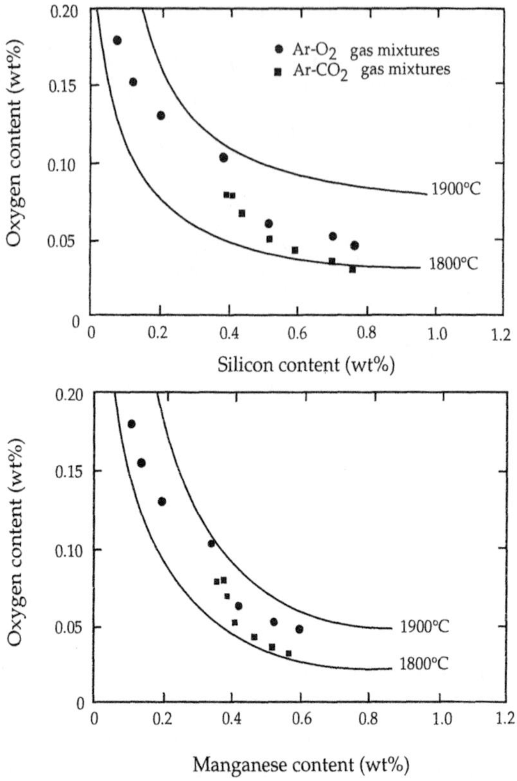

FIGURE 4.7. The oxygen content as a function of silicon and manganese in GMAW. The points represent measured values, while the solid lines represent thermodynamical calculations at the indicated temperatures. (From Grong, Ø. and Christensen, N., *Scand. J. Metall.*, 4, 155, 1983. © 1983 Munksgaard International Publishers Ltd., Copenhagen, Denmark. With permission.)

The elements that are supplied with the coating and can take part in the deoxidation process are (apart from silicon and manganese) usually magnesium, titanium, zirconium, calcium, and aluminum. The driving force for the possible reactions can be found from the diagram in Figure 4.11, showing the free energy change versus temperature. The sequence of deoxidation products in decreasing strength is CaO, MgO, Al_2O_3, TiO_2, SiO_2, and MnO. At very high temperatures, carbon can also act as a deoxidizer, forming CO. The deoxidation process is very efficient. It is estimated that at least 90% of the oxygen in the melt is removed before the weld solidifies.

4.3.3. INCLUSION GROWTH

The nucleation stage of the oxides is extremely difficult to study. However, considering the violent streaming of the fluid, formation of clusters should occur quite frequently. Thus, homogenous nucleation of particles should be the

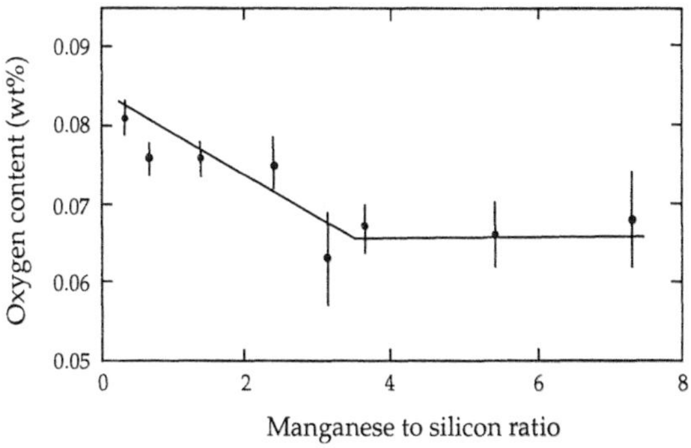

FIGURE 4.8. Oxygen content as a function of the manganese to silicon ratio. (From Grong, Ø., Siewert, T. A., Martins, G. P., and Olson, D. L., *Metall. Trans. A,* 17A(October), 1797, 1986. With permission.)

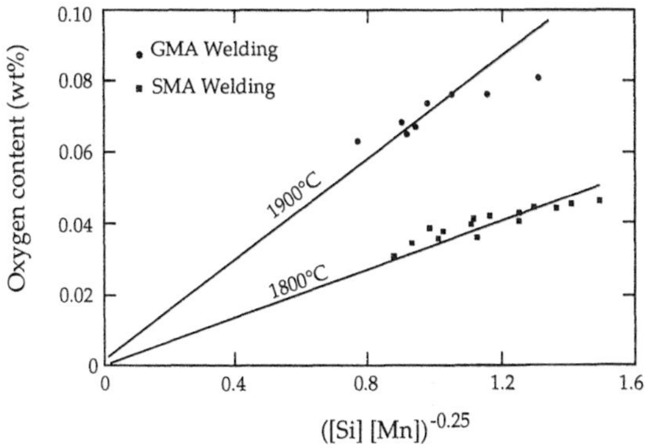

FIGURE 4.9. Correlation between the oxygen content and the deoxidation parameter $[\%Si][\%Mn]^{-0.25}$. The points represent measurements, while the solid lines represent thermodynamical calculations. Data for both GMAW and SMAW are shown. (From Grong, Ø., Siewert, T. A., Martins, G. P., and Olson, D. L., *Metall. Trans. A,* 17A(October), 1797, 1986. With permission.)

dominant process. This discussion will concentrate on inclusions that remain in the weld pool, i.e., those that grow in the cold zone. However, some experiments have been carried out that are more representative of inclusion growth in the hot zone. Here, the inclusions are much coarser than normally envisaged and the mode of growth is different.

Early work carried out by Lindborg and Torsell[7] on a steel melt held at a constant temperature of about 1650°C resulted in a growth model as illustrated in Figure 4.12, where it should be noted that the time scale extends to more than 1000 s. The major increase in particle size occurred after about 10 s and is initially due to gradient collision, followed by the Stokes' collision. "Gradient collisions" occur due to particles following the fluid flow and hitting each

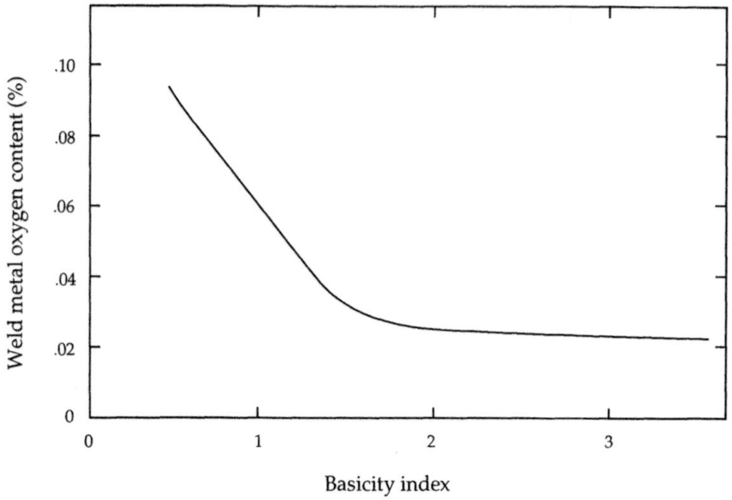

FIGURE 4.10. Influence of the basicity index on oxygen content. The oxygen content of the weld metal decreases rapidly when going from an acid to a medium basic slag. When all SiO_2 is used, no further reduction of the oxygen content occurs. (From Eager, T., *Weld. J.*, 57(March), 76s, 1978. With permission.)

other, while Stokes' collisions occur during the particle rise in the liquid, with a velocity predicted by Stokes' law. Larger particles in both cases are assumed to grow after hitting smaller particles. The fluid velocity assumed for this model was 10 mm/s. At 1650°C, a weld pool would be almost stagnant and growth would not be expected to occur due to gradient collision. In the work of Lindborg and Torsell the bath was agitated artificially, by induction stirring. The size of the particles is much larger than those remaining in the weld metals, with maximum sizes ranging up to 25 μm. After a long time, the largest particles will reach the surface of the steel melt and separate out. That the largest particles separate out is due to the fact that these particles have been moving for the longest period of time in the melt and have had many opportunities for collision. The larger the particle size, the higher the velocity due to Stokes' law and, thus, it is more likely that the largest particles reach the upper surface first. This in turn decreases the mean size of the particles that remain in the melt. Some slow growth of the inclusions was noted and assumed to be due to "diffusional coalescence" (also called Ostwald ripening).

In contrast to the model of Lindborg and Torsell, Grong et al.[6] found that Stokes' collisions in a weld pool make an insignificant contribution to the growth of the particles, because the fluid flow rate is much higher than the flow rate due to Stokes' law. The fluid flow rate in SAWs is estimated to be between 0.025 to 0.4 m/s, while the velocity of rising particles with a radius below 2 μm is estimated to be less than 2.4 μm/s.

Before discussing the growth of inclusions in the cold zone, some words

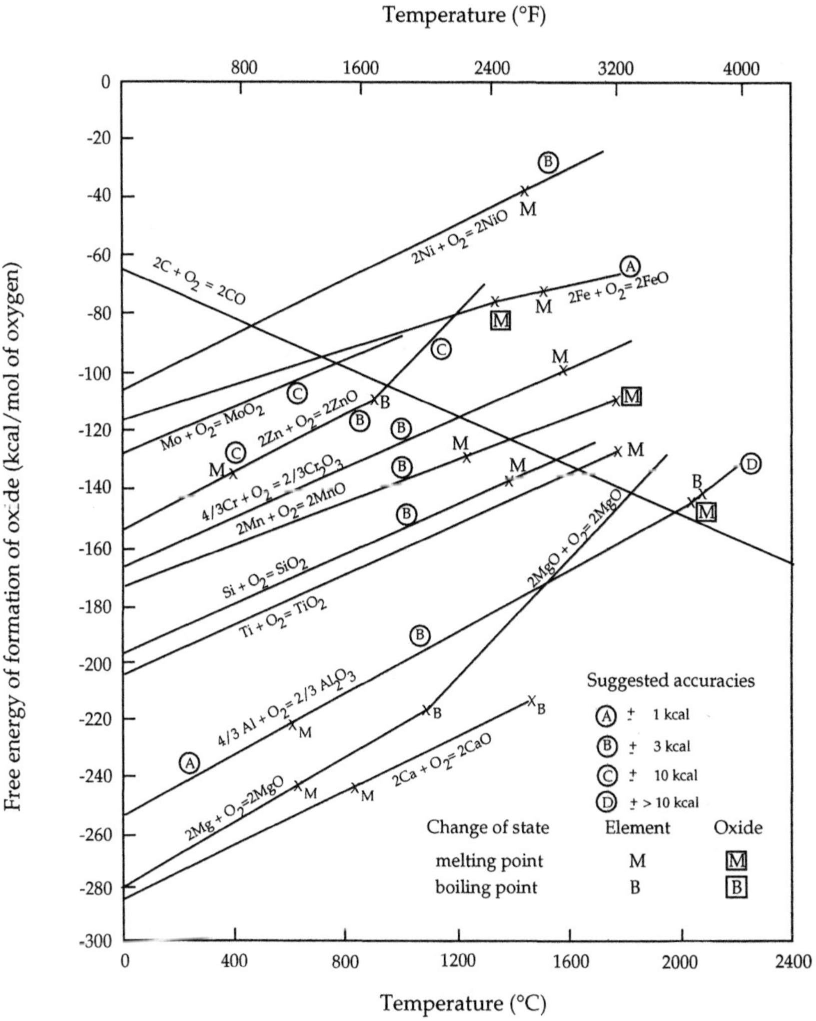

FIGURE 4.11. A diagram showing the free energy change as a function of temperature for a number of deoxidation reactions. (From Milner, D. R., *Br. Weld. J.*, 5, 98, 1958. With permission.)

about the microscopy techniques employed may be appropriate. The methods used to obtain size distributions for particles growing in the cold zone have been refined over the years. Optical microscopy has often been used. Later developments, using scanning electron microscopy (SEM), have enabled large quantities of data to be obtained at a higher resolution. Automated systems combining chemical and spatial information were first developed in the mid-1970s and this development has continued with more refined and more rapid systems. The size distributions obtained are dependent upon the lower resolution

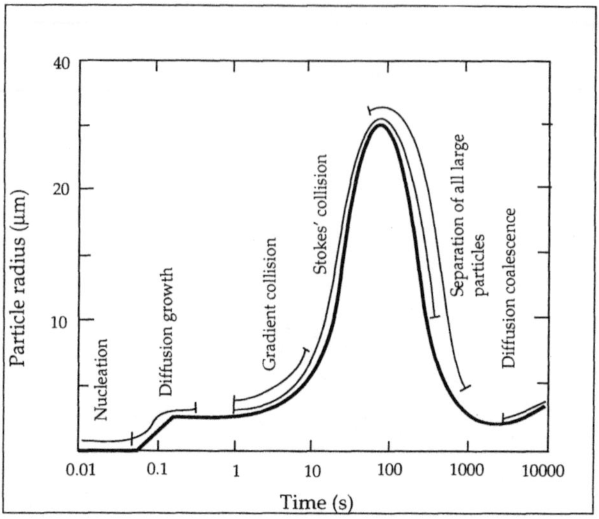

FIGURE 4.12. Growth model of oxide particles in an agitated steel melt at 1650°C. (From Lindborg, U. and Torsell, K. *Trans. Metall. Soc. AIME,* 242(January), 94, 1968. With permission.)

limit of the techniques used. The optical microscope has a resolution limit of about 0.2 μm, while the limit is ca. 0.05 μm for the SEM. Thus, much smaller particles can be detected with the SEM. However, if the system uses chemical information from the energy-dispersive X-ray (EDX) system, often attached to SEM, then the analysis is the average over a volume of approximately 5 μm^3, with a spatial resolution of about 1 μm. Particles embedded in a steel matrix will then be difficult to assess using a polished specimen. Recent developments have instead utilized extraction of particles on carbon replicas for examination in the SEM. With this method, the chemical analysis of closely spaced particles becomes feasible. It also becomes possible to measure the three-dimensional size distribution by tilting the specimen and measuring various dimensions. A complementary technique that has relatively recently come into use is the scanning transmission electron microscope (STEM), also commonly equipped with EDX facilities. With this instrument chemical analyses of very small particles can be obtained. Extraction replicas are also used to avoid interference with the matrix. Inclusion size distributions obtained in some different investigations are shown in Figure 4.13.

The size distributions obtained by Grong et al. (Figure 4.13a) came from measurements on experimental GMA welds, using metal cored wires. Their intention was to study the influence of the Mn/Si ratio on the growth of inclusions. The data were obtained by transmission electron microscopy (TEM) of particles extracted onto carbon replicas. A typical picture from such a weld metal is shown in Figure 4.14. The smallest size class used here was 0.1 μm and almost all particles have a diameter less than 1 μm. Few particles were observed having diameters above 1.2 μm. The variation in mean particle size with changing Mn/Si ratio was relatively small. At first, the mean particle diameter increased with increasing Mn/Si ratio, but in very high manganese (low silicon) welds, the distribution contained a dense population of very small particles, leading to a substantial decrease in average size.

Ahlblom et al.[8] used one of the first automated systems, particle analyzing scanning electron microscopy (PASEM), in the mid-1970s to study inclusion size distributions. They presented their data in the form of a cumulative distribution, but this has been replotted here as a normal distribution to facilitate comparison. They studied weld metals obtained by SAW with different current levels (Figure 4.13b). The lower detection limit of the particle diameter was 0.2 μm, so that the smallest particles are not measured. There were only minor differences in the size distribution between the two lower current levels (600 and 1000 A). With the highest current, the average size of the particles increased and the size distribution broadened.

Kluken[9] studied SAW metals, with systematic variations in the deoxidizing elements aluminum and titanium. He did not present the full size distribution, but only gave the mean diameters. The mean diameters were found to be constant, irrespective of variations in aluminum or titanium contents. However, he noted that a large aluminum content resulted in an increased number of coarse particles. Also, the two-dimensional arithmetic mean particle size was constant with increasing aluminum content. The ratio between the three-dimensional and two-dimensional diameters was found to be 1.47, relatively close to 1.57 predicted from the theory for a polydispersed system of spheres.

Thewlis[10] used optical microscopy to measure the size distribution of inclusions in SAW metals of the kind used for line-pipe fabrication. The lower detection limit was given as "better than 0.4 μm." He found that the majority of particles were 0.2 to 0.4 μm. The average diameters were fairly constant, about 0.45 μm when the heat input was 3.3 kJ/mm. The main variables studied were aluminum, calcium, titanium, and nitrogen contents. Aluminum was found to reduce the number of particles and increase the size. With increasing titanium content, the volume fraction of particles was reduced.

The mean particle sizes determined from the investigations discussed above have been plotted in Figure 4.15 as a function of the Mn/Si ratio. They have also been divided into groups with respect to heat input and whether other deoxidizing elements have been used. The overall picture is confusing, with no clear influence of the variables studied, except perhaps for the heat input. A rather coarse division of the inclusion sizes can be made:

- Below 0.3 μm, obtained with low heat input and strong deoxidation (mainly aluminum)
- Between 0.3 to 0.5 μm, the large majority of particle sizes
- Between 0.5 to 0.6 μm, without any seemingly rational explanation

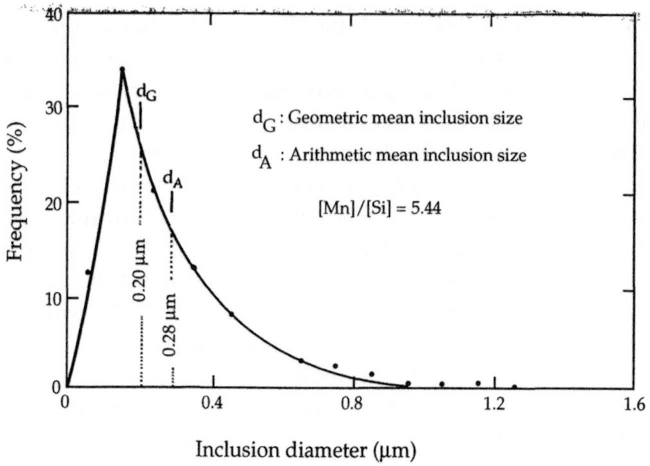

a

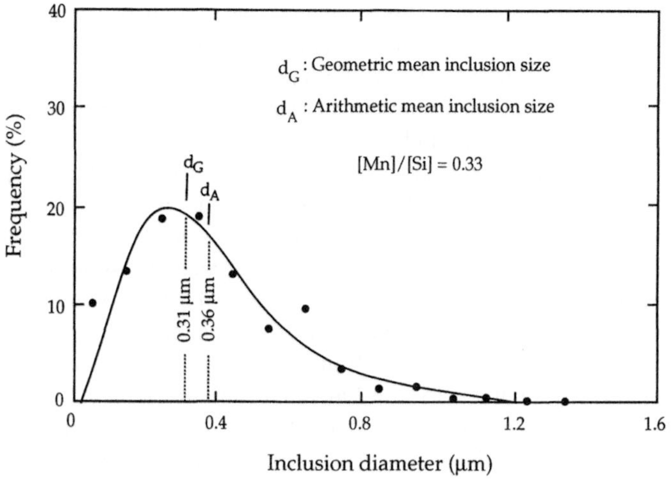

b

FIGURE 4.13. Size distribution as a function of the Mn/Si ratio of oxides formed in the cold part of the weld pool. (a to c) GMAW, using metal cored wires. (From Grong, Ø., Siewert, T. A., Martins, G. P., and Olson, D. L., *Metall. Trans. A,* 17A(October), 1797, 1986. With permission.) (d) SAW, with variation in welding current. (From Ahlblom, B., Bergström, U., and Werlefors, I., in *Proc. Int. Conf. Effect of Residual, Impurity and Micro-alloying Elements on Weldability and Weld Metal Properties,* The Welding Institute, London, 1983, paper 49. With permission.)

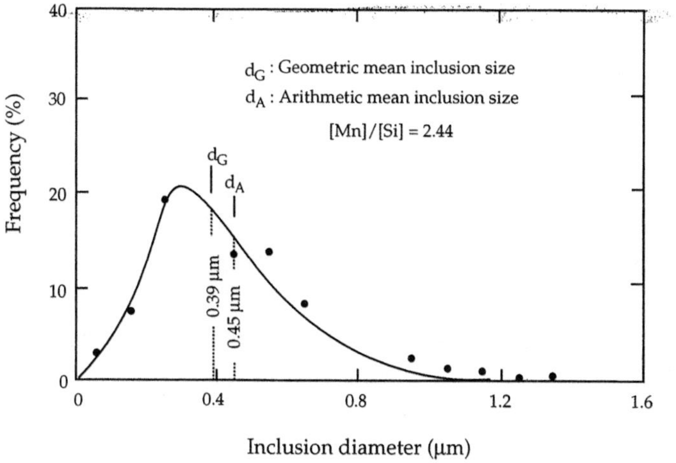

c

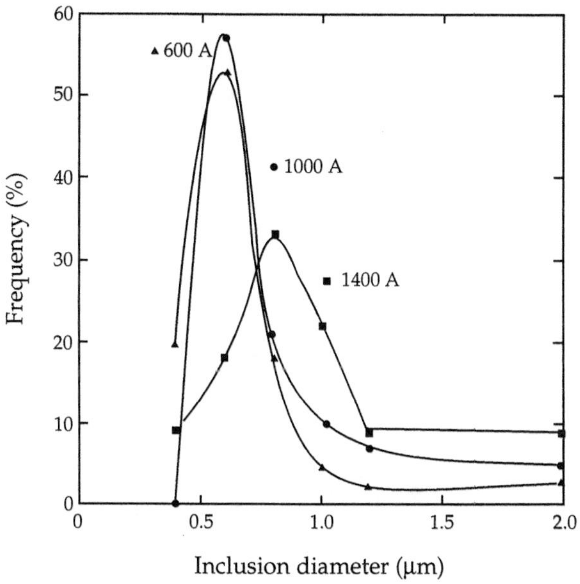

d

- Above 0.6 μm, when high heat inputs are used

There does not seem to be any strong influence of the Mn/Si ratio or any general effect of using aluminum or titanium deoxidation. The single value of 0.2 μm was obtained using aluminum deoxidation and low heat input.

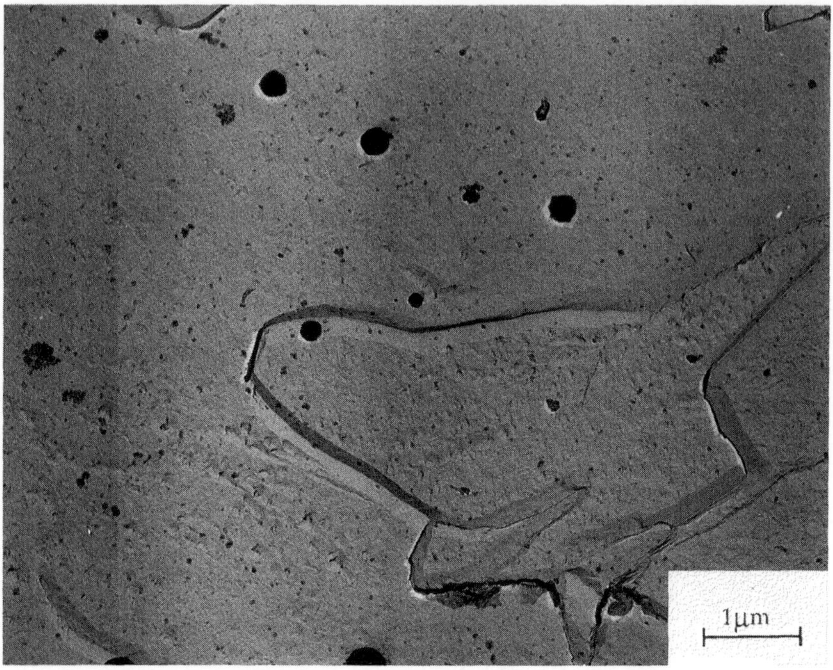

FIGURE 4.14. TEM of particles extracted onto a carbon replica. The particles come from a basic SMAW weld metal.

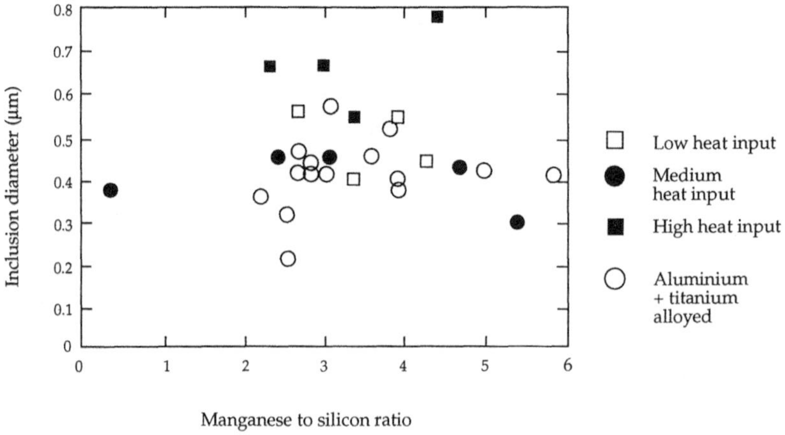

FIGURE 4.15. Plot of mean particle size as a function of the Mn/Si ratio. (Adapted from the data in Figure 4.13 and from Kluken.[9])

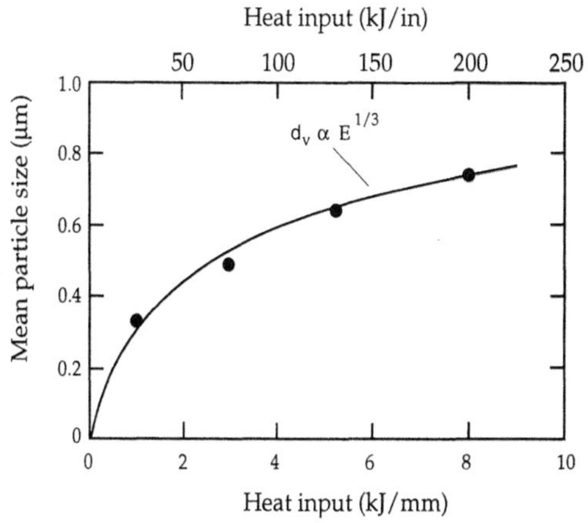

FIGURE 4.16. Relation between particle diameter and heat input, showing that the mean particle diameter is proportional to the third root of the heat input. It was shown by Kluken that this is equivalent to a similar dependence on the retention time. (From Kluken, A. O., Ph.D. thesis, NTH, Trondheim, Norway, 1991. With permission.)

The two growth mechanisms dominating in the hot zone (collision and diffusion) are discarded when it comes to the cold zone. The collision probability should be low, because the melt is virtually stagnant and the particles only move through buoyancy effects due to Stokes' law. Diffusional growth should be completed within a fraction of a second, because the density of nuclei is so very high (about $10^8/mm^3$) and the diffusion rates are so very large. Kluken found a linear relation between the mean diameter and the third root of the retention time (see Figure 4.16). This observation supports the assumption that Ostwald ripening is the dominant growth process in the cold zone. However, the shape of size distributions deviated somewhat from the requirements of a distribution obeying a Wagner coarsening equation. Ideally, the size distribution should be quasistationary and have a stable maximum particle diameter of about 1.5 times the mean diameter of the system.

4.3.4. INCLUSION COMPOSITION

The composition and crystal structure of the inclusions vary, depending on the deoxidation element content in relation to oxygen content. A list of the phases identified is presented in Table 4.2.

Several investigations have shown that the particles are multiphase. The core usually consists of the main deoxidation elements (i.e., manganese, silicon, aluminum, and sometimes titanium). In basic-type weld metals (i.e., with an oxygen content of the order of 200 to 400 ppm) without aluminum, glassy $MnOSiO_2$ particles are formed, and with high aluminum contents, γ-Al_2O_3 particles are found. In welds with moderate aluminum content, a spinel $MnOAl_2O_3$ (galaxite) is often formed. Particles have been found to have a very mixed composition, with manganese, silicon, aluminum, and titanium present

TABLE 4.2
Phases Identified in Slag Inclusions

Phase	Chemical formula	Structure type	Lattice parameter (Å)
Galaxite	$MnOAl_2O_3$	Cubic	8.27
Titanium monoxide	γ-TiO	Cubic	4.18
Titanium nitride	TiN	Cubic	4.25
Titanium carbide	TiC	Cubic	4.18
Rhodonite	$MnOSiO_2$	Glassy	
Alumina	γ-Al_2O_3	Cubic	7.85
Manganese sulfide	α-MnS	Cubic	5.23
Digenite I	$Cu_{1.8}S$	Cubic	5.70

simultaneously; with diffraction analysis, however, still only the spinel $MnOAl_2O_3$ and γ-Al_2O_3 were found. Many particles have surface layers that are titanium-rich or are different structures of MnS. Surface layers of CuS have also been reported. Measurements of the composition of some titanium-rich inclusion surface regions with wavelength-dispersive X-ray analysis have on occasion revealed high nitrogen concentrations. From diffraction analysis alone, it is not possible to distinguish between TiN, δ-TiO, or TiC. Moreover, the formation of δ-TiO would require strongly reducing conditions and it is therefore not likely to be an equilibrium product in weld metals. A suggestion of the buildup of particles is shown in Figure 4.17.

The composition of the particles can be estimated with reasonable accuracy, using the following set of equations. In these equations $[I]_i$ means the concentration in wt% of element I in the inclusion. The total volume fraction of inclusions (V_v) is given approximately by Equation 4.2. The inclusions are assumed to be oxides and sulfides. The solubility of sulfur is assumed to be 0.003 wt% and thus the sulfur content contributing to inclusion formation must be reduced by a corresponding amount:

$$V_v = 0.05\ \{[O] + 0.054\ ([S] - 0.003)\} \tag{4.2}$$

The aluminum content of the inclusions can be calculated as the difference between total and soluble aluminum content (ΔAl), divided by the mass fraction of inclusions. The mass fraction m_I is given as

$$m_I = V_v\ \rho_I/\rho_S \tag{4.3}$$

where ρ_I and ρ_S are the inclusion and steel densities, respectively. They are

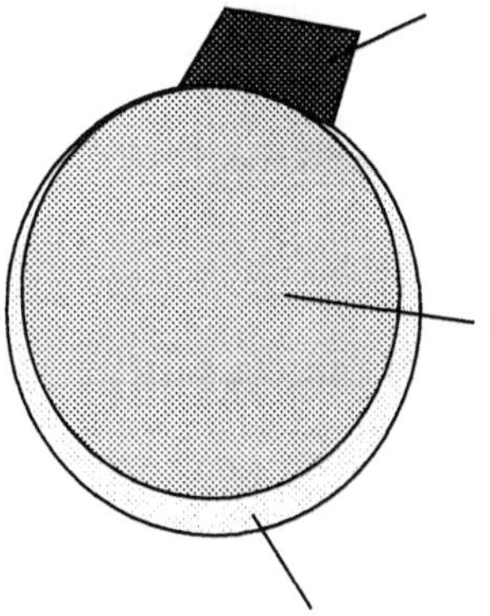

FIGURE 4.17. Schematic drawing, suggesting the buildup of a titanium oxide particle. (From Kluken, A. O., Ph.D. thesis, NTH, Trondheim, Norway, 1991. With permission.)

approximately 7.8 and 4.2 g/cm^3, giving a ratio of 1.86. Thus,

$$[Al]_i = 1.86\ [\Delta Al]/V_v \qquad (4.4)$$

(with the restriction $[\Delta Al] \leq 1.13\ [O]_w$). The restriction on the aluminum content comes from the stoichiometry of Al_2O_3.

The titanium content of the inclusions is calculated in the same manner as the aluminum content. However, unlike aluminum, titanium also forms nitrides easily and this must be taken into account. The amount of titanium in the form of nitrides can be calculated as

$$[Ti]_N = A_{Ti}([N]_T - [N]_{sol})/m_f A_N \qquad (4.5)$$

where $[Ti]_N$ is the titanium content in the nitrides, $[N]_T$ is the total nitrogen content in solution, and A_T and A_N are the atomic weights of the respective elements. The total nitrogen content can be estimated from the solubility product at a suitable temperature, e.g., just above the melting temperature of the steel. The titanium content in oxide inclusions $[Ti]_{oi}$ can now be estimated as

$$[Ti]_{oi} = 1.86\{[\Delta Ti]/V_v - [Ti]_N - [Ti]_{sol}\} \qquad (4.6)$$

The sulfur tied up in the inclusions is given by

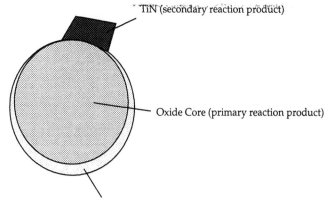

$$[S]_i = 1.86\ ([S] - 0.003)/V_v \qquad (4.7)$$

The silicon and manganese contents in the inclusions are calculated by correcting for the fact that oxygen first reacts with aluminum, and then titanium, before combining with either silicon or manganese. An assumption about the relative proportions of SiO_2 and MnO must also be made. If

$$\theta = \text{wt\% } SiO_2/\text{wt\% MnO} \tag{4.8}$$

and

$$\beta = (A_{Mn}/A_O + 1)\theta/[(A_{Si}/2A_O + 1) + (A_{Mn}/A_O + 1)] \tag{4.9}$$

where A_i is the atomic weight of element i, then

$$[Si]_i = \beta A_{Si}([O] - m_I[O]_{Al} - m_I[O]_{Ti})/2(m_I A_O) \tag{4.10}$$

$$[Mn]_i = (1 - \beta)A_{Mn}([O] - m_I[O]_{Al} - m_I[O]_{Ti})/(m_I A_O) \tag{4.11}$$

Figure 4.18 shows the correlation between measured and predicted concentrations in the oxide inclusions, using the above equations. These calculations can only be made with a knowledge of the solid solution concentration of aluminum, titanium, and sulfur. These values are difficult to estimate. Also, there are a number of assumptions behind the equations which make the calculations somewhat unreliable. The major weakness is the method for the partitioning of oxygen between different metallic elements. It is assumed that the strongest oxide former ties up as much oxygen as is permitted by its concentration and then the next strongest oxide former starts to combine with oxygen. However, in weld metals it is often found that manganese and silicon oxides exist when it might be expected that all of the oxygen should be tied up with aluminum and titanium.

4.3.5. NITROGEN AND HYDROGEN IN THE WELD METAL

Although the reactions with oxygen are the most important from the aspect of properties of the weld metal, nitrogen and hydrogen also have significant effects on the weld metal properties. The dissolution of these gases in the melt is described by Sievert's law. For nitrogen the following relation applies:

$$a_N = C\sqrt{p_{N2}} \tag{4.12}$$

where a_N is the activity of nitrogen in liquid steel, C is a temperature-dependent proportionality constant, and p_{N2} is the nitrogen partial pressure. The nitrogen concentration *[N]* is related to the activity by the relation

$$a_N = f[N] \tag{4.13}$$

where f is the activity coefficient given by:

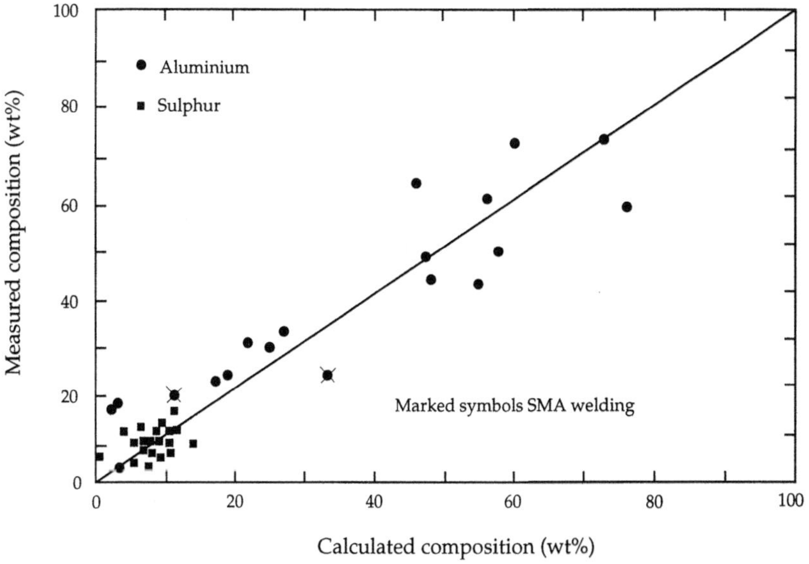

a

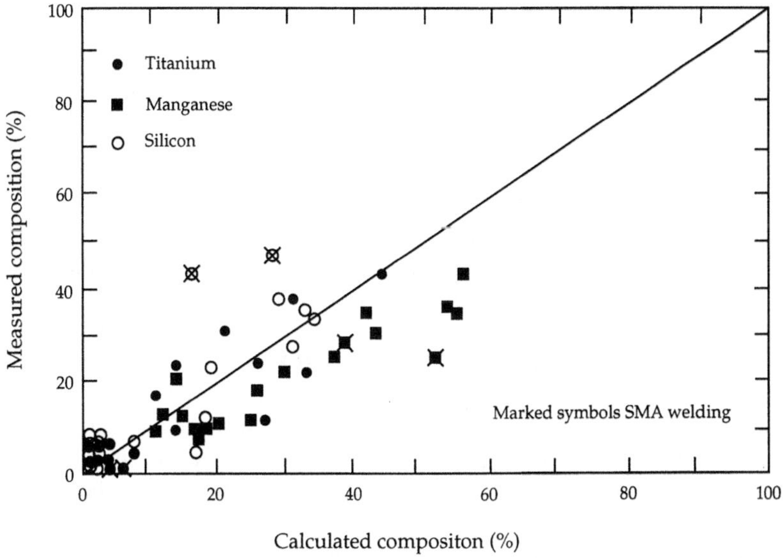

b

FIGURE 4.18. Correlation between measured and predicted concentrations of elements in oxide inclusions, using Equations 4.4 to 4.10. (a) Aluminum and sulfur; (b) titanium, manganese, and silicon. (From Kluken, A. O., Ph.D. thesis, NTH, Trondheim, Norway, 1991. With permission.)

$$\log \{f\} = \Sigma_i [Y] e_i \quad (4.14)$$

where $[Y]$ is the concentration of element I in the liquid steel and e_i is called the Wagner interaction parameter between the element concerned and nitrogen in dilute solutions.

Assuming that the nitrogen concentration at ambient temperature is related to its solubility in liquid steels, then the above equations can be used to crudely assess the effect of weld chemistry on the nitrogen content of the weld metal. The accuracy of the method is of course limited, because a factor such as arc length can significantly affect the nitrogen concentration, but this is not taken into account in the model. Figure 4.19 shows an example of the use of the method for analyzing the nitrogen content of SAWs. The absolute values differ between the measured and predicted concentrations, but the trends are predicted fairly well.

Weld metals from rutile SMAW electrodes usually have high contents of both oxygen and nitrogen, with nitrogen levels around 200 ppm. This is probably due to a comparatively low amount of shielding gas generated by this type of coating. Basic-type coatings give nitrogen contents of around 50 to 100 ppm. In SAW welds, the nitrogen content is the same as that in the wire. However, with some highly basic fluxes not containing carbonates, the nitrogen content can be influenced by the current type, with AC giving larger concentrations. Also, for solid wires and cored wires, the nitrogen content is dictated by what is supplied from the consumable, provided the shielding gas is not contaminated.

An expression similar to Equation 4.12 is also found for hydrogen. Hydrogen comes mainly from the decomposition of moisture in the consumables. Because it is the partial pressure and not the total available hydrogen that controls the amount of hydrogen in the weld metal, it is possible to decrease the hydrogen content by using a "dilution gas" such as CO_2. This is utilized in, for example, SAW fluxes where a small amount of carbonates in the flux generates CO_2 gas, giving very low weld metal hydrogen values.

4.4. SOLIDIFICATION

The solidification process influences both the grain size and the grain shape of the solid formed from the molten material. Further, the extent of segregation, both on a micro and macro scale, is determined by solidification. The inclusions that form in the molten material will be incorporated into the solid material during solidification. It has been found that inclusions are preferentially located in the primary grain boundaries, so there is an interaction between the solidification front and the inclusions.

Knowledge about weld pool solidification is very limited. It is mainly comprised of an extrapolation of the knowledge of the solidification of castings and related processes. However, in such cases the thermal gradient is much

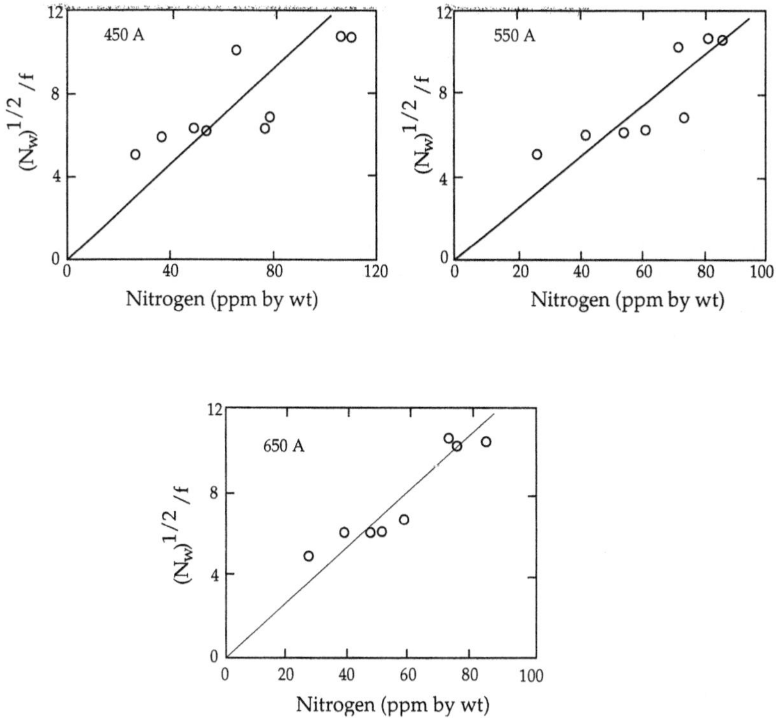

FIGURE 4.19. Correlation of calculated versus experimentally measured nitrogen concentration in SAW metals for different welding currents. N_W refers to the nitrogen content of the wire. (From Bhadeshia, H. K. D. H. and Svensson, L.-E., *J. Mater. Sci. Lett.*, 7, 610, 1988. With permission.)

lower than in welding. On the other hand, advances have recently been made in solidification theories describing nucleation, growth, and solute redistribution in castings and ingots. These theories must be investigated in relation to the welding process in order to test the applicability. What is needed is a correlation between the solidification parameters (growth rate, temperature gradient, and undercooling) and the microstructure developed. A recent review by David and Vitek[11] treats the solidification of weld metals in great detail and provides most of the information for this section.

The weld metals mainly solidify with a cellular or dendritic structure. The size of the primary grains is related to the grain size of the HAZ on which they grow. However, the crystallography of the growing grains complicates this relationship. The size of the grains is further influenced by the heat input.

4.4.1. PRIMARY SOLIDIFICATION MODES

The weld metal starts to solidify at temperatures below about 1500°C. The weld metal solidifies under conditions of constitutional supercooling. This means that the driving force for growth of solidified material is due to an enriched zone of alloying elements in the melt at the solid/liquid interface. The local liquidus temperature thus is different from that of the alloy as a whole. If the temperature gradient in the liquid at the solid/liquid interface is lower than that of the liquidus temperature, the material is said to be constitutionally supercooled.

The undercooling of a melt can be divided into kinetic undercooling due to the curvature of the solid/liquid interface, thermal undercooling, and constitutional undercooling. The undercoolings due to kinetic factors and to curvature are both present only at the solid/liquid interface. The contribution of these various factors is difficult to determine experimentally. The general opinion is that the constitutional supercooling effect is by far the largest effect. The undercooling due to curvature may be significant. It is related to the surface energy of the curved interface, and because the size of the crystal in welding is fairly small, surface energy effects can be considerable. Kinetic undercooling is usually less than 1 K for solidifying metals. Thermal undercooling does not normally occur in welding. This kind of undercooling appears in situations where there is a significant barrier for nucleation, but this is not the case in welding. Experimental measurements and theoretical calculations point to typical undercoolings at around 10 K.

The new grains develop directly from the growth of solid on the grains in the HAZ at the fusion boundary, i.e., there is no nucleation but epitaxial growth. This is strictly true only for weld metals having a composition identical to the base metal. When the weld metal has a composition that is radically different from that of the base plate, the surface energy between the weld metal and the base metal differs, and it becomes necessary for nucleation to occur.

It has also been suggested that solidification could occur on the oxides in the melt, in front of the epitaxially growing solidification front. Inoculated particles have been used to stimulate such nucleation. The reason for doing so is to avoid the columnar grain structure commonly found in favor of a more equiaxed grain structure. Successful results have been reported, but no commercial use for the method has been found.

The solidifying grains grow mainly along the maximum thermal gradient toward the weld center, resulting in a columnar grain shape. The width of the columnar grains is related to the size of the grains in the HAZ. However, because some unfavorably oriented grains will be stifled by those growing more rapidly, the successful grains will increase in size and are expected to be wider than the parent grains.

The grains separated by high-energy boundaries are usually referred to as primary grains. Inside these primary grains, there is a substructure that is divided by small-angle grain boundaries. This substructure can develop in different ways, depending on the solute content and the solidification parameter G/R, where G is the thermal gradient and R is the velocity of the solidification front. Usually, four different solidification modes are distinguished (Figure 4.20): planar front, cellular, cellular dendritic, and dendritic.

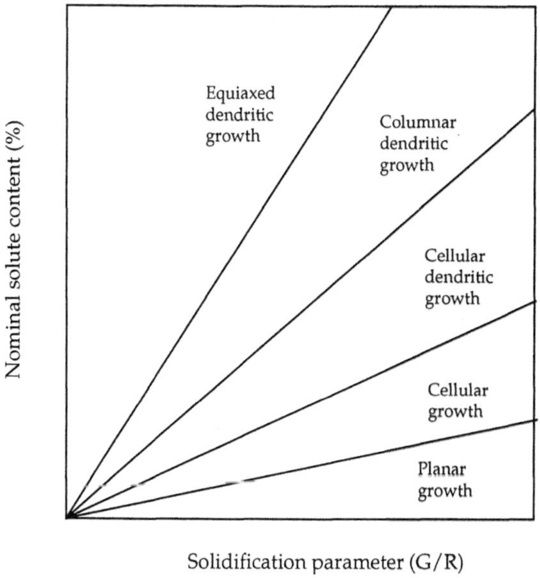

FIGURE 4.20. Diagram showing the solidification structure for different compositions and solidification parameters. (From Lancaster, J. F., *Metallurgy of Welding,* 3rd ed., Chapman & Hall, London, 1980. With permission.)

The planar front involves columnar grains which develop without any substructure. Growth occurs along the maximum thermal gradient and is not affected by any crystallographic preferences.

Cellular solidification occurs from the motion of an unstable solidification front. Also, here it is mainly the heat flow direction and not crystallography that determines the direction of growth. The cellular mode arises when several relatively closely spaced cells are growing parallel to each other within a primary grain.

Dendritic growth is different from the cellular or planar front growth in that the dendrites follow the easy growth direction along ⟨100⟩ planes, which means that the axis of a dendrite may deviate from the maximum thermal gradient direction. The development of dendrites is also due to an unstable growth front. Branching often occurs on dendrites, but may be more or less well developed. If the branching is poorly developed, then the structure is fairly similar to a cellular structure and is called cellular dendritic. With well-developed branching, the structure is called columnar dendritic. Figure 4.21 shows schematically the different structures.

The reason for the development of cellular or dendritic patterns is that the growth front can become unstable under conditions of constitutional supercooling. This occurs when solute builds up in front of the solid/liquid interface, giving a locally higher liquidus temperature. If the temperature gradient in the

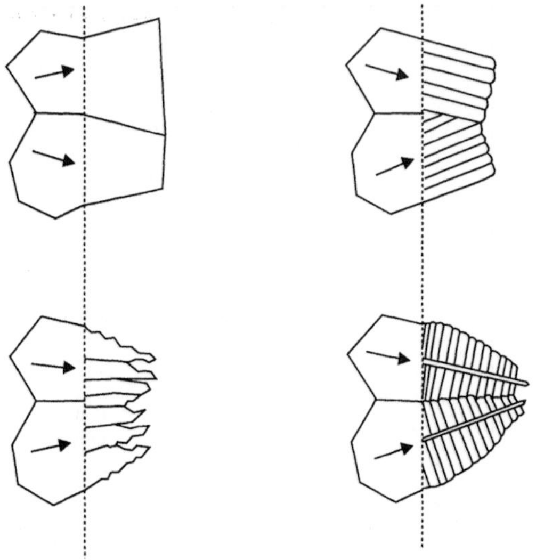

FIGURE 4.21. Schematic drawing of the morphology of the solidification structures. (From Lancaster, J. F., *Metallurgy of Welding,* 3rd ed., Chapman & Hall, London, 1980. With permission.)

melt is larger than the gradient due to the segregation, then any perturbation of the interface will melt back. If, however, the temperature gradient is smaller, then perturbation will be stable and continue to grow. This is illustrated in Figure 4.22. This condition is the same as was described for constitutional supercooling.

The condition under which the different growth modes develop thus depends both on the solute content and solidification parameter G/R. The temperature gradient in the liquid (G_L) is more important than the gradient in the solid for the development of the microstructure. G_L has been measured in several different weld metals and is of the order of 50 to 100 K/mm. The smaller the solidification parameter and the higher the solute content, the larger the risk for unstable growth. This means that a small temperature gradient and/or a high growth rate favor unstable growth.

It has been found experimentally that the dendrite arm spacings (d) can be related to the thermal gradient and the solidification rate by the following equations:

$$d_1 = a_1(G^2R)^{-1/4} \text{ (primary arm spacing)} \tag{4.15}$$

$$d_2 = a_2(GR)^{-n} \text{ (secondary arm spacing)} \tag{4.16}$$

where a_1 and a_2 are constants which depend on the alloy system. n varies between 1/3 to 1/2. Strictly speaking, the primary arm spacing cannot be

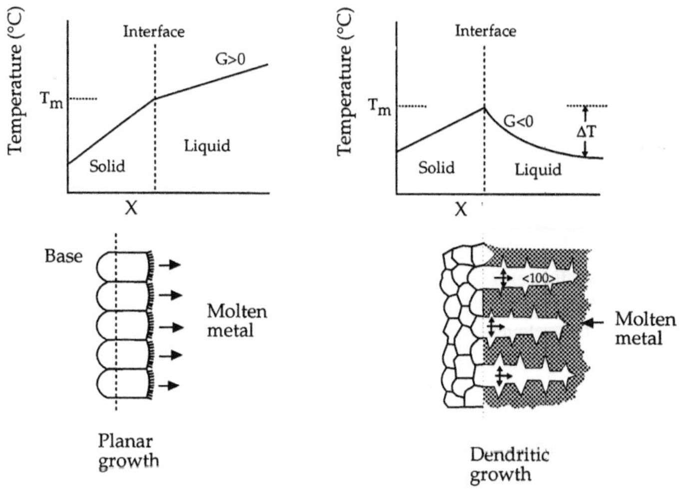

FIGURE 4.22. Schematic diagram showing how a positive thermal gradient in the melt will give a stable, planar front type of growth (left). When the thermal gradient in the melt is negative, unstable growth (as dendrites) will occur. (From Matsuda, F., Hashimoto, T., and Senda, T., *Trans. Nat. Inst. Res. Metall. (Japan),* 11(1), 43, 1969. With permission.)

characterized by the solidification parameter, because the dependence on G and R has different exponents.

Dependence of secondary arm spacing on heat input (q') has also been found. The relation is

$$d_2 = a_3(q'/V)^{1/2} \tag{4.17}$$

where V is the unit volume of the weld.

The growth rate R of the solidification front is related to the rate of motion of the heat source v by

$$R = v \cos\Theta \tag{4.18}$$

where Θ is the angle between the normal to the surface and the welding direction (Figure 4.23). The shape of the weld pool is influenced by the welding rate. At low and moderate rates, the weld pool as viewed from above will be elliptical in shape. With high welding speeds, it becomes increasingly difficult to dissipate the heat generated at the rear of the weld pool. The thermal gradient is smallest at the rear and largest at the sides of the weld pool. To minimize the area at the rear, the pool assumes a teardrop shape so that the heat can be more easily dissipated. However, this leads to a lower solidification growth rate, because the angle Θ will be greater than zero (Figure 4.24). A

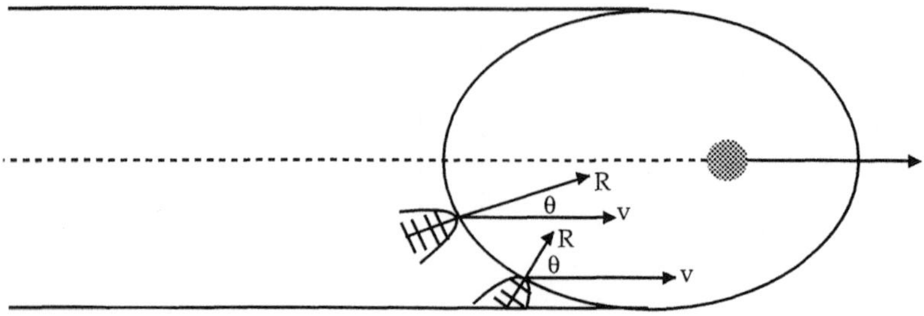

FIGURE 4.23. Illustration of the relation between crystal growth rate and welding speed. The crystal growth rate *(R)* is largest when growth occurs parallel with the welding direction and is smallest when 90° to the welding direction. (From Easterling, K. E., *Introduction to the Physical Metallurgy of Welding,* Butterworth-Heinemann Ltd., London, 1983. With permission.)

consequence of the variations in thermal gradient and growth rate with position is that different solidification modes can be found at various locations, as shown in Figure 4.25. Near the fusion line, the thermal gradient is large and the growth rate is small, giving a large solidification parameter. According to Figure 4.20 this favors a planar front growth mode. Near the weld centerline the thermal gradient is low but the growth rate is high, favoring a dendritic mode of growth. In between these modes a cellular growth mechanism can be expected.

It is difficult experimentally to observe the different growth modes in low-alloyed steels, because the solidification structure is masked by subsequent solid-state transformations. Studies of solidification structures have instead been on nontransforming alloys, such as aluminum and stainless steels. Many fundamental studies have also been carried out on single-crystal systems and metals such as iridium and niobium. Planar fronts are easily observed near the fusion line in stainless steel weld metals (Figure 4.26). Figure 4.27 shows an example of how the top of a bead has solidified in a dendritic mode, while the next bead deposited starts to solidify in a cellular mode. In this particular case no planar front growth was found.

4.4.2. ELEMENT SEGREGATION AND RELATED PHENOMENA

An important result of the solidification process is solute segregation. When solidification occurs at a plane front, solute redistribution only occurs during the initial and final transient stages. Thus, the segregation patterns in this case can be neglected. However, in most cases, the extent of the planar front growth mode is very limited and the major part of the weld solidifies either in the columnar or dendritic mode. In those cases, a much more complicated picture prevails. Due to the undercooling (resulting from constitutional undercooling or curvature effects), the dendrite tips may grow with a composition different from the equilibrium composition. The extent of deviation from equilibrium is a function of the temperature at the tip. However, this temperature is very

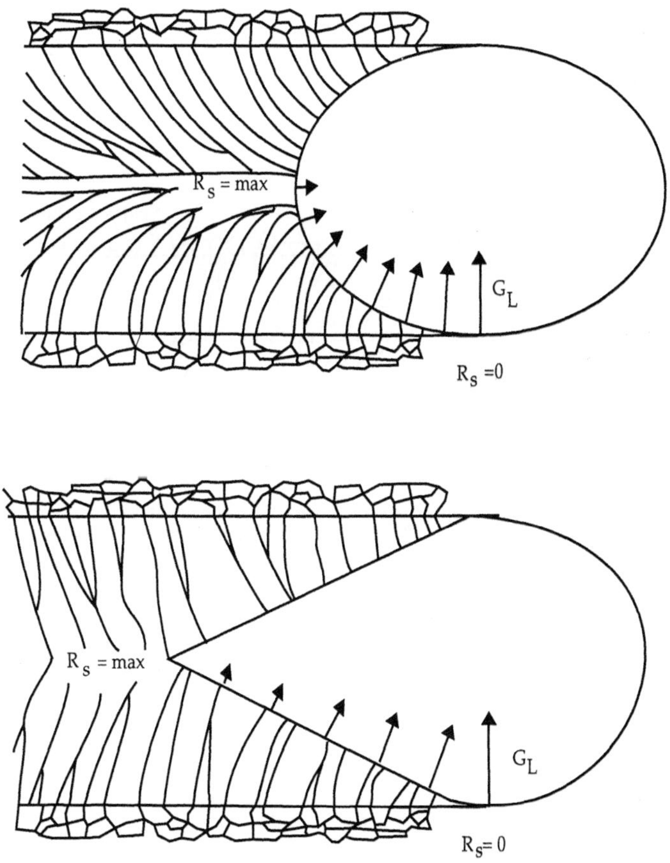

FIGURE 4.24. The relation between weld pool shape and welding speed. For very large welding speeds, the weld pool (when viewed from above) will assume a teardrop shape. The crystal growth rate will become slower because this growth must occur at an angle to the welding direction. (From Savage, W. F., *Weld. World,* 18, 89, 1980. With permission.)

difficult to calculate and even more difficult to determine experimentally. Measurements of the chemical composition in the case of the dendrites may give a hint of the undercooling at the dendrite tip, but the results of these measurements are not yet conclusive.

The solute redistribution that occurs between the dendrite arms is more easily analyzed. In these areas, the liquid and the solid coexist. This growth mode is similar to plane front growth. Two different cases can be assumed to occur. In one case, it is assumed that no diffusion in the liquid takes place in front of the growing solid. This leads to a composition profile as shown in Figure 4.28 (top). If, on the other hand, complete diffusion in the liquid is assumed, then as a second case the composition profile as shown in Figure 4.28

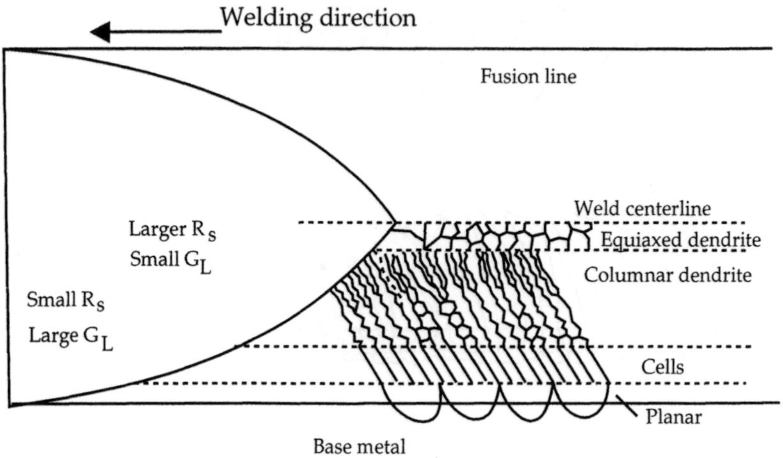

FIGURE 4.25. Different growth modes are dominant at different locations relative to the fusion line, due to variations in growth rate and thermal gradient. (From Matsuda, F., Hashimoto, T., and Senda, T., *Trans. Nat. Inst. Res. Metall. (Japan),* 11(1), 43, 1969. With permission.)

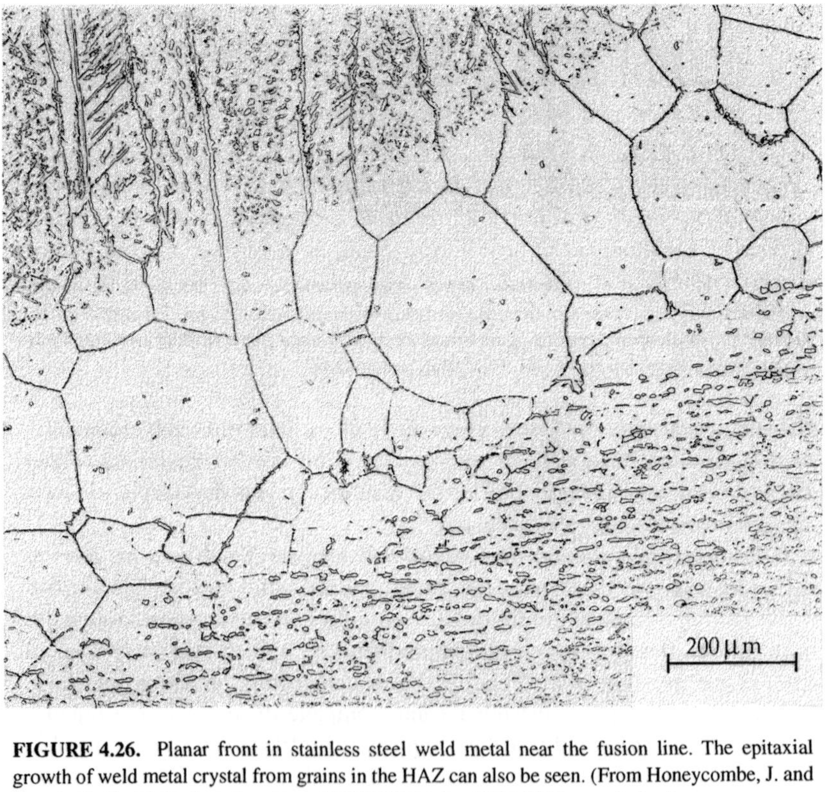

FIGURE 4.26. Planar front in stainless steel weld metal near the fusion line. The epitaxial growth of weld metal crystal from grains in the HAZ can also be seen. (From Honeycombe, J. and Gooch, T. G., *Weld. Inst. Res. Rep.*, 13/1976/IM, May 1976. With permission.)

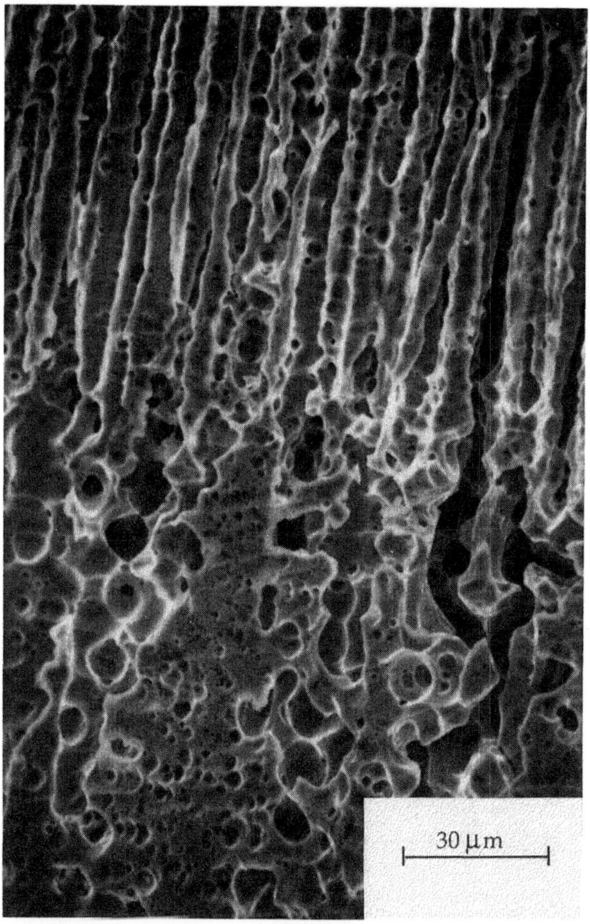

FIGURE 4.27. SEM showing how dendritic solidification has occurred near the top of a weld bead and how cellular solidification begins at the dendrite tips (from an austenitic stainless weld metal).

(bottom) is obtained. Experimental measurements of composition profiles lend support to both models in different alloy systems. More work is clearly needed to resolve this question.

For the second model, an analytical expression, known as the Scheil equation, has been developed to describe the variation of composition with distance

$$C_s^* = kC_0(1 - f_s)^{k-1} \tag{4.19}$$

where C_s^* = solid composition at a particular value of f_s, C_0 = initial alloy composition, f_s = volume fraction solid (related to the distance), and k = partition coefficient (defined as $k = C/C_0$).

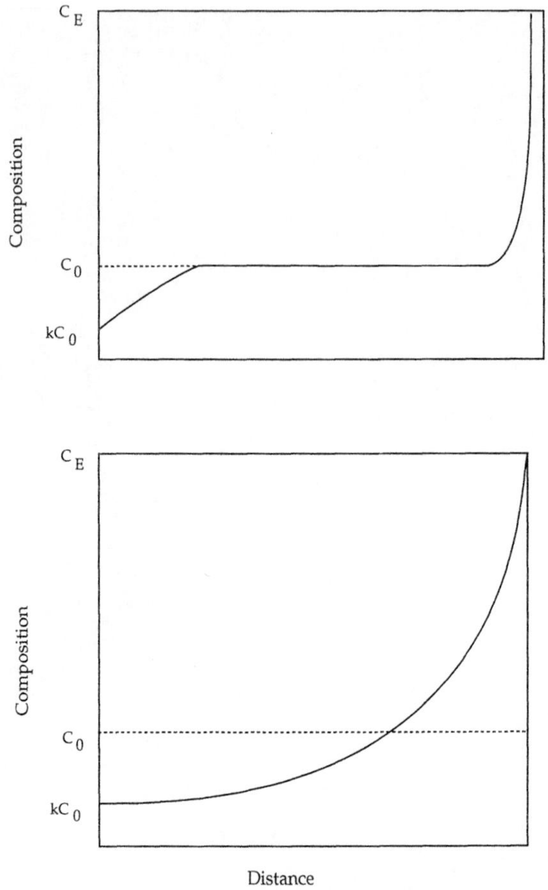

FIGURE 4.28. Schematic diagram showing the composition profiles for a volume element in a growing dendrite. (Top) Assuming no diffusion in the liquid; (bottom) assuming complete diffusion in the liquid. (From David, S. A. and Vitek, J. M., *Int. Met. Rev.*, 34(5), 213, 1989. With permission.)

The final melt to solidify will have an infinite composition, unless there is a limit on the solid solubility, such as a eutectic composition.

Another feature related to the solidification process is "banding," which is a macrosegregation phenomenon, i.e., the segregated area is much larger than the size of the dendrites. Banding is easily observed at low magnifications using optical microscopy (it can sometimes even be observed with the naked eye). There are different theories on the origin of banding. It may be due to a transition in the growth mode, from planar to dendrite. During planar growth, a solute layer is built up in front of the moving boundary. When the growth mode changes to a more rapid mode, this solute layer is "left behind" the growth front.

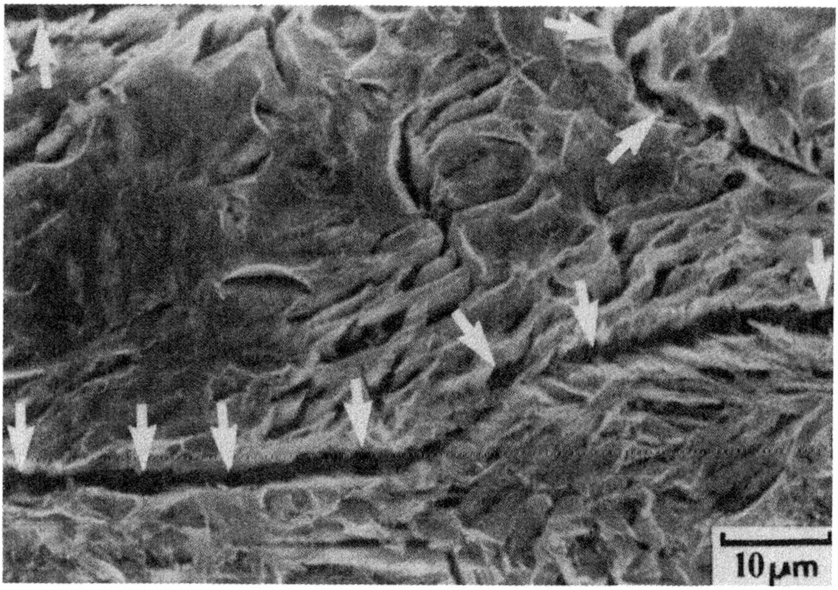

FIGURE 4.29. Incorporation of particles at advancing solidification front. (From Sugden, A. A. and Bhadeshia, H. K. D. H., *Metall. Trans. A,* 19A(March), 669, 1988. With permission.)

In certain cases, the banding is visible as continuous bands over the whole cross-section, while in other cases it has the appearance of local stringers. The banding is often situated close to the fusion line. The location of the banding makes it likely that it is a result of a change in growth mode, because the planar growth mode is known to operate for only a short period in the beginning of the solidification process. However, there are also other possibilities for the appearance of banding. During solidification there always exists a "mushy" zone, where liquid and solid coexist. Changes in the convective flow, which may result from local variation in the heat flow, can change the size of the mushy zone. The solute content of the mushy zone may then change, leading to banding.

The amount of banding seems to some extent to be process related. In SMAW, banding is observed occasionally, depending on coating type. With flux-cored wires banding occurs more frequently (mainly if the voltage is too high), while it is rarely found with SMAW. In plain C-Mn weld metals, chemical microanalysis with EDX systems usually does not show any significantly enhanced levels of elements detectable. Presumably, the absolute level of solute concentration is too low to be quantitatively measured with this technique, but it obviously is enough to change the appearance of the microstructure. However, in more alloyed weld metals, elements such as chromium and molybdenum can be found to be segregated in these areas.

The incorporation of the particles in the solid matrix has also been the subject of several investigations. As shown by Sugden and Bhadeshia,[12] particles were preferentially found in primary grain boundaries. They assumed that the particles were transported to these areas (i.e., pushed by the advancing solid interface) and then passively incorporated (see Figure 4.29).

In summary, the solidification process may give rise to several important structural effects that influence later development of the microstructure and also mechanical properties. To control the solidification process, a deep knowledge of two factors is essential: the influence of the welding procedure on the thermal gradient and the influence of chemistry on the solidification growth rate. In both these fields, our knowledge is still rather limited. Consequently, our ability to control the solidification process during welding is also limited. Factors that, at least to some extent, can be treated, such as the influence of particles on the solidification process and micro- and macrosegregation, certainly have an effect on the behavior of the weld metal. Up until now it is these factors that have been controlled, rather than the overall solidification process. There still appears to be room for further improvements in this field.

4.4.3. ETCHING TECHNIQUES TO REVEAL SOLIDIFICATION STRUCTURES

It is difficult to study the solidification structure in low-alloy steels, because the structure can be masked by subsequent transformations. However, there are some techniques whereby information about the solidification structure can be obtained. Etching on normalized samples using Stead's solution is the classical method. Stead's solution contains copper chloride, magnesium chloride, and hydrochloric acid. The etching reveals the phosphorus segregation pattern. Figure 4.30 illustrates the effects. It is possible to see how the solidification dendrites have grown without renucleation to accommodate the change in direction of the maximum thermal gradient. The ferrite microstructure is also shown by a subsequent etch with nital. The major axis of the prior austenite grains deviates significantly from the direction of the solidification pattern. Another way to reveal the solidification pattern, simultaneously with the general microstructure, is to use Klemm's reagent, which gives an interference layer on the specimen. Different colors result from different microstructural features. Particles between the dendrites appear white (see Plate 2),* and thus it is possible to see the connection between the solidification pattern and the general microstructure.

4.5. SOLID-STATE TRANSFORMATIONS

Carbon-manganese weld metals can solidify either as δ-ferrite or austenite. In most cases δ-ferrite appears. Two solid-state transformations will then occur

* Plate 2 appears following page 84.

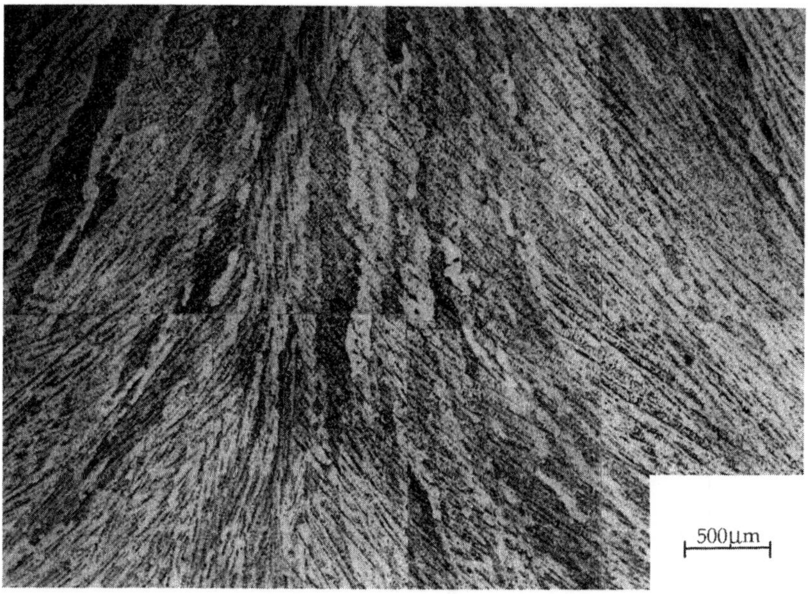

FIGURE 4.30. Use of Stead etching to reveal the solidification structure. The austenite grain structure was etched with a nital-type solution.

during cooling to room temperature. At high temperatures, the δ-ferrite transforms into austenite. This austenite then transforms back into α-ferrite as the temperature falls below the Ae_3 temperature (which might typically be around 800°C). In this section the first of these transformations will be described in more detail. The main importance of this transformation is the resulting size of the austenite grains, because this has a great influence on further transformation. First, however, the conditions for ferritic or austenitic solidification will be discussed.

The iron-carbon phase diagram shows that ferrite is the stable phase for carbon contents less than 0.18 wt%, and above this solidification occurs as austenite. Thus the common C-Mn weld metals used for joining should solidify as ferrite, because the carbon contents usually are less than 0.10 wt%. Alloying with manganese in concentrations typical for these weld metals (0.5 to 2 wt%) does not change the solidification mode. In some very highly alloyed weld metals with high concentrations of both manganese and nickel, austenite might form.

The occurrence of different solidification modes has been studied using differential scanning calorimetry (DSC), showing that both modes are possible (Figure 4.31). The solidification rate can influence the type of solidification, with higher cooling rates favoring austenite. However, this is more likely to be of significance in processes such as laser welding.

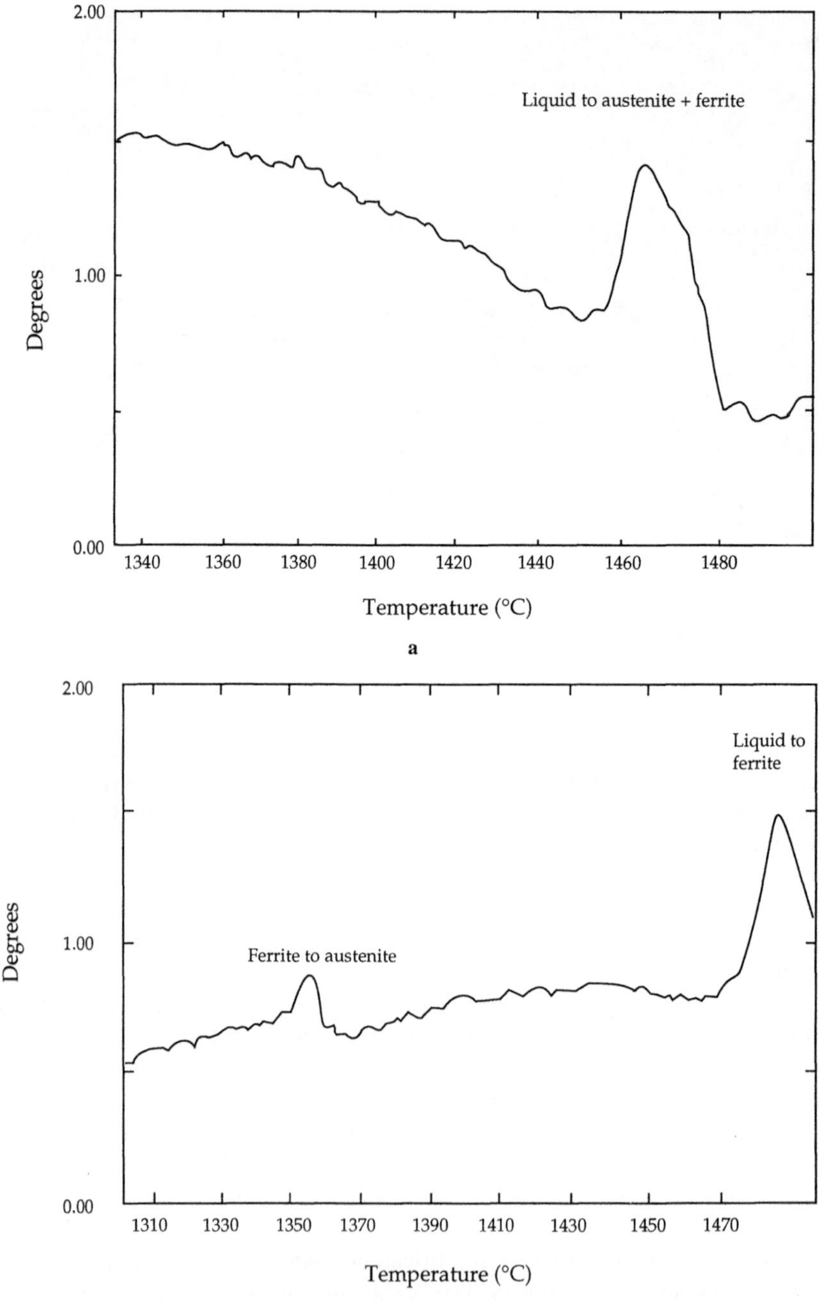

FIGURE 4.31. DSC study on solidification mode, showing the existence of both mixed austenitic/ferritic (a) and primary ferritic (b) solidification. (From Howden, D. G. and Park, S. M., Edison Weld. Inst. Rep. MP8818, November 1988. With permission.)

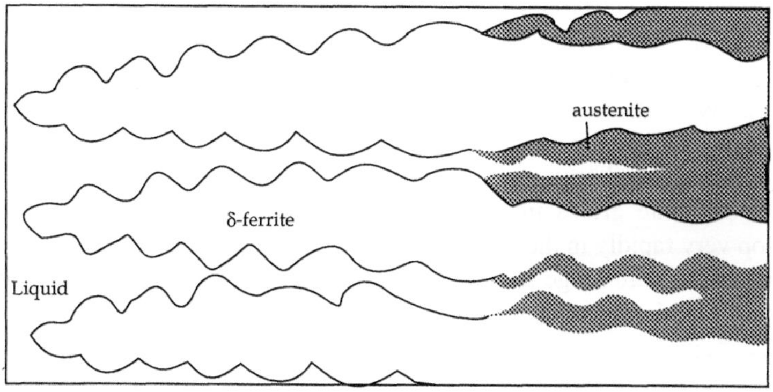

FIGURE 4.32. Schematic sketch showing primary ferrite solidification accompanied by the formation of austenite in a peritectic reaction.

4.5.1. THE δ-FERRITE TO AUSTENITE TRANSFORMATION

Because most weld metals solidify as δ-ferrite, the remainder of this section will focus on the δ-ferrite to austenite transformation. The δ-ferrite grains developed during solidification have the typical elongated or columnar structure. From the iron-carbon phase diagram, it is found that δ-ferrite begins to transform to austenite at around 1400 to 1500°C, depending on the alloy content. The austenite grains nucleate at the δ-δ grain boundaries. It is often envisaged that austenite forms as a peritectic reaction between the melt and the δ-ferrite in the regions between the δ-ferrite grains (Figure 4.32). The growth mechanism for the austenite is not clear because of the later austenite to α-ferrite transformation. Usually, it is only possible to see a trace of the prior austenite grain boundaries in fully transformed microstructures. In higher alloy steels, this latter transformation may be retarded, thus making it possible to follow the δ-ferrite to austenite change. However, there may of course be differences in the transformation reactions between low-alloyed and high-alloyed steels, so it is difficult to draw firm conclusions about the mechanisms of transformation.

Plate 3* shows the microstructure in a weld metal which was alloyed with about 2 wt% aluminum. This closes the austenite loop in the phase diagram and the majority of the weld metal then stays as δ-ferrite down to ambient temperature, with only a very small part transforming to austenite. This austenite transforms to martensite during subsequent cooling to room temperature. It is clearly seen how the austenite nucleates at the grain boundaries in the δ-ferrite. The growth mechanism is difficult to deduce from this micrograph, but in a few places small side plates of austenite are visible in addition to allotriomorphic austenite.

An alloy system that contains large amounts of both ferrite and austenite is the duplex grades of stainless steels. Keeping in mind the reservations stated

* Plates 3 and 4 appear following page 84.

above concerning different alloy systems, the similarities between Plates 3 and 4* are quite striking. In duplex steels, the austenite also nucleates along the δ-ferrite grain boundaries. A thin rim of austenite is formed, but the major part of the transformation occurs by the formation of side plates. Some austenite is also formed by nucleation at intragranular sites, leading to the development of fine, needle-shaped grains of austenite.

The austenite grains in both low-alloyed and high-alloyed weld metals develop very rapidly in the temperature range 1400 to 1500°C. The time spent in this temperature range for the weld metal during cooling is typically of the order of 1 s, almost independent of heat input.

The major axes of the austenite grains often deviate from those of the δ-ferrite. The deviation between the solidification structure and the austenite grain structure is often attributed to the fact that the heat source is moving and thus the temperature gradients shift directions as the heat source moves along and the temperature decreases. However, this is still puzzling, because nucleation seems to take place along the primary grains of the δ-ferrite. Unlike the solidification process, where atoms are added onto a solidification front, growth of austenite occurs from side to side, across the δ-ferrite grains. The first fully formed austenite naturally appears at the fusion line, because that is where the temperature first reaches the transformation start temperature. Because the austenite grains cross the original δ-ferrite grain boundaries, there must be a transformation front of austenite moving along the direction of maximum heat flow. The *austenite grain size* strongly influences further transformation to α-ferrite and is thus an extremely important parameter. However, because the details of austenite growth are not known, it is not currently possible to predict its grain size from first principles. The correlation between grain size and chemistry has been extensively studied and it has often been claimed that increasing amounts of nonmetallic inclusions lead to a smaller austenite grain size. Also, boronitrides have been seen to reduce the austenite grain size. This is thought to be due to a kind of Zener pinning mechanism, as in the HAZ. However, the driving force for the transformation from δ-ferrite to austenite in fact increases indefinitely as the temperature decreases and is in principle able to overcome any pinning effect. That particles can influence the grain size in this stage is very unlikely. However, when thickening of the grains occurs *after the transformation is completed,* it is possible that particles influence the austenite grain size. Thus, this is not a result of the δ-ferrite to austenite transformation, but a more general grain coarsening phenomenon. This growth occurs with a relatively low driving force, similar to grain growth under reheating conditions.

The most common way to study the metallography of weld metals is by making cross-sections. The austenite grains are seldom confined to this section, but deviate along the welding direction. Thus, to study the full appearance of the austenite grains, several nonparallel sections must be made. Figure 4.33

shows the grains in three sections: transverse, longitudinal, and a 45° section. This particular weld is made with SAW and the details may deviate if weld metals from other processes are studied, mainly due to differences in welding speed. The grains can be modeled approximately as space-filling arrays of hexagonal-shaped prisms, which are curved upward and along the direction of the moving heat source. The prisms can be characterized by the length c and the cross-sectional side length a. Normally it can be assumed that $c \gg a$ (typical value for a is 100 μm and for c several millimeters). The mean lineal intercept L_l, measured at random on a *longitudinal* section (showing equiaxed austenite grains), is given by

$$L_l = \pi a \cos [30°]/2 \tag{4.20}$$

On *transverse* sections, which are the most common, the size of the austenite grains is measured by measuring the width of the grains perpendicular to the major axis (L_{tn}). If it is assumed that the c-axes of the grains lie in the plane of the transverse section, then L_{tn} is identical to L_l.

To be able to make quantitative predictions, it is necessary to have correlation among austenite grain size, alloy content, and the welding parameters. The following regression equation has been obtained:

$$L_{tn}\ (\mu m) = 64.5 - 445.8[C] + 139[Si] - 7.6[Mn] + 16\ (\text{heat input, kJ/mm}) \tag{4.21}$$

where *[I]* indicates the concentration in wt% of element *I*.

4.5.2. THE AUSTENITE TO FERRITE TRANSFORMATION

The austenite to α-ferrite transformation follows in general the same pattern as described in Chapter 3 for transformation in the HAZ. However, there are some important differences between weld metals and plate material, making the resulting microstructures quite different. The main additional factors influencing the microstructure of the weld are the high content of slag particles and the columnar shape of the austenite grains. For weld metals of C-Mn, C-Mn-Ni, or C-Mn-Mo types, three ferritic constituents mainly appear, namely, allotriomorphic ferrite, Widmanstätten side plates, and acicular ferrite. Small amounts of so-called microphases (ferrite/carbide aggregates, bainite, martensite, or retained austenite) may also be found. For higher alloyed weld metals, such as C–1.5Mn–2Ni–0.5Mo–0.5Cr, the microstructure consists of a mixture of acicular ferrite and martensite. Because acicular ferrite is typical for weld metals and is very important for achieving good toughness, this constituent will be discussed in some detail. The formation of allotriomorphic ferrite and Widmanstätten ferrite occurs in the same manner as described for the HAZ. The principal development of microstructure in a weld metal is shown in Figure 4.34. If a lean alloy weld metal is assumed, a large fraction of the austenite will transform to allotriomorphic ferrite. The growth rate of the

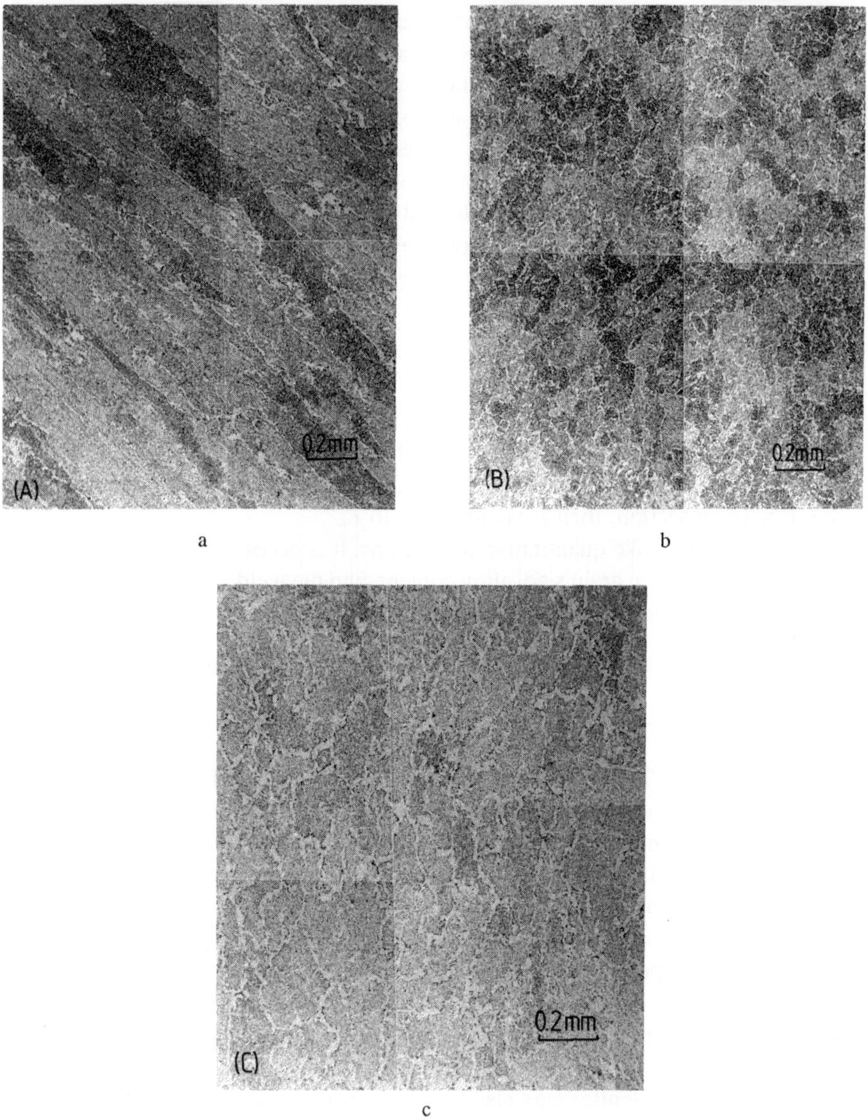

FIGURE 4.33. Sections of a weld metal showing the appearance of the austenite grains: (a) transverse, (b) longitudinal, and (c) 45°. (From Bhadeshia, H. K. D. H., Svensson, L.-E., and Grefoft, B., *J. Mater. Sci.*, 21, 1947, 1986. With permission.)

Widmanstätten side plates will also be high, and thus these two constituents will dominate the microstructure. With higher alloying content, as shown in the lower part of Figure 4.34, the growth rate of both allotriomorphic ferrite and side plates will be lower, leaving room for transformation to acicular ferrite. It should be noted that in this figure, the effect of composition on the austenite

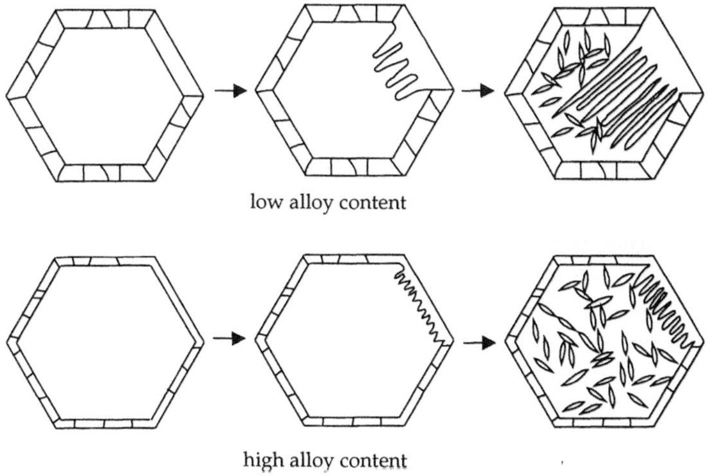

FIGURE 4.34. Sketch showing how the alloying content affects the microstructure in a weld metal. The austenite grains are assumed to have a hexagonal cross-sectional shape. With low alloying content, the microstructure is predominantly allotriomorphic ferrite and side plates. With higher alloying content, acicular ferrite can nucleate intragranularly and occupy a large fraction of the prior austenite grain. (From Bhadeshia, H. K. D. H., Svensson, L.-E., and Gretoft, B., *Acta Metall.*, 33(7), 1278, 1985. With permission.)

grain size has been neglected. It should also be noted that although allotriomorphic and Widmanstätten ferrite usually nucleate at prior austenite grain boundaries, they also can be nucleated intragranularly, e.g., at inclusions.

The nature and formation of acicular ferrite has been the subject of many investigations. The phase has been called acicular, because of the needle-shaped appearance in two-dimensional sections. It is generally recognized that in three dimensions, acicular ferrite has the morphology of thin, lenticular plates. The typical dimensions in metallographic sections are 5 to 10 μm long and about 1 μm wide. The acicular ferrite plates nucleate on inclusions inside the austenite grains. After initial nucleation, further plates may nucleate autocatalytically, so it is not expected to find a one-to-one correspondence between the number of inclusions and the number of acicular ferrite plates.

The mechanism by which acicular ferrite forms and grows is beginning to be understood. It appears that acicular ferrite is an intragranularly nucleated bainite. The evidence for this can be listed as follows:

- The shape change accompanying the transformation is (qualitatively) characterized as an invariant-plane strain with a large shear component, similar to that of bainite.
- The stored energy of transformation has been estimated to be around 400 J/mol, i.e., about the same as for bainite formation, while the formation of Widmanstätten side plates only involves a stored energy of about 50 J/mol.

- Microanalysis experiments indicate that there is no bulk partitioning of substitutional alloying elements during the transformation of austenite to acicular ferrite.
- The orientation relationship between the acicular ferrite grains and the austenite is *always* such that a close-packed plane of the austenite is parallel or almost parallel to a close-packed plane of acicular ferrite, and corresponding close-packed directions within these planes are within a few degrees from each other.
- The acicular ferrite transformation obeys the "incomplete-reaction phenomenon," the degree of reaction tending toward zero as the transformation temperature rises towards the bainite start (B_s) temperature.

The difference between acicular ferrite and classical bainite is that the acicular ferrite nucleates intragranularly as isolated plates radiating from the point nucleation site (i.e., the inclusion), instead of the sheaf morphology characteristic of bainite, which nucleates from austenite grain surfaces. The absence of sheaves of acicular ferrite is believed to be due to the stifling of growth by hard impingement between plates nucleated independently at adjacent sites. Bainite nucleates at the austenite/austenite grain surfaces and propagates by the repeated formation of subunits. Experiments by Yang and Bhadeshia[13] have shown that conventional bainite and acicular ferrite can be obtained in the same weld, simply by changing the prior austenite grain size. By decreasing the grain size, nucleation at grain boundaries dominates and the subsequent growth of bainitic sheaves completely overcomes the entire interior of the austenite grain, preventing the formation of acicular ferrite (see Figure 4.35).

In steel welds with relatively large concentrations of chromium (>1.5 wt%) or molybdenum (>0.5 wt%), bainite forms instead of acicular ferrite as the alloy concentration is increased. This is attributed to the absence of allotriomorphic ferrite at the grain boundaries in these alloys, making the grain boundaries available for the nucleation of bainite. In other alloy systems with relatively high concentrations of manganese and nickel, similar effects are also observed.

After the formation of acicular ferrite is complete, there may be some areas of austenite between the acicular ferrite grains, enriched in carbon, which have still not transformed. These areas generally are small regions, of the order of 1 μm in extent, which either are retained austenite or transform to a mixture of ferrite and carbides or to martensite. They are called "microphases" because the volume fraction is very low, often below 0.05. The microphases can also be associated with the Widmanstätten side plates, where it is found between the plates in an aligned manner. Microphases can also be found as a vein along the allotriomorphic ferrite grains. The microphases are illustrated in Figure 4.36.

A scheme has been developed within the International Institute of Welding (IIW) to enable a common description of the microstructure of weld metals. The scheme is shown in Figure 4.37. The microstructures are classified according

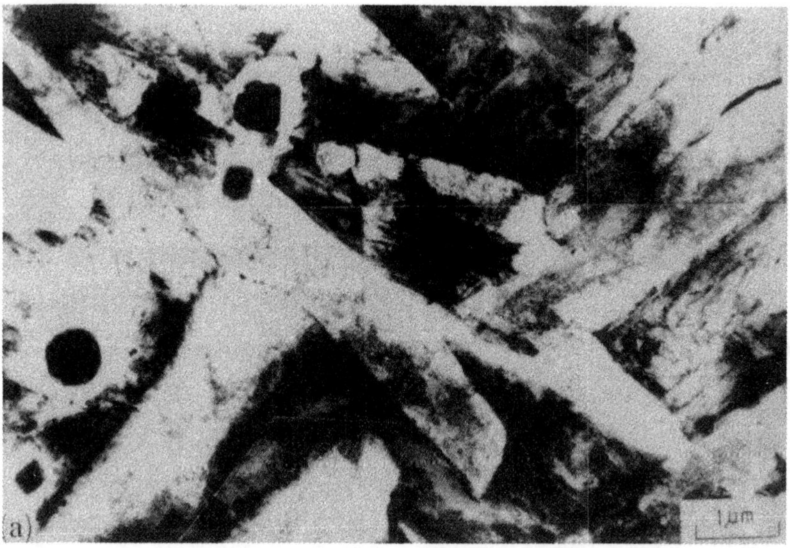

a

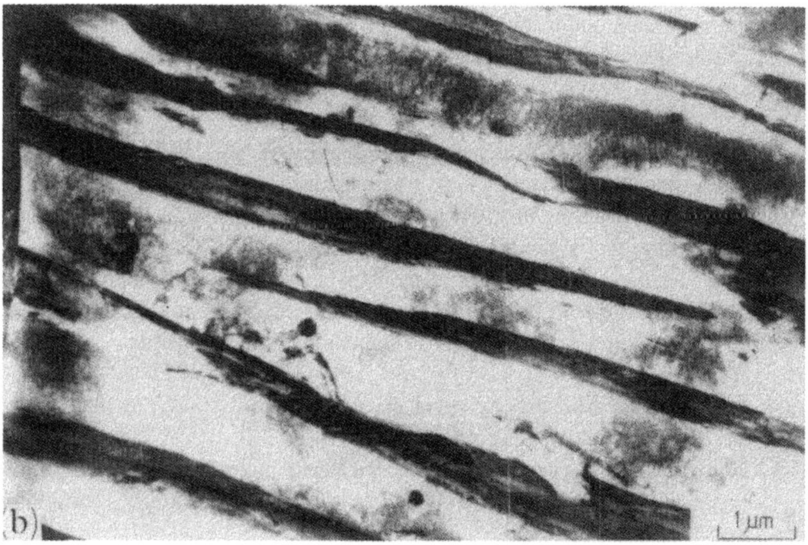

b

FIGURE 4.35. Formation of acicular ferrite and bainite in the same weld metal, depending upon the prior austenite grain size. (a) Formation of acicular ferrite after reheating to 1200°C, giving a coarse austenite grain size. (b) Bainite formed after reheating to 900°C, giving a small austenite grain size. (Courtesy of Yang, J.-R., National Taiwan University, Republic of China.)

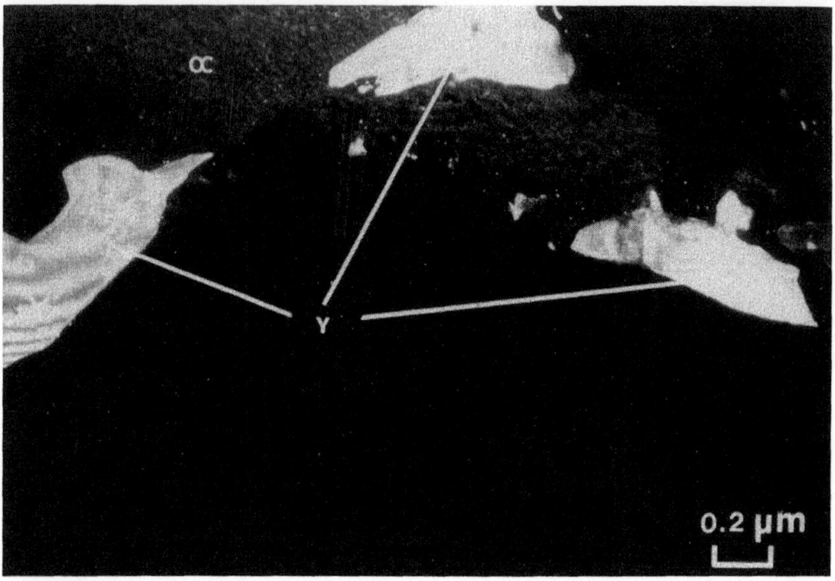

FIGURE 4.36. Dark field TEM of microphases (in this case retained austenite) in a C-Mn weld metal.

to their appearance under the optical microscope. However, ignoring details, there is a straightforward translation between this scheme and the Dubé classification.

4.5.3. ACICULAR FERRITE AND NONMETALLIC INCLUSIONS

An area that has attracted much interest during the 1980s is the role of nonmetallic inclusions on the formation of acicular ferrite. It was shown by Ricks et al.[14] that the inclusions are less effective as nucleants for ferrite when compared with austenite grain surfaces. This is of course consistent with the observation that ferrite first forms at the boundaries. There are basically three theories for the potency of particles in nucleating acicular ferrite:

1. A low lattice mismatch between the ferrite and the particles makes the inclusions a more potent nucleus.
2. Thermal strains around the particles (due to differences in the thermal expansion coefficients of the particle relative to the matrix) stimulate nucleation at inclusions.
3. Depletion of austenite stabilizing elements (particularly manganese) around the particles leads to easy nucleation there.

It is also possible that chemical reactions may occur between the particles and the matrix.

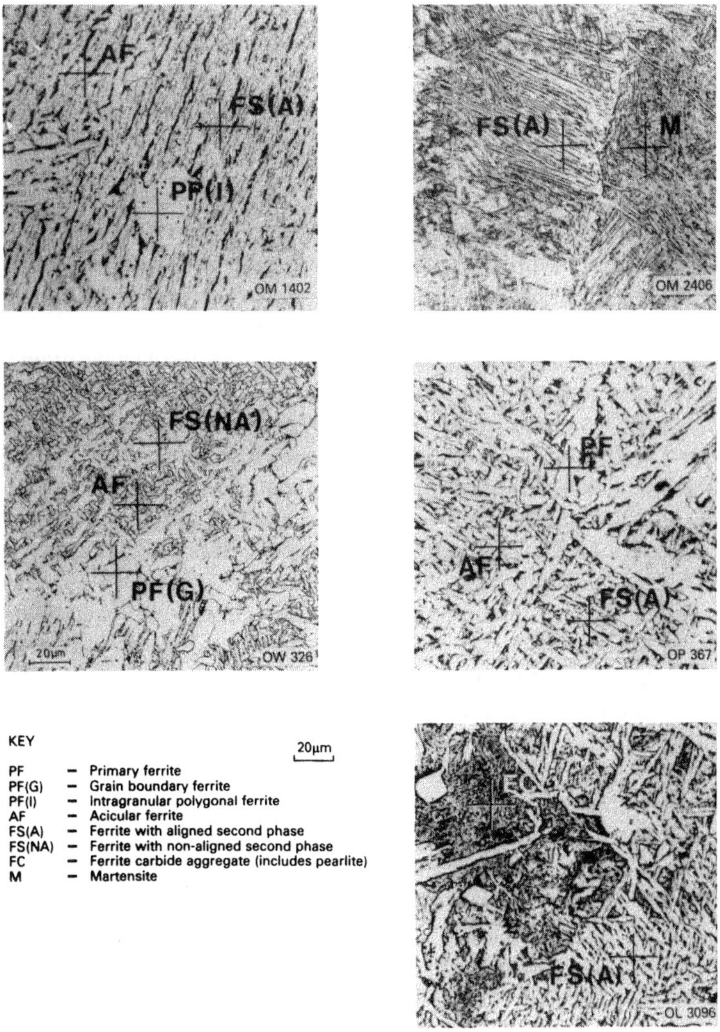

FIGURE 4.37. International Institute of Welding scheme for the classification of microstructures in C-Mn weld metals. (From IIW Doc. IX-1533-88, International Institute of Welding, London, 1988. With permission.)

The theory of low lattice mismatch is the most popular. The difficulty with this theory is that it assumes some kind of orientation relationship between the particle and the plate of acicular ferrite, while at the same time there is a Kurdjumov–Sachs orientation relationship between the austenite and the acicular ferrite plates. This implies that there also is a relationship between the particles and the austenite. However, this is quite unlikely, because the particles form in the melt with no obvious relationship to the solidifying structure.

One possible explanation would be that the δ-ferrite nucleates on the particles, but this would lead to equiaxed grains rather than the elongated grains observed.

The theory of thermal strains is difficult to verify and it is not established that inclusions with the largest thermal expansion difference relative to the matrix are the most efficient.

The theory of manganese depletion around inclusions has not been possible to verify using X-ray microanalysis in TEM. The spatial resolution of the technique may not be small enough to identify compositional changes in the vicinity of the particle/matrix interface; therefore, from the experiments carried out this theory is neither confirmed nor dismissed.

The particles that are most likely to nucleate acicular ferrite have often been considered to be various kinds of titanium oxide and nitrides. Both TiO and TiN have been suggested as the most likely nucleant. However, to form TiO requires strongly reducing conditions, circumstances which are quite unlikely. From thermodynamic data, titanium oxides should form at much higher temperatures than TiN. It has even been observed that TiN forms at the outside of oxide particles. Other suggestions for possible nucleants include Ti_2O_3, which is more likely to form from a thermodynamic point of view.

Aluminum is often present in the weld metal, either added from dilution of the weld by the base material or added deliberately as a deoxidizer. Aluminum has a much higher affinity to oxygen than does titanium, and therefore aluminum oxides are often found in the weld metal. These oxides are found to be very much less effective in nucleating acicular ferrite. One interesting observation was reported by Kluken,[9] who found that the amount of acicular ferrite increased with increasing amounts of aluminum in the weld metal. However, when all of the available oxygen was tied up by aluminum to form γ-alumina (when the Al:O ratio was 1:13), there was an abrupt decrease in the acicular ferrite content. This behavior probably occurs because at low aluminum concentrations, the aluminum oxide is in the form of galaxite ($MnOAl_2O_3$) rather than γ-alumina, the former being very effective as a nucleant according to lattice matching theory. On the other hand, it was observed that the inclusions often contained titanium-rich surface layers. The behavior can then be interpreted as titanium oxides forming an outer shell on the aluminum oxides as long as there was any oxygen left to form titanium oxides. With increasing aluminum content the amount of particles increased, raising the probability of nucleation of acicular ferrite. However, when the aluminum concentration became so large that all available oxygen was tied up in aluminum oxides, the nucleation probability was significantly reduced because titanium oxide shells could no longer form on the inclusion surfaces.

The importance of the presence of titanium oxides seems to be well founded. It has been reported by Bonnet and Charpentier[15] that if the titanium content was less than 0.004 to 0.005 wt%, no acicular ferrite was formed. However, there are some complicating observations. First, Thewlis et al.[16] reported that the "active" particle can be a galaxite $MnOAl_2O_3$ rather than titanium oxides. Second, surface layers on the particles have been found and these may well be the actual nucleating agent. Kluken reported TiN and MnS on the surface of the particles and Devillers et al.[17] found CuS on the particle surfaces. In the latter case, CuS hampered acicular ferrite formation, while Kluken attributed the nucleating potency to the presence of the TiN. The experimental difficulties in determining the crystal structure of the "substrate particle," the surrounding matrix, and any possible surface layers are very significant, because the scale of the components makes the use of a single microscopy technique almost impossible.

Thewlis[18] made a thorough investigation of the relation between austenite grain size, number density and size of particles, particle composition, and microstructure using thermal cycling in a dilatometer. The weld metals he studied were of Ti-B type, with different amounts and kinds of particles. He found a complex relation between the parameters studied and the transformation temperatures and resulting microstructures. He concluded that the transformation temperature and microstructure could not be described just by the alloying content, but that the inclusion characteristics were of vital importance to microstructural development. He also found that, depending on the type of inclusion, there was a certain austenite grain size above which the ferrite nucleation site shifted from the austenite grain boundaries to inclusions. In some cases this austenite grain size was as small as 20 μm and this was connected to the presence of inclusions with a very low energy barrier to nucleation. At the same time, it must be pointed out that the inclusions are also present at the grain boundaries and may aid nucleation there. Understanding the role of inclusions in affecting the nucleation of acicular ferrite is still far from complete. As will be shown in Chapter 6, the microstructure of weld metals of C-Mn type can be predicted relatively well, using a model that takes only the thermodynamic and kinetic influences of alloying elements into account and neglects the influence of particles. This indicates that in most commercial welds, there are sufficient particles of the right kind, capable of nucleating acicular ferrite to the full extent. The observations of Terashima and Hart[19] on the effect of small variations of aluminum on impact toughness in SAW metals are however an indication that there is a practical problem associated with obtaining the correct type of particles. However, Thewlis[18] also studied the effect of aluminum and attributed much of the negative effects to soluble aluminum rather than γ-alumina, which is a poor nucleant for acicular ferrite. As will be discussed in more detail in Chapter 5, particles can be negative because they can induce fracture, but at the same time they are necessary to create a fracture-resistant microstructure with a high proportion of acicular ferrite.

FIGURE 4.38. Dark field TEM of twinned martensite in the intercritically reheated zone of the weld metal.

4.5.4. TRANSFORMATIONS IN UNDERLYING BEADS

Most joints are completed using several beads. Adjacent beads then receive a heat treatment whenever a new bead is deposited, giving HAZs similar to those found for the base material. In the coarse-grained zone, the base material transforms to a bainitic or martensitic structure, while in the weld metal allotriomorphic ferrite, Widmanstätten ferrite, and acicular ferrite are found. The weld metal thus transforms back to basically the same structure as in the as-deposited region, but with a different shape and size of the austenite grains. The proportions between the various phases are different, due to the differences in austenite grain size and shape. The similarity between the as-deposited regions and the coarse-grained zones is expected, because the hardenability of the weld metal is low due to the low carbon content.

The normalized zone consists of a fine-grained equiaxed ferrite. In the partly transformed zone the microphases have transformed to austenite, while the ferrite is to a large extent untransformed. The austenitic areas can transform back to twinned martensite (see Figure 4.38) or other types of microphases. In both the normalized and the partly transformed zones segregations of carbon-rich phases can be found, especially in weld metals with higher alloying contents (Figure 4.39).

The transformed areas often have better mechanical properties than the as-deposited regions and it is therefore of interest to control the welding procedure in order to maximize the amount of transformed microstructures. This, however,

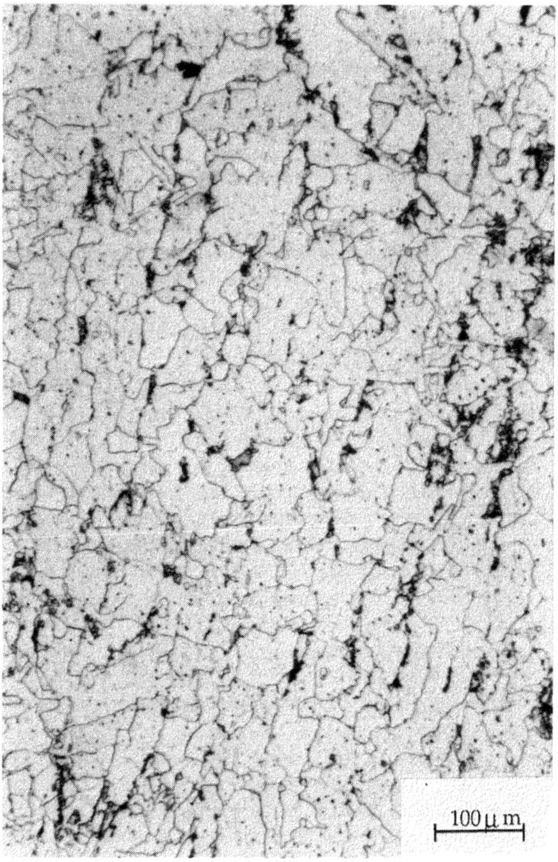

FIGURE 4.39. The black dots in this micrograph are segregated areas (having increased amounts of nickel) in a C-Mn 2 wt% nickel weld metal. These dots are seen in the reheated regions. In these areas the transformation from austenite to ferrite has been delayed, which has led to an increased carbon content. The black dots thus contain a greater carbide phase.

is not easily done, because if a large heat input is required to enable the temperature to rise to say Ae_1 at the fusion line of the underlying bead, this usually means that a large volume of weld metal is deposited. This makes refinement from the next bead difficult. As a rule of thumb, about 50% of the area of a bead is transformed as a consequence of the deposition of another adjacent bead. However, large variations surround this value and a complete transformation of the underlying beads can take place, especially when small beads are deposited using small-diameter electrodes. In Chapter 6, a method for controlling the degree of transformation of the beads will be described.

REFERENCES

1. **Lancaster, J. F.,** Metal transfer in fusion welding, in *Proc. Int. Conf. Arc Physics and Weld Pool Behaviour,* The Welding Institute, London, 1979, 135.
2. **Becken, O.,** Metal Transfer from Welding Electrodes, IIW Doc. 212-179-69, International Institute of Welding, London, 1969.
3. **Jelmorini, G., Tichelaar, G. W., and van den Heuvel, G. J. P. M.,** Droplet Temperature Measurements in Arc Welding, IIW Doc. 212-411-77, International Institute of Welding, London, 1977.
4. **Halmøy, E.,** Wire melting rate, droplet temperature and effective anode melting potential, in *Proc. Int. Conf. Arc Physics and Weld Pool Behaviour,* The Welding Institute, London, 1979, 49.
5. **Grong, Ø. and Christensen, N.,** Factors controlling MIG weld metal chemistry, *Scand. J. Metall.,* 4, 155, 1983.
6. **Grong, Ø., Siewert, T. A., Martins, G. P., and Olson, D. L.,** A model for the silicon-manganese deoxidation of steel weld metal, *Metall. Trans. A,* 17A(October) 1797, 1986.
7. **Lindborg, U. and Torsell, K.,** A collision model for the growth and separation of deoxidation products, *Trans. Metall. Soc. AIME,* 242(January), 94, 1968.
8. **Ahlblom, B., Bergström, U., Hannerz, N.-E., and Werlefors, I.,** Influence of welding parameters on nitrogen content and microstructure of submerged-arc weld metal, in *Proc. Int. Conf.: The Effect of Residual, Impurity and Micro-alloying Elements on Weldability and Weld Metal Properties,* The Welding Institute, London, 1983, paper 49.
9. **Kluken, A. O.,** Modelling of the Reaction Sequence during Deoxidation and Solidification of Steel Weld Metals, Ph.D. thesis, Trondheim University of Technology, Norway, 1990.
10. **Thewlis, G.,** Pipe-line welds — effects of pipe material and consumable composition, *Joining Mater.,* January, p. 25 and March, p. 125, 1989.
11. **David, S. A. and Vitek, J. M.,** Correlation between solidification parameters and weld microstructures, *Int. Metall. Rev.,* 34(5), 213, 1989.
12. **Sugden, A. A. and Bhadeshia, H. K. D. H.,** The non-uniform distribution of inclusions in low-alloy steel weld deposits, *Metall. Trans. A,* 19A(March), 669, 1988.
13. **Yang, J.-R. and Bhadeshia, H. K. D. H.,** Thermodynamics of the acicular ferrite transformation in alloy-steel weld metals, in *Advances in Welding Science and Technology,* David, S. A., Ed., ASM International, Metals Park, OH, 1987, 187.
14. **Ricks, R. A., Barrite, G. S., and Howell, P. R.,** Influence of second phase particles on diffusional transformations in steels, in *Solid State Phase Transformations,* Aaronson, H. I. and Wayman, C. M., Eds., Metallurgical Society of AIME, Pittsburgh, 1981.
15. **Mills, A. R., Thewlis, G., and Whiteman, J. A.,** Nature of inclusions in steel weld metals and their influence on formation of acicular ferrite, *Mater. Sci. Technol.,* 3(December), 1051, 1987.
16. **Bonnet, C. and Charpentier, J.-P.,** Effect of deoxidation residues in wire and in some particular oxides in CS fused fluxes on the microstructure of submerged-arc weld metals, in *Proc. Int. Conf. Effect of Residual, Impurity and Micro-Alloying Elements on Weldability and Weld Metal Properties,* The Welding Institute, London, 1983, paper 8.
17. **Devillers, L., Kaplan, D., Ribes, A., and Riboud, P. V.,** The effect of low level concentrations of some elements on the toughness of submerged-arc welded C Mn steel welds, in *Proc. Int. Conf. Effect of Residual, Impurity and Micro-Alloying Elements on Weldability and Weld Metal Properties,* The Welding Institute, London, 1983, paper 1.
18. **Thewlis, G.,** private communication.
19. **Terashima, H. and Hart, P. H. M.,** Effect of aluminium on C-Mn steel submerged-arc weld metal properties, *Weld. J.,* 63(June), 173-s, 1984.

Chapter 5

RELATION BETWEEN MICROSTRUCTURE AND MECHANICAL PROPERTIES

5.1. INTRODUCTION

The safe use of an engineering structure relies on each of its components possessing the necessary mechanical properties, the most important of these properties usually being strength and toughness. The main points described in this chapter are how these properties are measured and how they can be influenced by changes in the microstructure. Tensile testing alone is not enough to characterize the properties of the steel because the tendency for brittleness, which occurs at lower temperatures, also must be accounted for. Toughness testing is thus necessary. Impact toughness testing is often used, but a fracture mechanics approach is frequently necessary. In the heat-affected zone (HAZ), brittle behavior can be found in several zones, such as the coarse-grained zone, the intercritically heated zone, and the subcritical zone. A special problem relates to the so-called local brittle zones (LBZs) that appear in the intercritically heated zone or in the intercritically reheated coarse-grained regions. In the weld metal, the same fundamental correlation between microstructure and properties exists as in the HAZ. However, additional complications may arise due to the relatively high content of nonmetallic inclusions. Also, the fact that the weld metal is a cast structure that leads to pronounced chemical segregation can affect the mechanical properties, especially toughness.

5.2. TEST METHODS

The two most common testing methods are tensile and impact toughness testing. Other tests include bend testing and fracture mechanics. Uniaxial tensile tests use round, smooth tensile bars. Four different values are measured: yield strength, ultimate tensile strength, fracture elongation, and cross-sectional area reduction at fracture. The strength values can be found from the stress-strain curve (Figure 5.1). The yield point is reached after approximately 0.1 to 0.5% plastic strain. For many steels there is an upper (R_{eH}) and a lower (R_{eL}) yield point. There can be a difference of 20 to 40 MPa between R_{eH} and R_{eL} for an ordinary mild steel. For higher alloyed steels and for heat-treated samples, the stress-strain curve does not show a clearly defined yield point, but a smooth transition from an elastic to a plastic deformation. In such cases, the yield stress is defined as the stress at which 0.2% plastic stress has occurred, $R_{p0.2}$. To measure this, a more accurate record of the stress-strain curve is necessary.

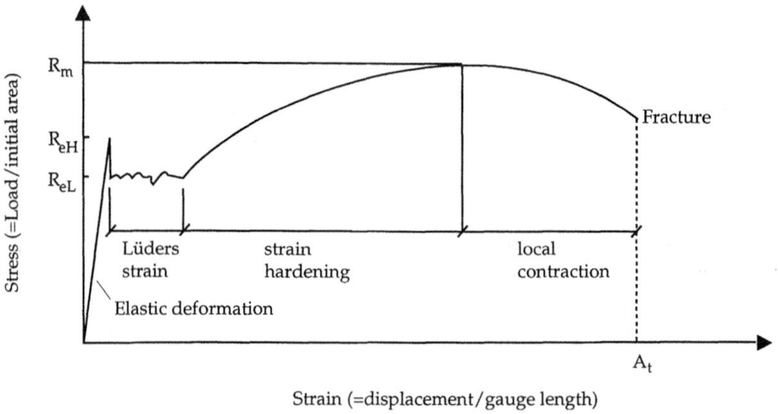

FIGURE 5.1. A typical stress-strain curve, with strain on the horizontal axis and stress on the vertical axis. The initial deformation is elastic, up to the upper yield point (R_{eH}). In most steels, a lower yield point (R_{eL}) is found. The plastic deformation starts with a Lüders strain immediately following the lower yield point. When the steel strain hardens, increasing stress is needed to continue the plastic deformation. After maximum stress is reached, local contraction takes place until the final failure.

Elongation and reduction in cross-sectional area are measures of the *ductility* of the material. They are usually determined manually. The elongation at fracture is measured by marking a gauge length (L_0) by slight scratches on the specimen prior to testing. The gauge length is usually five times the diameter of the tensile bar and the corresponding fracture elongation is denoted A_5. After fracture the two halves are fitted together and the distance between the scratches is measured again (L_f). The fracture elongation is then given by

$$A_5 = 100\ (L_f - L_0)/L_0 \tag{5.1}$$

Naturally, there is a degree of scatter in fracture elongation, depending on the material, but in general values of 20 to 25% are found for common steels and weld metals.

The area reduction at fracture is found by recording the diameter of the bar before and after testing (A_0 and A_f). The area reduction at fracture (Z) is then given by

$$Z = 100\ (A_f - A_0)/A_f \tag{5.2}$$

This also shows some scatter, but typical values are around 60 to 70%. Minimum values or a range of values are specified for strength, while minimum values of ductility are specified in mandatory requirements.

For a welded joint, transverse tensile testing with the axis of the sample normal to the welding direction is common. This is done to ensure that the weldment has a higher strength than the base material, i.e., that the weld metal

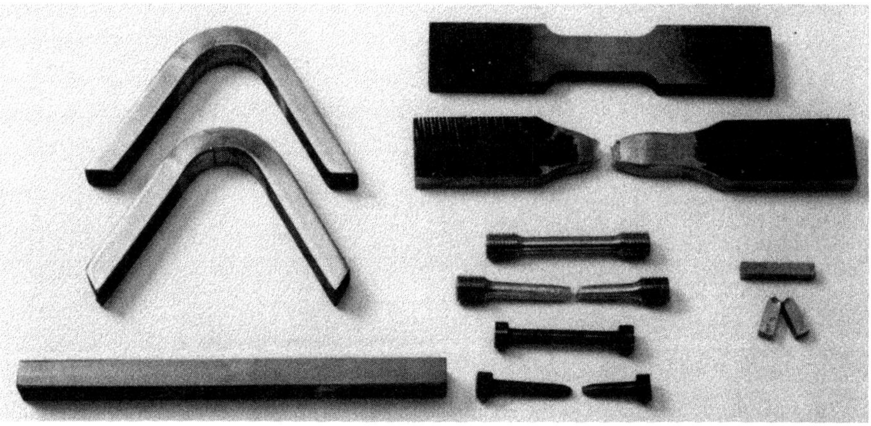

FIGURE 5.2. Typical test pieces used for mechanical testing. The test pieces shown are (1) flat transverse tensile test specimen, (2) bend test specimen, (3) round tensile specimen for longitudinal testing (for measuring $R_{p0.2}$), (4) round tensile specimen for longitudinal testing, and (5) impact test specimen.

is *overmatching,* by stipulating that fracture must take place in the base material. The specimens in this case are of a flat type. Generally only the ultimate tensile strength is determined. Another common test is bend testing, where the weld is bent over a die with a certain radius. Both side bend tests, where the axis of the specimen is perpendicular to the welding direction, and longitudinal bend tests are made. In both cases either the face or the root of the weld can be stretched. This test mainly reveals the presence of defects, and it also gives some indication of the ductility of the material. Typical test pieces used for mechanical testing are illustrated in Figure 5.2.

The ductility measured by tensile testing of a smooth tensile bar does not correlate with the toughness of ferritic steels, because they can show brittle behavior, with little or no plastic deformation at low temperatures or high strain rates. There are several ways of measuring toughness. The most common is by *impact testing,* in which a large hammer hits a small notched sample. The quantity measured by impact toughness testing is the *energy absorbed* during fracture. By recording this at a variety of temperatures, a curve such as the one shown in Figure 5.3 is obtained for most ferritic steels. Examples of impact specimens and their fracture surfaces when tested at different temperatures are shown in Figure 5.4. The *ductile/brittle transition temperature,* where the fracture mode changes from one involving gross plastic deformation to brittle cleavage, is usually the most interesting property to monitor. This transition takes place over a certain temperature interval and it is customary to define the transition temperature with respect to a reasonable impact energy level. A common choice is 27 J (20 ft-lb), but other levels, such as 40 J (30 ft-lb), are also often used. The particular choice is dictated by several factors, the most

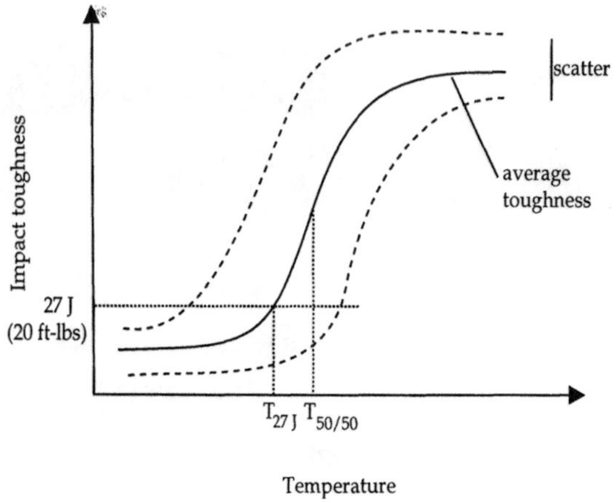

FIGURE 5.3. Impact toughness as a function of temperature, showing the characteristic drop in toughness as the temperature decreases. The scatter is low at the upper and lower shelf, but quite large in the transition region.

FIGURE 5.4. Examples of impact specimens and their fracture surfaces from specimens tested at different temperatures.

important being the strength of the steel. Higher strength steels require higher impact toughness.

Another measure of the transition temperature is FATT, the fracture appearance transition temperature. FATT is determined by inspection of the fracture surfaces and defined as the temperature at which 50% of the surface is covered by ductile fracture and the rest by brittle fracture. This is perhaps a more physically sound way of determining the transition temperature, but the method is used only to a limited extent. It is of course more time consuming and it can also in some cases be difficult to estimate the area fraction of the different kinds of fracture. Brittle and ductile fracture can be mixed over a large part of the fracture surface, although to the naked eye it might seem that one or another fracture mode is dominant.

The impact toughness data are notorious for their scatter, particularly in the transition temperature range where the fracture mode changes from ductile to brittle. Most codes require that three specimens are tested at each temperature. The average values are then compared to the requirements. Apart from the average considerations, limits are also placed on the lowest values to be accepted. Usually, no single value lower than 70% of the average value is allowed.

Impact testing is an inexpensive and simple method for measuring toughness. The drawbacks of the method are the small size of the sample (the method thus may not be representative of service) and the high strain rate during testing, which is not necessarily encountered in practice. The notch is also smooth and blunt. The measured toughness may not be used for design purposes. The test is nevertheless useful in quality control and as a ranking procedure for the comparison of different materials. It should however be stressed that impact testing is not an engineering design method. If 40 J (30 ft-lb) has been achieved at –40°C (–40°F) for a certain material, it does not mean that the material can be safely used at –40°C; it only means that the material has a better toughness than another material giving 40 J at –20°C (–4°F).

Hence, impact toughness testing is mainly a ranking technique (although it may not always give the same ranking order as fracture mechanics testing). However, in many cases methods are needed that can give data which are useful in an engineering analysis of a construction. One example of such a case is in the design of a structure where a weld can be assumed to contain a defect (e.g., an undercut) of a certain size. The tolerable stresses must be calculated. Another example may be in the assessment of the repair of a component in which a defect of a certain size (e.g., a crack) has been found. In both of these cases, it is necessary to obtain quantitative data on the material *fracture toughness.* There are three well-established methods: linear elastic fracture mechanics (LEFM), crack-tip opening displacement (CTOD), and J-integral measurements. An in-depth treatment of the application of fracture mechanics has been given by Knott.[1]

In LEFM the material property K_c (the critical stress intensity) is determined. K_c is measured under a plane strain condition, i.e., one dimension of the test piece is so much larger than the other dimensions that the strain is concentrated in a plane. Three modes of loading have been defined (*I, II,* and *III*), illustrated in Figure 5.5. The most common loading mode is *I.* The fracture

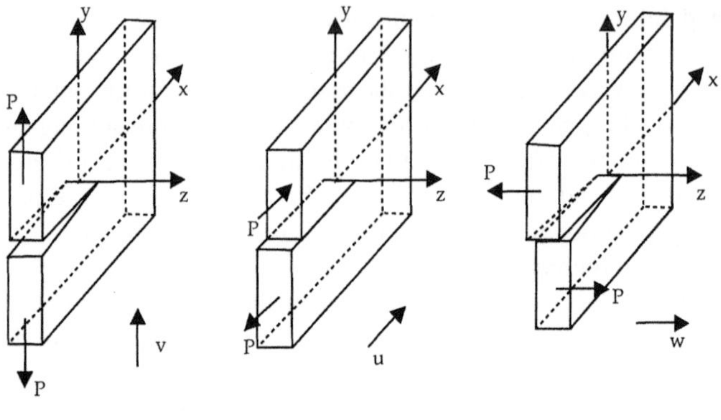

FIGURE 5.5. The three different modes of loading.

toughness is then denoted K_{Ic}. There are two requirements for K_{Ic} measurements. First, the section of the test piece must be thick enough so that any contribution from the shear lips to the measurements is minimized. Second, the fracture should take place under quasielastic conditions, i.e., there should not be any gross plastic deformation preceding fracture, except for a very small zone adjacent to the crack tip. Further, this zone must be much smaller than the cross-section of the specimen. To be able to characterize the fracture process with a single variable (K_{Ic}), the "process region" at the front of the crack tip must be much smaller than the crack length.

K_{Ic} tests can be conducted using different geometries of specimens. Figure 5.6 shows a single-edge-notched specimen. These can be loaded in three-point bending or in "compact tension" testing.

Some examples of K_{Ic} measurements are shown in Figure 5.7. The tests were made on both austenitic and ferritic steels. As can be seen, for the alloys tested, K_{Ic} decreases with increasing strength. Typical K_{Ic} values for steels are similar to those in Figure 5.7. There is also a transition in fracture toughness with test temperature, which is analogous to that found during impact toughness experiments (Figure 5.8). The difficulty with K_{Ic} measurements is keeping the plastic zone small enough relative to specimen cross-section. As an example, Knott mentions a 500-MPa (70,000-psi) yield strength steel, where testing at room temperature would require a specimen thickness of 225 mm (9 in.). Decreasing the test temperature to –100°C (–145°F) allows valid testing of 17-mm (0.67-in.) thick specimens.

K_{Ic} testing is not feasible in practice for many of the common steels or steel weld metals, because they have so much ductility that excessively large specimen thicknesses are required. To cope with situations where gross plastic yielding accompanies fracture, two different more practical tests have been suggested: the opening of the crack tip before the crack propagates (CTOD) or the strain energy release rate (J_{Ic}). The advantage of using these methods is that much smaller test pieces can be used.

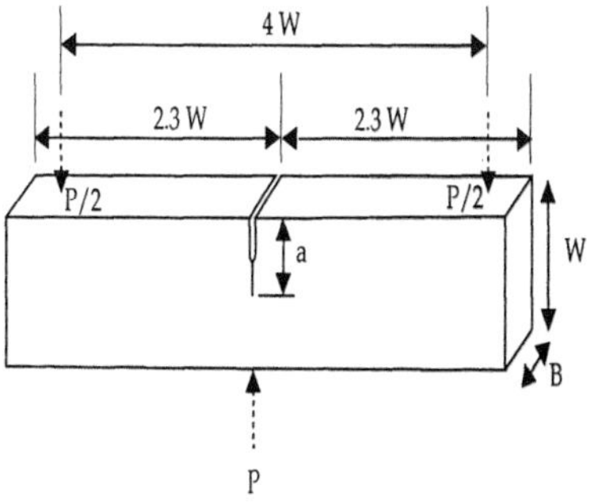

FIGURE 5.6. The dimensions of single-edge notched specimens used for fracture mechanics testing.

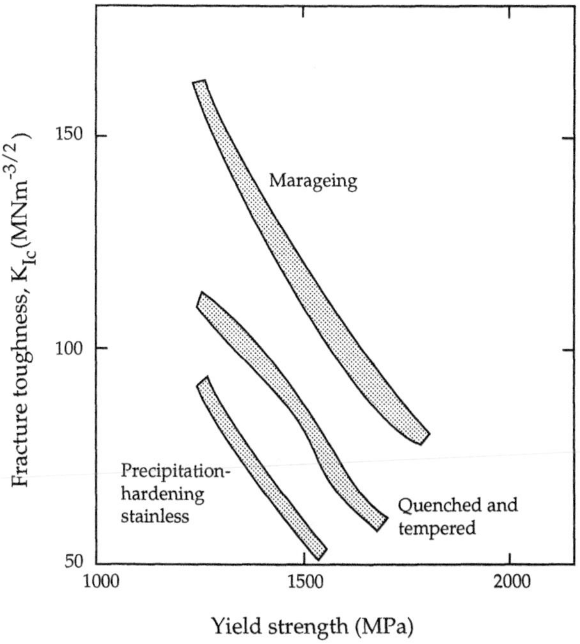

FIGURE 5.7. K_{Ic} measurements from three different steel types, showing that the yield strength has a great influence on the fracture toughness. (From Knott, J. F., *Fundamentals of Fracture Mechanics,* Butterworth-Heinemann Ltd., London, 1973. With permission.)

Measurement of CTOD is made on single-edge-notched specimens, loaded in three-point bending. Following the British standard BS 7448:1992, the opening of the crack tip is found by measuring the opening of the notch at the specimen surface and then calculating the CTOD value using the following equation:

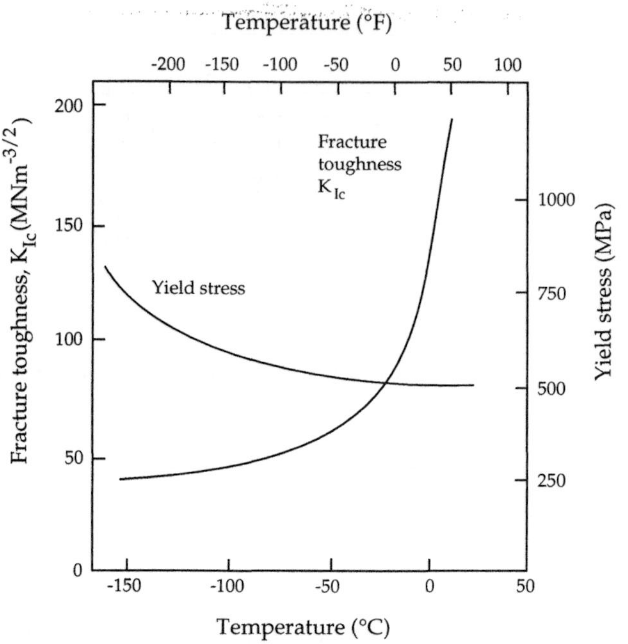

FIGURE 5.8. Variation of fracture toughness with temperature for a low-alloy steel. The sharp transition in fracture toughness, from low toughness at low temperatures to a high toughness at temperatures above approximately –50°C, is analogous to that observed during impact toughness testing. (From Knott, J. F., *Fundamentals of Fracture Mechanics,* Butterworth-Heinemann Ltd., London, 1973. With permission.)

$$\delta = K^2(1 - \upsilon)/2\sigma_y E + 0.4(W - a)V_p/(0.4W + 0.6a + z) \qquad (5.3)$$

Here, δ is the value of the CTOD, K is the stress intensity factor (calculated from the critical values of the applied load), υ is Poisson's ratio, σ_y is the yield stress, E is Young's modulus, V_p is the plastic component of clip gauge displacement, W is the specimen width, a is the crack length, and z is the distance of the clip gauge location from the test piece surface. The stress intensity, K, is calculated as

$$K = YP/BW^{1/2} \qquad (5.4)$$

where B is the specimen thickness and Y is a compliance function which depends on the ratio a/W. The values of the function are tabulated by the above BS standard.

Typical load-displacement curves are shown in Figure 5.9. Several possible events may take place. If fracture occurs before general yield, this is called a *critical* event, denoted by P_c and V_c, giving a critical CTOD value δ_c. If fracture occurs after general yield has started but before a maximum load has been

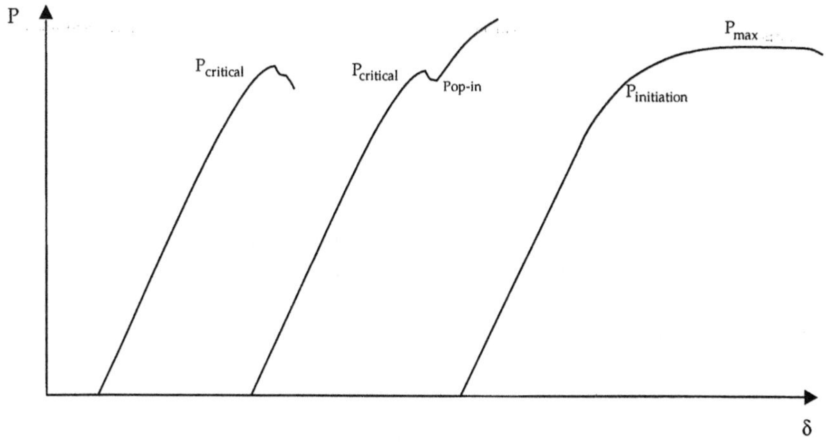

FIGURE 5.9. Typical load-displacement curves from CTOD testing. The curves illustrate critical fracture (fracture without any evidence of slow crack growth) (left curve), as above, with pop-in (middle curve), and fracture at maximum load (right curve).

reached, then this is denoted by the index *u* on the load, displacement, and CTOD parameters, for *unstable.* Finally, if fracture occurs at *maximum* load, the index will be *m.* In the middle curve in Figure 5.9 a so-called "pop-in" has occurred, i.e., there has been a small, unstable propagation of the crack that has stopped and thus the loading can continue in the normal manner. Pop-ins are treated as the onset of unstable crack growth and the CTOD value is calculated on the basis of the pop-in value.

The CTOD value δ can be related to K_{Ic} by the equation

$$K_{Ic} \approx K_{\delta c} \approx \sqrt{1.5\sigma_y E\delta} \quad (5.5)$$

Here, σ_y is the yield stress of the material.

The J-integral method is an alternative to CTOD testing. It determines the fracture toughness of a material breaking outside the linear elastic range. In the J-integral method, the change in potential energy during crack advance is measured. A load-displacement diagram is recorded for several values of the crack length. Three specimens with different crack lengths are commonly used. The potential energy *U* is calculated as

$$U(a) = \int_0 \Delta P(a) d\Delta \quad (5.6)$$

Calculation of the potential energy for different crack lengths makes differentiation with respect to crack length possible and the J-integral is obtained as

$$J = -1/B \; \Delta U/\Delta a \quad (5.7)$$

where B is the specimen width. The critical value of the J-integral, when unstable crack propagation takes place, J_c, is related to the fracture toughness by

$$K_c = \sqrt{J_c E} \tag{5.8}$$

It has long been debated whether impact toughness data can be converted to fracture mechanics toughness data. A general method to transform impact toughness data to fracture toughness does not exist. The best correlation has been found between the transition temperatures of the respective tests. However, when local brittle zones appear in fracture mechanics testing, the correlation is not valid.

Fracture toughness testing is made in plate thickness from 15 mm (0.59 in.) and thicker. In connection with offshore it is usually carried out on plates thicker than 50 mm (2 in.) and the test temperature is set to the design temperature. For offshore installations in the North Sea, the design temperature is –10°C (14°F) and this has so far been the common test temperature. A thickness of $\delta \geq 0.25$ mm (0.01 in.) is most often required in offshore. With offshore installations in colder regions, test temperatures of –15°C (5°F) are used. The drawback to fracture toughness testing is mainly cost, especially when testing is made on welded components. The welding of a thick plate by shielded metal arc welding (SMAW) may well take over 12 hours. The test specimens are then machined, including careful notching in the correct position, within close tolerances. The specimens are then subjected to fatigue loading, to obtain a sharp crack as a starting point for the crack propagation. Creating the fatigue crack is often the most critical step. The crack front must be straight, with only small deviations, in order to fulfill the requirements of the codes. The straightness of the fatigue crack can be improved by reducing the residual stresses from welding. This can be done either through compression of the sides of the specimen in front of the notch or by backbending the specimen prior to fatigue.

A simple and rapid way to obtain important information is by *hardness testing*. To find the high hardnesses that may arise in regions of the HAZ, a method that samples relatively small volumes is used. The Vickers hardness test is popular with a 10-kg load (HV10). The hardness measurement is made from the base plate, through the HAZ across the weld metal to the other base plate (as illustrated in Figure 5.10). The distance between the indentions is dependent upon the size of the indents. The center-to-center distance between two indents should be at least 3 times the size of each indent. If the material is so soft that the distance will be too large, then a smaller load can be used, although smaller loads give larger scatter in hardness data. Other hardness methods are also sometimes specified, such as Rockwell or Brinell tests. However, the indention sizes of these methods are relatively large and do not

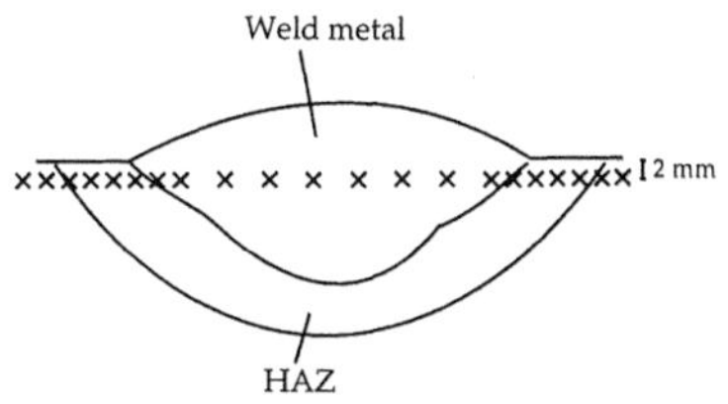

a

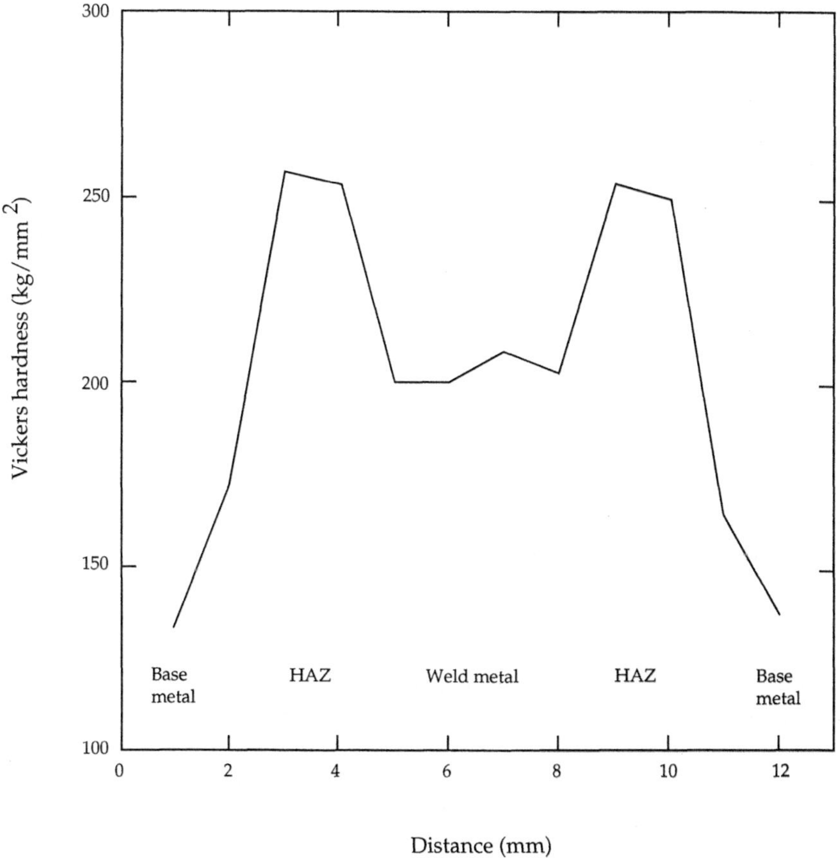

b

FIGURE 5.10. (a) Hardness measurement across a weld. (b) Typical hardness trace when going from the base plate, through the HAZ, across the weld, and out to the other base plate. In this case, a normalized steel has been welded with a C-Mn electrode and the highest hardness is found in the coarse-grained region of the HAZ.

exclusively sample the HAZ region. It is therefore not advisable to use these methods for assessing HAZ properties through correlation studies.

5.3. MECHANICAL PROPERTIES OF THE HEAT-AFFECTED ZONE

5.3.1. STRENGTH

In an ordinary weld, the size of the HAZ is too small to allow the determination of the strength and ductility by extracting tensile specimens. Some measure of the strength can be obtained from hardness data. The other possibility is to use simulation techniques, by which a certain part of the HAZ can be studied. A specimen is subjected to the same thermal cycle that the area of the HAZ in question would undergo. Although this method gives valuable information, there is always the drawback that the influence of neighboring areas cannot be accounted for. Simulation techniques have been used mainly for the assessment of toughness.

A thorough investigation of the strength and ductility of the HAZ was conducted by Akselsen et al.[2,3] using specimens that had been subjected to weld simulation as well as real welds. This investigation revealed several important aspects about the connection between microstructure, strength, and hardness and will therefore be discussed in some detail. Several different steels were used in that investigation:

- Two medium-strength steels, one with 0.17 wt% carbon and the other with 0.10 wt% carbon, the latter being microalloyed
- One 430 MPa (60,000 psi) yield strength steel with 0.09 wt% carbon, made with accelerated cooling
- Two high-strength quench and tempered steels with yield strengths around 600 MPa (90,000 psi), with carbon contents of about 0.14 wt%

The investigation concentrated mainly on the coarse-grained region of the HAZ. With simulated specimens, the relation between cooling time from 800 to 500°C and the martensite content could be found for each steel (Figure 5.11). The tensile properties were also measured on simulated specimens. Hardness measurements on real welds and on simulated specimens showed good correlation (Figure 5.12), and the hardness could also be calculated using Suzuki's BL 70 formula (see Table 5.1). From the hardness values, the yield stress, the ultimate tensile strength, and the ductility can be calculated using the following equations:

$$R_{p0.2} = 3.1HV_m\,(0.1)^n - 80 \qquad \text{(MPa)} \tag{5.9}$$

where n is the work hardening exponent, given as:

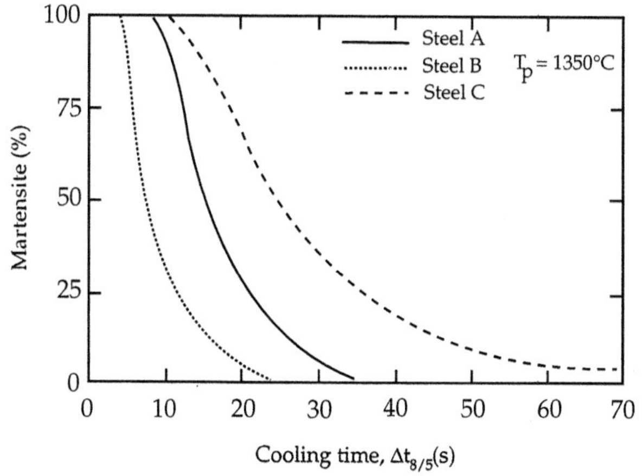

FIGURE 5.11. The amount of martensite as a function of the cooling time from 800 to 500°C. (From Akselsen, O. M., Rørvik, G., Onsøien, M. I., and Grong, Ø., *Weld. Res. Suppl.*, September, 356-s, 1989. With permission.)

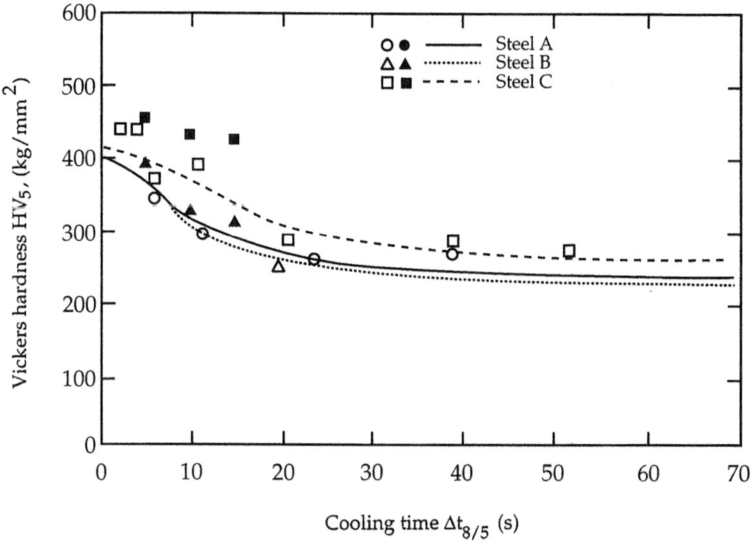

FIGURE 5.12. Hardness as a function of the 800 to 500°C cooling time. Full lines show values calculated according to Suzuki's BL 70 formula, open symbols show weld simulated samples, and filled symbols show bead on plate welds. (From Akselsen, O. M., Rørvik, G., Onsøien, M. I., and Grong, Ø., *Weld. Res. Suppl.*, September, 356-s, 1989. With permission.)

TABLE 5.1
Hardness Formulas for Calculating Maximum Hardness of the HAZ[4] (All Concentrations in wt%)

Modified NSC-SM (P_{cm}) formula

H_{max} (HV10) = (189 + 67C + 507 P_{cm}) – (101 + 711C – 461P_{cm}) arctan X

X = (log $t_{8/5}$ + (0.501 + 7.90C – 11.01P_{cm}))/(0.543 + 0.55C – 0.76P_{cm})

P_{cm} = C + Si/30 + (Mn + Cu + Cr)/20 Ni/60 + Mo/15 + V/10 + 5B

BL 70 formula

H_{max} (HV10) = H_∞ + K/(1 + exp (α(Y – Y_5)))

Y = log $t_{8/5}$ (in seconds)

H_∞ = 884C + 287 – K

K = 269 + 454C – 36Si – 79Mn – 57Cu – 12Ni – 53Cr – 122Mo – 169Nb – 7089B

αK = 478 + 3364C – 256Si + 66Ni – 408Mo – 1321V – 1559Nb

Y_5 = –0.085 + 2.070C + 0.459Mn + 0.655Cu + 0.122Ni + 0.222Cr + 0.788Mo + 30B

BL 70 S formula

H_{max} (HV10) = H_∞ + K/(1 + exp (α(Y – Y_5)))

Y = log $t_{8/5}$ (in seconds)

H_∞ = 884C + 287 – K

K = 237 + 1633C – 1157P_{cm}

αK = 566 + 5532C – 2280P_{cm}

Y_5 0 – 0.0300 – 6.00C + 7.77P_{cm}

MW formula–100% Martensite

HV_M (HV10) = 802C + 305

MW formula–100% Bainite

HV_B = 350 (C + Si/11 + Mn/8 + Cu/9 + Cr/5 + Ni/17 + Mo/6 + V/3) + 101

MW formula 0 < % Martensite < 100

HV_x = 2019 [(C(1 – 0.5 log $t_{8/5}$) + 0.3 (Si/11 + Mn/8 + Cu/9 + Cr/5 + Ni/17 + Mo/6 + V/3)] + 66 (1 – 0.8 log $t_{8/5}$)

MW general formula

A = (100% Martensite)/100 ≈ (HV_M – HV_x)/(HV_M – HV_B); 0 < A < 1; A < 0 ⇒ A = 0; A > 1 ⇒ A = 1

HV_c = 802C – 452C A + 350A (Si/11 + Mn/8 + Cu/9 + Cr/5 + Ni/17 + Mo/6 + V/3) + 305 (1 – 0.67A)

$$n = 0.065\ (\Delta t_{8/5})^{0.17} \tag{5.10}$$

The strain hardening exponent is independent of the chemical composition, but depends on the cooling time. This is due to a difference in strain hardening exponent between martensitic and side plate microstructures.

$$R_m = 3.5HV_m\ (1 - n)[12.5/(1 - n)]^n - 92 \qquad \text{(MPa)} \tag{5.11}$$

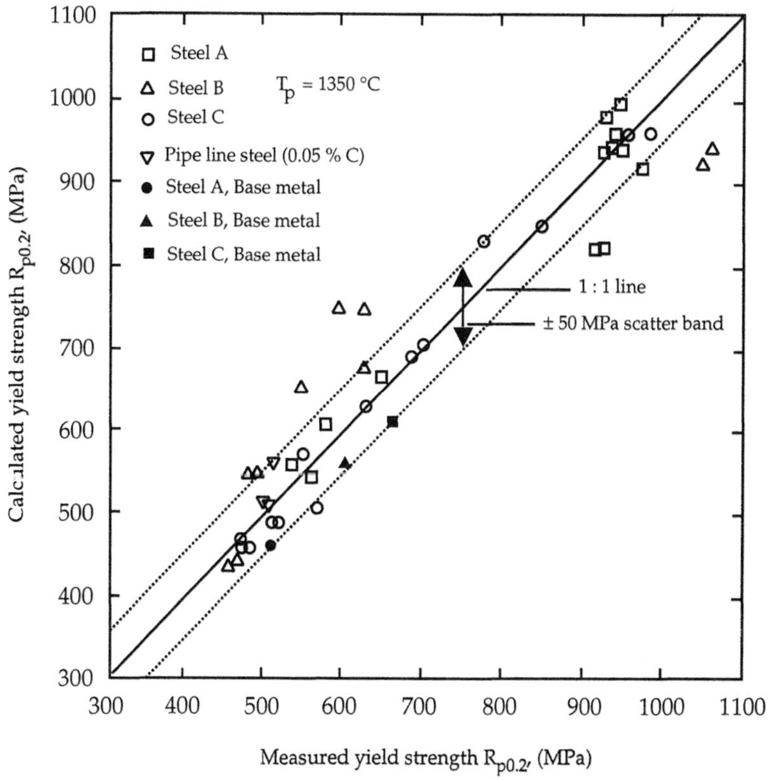

FIGURE 5.13. The relation between measured and calculated yield strength, using Equations 5.10 and 5.11. (From Akselsen, O. M., Rørvik, G., Onsøien, M. I., and Grong, Ø., *Weld. Res. Suppl.*, September, 356-s, 1989. With permission.)

$$A = 5.75 \times 10^4 \, [R_m]^{-1.25} \qquad (\%) \tag{5.12}$$

The agreement between measured and predicted values is shown in Figure 5.13. The yield strength can in general be predicted from hardness measurements to lie within a scatterband of ±50 MPa.

The strength values are closely related to the volume fraction of martensite in the microstructure. In Figure 5.14 the variation in strength over the complete HAZ is shown for a medium-strength steel with low carbon content (left side) and a high-strength steel (right side) for various welding conditions. For low heat inputs (1 to 2 kJ/mm, 25 to 50 kJ/in.), high strengths were obtained in the coarse-grained zone for both steels due to the formation of bainite and martensite. With higher heat inputs, the yield strength was still higher than in the base material for the medium-strength steel, but not at all as high as with low heat input. Naturally, this is due to less martensite formation. The high-strength steels were actually softer in the HAZ than in the base material. This kind of

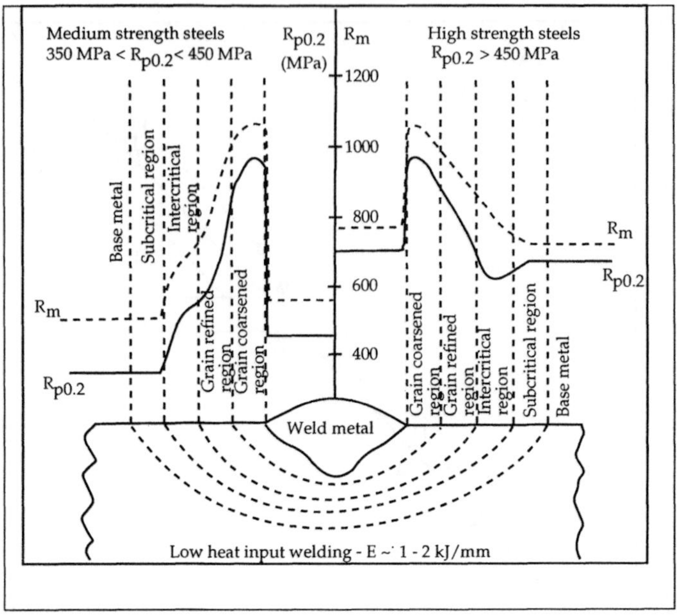

a

FIGURE 5.14. The variation in yield strength across a welded joint. The left side of the weld relates to a medium-strength steel and the right side to a high-strength steel. (a) The situation for low heat input (1 kJ/mm). (b) High heat input (>4 kJ/mm). For the medium-strength steel, an overmatching weld metal was used. The influence of heat input in reducing the yield strength (and the hardness) can be noted. For the high-strength steel a matching weld metal was used. With low heat input, the coarse-grained zone has a higher yield strength than the weld metal and the base metal. However, with high heat input, the HAZ is softer than both the weld metal and the base metal. (From Akselsen, O. M. and Rørvik, G., *Mater. Sci. Technol.*, 6(April), 383, 1990. With permission.)

"soft zone" is often noticed in high-strength steels because they are sensitive to tempering.

The main factor influencing strength is thus the amount of martensite. Other factors that can influence strength are elements in solid solution, grain size, and precipitation of particles. The strength of martensite is a combination of fine grain size and carbon in solid solution. Solid solution elements otherwise have a fairly small influence on strength. The other constituents in the HAZ (laths and allotriomorphic ferrite) have a relatively large effective grain size and a lower dislocation density, which explains a large part of the difference between a martensitic HAZ and a HAZ without martensite.

In the coarse-grained zone, most particles from microalloying elements (except for possibly TiN) are dissolved. Reprecipitation during the austenite to ferrite transformation as the metal cools may occur. The particles then usually

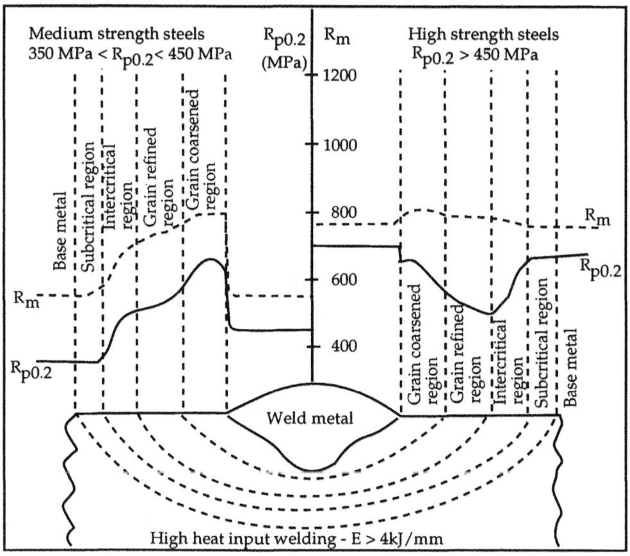

FIGURE 5.14.b

precipitate as an interphase reaction, which leads to a considerable increase in strength. In the grain refined zone (i.e., where the maximum temperature has been lower than ca. 1100°C, 2000°F) the particles do not fully dissolve, but probably coarsen. Consequently, a lower contribution to strength from the precipitates can be expected there.

As shown by the example above, hardness can be used as a good alternative to tensile testing for the determination of strength. There are quite a number of models which try to predict the maximum hardness in the HAZ from a knowledge of steel chemistry and welding condition. A summary of the most recent formulas is given in Table 5.1.[4]

5.3.2. TOUGHNESS

Toughness is considered to be a much more critical property of the HAZ than strength. As shown above, the strength of the HAZ is in general higher than that of the base material. Thus the design of a structure from the point of view of strength is not problematic. The toughness of the material, which is linked more closely with the ability to withstand cracking and fracture, is more difficult to design against. There are two zones in the HAZ which are of prime concern, namely the coarse-grained zone and the intercritically heated zone. Under some circumstances, the subcritically heated zone can also show low toughness. The majority of this section will deal with the coarse-grained zone. A further complication is that most welds are built up by many passes, so that the HAZ consists of a complicated pattern of zones that have been reheated again to various degrees. To assess the effect of metallurgical changes on the HAZ properties toughness, testing is therefore sometimes made on a single-pass bead in groove samples, where there has been no further reheating of the HAZ. To study the toughness of an individual zone, the thermal cycle corresponding to that zone is obtained in a thermal simulator. The size of each zone is so small that in a real welded joint a notch will always sample several microstructures.

The theory of the connection between microstructure and toughness has been described by Knott and co-workers.[1,5,6] Their work will be reviewed briefly here. Low toughness in ferritic steels is usually connected with fracture occurring by a cleavage mechanism. The condition for the nucleation and propagation of a cleavage crack must therefore be investigated. From the analysis of Griffith, in a material containing a defect of length $2a$, the crack will propagate if the total energy of the system decreases during propagation. As the crack grows, the stored energy will decrease, but instead the surface energy per unit area (γ) will increase. The condition for crack propagation can be given as

$$\sigma_F = [2E\gamma/\pi a(1 - \upsilon)]^{1/2} \qquad \text{(MPa)} \tag{5.13}$$

where σ_F is the *fracture stress,* E is Young's modulus, and υ is Poisson's ratio. This equation is applicable to plane strain conditions.

For ductile materials much of the energy is used for plastic flow around the crack tip and this energy term, γ_p, is considerably larger than the surface energy per unit area. For these materials, which are the most common in engineering practice, the fracture stress can be written

$$\sigma_F = [E(2\gamma + \gamma_p)/\pi a(1 - \upsilon)]^{1/2} \qquad \text{(MPa)} \tag{5.14}$$

It has been found that cleavage fracture is controlled by tensile stress rather than by shear stress, implying that the nucleation of a cleavage crack is an "easy event," while propagation is the controlling step. It is assumed that a small crack nucleates in, for example, a grain boundary carbide of thickness l. The critical event is the propagation of this crack into the surrounding ferritic matrix. The expression for the fracture stress is then given by

$$\sigma_F = [4E\gamma_p/\pi(1 - \upsilon^2)l]^{1/2} \tag{5.15}$$

It can be noted that the fracture stress is independent of grain size, which is surprising because grain size is known to be the strongest factor in preventing cleavage fracture. This is explained by the fact that a smaller grain size gives more grain boundary area, which in turn reduces the size of the carbides which initiate fracture. Thus, there is an indirect influence of grain size.

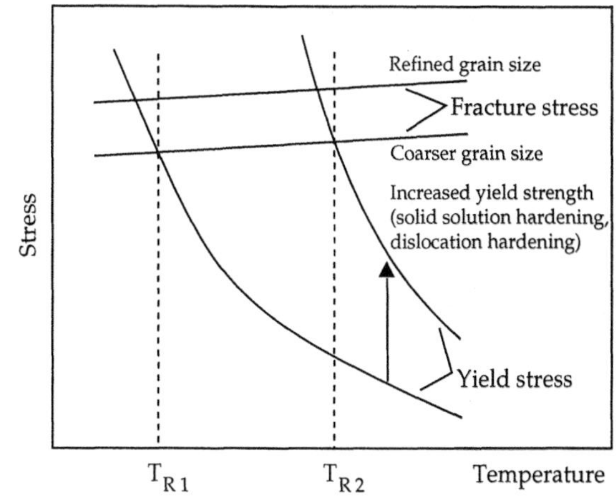

FIGURE 5.15. A schematic diagram explaining the relation among yield strength, fracture stress, and mode of fracture. When the temperature is lowered the yield stress increases, while the fracture stress is independent of temperature. Thus, when the yield stress becomes higher than the fracture stress, fracture occurs without any plastic deformation, i.e., it is brittle. If the yield strength is increased, then brittle fracture will take place at a higher temperature. The same effect arises if the deformation rate is increased.

The fracture will be brittle when the yield stress is higher than the fracture stress, while if the yield stress is lower than the fracture stress, the fracture will be ductile, as illustrated in Figure 5.15. This implies that increased strength leads to decreased toughness. This is usually true, but not always. Smaller grain size increases both the yield and fracture stress so that an improved toughness can be found. Other mechanisms to increase strength, such as solid solution hardening or precipitation, will lead to decreased toughness.

The role of various alloying elements must thus be judged with respect to their influence on the microstructure and by what mechanism they influence strength. Elements that act to refine the grain size have a positive influence on toughness. In general, manganese, molybdenum, copper, nickel, vanadium, and chromium, when added in carefully controlled quantities, can influence the austenite to ferrite transformation so that a fine-grained structure is achieved.

Reduction of carbon almost always has a positive effect on toughness at constant strength, because of the reduction in the content of brittle carbides and microphases. A martensitic microstructure with low carbon content has appreciable toughness, whereas high carbon martensite is brittle. Due to the high M_s temperature, this low carbon martensite will be autotempered during cooling, improving toughness. The reduction in the carbon content of steels that has taken place during the 1980s probably has been the largest single factor responsible for improvement in toughness in the HAZ. However, the relation is not entirely straightforward. As shown by Harrison and Hart,[7] low heat input welding (1 kJ/mm, 25 kJ/in.) gives better toughness in steels with higher

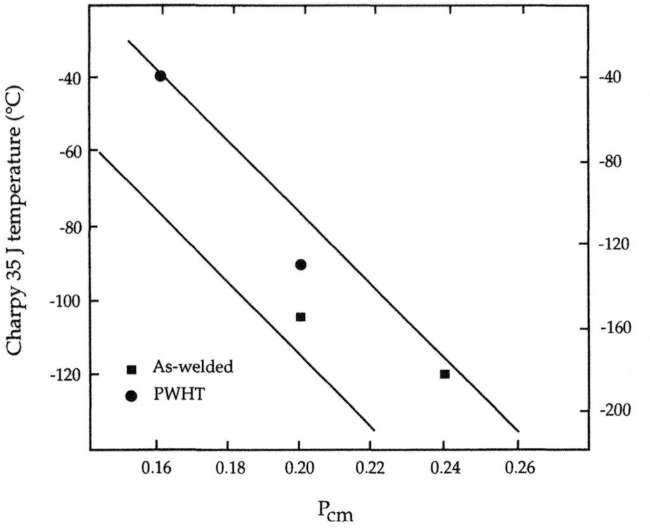

a

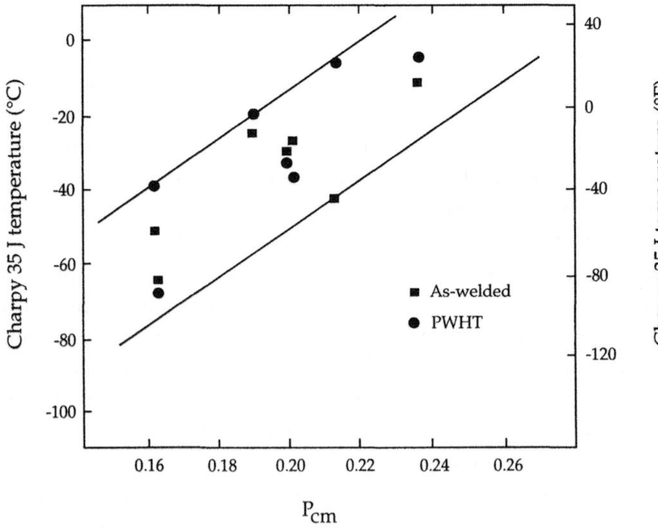

b

FIGURE 5.16. The 35-J transition temperature in the coarse-grained zone as a function of the hardenability of the steels, expressed as P_{cm} (P_{cm} is given in Equation 1.7). (a) The relation for a low heat input (1 kJ/mm FCAW). (b) The relation for 5 kJ/mm SAW. (From Harrison, P. L. and Hart, P. H. M., in *Proc. 8th Int. Conf. Offshore Mechanics and Arctic Engineering,* The Welding Institute, London, 1989. With permission.)

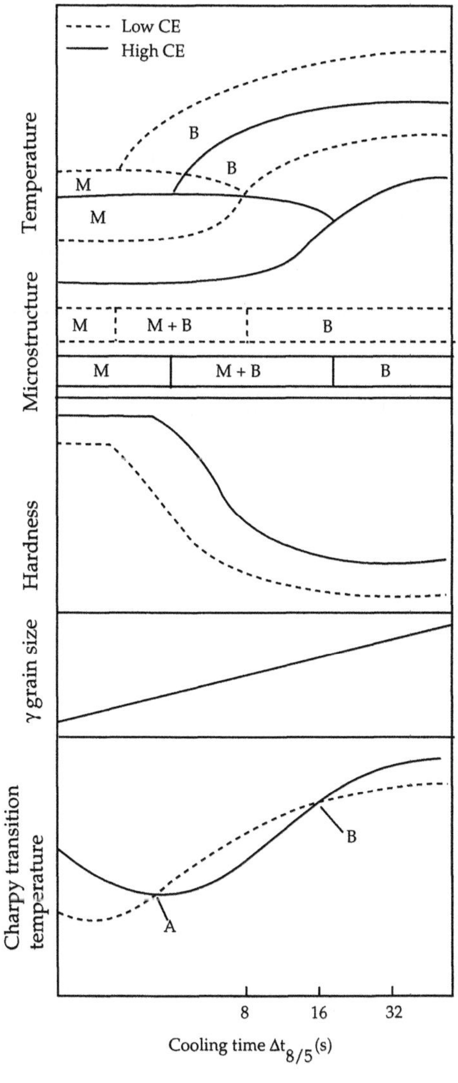

FIGURE 5.17. An explanation for the toughness-hardenability results shown in Figure 5.16. Steels with high hardenability will have an autotempered martensite when welded with low heat input (because the bainite nose is moved to the left and the M_s temperature is relatively high), as can be deduced from the schematic CCT diagram. The low hardenability steels will have a bainitic structure. Cross-over point A corresponds to such low heat input that in the low hardenability steels autotempered martensite is also formed. The critical value of heat input is below 1 kJ/mm. Point B corresponds to the point where the microstructures of all steels are bainitic and the steels with lower hardenability will then be softer, which should give them a better toughness. (From Harrison, P. L. and Hart, P. H. M., in *Proc. 8th Int. Conf. Offshore Mechanics and Arctic Engineering,* The Welding Institute, London, 1989. With permission.)

hardenability, while high heat inputs (5 kJ/mm, 125 kJ/in.) give the opposite result (Figure 5.16). This is explained by the schematic diagram in Figure 5.17, where at high heat inputs steels with lower hardenability in general are softer and thus have better toughness. At low heat inputs, steels with a higher hardenability will have an autotempered martensitic microstructure, while those with lower hardenability will be bainitic. It is not until the heat input is lowered even further that the low hardenability steels will become martensitic and then develop better toughness. Thus there will be two crossover points in the schematic diagram.

Boron can be added to the steels to suppress the formation of ferrite at the austenite grain boundaries. There is a specific product of boron concentration and austenite grain size $[B] \times d_\gamma$ that produces a fully martensitic microstructure, where optimum toughness is achieved. If $[B]$ is given in parts per million and d_γ in millimeters, then the product should be around 10. For lower values, insufficient hardenability arises and for higher values, borocarbides precipitate. Because the austenite grain size is dependent on the heat input, the boron content should be individually tuned for each application, making the concept difficult to adopt.

Microalloying elements mainly have a detrimental effect on toughness, probably due to precipitation hardening. The microalloying carbides dissolve during the high-temperature cycle and then reprecipitate in more unfavorable shapes. The interphase type of precipitation is likely to give more brittle behavior than a more random dispersion of precipitates. However, as discussed in Chapter 3, vanadium can promote intragranular fine-grained ferrite and thus be beneficial. Titanium, which is used to restrict austenite grain growth by TiN precipitates, also has a positive influence on toughness, for two reasons. First, the amount of nitrogen in solid solution is decreased, and second, less martensite or bainite is formed because of the smaller austenite grain size. Instead, Widmanstätten ferrite side plates are formed which have better cleavage resistance than martensite or bainite, at least for ordinary carbon contents (around 0.18 wt%).

However, not even the side plates have enough cleavage resistance for the most demanding applications. Experiments have been conducted to further decrease the grain size in the HAZ by using Ti_2O_3 particles as nucleants to form acicular ferrite in the austenite grain interiors, rather than bainite. The dispersion of the particles must not be too dense to restrict grain growth, because nucleation of acicular ferrite is favored by large austenite grains. However, toughness is also related to the presence of nonmetallic inclusions, as will be discussed in more detail for the properties of weld metals. The size distribution of the particles must therefore be carefully controlled.

Low fracture toughness values may sometimes occur due to impurities such as nitrogen, sulfur, and phosphorus. Nitrogen contents are controlled by the casting practice and also by using titanium to tie up free nitrogen. With calcium treatment of the steels, a significant improvement in transition temperature has

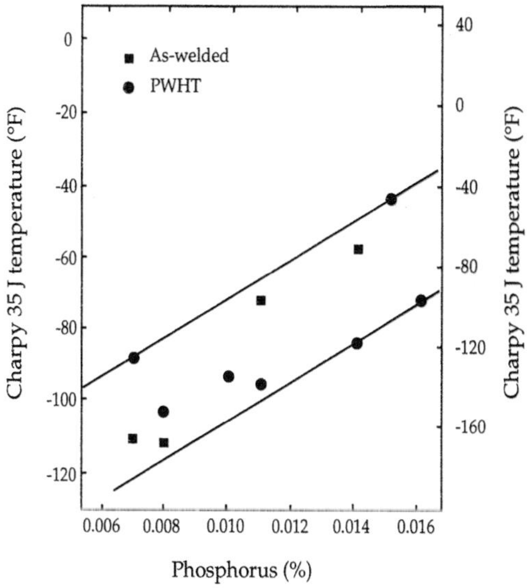

FIGURE 5.18. Reduction of the phosphorus level also improves fracture toughness. (From Harrison, P. L. and Hart, P. H. M., in *Proc. 8th Int. Conf. Offshore Mechanics and Arctic Engineering,* The Welding Institute, London, 1989. With permission.)

been found, due to lower sulfur content. Reduction of the phosphorus level also results in a significant improvement in fracture toughness (Figure 5.18). Phosphorus probably segregates to the ferrite/carbide interface and decreases the cohesion, which increases the risk of nucleation of cleavage cracks.

The concept of local brittle zones (LBZs) is frequently used to explain unexpected drops in fracture toughness. The concept has been given different meanings in different investigations. It has sometimes been used to describe the whole of a brittle coarse-grained zone, but also small islands of martensite or bainite that can be found in intercritically reheated coarse-grained zones.

The discovery of LBZs largely coincided with the development of steels and testing procedures for the offshore industry. However, investigations on older steels have also revealed LBZs. In practice, very few incidents of cracking have been reported that can be connected to LBZs. The reason for this is still open to speculation, but it may well be that the much larger constraints found in fracture toughness testing (especially in CTOD testing) than in a real fabrication can explain this. It has also been shown that low toughness due to LBZ appears when the steel has been subjected to two subsequent thermal cycles, but when a third thermal cycle is used, toughness increases again.

In the subcritical zone, low toughness can be found due to several reasons. If the peak temperature has been just below the Ae_1 temperature, formation of alloy carbides can take place. This is perhaps most common in microalloyed steels, which have first been reheated into the coarse-grained region, with concomitant dissolution of the carbides. If reprecipitation does not take place, a second thermal cycle will cause precipitation. If the peak temperature has been somewhat lower (e.g., 400°C, 750°F), coarsening of grain boundary cementite can result in decreased toughness, in accordance with Knott's theory above. Finally, when reheated to around 200°C (400°F), strain aging can occur, especially in steels with a relatively high nitrogen content without titanium additions. Alloying with titanium ties up the nitrogen. Also, aluminum ties up the nitrogen, but AlN dissolves during high-temperature reheating, meaning that a coarse-grained zone being reheated to about 200°C (400°F) can show reduced toughness due to strain aging.

5.4. MECHANICAL PROPERTIES OF THE WELD METAL

5.4.1. STRENGTH

The tensile strength of the weld metal is usually set to be higher than for the corresponding base material. The strength in the as-deposited weld metal naturally is built up by the same components as in the base metal or the HAZ. The most important components for the weld metal are

- A fine grain size (acicular ferrite)
- Solid solution hardening elements, e.g., manganese and nickel
- Dislocation hardening (acicular ferrite is essentially a bainitic structure)

The content of microalloying elements is usually kept very low so there is hardly any contribution from precipitation hardening. One possible candidate for precipitation hardening is molybdenum, which is frequently used in concentrations around 0.2 to 0.5 wt%. However, the main effect of molybdenum is to shift the curves in the continuous cooling transformation (CCT) diagrams to the right in order to increase hardenability. Precipitates of molybdenum carbides have not been found in as-deposited weld metals. The oxide inclusions are too large to have any hardening effect.

In multirun weld metals, the situation is somewhat more complex. The various HAZs all have their own strength profiles. Investigations similar to those done on base material HAZ by Akselsen et al. have not been done on weld metals. However, using hardness traces across the different zones and converting this to yield strength by application of Equation 5.6 provides a guideline about the yield strength variation. By calculating the volume fractions of each zone, an estimate of the total yield strength can be obtained. This method has been tested on data presented by Evans[8–13] and the correspondence between measured and predicted values is fairly good (Figure 5.19). Of course, there are several error sources in this method, e.g., the equation given by Akselsen et al. has a certain scatter and the calculation of the volume fractions of different zones is very approximative.

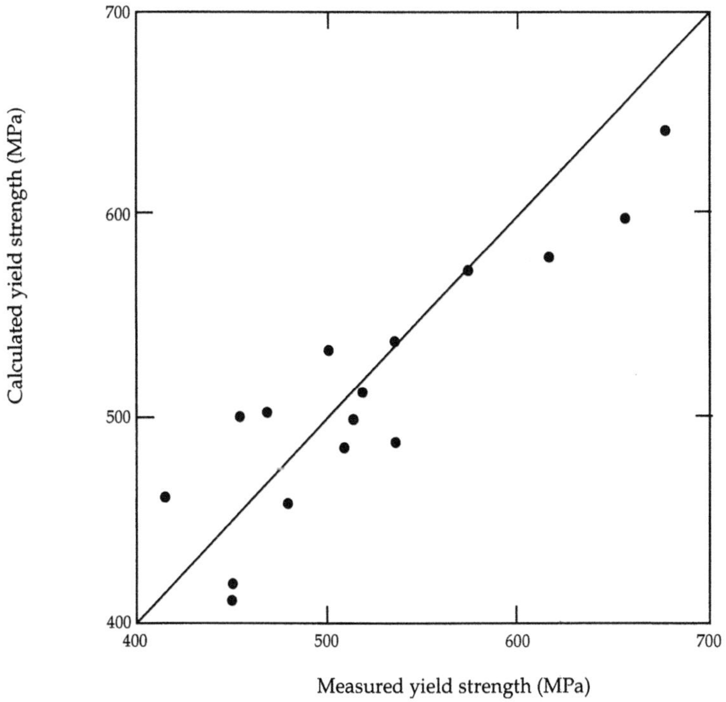

FIGURE 5.19. Hardness data by Evans[8–13] converted to yield strength by using Equations 5.10 and 5.11, assuming that the primary microstructure occupies about 50% of the structure, the coarse-grained zone 20%, and the intercritically and subcritically reheated zones together occupy 30%.

In many investigations, strength has been related to the chemistry of the weld metal by regression analysis. A summary of these regression equations is given in Table 5.2. Using these equations, a rapid estimate of the yield strength can be found. However, the equations can only be used within the limits of the chemical compositions for which they were developed and for the welding conditions used (mostly a heat input of 1 kJ/mm, 25 kJ/in.).

Of some interest is the lowest strength level that can be achieved in a weld metal. One SMAW electrode with a very low carbon content and reduced manganese and silicon concentrations (for deoxidation) has been developed. The microstructure of the weld metal consists of massive ferrite (Plate 5*) and the strength of a multirun all-weld metal sample is around 350 MPa (50,000 psi). This can be regarded as the minimum yield strength level that can be obtained in a weld metal.

* Plate 5 appears following page 84.

TABLE 5.2
Summary of Different Regression Equations, Relating Yield (σ_y) and Ultimate Tensile (σ_R) Strength to Weld Metal Chemical Composition (Strength in MPa and Concentration of Elements in wt%)

Yield and tensile strength	
As-welded condition	**Stress-relieved condition**
$\sigma_y = 335 + 439C + 60Mn + 361C \cdot Mn$ $\sigma_R = 379 + 754C + 63Mn + 337C \cdot Mn$ ($0.04 < C < 0.15$, $0.6 < Mn < 1.8$) (Ref. 8)	$\sigma_y = 288 + 91Mn + 95Si - 10Si^2$ $\sigma_R = 344 + 89Mn + 212Si - 79Si^2$ (C 0.06 – 0.07, $0.6 < Mn < 1.8$, $0.2 < Si < 0.9$) (Ref. 9)
$\sigma_y = 293 + 91Mn + 228Si - 122Si^2$ $\sigma_R = 365 + 89Mn + 169Si - 44Si^2$ (C 0.06 – 0.07, $0.6 < Mn < 1.8$, $0.2 < Si < 0.9$) (Ref. 9)	$\sigma_y = 287 + 113Mn + 193Mo + 29Mn \cdot Mo$ $\sigma_R = 373 + 113Mn + 167Mo + 37Mn \cdot Mo$ (C 0.04, $0.6 < Mn < 1.8$, $0 < Mo < 1.1$) (Ref. 10)
$\sigma_y = 305 + 121Mn + 137Mo + 8Mn \cdot Mo$ $\sigma_R = 383 + 116Mn + 150Mo + 8Mn \cdot Mo$ (C 0.04, $0.6 < Mn < 1.8$, $0 < Mo < 1.1$) (Ref. 10)	$\sigma_y = 312 + 100Mn + 58Cr + 22Mn \cdot Cr$ $\sigma_R = 393 + 106Mn + 66Cr + 10Mn \cdot Cr$ (C 0.04, $0.6 < Mn < 1.8$, $0 < Cr < 2.4$) (Ref. 11)
$\sigma_y = 320 + 113Mn + 64Cr + 42Mn \cdot Cr$ $\sigma_R = 395 + 107Mn + 63Cr + 36Mn \cdot Cr$ (C 0.04, $0.6 < Mn < 1.8$, $0 < Cr < 2.4$) (Ref. 11)	$\sigma_y = 319 + 85Mn + 17Ni + 21Mn \cdot Ni$ $\sigma_R = 393 + 95Mn + 17Ni + 19Mn \cdot Ni$ (C 0.04, $0.6 < Mn < 1.8$, $0 < Ni < 3.5$) (Ref. 12)
$\sigma_y = 332 + 99Mn + 9Ni + 21Mn \cdot Ni$ $\sigma_R = 401 + 102Mn + 16Ni + 15Mn \cdot Ni$ (C 0.04, $0.6 < Mn < 1.8$, $0 < Ni < 3.5$) (Ref. 12)	
$\sigma_y = 484 + 57Cu$ $\sigma_R = 561 + 59Cu$ (C 0.07, Mn 1.5, $0 < Cu < 1.4$) (Ref. 13)	

5.4.2. TOUGHNESS

The toughness of weld metals is influenced by a number of metallurgical factors. The position of the notch relative to the different zones in a multirun weld is also an influence. First, a description of the fracture toughness of a single as-deposited bead in terms of metallurgical factors will be given, followed by a description of the effect of multipass welding.

Examination of impact toughness test specimens from weld metals having high impact toughness (i.e., situated at the upper shelf level of the impact curve) shows that the fracture takes place by ductile void coalescence (Figure 5.20). The voids nucleate on inclusions, mainly the oxide particles. Naturally, this leads to higher upper shelf values for weld metals from a basic-type consumable than from a rutile type, because the oxygen content of the rutile weld metals is much higher.

Specimens extracted from the transition region show ductile fracture close to the notch, but at some distance away from the notch a brittle cleavage fracture instead appears (Figure 5.21). Ductile fracture is also found in the shear lips at the sides of the specimen. In the lower shelf region of the impact

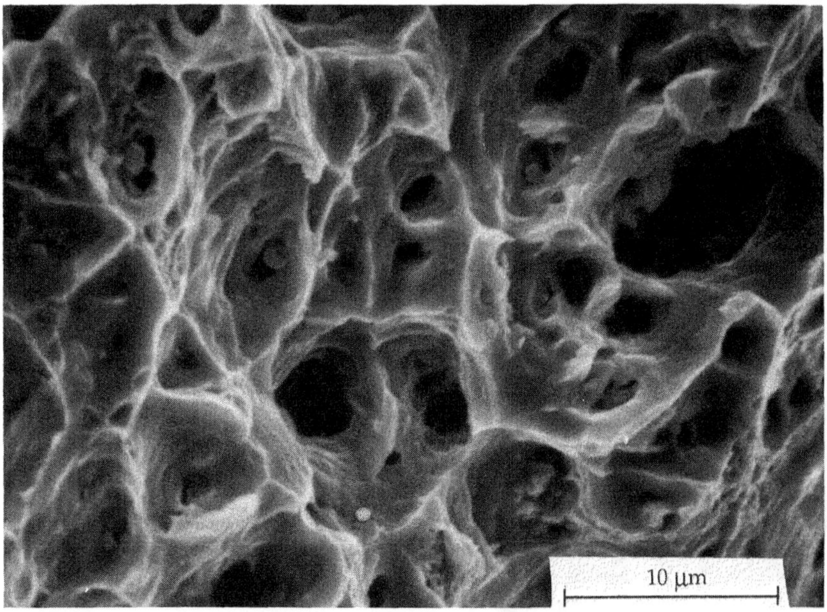

FIGURE 5.20. Fracture taking place by ductile void coalescence. Scanning electron micrograph.

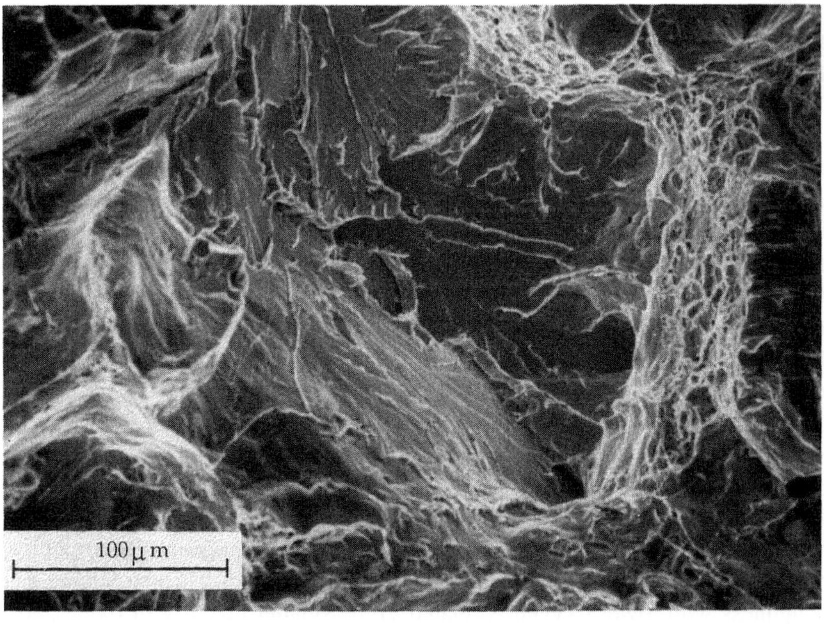

FIGURE 5.21. Typical appearance of the fracture from a brittle specimen. Large areas of cleavage fracture can be seen, together with small parts of ductile fracture. Scanning electron micrograph.

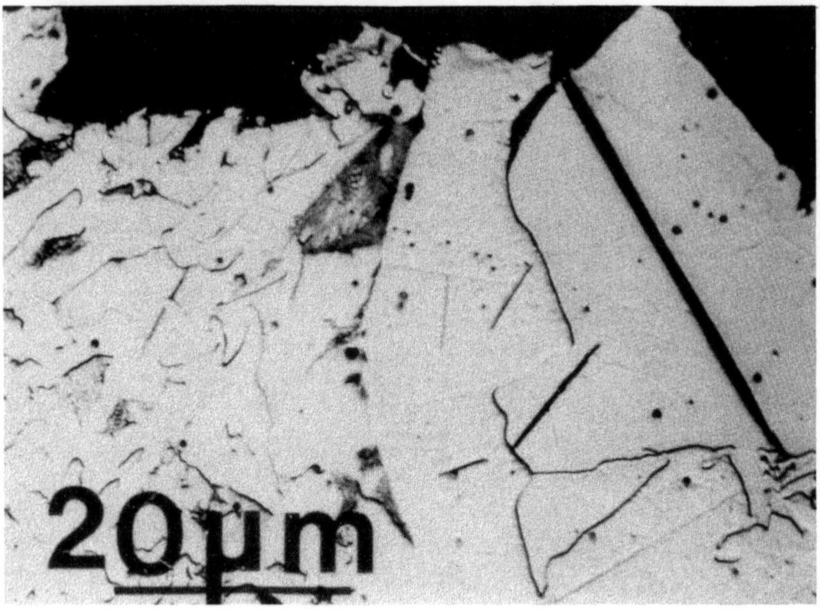

FIGURE 5.22. Cleavage cracks following the coarse-grained allotriomorphic ferrite.

toughness curve almost all of the fracture takes place by cleavage. To extend the useful temperature range of a weld metal, brittle fracture must be avoided as much as possible.

The conditions that favor cleavage cracks are the presence of ferrite phases that nucleate on prior austenite grain boundaries (i.e., allotriomorphic ferrite and Widmanstätten side plates), inclusions, and segregated microphases. The cleavage cracks follow a more or less continuous path of the allotriomorphic ferrite (Figure 5.22) and propagate relatively easily in the side plate microstructure, because the plates are separated only by low angle boundaries, making the effective grain size much larger than the packet size. Acicular ferrite has the best resistance to cleavage fracture through its fine grain size and myriad of crystallographic orientations.

The impact toughness (measured as a transition temperature) improves steadily with decreasing oxygen content, until a certain oxygen concentration, where the toughness drops again. The exact oxygen concentration where the toughness starts to fall again is dependent on several factors. In high-current GMAW the transition takes place at around 120 to 150 ppm oxygen, and this value has often been quoted as a general transition value. The improvement in toughness with lower oxygen is related to the smaller quantity of oxide particles. Both the upper shelf energy and the transition temperature are positively influenced by a lower oxygen content. The drop in toughness at very low

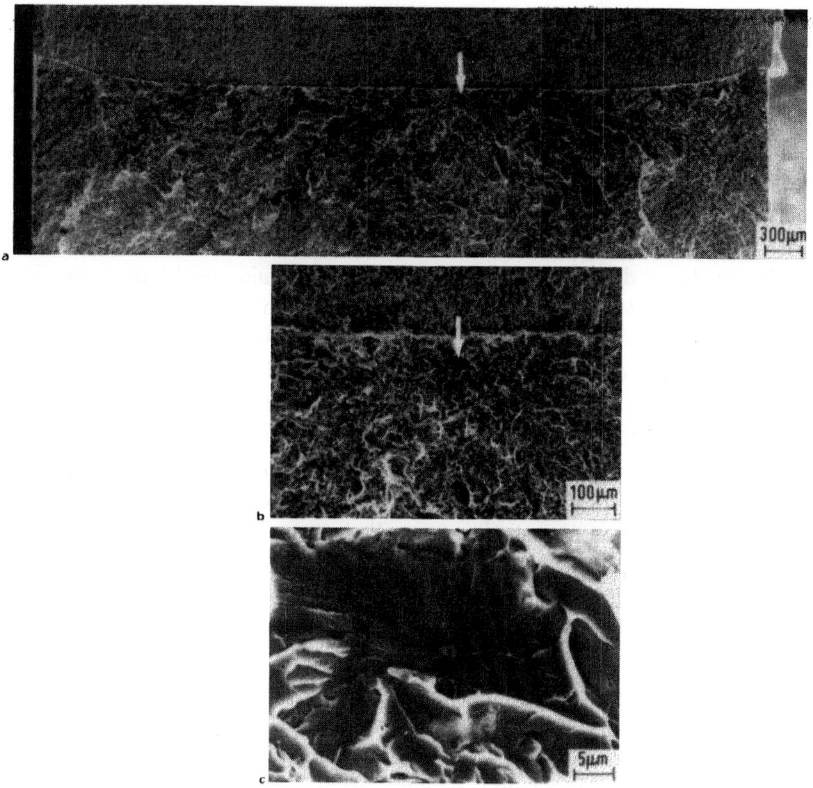

FIGURE 5.23. Cleavage cracks initiation at inclusion. (After McRobie, D. E. and Knott, J. F., *Mater. Sci. Technol.*, 1(May), 357, 1985. With permission.)

oxygen concentrations is related to the decrease in acicular ferrite content, which takes place when there are either too few particles to nucleate acicular ferrite or the particles have a composition that makes them poor nuclei. In the latter case, the oxygen content at which the transition occurs is affected by the ncentration of oxide formers, such as aluminum and titanium. If the alumi-m content is adjusted when the oxygen content is reduced, the condition for icular ferrite nucleation may still be fulfilled, and consequently, the tough-ss remains at a high level. On the other hand, if the possibility to nucleate ular ferrite for some reason is significantly reduced, then bainite which has a lower cleavage resistance, will form instead, and then the toughness falls.

The influence of inclusions (and hence oxygen content) on toughness has thoroughly been studied by Knott and co-workers[6,14] using small CTOD test bars, which were subjected to simulated thermal cycles. Cleavage cracks were found to initiate in inclusions (Figure 5.23), explaining the dependence on oxygen content. For the base plates it was suggested[5] that the cleavage cracks nucleated in grain boundary carbides. The general lower toughness of weld metals compared to base metal can probably partly be explained by the oxides being on average larger than the carbides. Although the particles were found to have a fairly stable *average* size (see Section 4.3.2), it is the *maximum* size that is most important for the fracture properties. It is especially the inclusions situated in soft components, such as allotriomorphic ferrite, that crack most easily, because strain concentrates around these inclusions and causes them to crack.[6]

Obviously, a delicate balance is needed to obtain the highest possible toughness in weld metals, because the particles are needed for the nucleation of acicular ferrite, which hinders cleavage fracture; at the same time however the particles induce cleavage. To explain the beneficial effect of fine grains, it is assumed that the carbides become thinner with smaller grains. This argument is not applicable to weld metals. Instead, a high content of fine grains means that there are less coarse grains in which the cleavage cracks can nucleate. However, this should mean that brittle fracture in weld metals is *nucleation controlled* rather than propagation controlled, as for the base metal.

With this model, it is predicted that a weld metal with high oxygen content should have lower fracture toughness, both in the upper shelf region and in a higher transition temperature. Figure 5.24 shows an example of SAW metals, made with fluxes that have various degrees of basicity. Two types of weld metals have been used, one with high hardenability and one with lower hardenability (giving different yield strengths). By changing the basicity of the fluxes, the oxygen content was varied. Simultaneously, the aluminum and titanium (but no other elements) contents varied; thus the hardenability within the same type of weld metal was essentially constant. As can be seen, the impact toughness varied with both strength level and oxygen content. The upper shelf level was significantly affected, but the transition temperature was also influenced by the oxygen content.

Thus, the general microstructure and the inclusions are the two basic factors determining fracture toughness. As with the base metal HAZ, there are some additional factors that cause embrittlement of the weld metal: segregated microphases, nitrogen, and impurity elements. Segregated bands of microphases appear in weld metals with too high a manganese content. The last liquid to solidify may contain so much manganese that these areas form microphases in the final microstructure. The microphases can be bainite, martensite, or retained austenite. All promote low fracture toughness, even the retained austenite, which can transform to untempered martensite during testing. The high strain rates can induce this transformation, especially during impact testing. The more or less continuous paths of brittle material thus formed can lead to a decreasing fracture toughness, although the amount of acicular ferrite may increase (Figure 5.25).

Another well-known element that can cause embrittlement is nitrogen. Nitrogen can be picked up from the surrounding air due to poor protection of

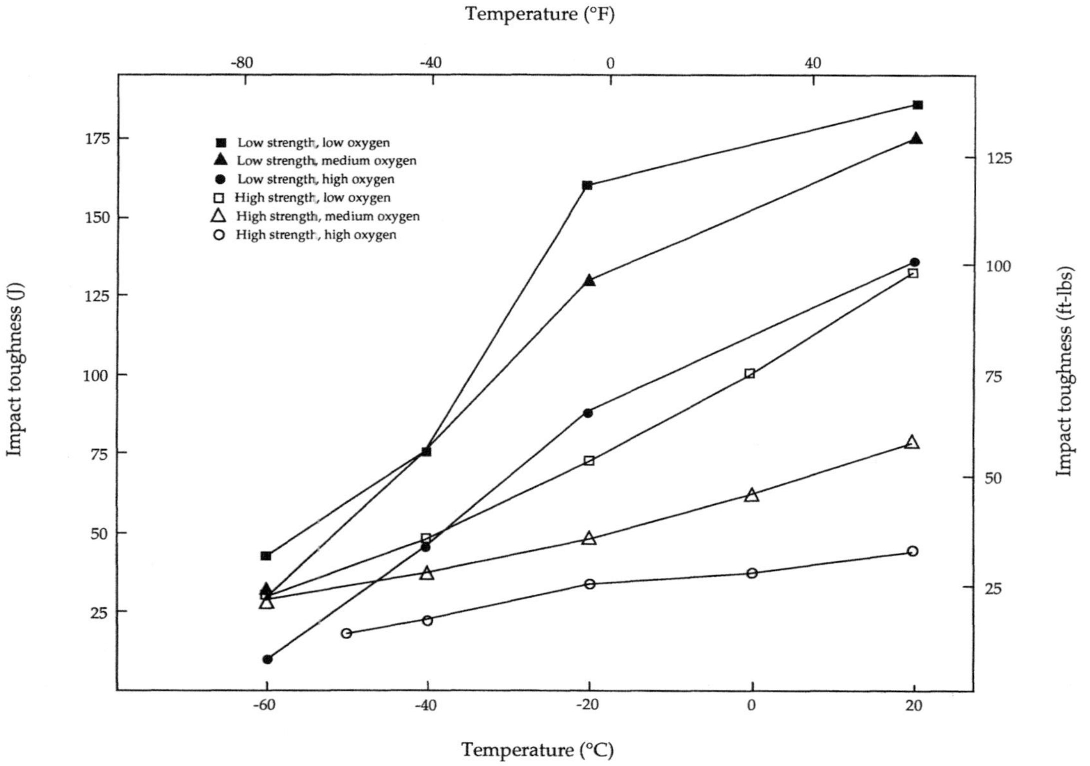

FIGURE 5.24. The variation in impact toughness of all-weld metal samples for a high hardenability alloy (yield strength 700 MPa) and an alloy with moderate strength (yield strength 450 MPa). Different fluxes have resulted in variation in oxygen content. Oxygen influences both upper shelf energies as well as the transition temperature.

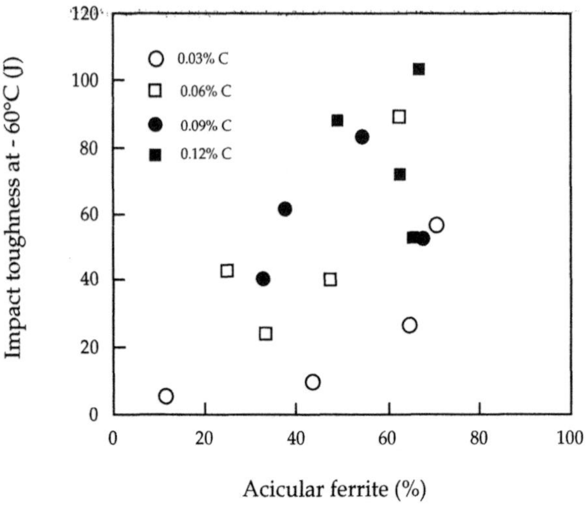

FIGURE 5.25. Variation of impact toughness with acicular ferrite content. The initial improvement of toughness is turned to a decrease of around 70% acicular ferrite due to the formation of continuous layers of microphases. (From Svensson, L.-E. and Gretoft, B., *Weld. Res. Suppl.*, December, 454-s, 1990. With permission.)

the arc and the weld pool, but also from the base metal if it is alloyed with nitrogen, through dilution. The exact mechanism by which nitrogen embrittles weld metals is not clear. A rule of thumb is that for basic types of weld metals, intended to have good impact properties at –40°C (–40°F), more than 100 ppm nitrogen cannot be accepted. For every 10-ppm increase in nitrogen, the transition temperature increases 2 to 3°C.

Impurity elements naturally decrease toughness, just as for the base material. Sulfur and phosphorus are the most common impurities. In weld metals for critical applications, the concentration of these elements is now in general kept below 0.010 wt%. However, the improvement in toughness from reduction of these elements has not been quantified at these low levels. Other impurity elements that can significantly decrease the toughness are antimony, tin, and arsenic. The effect of antimony on the impact toughness is shown in Figure 5.26, where the large effect on toughness of very small additions can be seen.

Another problem associated with impurity elements is the occurrence of intergranular fracture, which can be found after postweld heat treatment (e.g., stress relieving). It is most common when the heat treatment has been made at relatively low temperatures, between 500 to 600°C (900 to 1100°F). It happens because impurity elements segregate to the grain boundaries, decreasing the cohesion and promoting easy fracture there. The natural way to avoid this type of embrittlement is to decrease the impurity element content. The maximum permissible content depends on the alloying content of the weld metal. In general phosphorus and sulfur contents below 0.010 wt% are sufficient, pro-

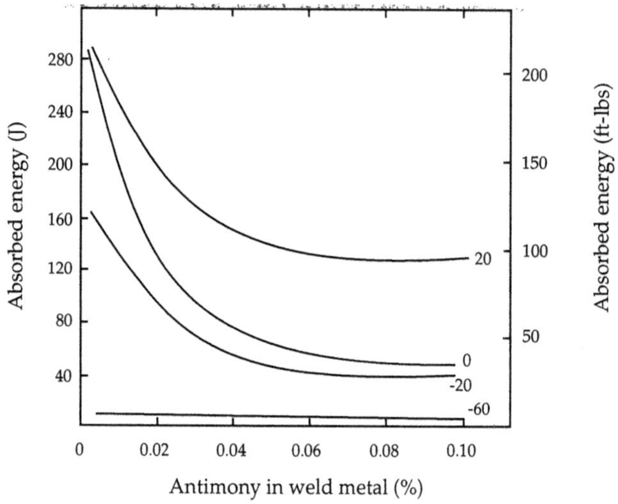

FIGURE 5.26. The effect of antimony on the impact toughness. (From Almquist, G., Gretoft, B., Svensson, L.-E., and Wittung, L., *Proc. Int. Conf. Effects of Residual, Impurity and Microalloying Elements on Weldability and Weld Properties,* The Welding Institute, London, 1983, paper 21. With permission.)

vided that arsenic, tin, and antimony are kept below 0.020 wt%. However, in certain Ti-B-alloyed weld metals, as well as in Cr-Mo-Ni- alloyed weld metals, the phosphorus content in particular should be decreased even further.

This type of embrittlement is called reversible temper embrittlement, because good toughness can be restored by an additional heat treatment at around 600 to 650°C (1100 to 1200°F), whereby the impurity elements diffuse away from the grain boundaries. It is also possible to prevent segregation by adding elements that have positive interaction energy with the impurities, preventing them from segregating. Molybdenum is often used for this purpose. Also, carbon has a positive effect on phosphorus segregation.

The segregation of impurity elements to the grain boundaries is studied using surface-sensitive analytical instruments such as Auger electron spectroscopy or ESCA (electron spectroscopy for chemical analysis). With these methods a monolayer of atoms on a fracture surface, for example, can be detected. However, for nonalloy and low-alloy steels, it is usually necessary to fracture the specimen in a vacuum chamber in order to avoid oxidation of the surfaces. Thus, for investigation of fracture surfaces from mechanical test pieces or from cracked components, these methods generally are of little help.

Just as for the base metal, various zones in the weld metal HAZ have different toughness properties. The fine-grained zone is considered to have the highest toughness, due to its fine grain size, and the as-deposited structure the lowest toughness. Contrary to the HAZ in the base metal, the partially transformed zone is usually not particularly susceptible to low toughness, nor is the coarse-grained zone. Simulation experiments by Chen et al.[15] indicated that the lowest toughness actually was found for specimens reheated to ca. 700°C (1300°F), but the metallurgical reason for this is not known. Thus, to have a high toughness, the welding procedure should be designed so that as little as-deposited structure as possible is found in the weld metal. The influence of the as-deposited regions on the toughness can be illustrated by the following example.

Weld metals having a low alloying content generally show a larger difference in toughness between the as-deposited and the reheated weld metal than weld metals with, say, 1.5 wt% manganese. Impact toughness is mainly determined by the type of microstructure that appears in the central part of the specimen. This is due to the fact that the triaxial state of stress is highest in the central part of the bar, and thus with a susceptible microstructure, brittle fracture easily starts there. This is illustrated in Figure 5.27. The top part of the figure shows a weld metal with a relatively lean chemical analysis. The left part of the figure shows drawings of impact bars, where the streaked areas represent as-deposited regions. The vertical line indicates the position of the notch. The impact bars have been selected from welds made with SAW, with three different current levels: 450, 550, and 650 A. To the right, the result of the impact testing is shown. As can be seen, the impact toughness is very sensitive to the presence of as-deposited regions in the central part of the impact bars, resulting in the weld metal made with 450 A having a lower transition temperature. With higher alloying contents (shown in the lower part of the figure) the difference in toughness between the as-deposited and the reheated areas diminishes, and thus, the influence of the notch position relative to as-deposited regions is less.

Nevertheless, scatter in impact toughness data can be related to variations in the position of the notch relative to the various zones on the weld metal. The scatter in toughness over time during a project, using the same products, has often been a concern to fabricators. It can often be related to the placement of the notch and not to any embrittlement of the weld metal. As long as the toughness values stay within acceptable limits, this scatter in toughness should not be considered alarming. This reason for scatter is naturally much more common in manually made welds.

In one special case, there is a negative influence of multipass welding and this relates to the presence of carbide-forming elements. Most of the alloying elements in a weld metal are added to increase hardenability, i.e., to decrease the amount of allotriomorphic ferrite and increase the amount of acicular ferrite. Molybdenum (and in some odd cases chromium) is the only element deliberately added, having the dual role of promoting acicular ferrite and also being a carbide former. In multipass welding, the amount of carbides (or carbonitrides) is so low that it has no significant effect on the toughness. However, in two-pass welding, it was found that the impact toughness decreased as a result of precipitation.[16] In this case, molybdenum was added

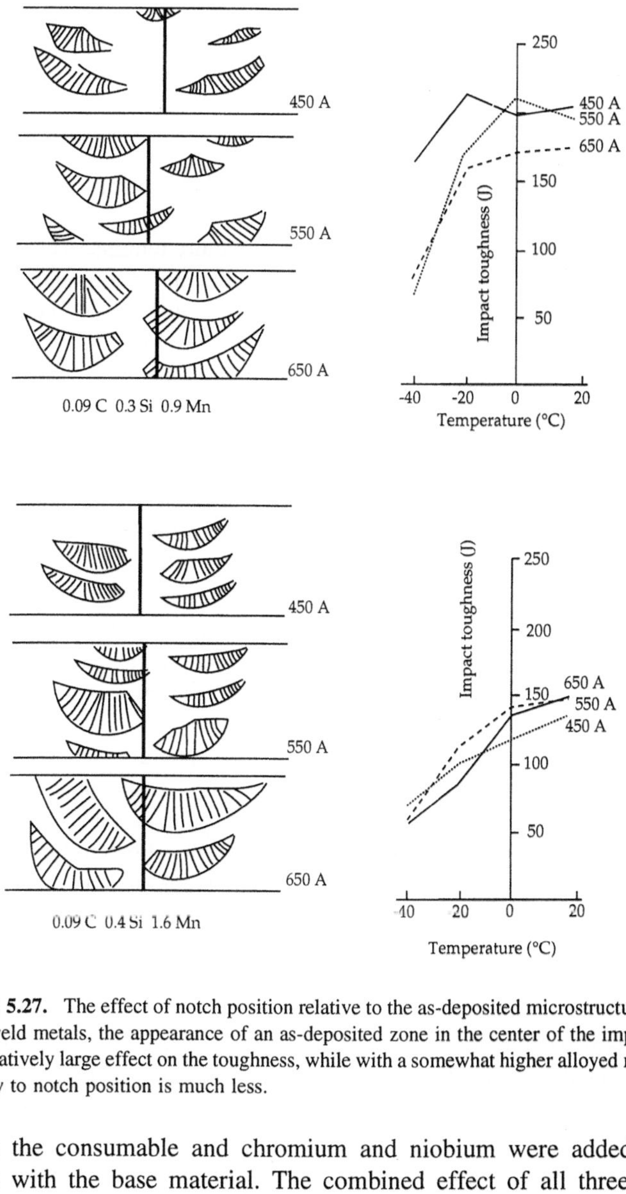

FIGURE 5.27. The effect of notch position relative to the as-deposited microstructure. For lean alloyed weld metals, the appearance of an as-deposited zone in the center of the impact bar can have a relatively large effect on the toughness, while with a somewhat higher alloyed material, the sensitivity to notch position is much less.

through the consumable and chromium and niobium were added through dilution with the base material. The combined effect of all three carbide-forming elements led to the precipitation of so many particles that the toughness was affected. The composition of the particles were determined using field-ion microscopy and atom probe microanalysis. They were found to be of M_2X type, where M = Cr, Mo, Nb and X = C, N. The microalloying elements niobium and vanadium are in general regarded as harmful with respect to toughness, although Dolby,[17,18] when reviewing the literature, found indications that low levels of either vanadium or niobium could favor acicular ferrite formation during cooling. Carbonitrides are not formed in the as-deposited weld metal if only small concentrations of the carbide-forming elements are added. However, with high concentrations (of the order of 0.1 wt%) interphase precipitation of niobium carbides, but not vanadium carbides, has been found. Even if no or very little precipitation occurs during multipass welding, heat treatments such as stress relieving will certainly enhance the precipitation and lead to embrittlement.

The discussion so far has mainly dealt with fracture toughness as measured by impact testing. Metallurgically, the same factors are of importance during fracture mechanics testing. As discussed earlier, it is difficult to make a direct comparison between impact and fracture mechanics tests. This is because factors that do not easily show up in impact toughness specimens can influence the CTOD properties. Some factors that have been found to influence the CTOD properties are discussed below.

When welding, it is of utmost importance to grind out the first root beads because severe embrittlement can occur there. Nitrogen pickup due to the use of thin electrodes and the associated inferior gas protection has sometimes been observed. The welder may also be tempted to use too long an arc, increasing the risk of air entrapment. Distortion of the plates during welding always occurs, although strongbacks are welded to minimize movement. The distortion causes deformation of the weld metal. Deformation together with nitrogen can cause strain aging embrittlement and it is therefore necessary to carefully remove the root bead.

For K-joints, where the root area is close to the center of the plate, the effect of dilution is more pronounced than in V-joints. As with impact toughness testing, the highest triaxial stress occurs in the plate center and any embrittlement in this area immediately results in low toughness. Embrittlement that may arise from dilution effects is due to increased carbon content, increased amounts of microalloying elements, and increasing amounts of aluminum. Excessive carbon manifests itself in high levels of microphases, while microalloying elements give rise to precipitation. Excessive aluminum, finally, can change the type and size distribution of particles, thereby reducing the amount of acicular ferrite. It has also been found that in continuously cast steels a segregation band exists in the center of the plate, containing larger amounts of impurities. High dilution of the base plate into the weld pool gives increased risk for low toughness.

In a recent study[19] it was shown that the CTOD test results from a 700 MPa (100,000 psi) yield strength welded steel could be described by a Weibull distribution with three parameters:

$$F(\delta) = 1 - \exp[-\{(\delta - \delta_a)/\beta\}^{\alpha}] \tag{5.16}$$

where α is called a shape parameter, β is a scale parameter, and δ_a is a shift parameter corresponding to the lowest CTOD value. By letting $z = \delta - \delta_a$ and

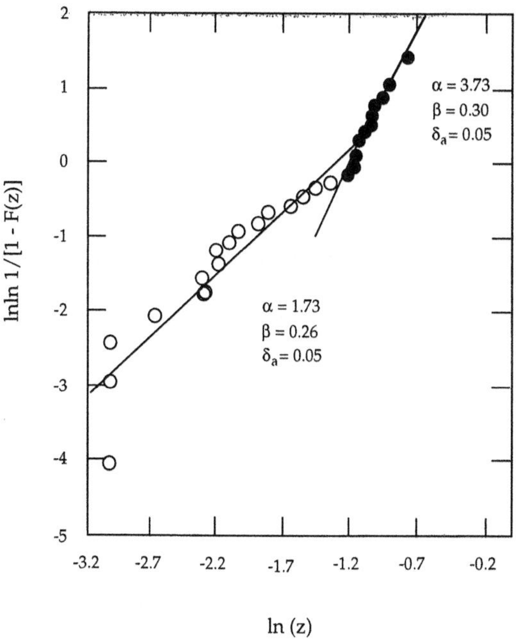

FIGURE 5.28. Plot of the Weibull distribution against the CTOD test results in a welded 700-MPa steel. The results fall into two regimes, each described by a set of values of parameters α, β, and δ_a. The transition point from one regime to the other is $\delta = 0.34$ mm. The asymptotic lowest CTOD value is 0.05 mm. (From Zhou Zhiliang, Lic thesis, The Royal Institute of Technology, Stockholm, Sweden. With permission.)

taking the logarithm of the equation, a straight line between lnln $1/(1 - F(z))$ and $\alpha(\ln z - \ln \beta)$ is obtained. A plot of this kind, with experimental values, is shown in Figure 5.28. As can be seen, the results fall into two groups, each having its own parameter values. The scale parameter, β, is fairly similar between the two groups, while the shape parameter differs significantly. The results were explained by the higher values being due to a ductile mechanism both for initiation and crack propagation, while the lower values were found when the crack propagated in a brittle manner.

REFERENCES

1. **Knott, J. F.,** *Fundamentals of Fracture Mechanics,* Butterworths, London, 1973.
2. **Akselsen, O. M., Rørvik, G., Onsøien, M. I., and Grong, Ø.,** Assessment and prediction of HAZ tensile properties of high-strength steels, *Weld. Res. Suppl.,* September, 356-s, 1989.
3. **Akselsen, O. M. and Rørvik, G.,** Tensile properties of heat affected zone of medium strength low carbon, C-Mn and 2.25Cr-1Mo steels, *Mater. Sci. Technol.,* 6(April), 383, 1990.
4. **Düren, C.,** Formulae for Calculating the Maximum Hardness in the Heat-Affected Zone of Welded Joints, IIW Doc. XI-1437-86, International Institute of Welding, London, 1986.

5. **Curry, D. C. and Knott, J. F.,** *Met. Sci.,* 12, 511, 1978.
6. **Tweed, J. H. and Knott, J. F.,** Micromechanisms of failure in C-Mn weld metals, *Acta Metall.,* 35(7), 1401, 1987.
7. **Harrison, P. L. and Hart, P. H. M.,** Influences of steel composition and welding procedure on the HAZ toughness of thick section structural steels, in *Proc. 8th Int. Conf. Offshore Mechanics and Arctic Engineering,* The Hague, The Netherlands, March 19 to 23, 1989.
8. **Evans, G. M.,** The effect of carbon on the microstructure and properties of C-Mn all-weld metal deposits, *Weld. J.,* 62(11), 313, 1983.
9. **Evans, G. M.,** Effect of silicon on the microstructure and properties of C-Mn all-weld-metal deposits, *Met. Constr.,* July, 438R, 1986.
10. **Evans, G. M.,** The effect of molybdenum on the microstructure and properties of C-Mn all-weld metal deposits, *Joining Mater.,* 1(5), 239, 1988.
11. **Evans, G. M.,** The effect of chromium on the microstructure and properties of C-Mn all-weld metal deposits, *Weld. Met. Fabr.,* 57(7), 346, 1989.
12. **Evans, G. M.,** The effect of nickel on the microstructure and properties of C-Mn all-weld metal deposits, *Oerlikon Schweissmitt.,* 48(122), 18, 1989.
13. **Es-Souni, M., Beaven, P. A., and Evans, G. M.,** The Effect of Copper on the Microstructure and Properties of C-Mn All-Weld Metal Deposits, IIW Doc. IIA-768-89, International Institute of Welding, London, 1989.
14. **McRobie, D. E. and Knott, J. F.,** Effects of strain and strain aging on fracture toughness of C-Mn weld metal, *Mater. Sci. Technol.,* 1(May), 357, 1985.
15. **Chen, J. H., Wang, G. Z., Wang, Z., Zhu, L., and Gao, Y. Y.,** Further study on the scattering of the local fracture stress and allied toughness value, *Metall. Trans. A,* 22A(October), 2287, 1991.
16. **Svensson, L.-E. and Henjered, A.,** Microanalysis of fine precipitates in a two-pass C-Mn submerged arc weld metal, *Mater. Sci. Technol.,* 1(December), 1094, 1985.
17. **Dolby, R. E.,** The influence of niobium on the microstructure and toughness of ferritic weld metal — a review, *Met. Constr.,* 13(11), 699, 1981.
18. **Dolby, R. E.,** Review of Work on the Influence of Vanadium on the Microstructure and Toughness of Ferritic Weld Metals, IIW Doc. IX-1213-81, International Institute of Welding, London, 1981.
19. **Zhou Zhiliang,** CTOD Toughness of 700 MPa Yield Strength Steel HAZ and Weld Metal, Lic. thesis, Paper C, The Royal Institute of Technology, Stockholm, Sweden, 1992.

Chapter 6

CONTROL OF MICROSTRUCTURE AND PROPERTIES

6.1. INTRODUCTION

The theory presented in the previous chapters will now be used to more closely examine some welded joints in an attempt to deduce the microstructures and properties that are likely to appear. This is done by looking at some specific examples and analyzing the thermal cycles and the choice of base material and consumables. The risks of cracking will also be assessed. We begin by focusing on the thermal cycle.

6.2. PREDICTIONS FROM THE THERMAL CYCLE

Two typical welding processes are considered to illustrate the problem. The first represents the use of relatively high heat input welding for thin plates, while the second relates to low heat input welding in relatively thick plates. The relevant equations were presented in Section 1.7.

The joint configurations used are shown in Figure 6.1. In the first case the plate thickness is 12.5 mm, and the welding process is single-wire submerged arc welding (SAW). The configuration shown in Figure 6.1, an I-joint, is used when the mechanical properties demands are moderate. If better mechanical properties are required, different variants of Y-joints are used. In the second case gas-metal arc welding (GMAW) is used for joining a 35-mm-thick plate. Here, a V-joint is assumed. This joint type is used when the welding can only be made from one side. Otherwise, it is common to use X-joints. However, for the analysis made here, the exact choice of joint geometry is irrelevant. A first question may be how accurately the positions of the isotherms can be found, due to differences in the values of the physical constants between different materials. This will now be examined by looking at three different steels.

It is necessary to determine whether the welding conditions will lead to two- or three-dimensional cooling conditions. As pointed out in Section 1.7, the heat flow equations can be simplified considerably if it is assumed that the welding speed is so high that the heat flow in the direction of welding can be neglected. This means that the heat flow will be either one-dimensional (in thin plates, where heat is only flowing sideways) or two-dimensional (in thick plates, where the heat flow is directed both downward and sideways).

To quickly determine which heat flow mode operates, the diagram of Myhr and Grong, shown in Figure 1.39 and reproduced in Figure 6.2, is used. The dimensionless parameters are $\delta = vd/2\kappa$ and θ_p/n. Here, θ_p is the normalized peak temperature $(T_p - T_0)/(T_m - T_0)$, T_p is the peak temperature, T_m is the melting temperature, T_0 is the preheat temperature, and $n = (qv)/(4\pi\kappa^2\rho c(T_m - T_0))$.

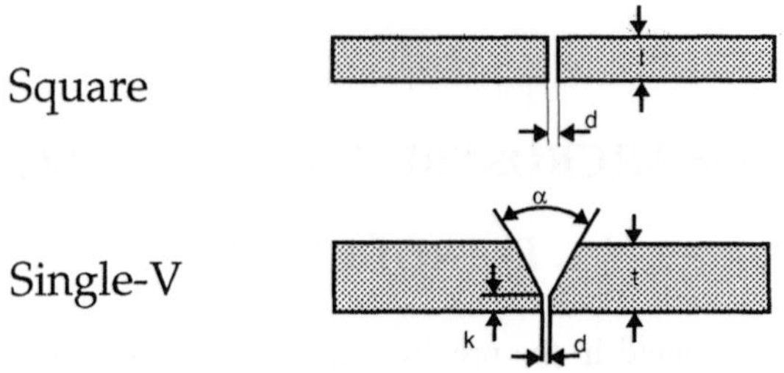

FIGURE 6.1. The joint configurations used for the two case studies. An I-joint is often used in SAW of relatively thin plates, when the demands on mechanical properties (especially toughness) are moderate. The second joint configuration is a 60° V-joint, which is relatively common when welding thicker plates.

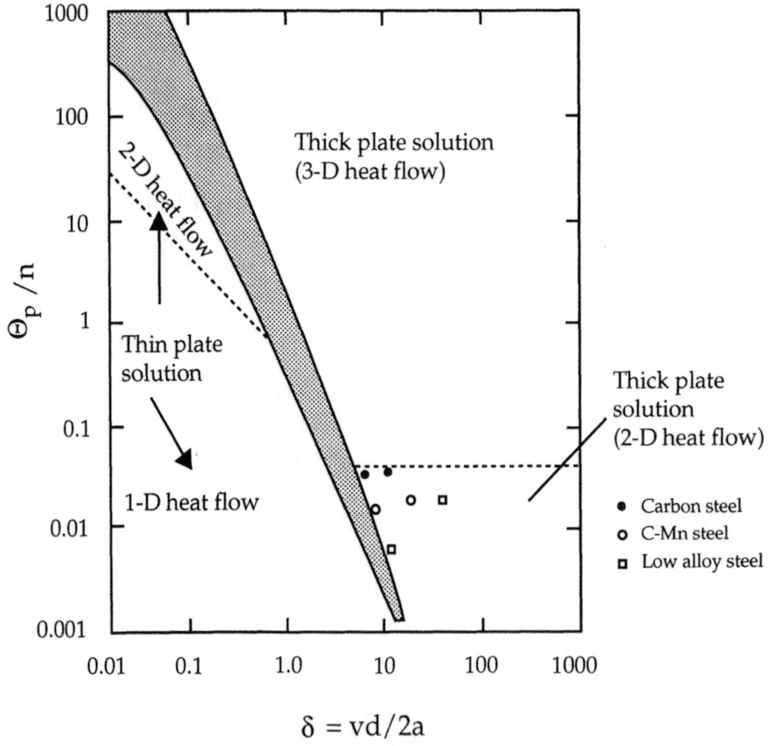

FIGURE 6.2. Heat flow map, showing the dominant modes of heat flow. The points indicated show the calculated values for SAW and GMAW of the three different kind of steels. The dominant mode is the thick-plate solution, two-dimensional heat flow.

TABLE 6.1
Values of the Physical Constants

Alloy	κ (mm^2/s)	c(J/°C g)	λ (W/mm) (°C)	ρ (g/mm^3)
Ordinary carbon steel	8	6.1×10^{-7}	0.038	7800
C-Mn steel	4.6	7.2×10^{-7}	0.026	7800
Low-alloy steel	3	8.1×10^{-7}	0.019	7800

TABLE 6.2
Welding Conditions for Two Cases

Process	Joint	Voltage (V)	Current (A)	Welding speed (mm/s)	Preheat temp (°C)
SAW	I	30	600	6.8	25
GMAW (root bead)	V	24	180	4.5	150
GMAW (fill beads)	V	30	300	4.5	150

The three different steels considered are a plain carbon steel, a C-Mn steel, and one low-alloyed steel. The values of the relevant physical constants are given in Table 6.1. The welding conditions are summarized in Table 6.2.

Figure 6.2 gives the results of the calculations for the three steels and the two welding conditions, for a peak temperature of 1300°C (2350°F). As can be seen, all points fall in the area of thick-plate solution, two-dimensional heat flow. The equation used to calculate the positions of the isotherms of different peak temperatures is then the same as Equation 1.13:

$$r_p = (2/\pi e)^{1/2}\ [(q'/v)/(\rho c(T_p - T_0))]^{1/2} \tag{6.1}$$

The calculated positions of the isotherms for the SAW in an ordinary carbon steel are shown in Figure 6.3. It is assumed that the isotherms are semicircular in shape. This is a good approximation for the isotherms corresponding to temperatures some distance away from the fusion line. However, the fusion line itself often deviates from the ideal shape near the top side of the plate. A more common shape of the fusion line is indicated in Figure 6.3a.

Figure 6.3b shows the isotherms corresponding to three temperatures (1500, 1100, and 700°C; 2700, 2000, and 1300°F) for the three different steels. As can be seen, the differences are relatively minor (1 to 2 mm), but the limitations on how accurately the isotherms can be calculated must always be noted. The exact position of the isotherms is further affected by the temperature dependence of the physical constants.

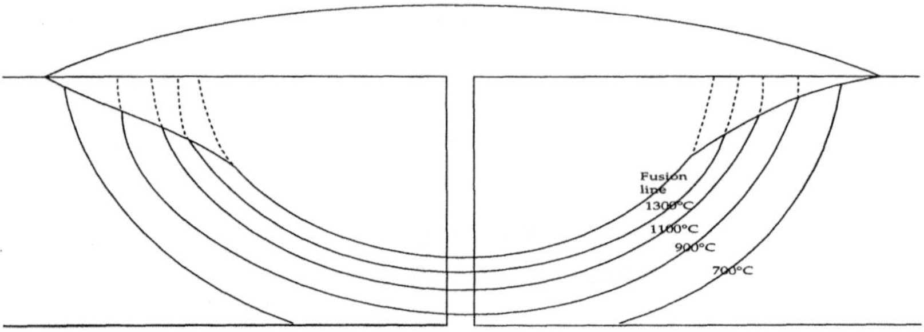

a

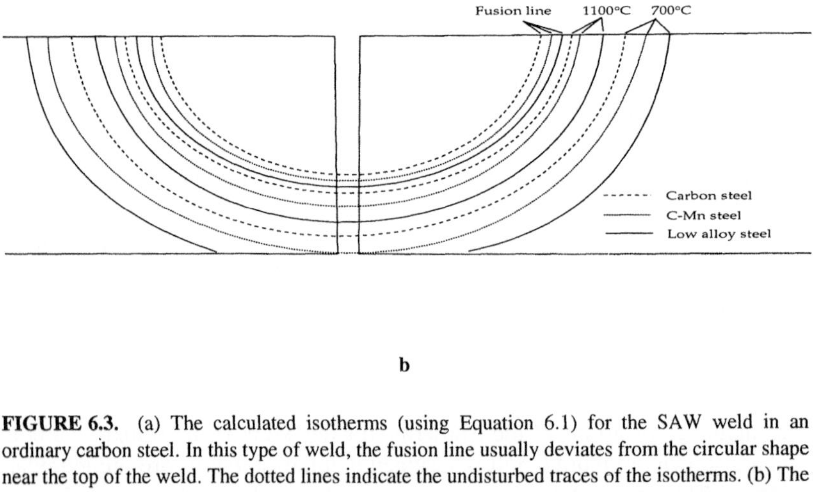

b

FIGURE 6.3. (a) The calculated isotherms (using Equation 6.1) for the SAW weld in an ordinary carbon steel. In this type of weld, the fusion line usually deviates from the circular shape near the top of the weld. The dotted lines indicate the undisturbed traces of the isotherms. (b) The isotherms corresponding to three temperatures (1500, 1100, and 700°C) (2700, 2000, and 1300°F) for three different steels. A circular shape of the fusion line was assumed. The carbon and the C-Mn steels have fairly close isotherms, while the low-alloy steel deviates significantly from the other two.

When the approximate position of an isotherm has been determined, the thermal cycle in a specific point can be determined, using Equation 1.11

$$T = T_0 + (q'/v)/(2\pi\lambda t)\exp(-b/4\kappa t) \qquad (6.2)$$

where $b = y^2 + z^2$.

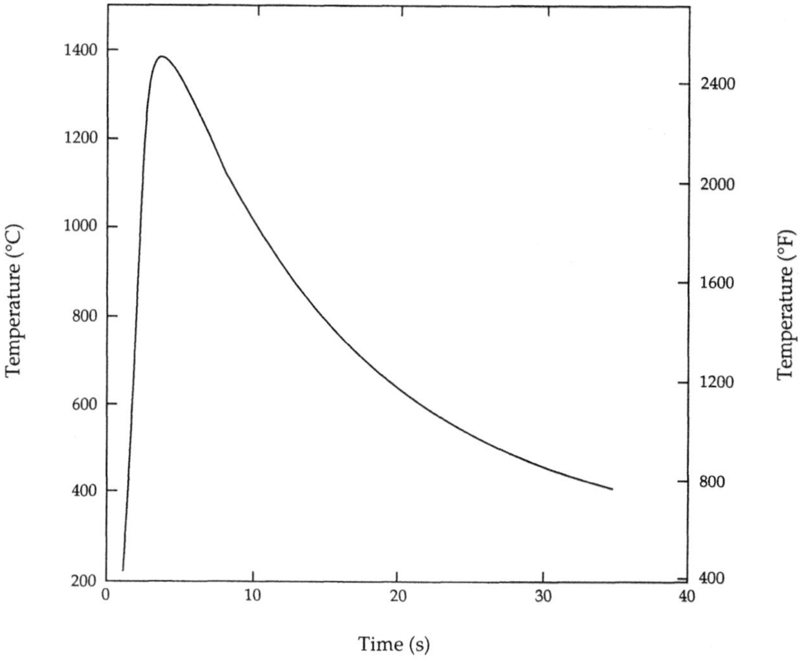

FIGURE 6.4. The calculated thermal cycle at $r = 9$ mm (corresponding to a peak temperature of 1300°C, 2350°F) for a SAW C-Mn steel (using Equation 6.2 and the welding conditions from Table 6.2).

Taking the data for a C-Mn steel and analyzing the point $r = 9$ mm (corresponding to a peak temperature of 1300°C, 2350°F) gives the thermal cycle shown in Figure 6.4. The cooling time from 800 to 500°C can then be calculated using Equation 6.3, which is the same as Equation 1.15:

$$\Delta t_{8/5} = (q'/v)/(2\pi\lambda)[1/(500 - T_0) - 1/(800 - T_0)] \qquad (6.3)$$

giving $\Delta t_{8/5}$ as 12.5 s. The cooling time will vary from 8.6 s in an ordinary carbon steel to 17.1 s in a low-alloy steel. This of course is a relatively large variation in cooling time and can significantly alter the microstructure and properties of the heat-affected zone (HAZ).

The thick-plate solution with two-dimensional heat flow is also applicable in the second joint. In the root bead $\Delta t_{8/5}$ can be calculated to 6 s, while it is 12 s for the filling passes (for a C-Mn steel). The heat input rate is only about 0.7 kJ/mm in the root run and about 1.5 kJ/mm for the other runs. The thermal cycles for the root and fill runs are shown in Figure 6.5.

From Figure 6.1, the circumstances under which one-dimensional heat flow exists in steel welds can be speculated. The value of the δ-parameter

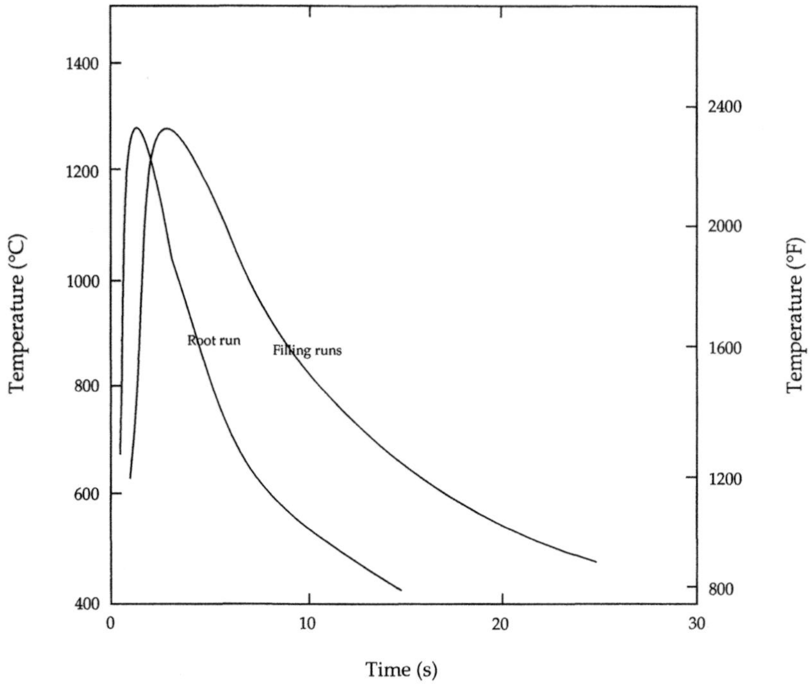

FIGURE 6.5. The calculated thermal cycles for the root and fill runs (peak temperature 1300°C, 2350°F) for GMAW C-Mn steel. The welding parameters are given in Table 6.2.

should be significantly less than 10. Taking $\delta = 2$ as a reasonable value, then, because v often is around 4 mm/s or above, the plate thickness (in mm) will numerically be of the same order as κ (in mm^2/s), i.e., between 2 and 8 mm. Because thin plates are welded with a lower heat input, the value of θ_p/n will be high, and although the value of δ is low, it is possible that the welding conditions still will differ from the one-dimensional heat flow area.

Using these fairly simple calculations, which can be made easily on a programmable pocket calculator, a sense of the thermal cycle the material has experienced can be gained. However, it must be stressed that these values are only for guidance, because

- The shape of the weld pool is dependent upon the current and voltage balance; thus calibration against a weld made with the actual procedure should be made.
- The values of the physical constants vary with temperature and material.

6.3. METALLURGICAL EFFECTS

Once the thermal cycle for a certain procedure has been determined as closely as possible, the metallurgical reactions can be assessed. To exemplify the analysis, three steels of different qualities will be chosen and welded according to two different procedures. The selection of consumables will also be discussed, in order to assess the reactions in the weld metal. The metallurgical features that will be discussed are microstructure, mechanical properties, and defects. The following three steels are selected:

1. An ordinary line pipe steel quality, according to API X-60 specification, produced by a thermomechanical controlled processing (TMCP) rolling procedure
2. A normalized, fine-grain-treated C-Mn steel
3. A titanium-treated TMCP steel

It is emphasized that these steels are not interchangable in practice. For the line pipe application a steel of the first type mentioned above is naturally selected, while the other steel types are used in other structural applications. The third steel has a composition which is typical for TMCP steels in larger thicknesses. The steels are selected to illustrate how the selection of steels and consumables can be analyzed and not how they are applied in practical constructions. The chemical composition and mechanical properties of the steels are given in Table 6.3.

The steels may not be directly comparable, because the normalized steel has a lower yield strength and perhaps should require a thicker plate in its construction. The steels are assumed to be of good quality (i.e., having low impurity content, although the contents of arsenic, tin, and antimony are not given).

6.3.1. HIGH HEAT INPUT WELDING

6.3.1.1. Heat-Affected Zone Effects

Two welding procedures will be analyzed: one using high heat input, resulting in a slow cooling, and one with a fairly moderate heat input, resulting in a relatively rapid cooling. As shown in Section 6.2, two-dimensional heat flow is often the most common mode for heat transport. This means that the cooling time of a weld is independent of plate thickness. The first welding procedure assumed here is SAW of a 25-mm-thick plate, using three electrodes, which gives in total a heat input rate of 4.5 kJ/mm (115 kJ/in.). $\Delta t_{8/5}$ will then be around 22 s.

Because the thermal cycle in the HAZ is known, the grain growth behavior can be examined. Following the outline of Section 3.2, the austenite grain size in a steel without titanium can be found from Figure 3.8. There is a certain

TABLE 6.3
Composition (wt%) and Mechanical Properties of Steels (E_w and P_{cm} Calculated According to Equations 1.8 and 1.9)

Steel	C	Si	Mn	P	S	Nb	V	Ti	Ni	Al	Mo
X-60	0.06	0.08	1.47	0.010	0.003	0.015	0.005	0.015	0.37	0.025	0.12
Normalized	0.17	0.30	1.45	0.015	0.011	0.002	0.025	0.005	—	0.025	—
TMCP	0.10	0.30	1.24	0.009	0.005	0.025	0.004	0.020	—	0.002	—

Steel	R_{eL} (MPa)	R_m (MPa)	KV (J)/–40°C	E_w	P_{cm}
X-60	420	500	40	0.36	0.15
Normalized	360	450	27	0.42	0.26
TMCP	420	550	40	0.31	0.17

variation from steel to steel, mainly due to the influence of the chemical composition on the activation energy. However, this is neglected. Thus for the second steel, Figure 3.8 shows that an austenite grain size of ca. 300 μm is achieved just beside the fusion line, ca. 150 μm at a peak temperature of 1300°C (2350°F) and ca. 50 μm at 1100°C (2000°F). The lower temperature of the coarse-grained region of the HAZ is often considered to be 1100°C (2000°F). For the titanium-stabilized steels, Figure 3.13 is applicable. At the fusion line the austenite grain size is ca. 100 μm, at 1300°C (2350°F) peak temperature about 50 μm, and at 1100°C (2000°F) about 30 μm. Thus, at low peak temperatures there is no significant benefit of microalloying with titanium.

The next step is to assess the likely microstructures that will appear. This is most correctly made using a continuous cooling transformation (CCT) diagram. However, such diagrams must be obtained experimentally and are seldom at hand. From a time-temperature transformation (TTT) diagram, which can be calculated using the method proposed by Bhadeshia,[1] a first check can be made, although the transformation described by these diagrams is only for isothermal conditions. TTT diagrams for the three steels are shown in Figure 6.6. It should be noted that it is only the start of the transformation that is calculated. This is almost independent of austenite grain size and thus no influence on the diagrams is seen from the differences in austenite grain size resulting from the addition of titanium. The following characteristics may be noted (in the approximation in which isothermal diagrams are used):

- The nose of the diffusional transformation curve appears at approximately 700°C for all steels.
- In steels 1 and 2 the nose appears at 4 s, while in steel 3 it appears at 1.5 s.
- The shear transformation curve is moved slightly to the left in steel 2 compared to steel 3.
- The effect of the higher carbon content of steel 2 is only to lower the M_s temperature. The position of the transformation curves is hardly affected.

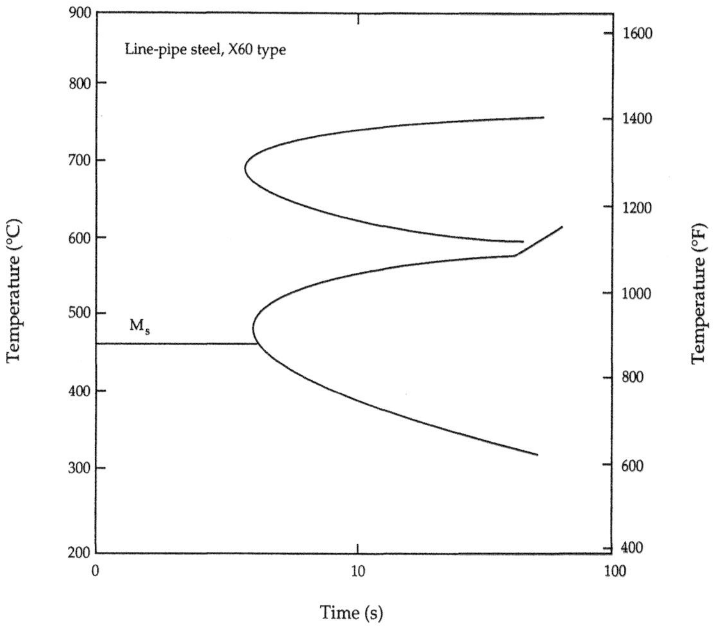

a

FIGURE 6.6. Calculated TTT diagrams for the three steels presented in Table 6.3: (a) X-60 line pipe steel, (b) normalized steel, and (c) TMCP steel. The calculations were made using the method of Bhadeshia.[1] Steels a and b are very similar, except for the M_s temperature. Steel c, having a lower alloying content, has the C-curve for diffusional transformation more to the left, meaning that allotriomorphic ferrite more easily forms in this steel. The M_s temperature is on the same level as for steel a, due to the low carbon content in these steels.

What consequences will this have on the microstructure? With relatively slow cooling, it is likely that some allotriomorphic ferrite is formed in all the steels, but most probably in steel 3. However, the main part of the microstructure will be lath ferrite. In all three steels the laths are most likely a mixture of Widmanstätten side plates and bainite. The higher carbon content of steel 2 will lead to a higher hardness of the bainite due to an increased proportion of carbides.

The TMCP steels will have a much finer grain size in the coarse-grained region, meaning that the chance of forming allotriomorphic ferrite is higher. Even if the starting temperature of the transformation is independent of austenite grain size, the total amount naturally is affected. Smaller austenite grains means a higher density of nucleation sites for grain boundary ferrite, leading to a higher volume fraction of allotriomorphic ferrite. Not only is the allotriomorphic ferrite affected, but laths that appear will also be finer in the titanium-alloyed steels. Thus, the normalized steel will be harder due to the higher carbon content and also more brittle due to the presence of coarser laths. On the other hand, the allotriomorphic ferrite can also induce brittleness, but

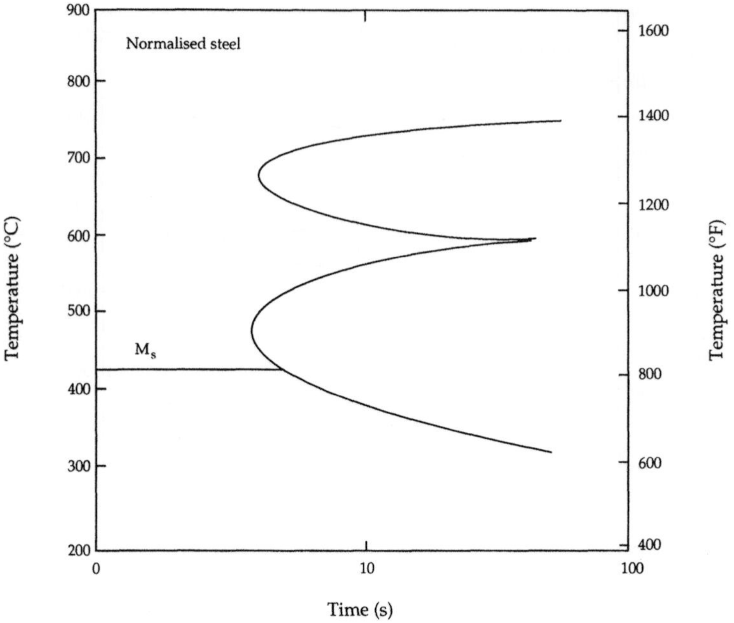

FIGURE 6.6.b

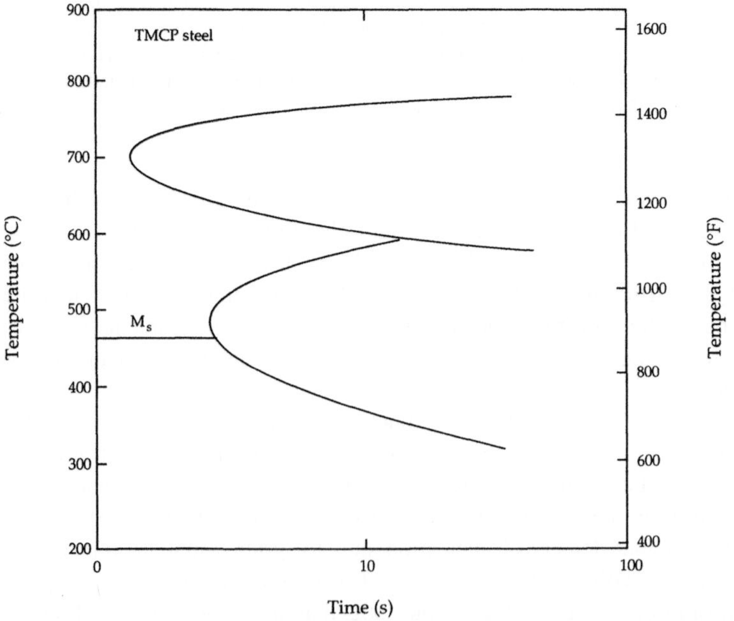

FIGURE 6.6.c

because it is softer, the overall effect is likely to be in favor of the titanium-stabilized low carbon content steels.

In the regions away from the fusion line the austenite grain size will be smaller in all steels, enhancing the probability of allotriomorphic ferrite formation. Because there is practically no difference in austenite grain size between the steels here, the microstructures will be fairly similar.

In summary, this means that the lower carbon content steels will have a softer HAZ than steels with a higher carbon content. There will not be any ferrite grain refining advantages associated with this higher hardness; thus toughness of the high carbon content steel is likely to be lower. Any difference in toughness between 0.1 wt% carbon and 0.06 wt% carbon is difficult to judge. There are other factors here that also must be considered, such as differences in manganese and nickel content.

The maximum hardness of the three steels can be calculated according to the BL 70 formula of Suzuki. A common specification in offshore industry is a maximum hardness of 248 HV, to avoid the risk of stress corrosion cracking. The two low-carbon steels easily fulfill this requirement for this procedure, having calculated hardnesses of 191 (TMCP) and 205 (X-60) HV. The normalized steel has a calculated hardness of 248 HV, which is exactly the limit of the specification.

6.3.1.2. The Weld Metal

The choice of weld metal is dependent on several factors:

- The requirements for mechanical properties must naturally be met. In welds for offshore use these are typically 40 J (30 ft-lb) at –40°C (–40°F).
- The productivity must be high, as in this example obtained by using several wires.
- The profile of the weld bead must give a smooth transition to the base plate, in order to avoid fatigue cracking problems during service.

To obtain the toughness requirements, a basic flux is the natural choice. However, in many cases a semibasic flux can give satisfactory properties. This may then be a better choice, because semibasic fluxes generally have better operating characteristics for high heat input welding.

The alloy content of the weld metal is determined by the strength and toughness levels required. The most common alloying concepts used for high heat input welds are either C-Mn, C-Mn-Mo, or C-Mn-Ti-B alloying. However, irrespective of the choice of alloying elements from the consumable, there is such a large dilution with the base plate that this has a very significant influence on the composition and microstructure of the weld metal. The dilution in this type of procedure is estimated to be around 70%, i.e., 70% of the weld metal is made up from base plate material and 30% from the welding consumables.

TABLE 6.4
Chemical Composition of All-Weld Metal Samples

Alloy	C	Si	Mn	P	S	Nb	V	Ti	Al	Mo	B
C-Mn	0.07	0.30	1.45	0.013	0.012	0.002	0.005	0.005	0.025	—	—
C-Mn-Mo	0.07	0.30	1.45	0.013	0.011	0.002	0.005	0.005	0.025	0.5	—
C-Mn-Ti-B	0.07	0.30	1.25	0.013	0.011	0.005	0.005	0.050	0.002	0.25	50

Note: All figures in wt%, except for boron, which is given in ppm of weight. The oxygen content is generally 400 ppm for a semibasic flux and 300 ppm for a basic flux. The nitrogen content is around 75 ppm.

The chemical composition of a weld metal in an all-weld metal test differs slightly from the chemical composition of the wire. This can be due to the fact that some fluxes can be alloying, e.g., in manganese, chromium, or other elements. Another factor is the creation of a gas-metal-slag equilibrium which mainly affects the carbon content. A typical all-weld metal composition is given in Table 6.4 for the three types of weld metals commonly used.

Thus, for each of the three steel types, there will be three possible compositions of the weld metal. This gives nine possible weld metal compositions, which are listed in Table 6.5, assuming a dilution of 70%.

What can be noted from Table 6.5 is the large influence of the base plate composition. The calculations made are purely arithmetic, but are in agreement with experimental results. The carbon content may be adjusted slightly by the slag-metal equilibrium, but not to such a degree that the conclusions from this exercise are violated.

The microstructure of the weld metal is determined partly by the hardenability of the alloy (mainly determined by the amounts of carbon, manganese, molybdenum, and boron) and partly by the size and type of inclusions. The toughness in turn is determined by the general microstructure, the size of the inclusion, and also the impurity element content.

A passing comment can be made about a common misunderstanding of the homogeneity of weld metal composition. It is sometimes believed that there is a gradient in chemical composition in the weld metal, due to dilution effects, so that near the fusion line there is a concentration of elements from the base plate and near the center of the weld there is a concentration of elements from the consumables. However, the mixing of elements in the weld pool is very effective due to fluid streaming in the pool, so that within a single bead no such inhomogeneities can be found. Any inhomogeneities are mainly due to segregation effects, which exist on very local levels (between solidification dendrites). One type of gradient that may occur is of course between different beads. The beads lying close to the base metal will be richer in alloying elements diluted from the base plate.

Starting with the type of particles, Mills et al.[2] found that the presence of galaxite $MnOAl_2O_3$ is highly beneficial. Although the reaction sequence in the

TABLE 6.5
Chemical Composition of Weld Metal Sample, Assuming a Dilution of 70%

Weld metal	C	Si	Mn	Ni	Ti	Al	Mo	B
X-60/C-Mn	0.07	0.15	1.47	0.26	0.012	0.025	0.08	—
X-60/C-Mn-Mo	0.07	0.15	1.47	0.26	0.012	0.025	0.23	—
X-60/Ti-B	0.07	0.15	1.40	0.26	0.026	0.018	0.16	15
Norm./C-Mn	0.14	0.30	1.45	—	0.005	0.025	—	—
Norm./C-Mn-Mo	0.14	0.30	1.45	—	0.005	0.025	0.15	—
Norm./Ti-B	0.14	0.30	1.39	—	0.019	0.018	0.075	15
TMCP/C-Mn	0.091	0.30	1.30	—	0.016	0.009	—	—
TMCP/C-Mn-Mo	0.091	0.30	1.30	—	0.016	0.009	0.15	—
TMCP/Ti-B	0.091	0.30	1.25	0.029	0.002	0.075	15	

Note: All figures are in wt%, except for boron, which is given in ppm of weight. Assuming a semibasic flux, the oxygen content of the weld metal will be about 150 ppm and about 100 ppm with a high basic flux.

weld pool for oxide inclusion formation is not known in detail, a simple model can be used, in which it is assumed that aluminum first reacts with oxygen, then titanium, and then manganese, as outlined in Section 4.3.

Assuming that the soluble aluminum content is 0.006 wt%, then Table 6.6 can be created. Here the amount of oxygen tied up in alumina is calculated, assuming that the oxygen content of the Al_2O_3 is given by 1.13 times the aluminum content. The remaining oxygen is then found by subtracting the amount tied up in alumina from the total oxygen.

With the highest aluminum content (0.025 wt%) there will be an excess of free aluminum. This has two negative consequences. First, only Al_2O_3 will form and this particle is considered to be a poor nucleant for acicular ferrite. Second, the free excess aluminum is suspected to be detrimental to the impact toughness properties.[3] The optimum aluminum content is around 0.010 wt% if the oxygen content is around 150 ppm. Then there is enough oxygen to form both Al_2O_3 and MnO, leading to a tendency to form galaxite. This, however, also requires that the titanium content is low; otherwise, titanium oxides are formed in preference to MnO and thus no galaxite is formed.

If the titanium content is high, as when a Ti-B consumable is used, then titanium oxides probably are the nucleants for acicular ferrite, instead of galaxite. The aluminum content must then be kept low (<0.005 wt%) in order to ensure maximum formation of titanium oxides. It is still unclear which titanium oxide type is actually the most effective ferrite nucleant and therefore the optimum oxygen to titanium ratio cannot be stated. It must also be considered that some titanium is tied up with nitrogen (Equation 4.4). However, TiN is also considered to be an effective nucleant, so from this viewpoint, it may not present any drawback if some of the titanium is used for nitride formation.

TABLE 6.6
Oxygen Content Tied Up in Aluminum Inclusions ($[O]_{i,Al}$)

[ΔAl]	$[O]_{i,Al}$	[ΔO]
0.019	215	—
0.012	136	14
0.003	34	116

Note: [ΔAl] is the total aluminum content less the soluble aluminum content and [ΔO] is the remaining oxygen, which can form oxides with other elements.

This also has the positive effect of removing some nitrogen from solid solution, which should improve the toughness. Thus, to ensure that the amount of acicular ferrite is maximized, it is important that the content of the microalloying elements both in the plate and in the consumable is adjusted so that particles of the correct kind can be formed and that the ratio between elements such as aluminum, titanium, oxygen, and nitrogen is kept close to the optimum value. Knowledge in this area is still rather limited and much more research is clearly needed.

The hardenability of the alloys must be adjusted to ensure that high amounts of acicular ferrite are formed. However, carbon content in excess of about 0.10 wt% is generally avoided. The microstructure of the nine weld metals from Table 6.5 has been calculated with the model of Bhadeshia et al.[4] for the welding conditions specified above and the result is shown in Figure 6.7. The large effect of the carbon content can easily be seen. However, 0.14 wt% carbon is an unusual and unrealistic value. There is no effect of molybdenum on the microstructure, which is somewhat surprising, because this element is frequently used in this kind of application. However, with the high manganese contents present here, the hardenability is still so high that the small amount of molybdenum does not influence the microstructure.

The most effective way to maximize the acicular ferrite content is by using titanium and boron. Boron prevents the formation of allotriomorphic ferrite, enhancing the possibility for formation of acicular ferrite. However, it has been found that addition of titanium is necessary. Without titanium, bainite easily forms instead of acicular ferrite. In the alloys above, the boron content is too low to achieve maximum effect. This is due to the high dilution and it is customary to have special wires that give about 100 ppm of boron in an undiluted weld metal, resulting in about 30 ppm of boron in the diluted weld metal.

The tensile properties of the weld metal can be calculated by the method of Svensson et al.[5] The values are shown in Table 6.7. In this case it is assumed

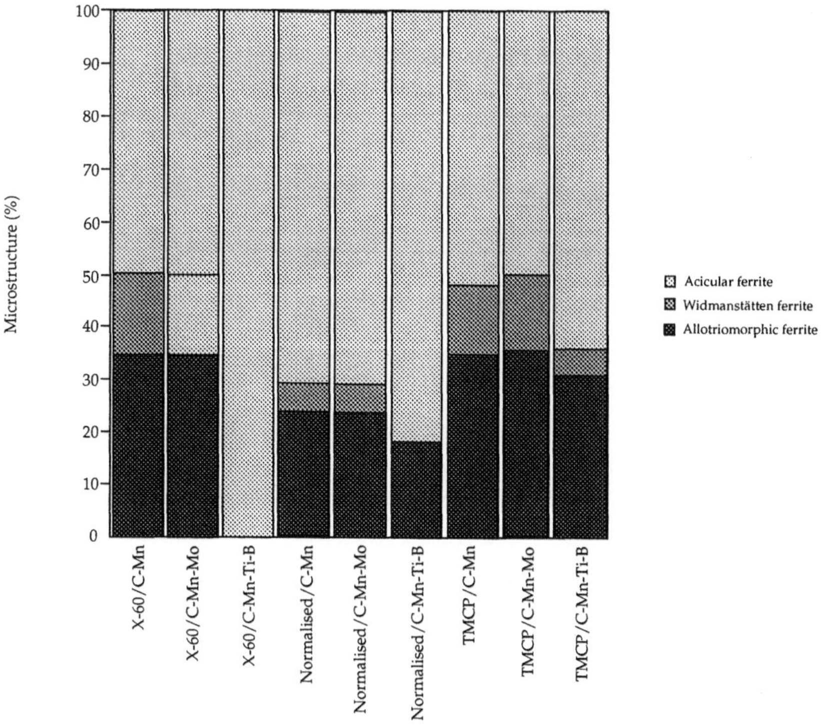

FIGURE 6.7. The microstructure of the nine weld metals from Table 6.5 as calculated using the model of Bhadeshia et al.[4]

that the testing is made in the last deposited bead. This means that only the primary structure of the weld metal will contribute to strength and not the reheated zones.

The impact properties can be assumed to be proportional to the amount of acicular ferrite, because the size of the particles is probably similar in all the weld metals. The size of the particles is mainly determined by the heat input. The arithmetic mean three-dimensional diameter can be estimated from Figure 4.15 to be about 0.6 μm.

Finally, the risk for solidification cracking must be discussed. In modern steels such as the ones used in this example, which have low impurity content, this risk is very low. However, under certain circumstances, as when the depth-to-width ratio is larger than one, the risk may be large even for these steels. The UCS parameter, calculated according to Equation 1.7, gives the values shown in Table 6.8.

The highest risk for solidification cracking exists in the weld metal in the normalized steel, mainly due to the high carbon content. No single weld metal has a UCS value above 30, where the solidification cracking risk is very large.

TABLE 6.7
Tensile Properties of Weld Metals, Calculated by the Method of Svensson et al.[5]

Weld metal	Yield strength (MPa)
X-60/C-Mn	614
X-60/C-Mn-Mo	617
X-60/Ti-B	736
Norm./C-Mn	656
Norm./C-Mn-Mo	658
Norm./Ti-B	674
TMCP/C-Mn	616
TMCP/C-Mn-Mo	616
TMCP/Ti-B	619

Note: It is assumed that the tensile specimens are extracted from the last deposited bead and that no reheated zones will influence the results.

However, values around 20 also call for a careful inspection of the welding procedure to ensure that no circumstances enforcing cracking are present. Normally, when making these kinds of welds, with one run from either side, the welds are relatively deep to ensure penetration, which increases the solidification cracking risk.

6.3.1.3. Further Considerations

Increased productivity is usually associated with increased heat input. The mechanical properties, and most notably toughness of the welded joint, are influenced significantly by this variation in heat input. Moreover, different steels respond differently to heat input variations due to differences in the transformation characteristics. This means that a variety of transformation products appear when the cooling time is varied.

A number of investigations that discuss the toughness of some different steels and weld metals as a function of heat input will be presented in this section. Dolby[6] reported a major investigation on normalized steels. The toughness was reported as crack-tip opening displacement (CTOD) values of 25-mm-thick plates. Figure 6.8 shows the toughness at –60°C (–76°F) in the coarse-grained HAZ for two different steel types, one plain C-Mn steel with 0.17C-1.1Mn (wt%) and one 0.15C-1.4Mn-Nb steel. The niobium content was fairly high, about 0.06 wt%. As can be seen, the plain C-Mn steel had a low toughness for low heat inputs (due to martensite formation), but for heat inputs between 3 and 7 kJ/mm (75 and 175 kJ/in.), the toughness was good. An extremely high heat input (25 kJ/mm, 635 kJ/in.) led to a decreasing toughness. In the other steel, the toughness was low for low heat inputs, just as for the C-Mn steel. However, increasing heat input led to an increase in toughness, but

TABLE 6.8
Value of the UCS Parameter for Nine Weld Metals

Weld metal	UCS
X-60/C-Mn	7.8
X-60/C-Mn-Mo	7.8
X-60/Ti-B	8.2
Norm./C-Mn	23.0
Norm./C-Mn-Mo	23.0
Norm./Ti-B	23.4
TMCP/C-Mn	12.2
TMCP/C-Mn-Mo	12.2
TMCP/Ti-B	12.5

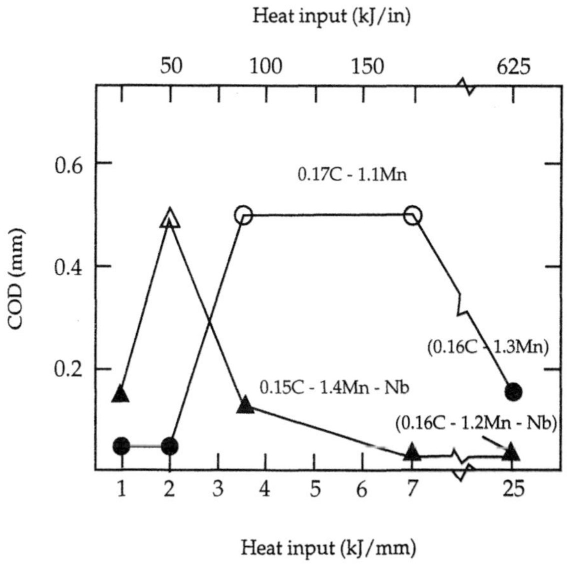

FIGURE 6.8. Toughness at –60°C in the coarse-grained HAZ for two different steel types, one with 0.17C-1.1Mn and one with 0.15C-1.4Mn-Nb. (From Dolby, R. E., *Weld. Res. Suppl.*, 58 (August), 225-s, 1979. With permission.)

only up to 2 kJ/mm (50 kJ/in.). Higher heat inputs led to a rapid decrease in toughness.

In the C-Mn steel the microstructure consisted of side plates at high heat inputs. However, these were fairly soft (the hardness was below 200 HV10), explaining the good toughness. In the C-Mn-Nb steel, niobium was assumed to promote an upper bainite-type microstructure with a somewhat higher hardness (20 to 40 HV10 harder than a nonniobium steel) and this was

TABLE 6.9
Chemical Composition (wt%) and Mechanical Properties of TMCP Steel Used in the Investigation by Nevasmaa et al.[7]

C	Si	Mn	Cu	Ni	Ti	Al	P	S
0.08	0.17	1.45	0.23	0.17	0.008	0.029	0.006	0.002

R_e (MPa)	R_m (MPa)	A_5 (%)	*CVE* (–40°C) (J)
420 (min)	620 (max)	24–28	>120 (min)

expected to yield lower toughness. Precipitation of niobium carbides and nitrides is commonly expected, but according to Dolby it was not possible to verify precipitation.

In a recent investigation, Nevasmaa et al.[7] looked at the impact toughness of the HAZ in a TMCP accelerated cooled steel. The chemical composition and mechanical properties are given in Table 6.9. The steel, 35 mm thick, was welded both with flux-cored wires and SAW. The heat input varied from 1 to 5 kJ/mm (25 to 125 kJ/in.). The result is shown in Figure 6.9. As can be seen, there is no straight relationship between heat input and toughness. However, it can be noted that, except for a few odd values, the impact toughness was above the 40-J (30-ft-lb) level, irrespective of heat input. It can further be seen that the impact toughness average values are somewhat lower for low heat inputs (1 and 2 kJ/mm, 25 and 50 kJ/in.) (although there are some exceptions) than for high heat inputs. On the other hand, the scatter in impact toughness is much higher for high heat inputs. There are two points that deviate from the general pattern. These were welded with a high heat input, but still show the features typical of low heat input (i.e., somewhat lower toughness and small scatter). In these specimens, the addition of metal powder was used to increase productivity. To obtain the same productivity without addition of metal powder, the heat input must be approximately doubled. The melting of the metal powder requires some energy, and thus the welding is effectively carried out with a lower heat input than that calculated from the welding parameters. The good impact toughness found was related to a fine-grained ferritic microstructure, partly brought about by a fine austenite grain size, due to particle-inhibited grain growth (Figure 6.10).

In the two investigations reported above, there is only one case where a drawback to high heat inputs was found with regard to HAZ toughness: when steels with high microalloying contents are used. This is true at least when the heat input is below 7 kJ/mm (175 kJ/in.).

In an investigation similar to that on the accelerated cooled TMCP steel, a direct quench and tempered (DQT) steel of higher strength (about 690 MPa,

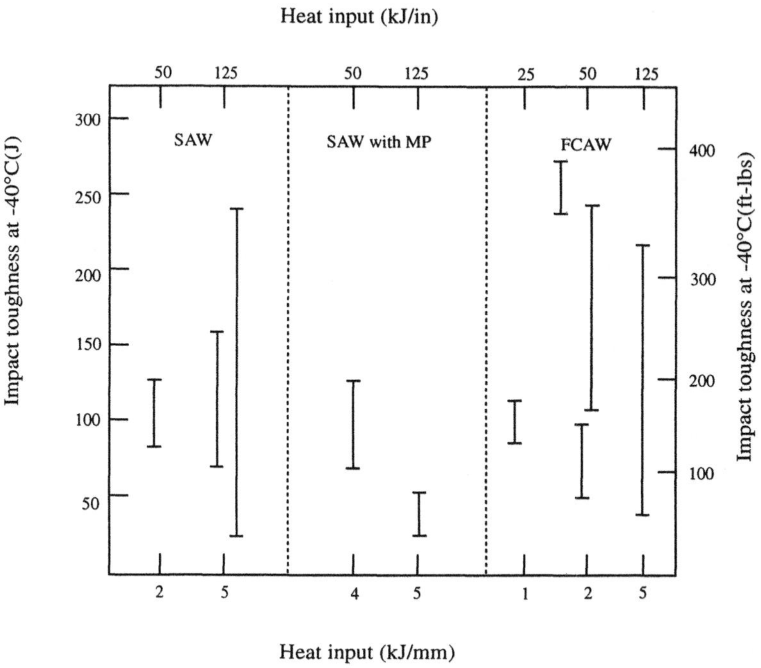

FIGURE 6.9. Toughness in the HAZ of the TMCP accelerated cooled steel as a function of heat input. (From Nevasmaa, P. et al., VTT Res. Notes 1410, VTT, Espoo, Finland, 1992. With permission.)

100,000 psi) was welded with different heat inputs.[8] The plate thickness was 40 mm and the chemical composition is given in Table 6.10. The impact toughness results are shown in Figure 6.11. The impact toughness was in general on a lower level than for the lower strength steel, which is not surprising. However, there is no trend at all in the relation between toughness and heat input, although it seems to be slightly better to use a low heat input.

Changes in productivity also affect the weld metal properties. For the cases reported above, the requirements on toughness can be met by using C-Mn-Ni-alloyed weld metals for the lower strength level, while a C-Mn-Ni-Mo-Cr-alloyed weld metal is needed to match the strength of the 690 MPa strength level. Both of these weld metals also match the toughness properties of the HAZ.

Another example where productivity requirements can affect the properties is when changing from single-wire SAW to welding with parallel wire. Figure 6.12 shows the relation between impact toughness at –60°C (–76°F) with heat input for four different welding procedures. As can be seen in Figure 6.13a to d, there is a difference in the amount of refined microstructure between the tests. With increasing heat input in the parallel wire procedures the amount of

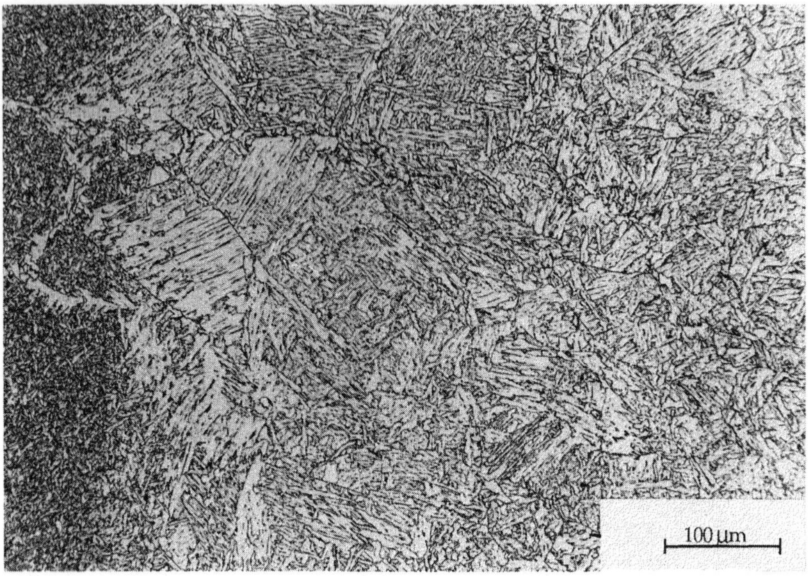

FIGURE 6.10. A fine-grained ferritic microstructure, brought about partly by a fine austenite grain size, due to particle-inhibited grain growth. (From Nevasmaa, P. et al., VTT Res. Notes 1410, VTT, Espoo, Finland, 1992. With permission.)

TABLE 6.10
Chemical Composition (wt%) and Mechanical Properties of DQT Steel Used by Nevasmaa et al.[8]

C	Si	Mn	Cu	Ni	Cr	Mo	P	S
0.10	0.28	0.91	0.22	1.00	0.49	0.27	0.009	0.002

R_e (MPa)	R_m (MPa)	A_5 (%)	*CVE* (–40°C) (J)
715 (min)	820 (max)	23–24	154 (min)

primary, unrefined microstructure increases. This is probably the most likely explanation for the variation in toughness. It should however be noted that in all procedures a very high toughness was found. The increased productivity of the parallel wire method can certainly be used with confidence.

6.3.2. MULTIPASS WELDING

6.3.2.1. Heat-Affected Zone Effects

If the same three steels used for the example above in high heat input welding are subjected to a different welding procedure (multipass welding

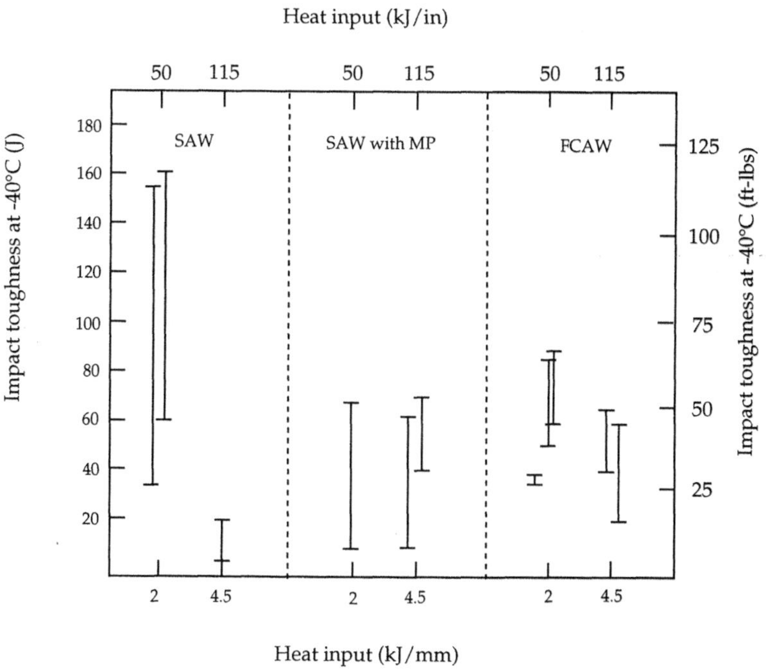

FIGURE 6.11. Impact toughness in the HAZ of a DQT steel, as a function of heat input. (From Nevasmaa, P. et al., VTT Res. Notes 1406, VTT, Espoo, Finland, 1992. With permission.)

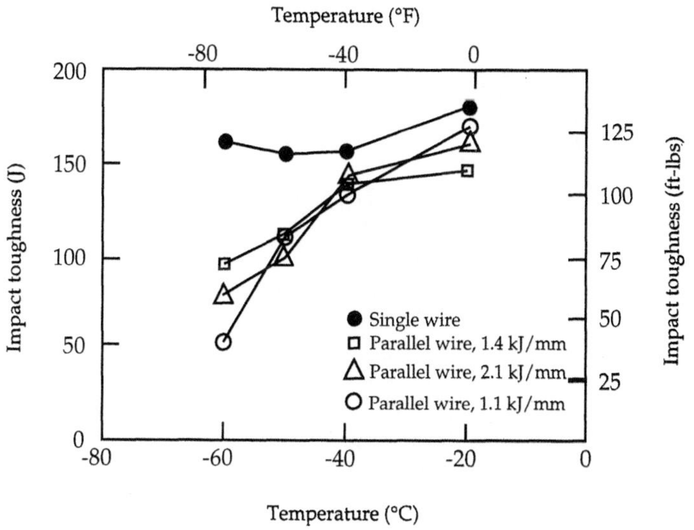

FIGURE 6.12. The relation between impact toughness at –60°C (–76°F) and heat input for four different welding procedures.

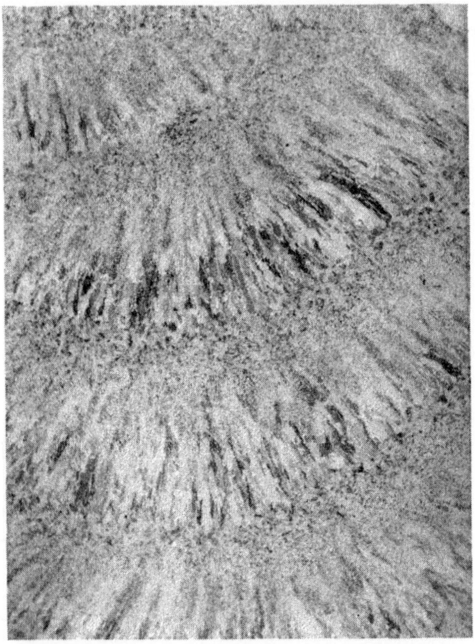

a

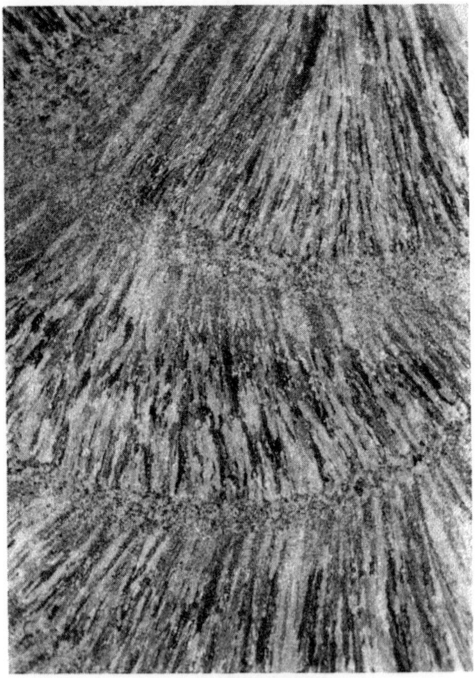

b

FIGURE 6.13. The difference in the amount of refined microstructure between four welding procedures: (a) single wire; (b) parallel wire, 1.1 kJ/mm heat input; (c) parallel wire, 1.4 kJ/mm heat input; (d) parallel wire, 2.1 kJ/mm heat input.

c

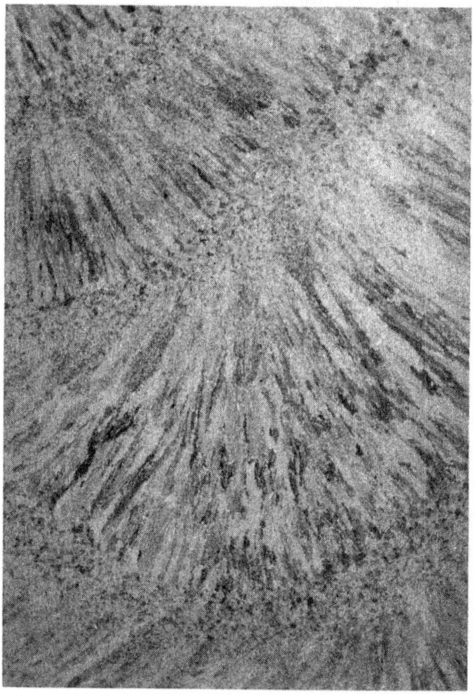

d

FIGURE 6.13 (continued)

TABLE 6.11
Cooling Times from 800 to 500°C for the GMAW Procedure, Specified in Table 6.2, but with 100°C (200°F) Initial Temperature for the Root Run in the Normalized Steel and 25°C (80°F) Otherwise

Steel	Root run	Fill run
X-60 and TMCP	3.6	7.5
Normalized	4.7	7.5

using GMAW, similar to that used in Section 6.2), the cooling times will be much shorter, especially for the root runs. In Section 6.2, the $\Delta t_{8/5}$ was found to be 6 s for the root run if a preheat temperature of 150°C (300°F) was used. From BS 5135:1984, it can be found that no preheat is necessary for either plate, provided the hydrogen content is below 5 ml/100 g weld metal. If the hydrogen content is between 5 and 10 ml/100 g weld metal, then 100°C (200°F) preheat is necessary for the root run in the normalized steel. When a heat input rate of 1.5 kJ/mm (38 kJ/in.) is used, no preheat is necessary. Thus, to determine the cooling time for this actual case, T_0 is set to 25°C (80°F) in general usage and to 100°C (200°F) for the root run in the normalized steel. The result is given in Table 6.11. In practice, the cooling times for the fill runs will be longer than those given in Table 6.11, because the interpass temperature will be higher than 25°C (80°F). Short cooling times may be found if the welding is temporarily stopped (e.g., overnight) and then restarted without any preheating.

The austenite grain growth behavior is examined using Figures 3.8 and 3.13. A grain size of 50 μm is found in the titanium steels beside the root beads at the fusion line and about 60 μm for the other passes. For the non-titanium steel the austenite grain size is about 100 μm in the root passes and about 200 μm for the filling passes. The effect of titanium on the austenite grain size is much larger for this welding procedure than for the high heat input weld. This is because during high heat input welding, the titanium particles coarsen and are less effective in restricting grain growth.

There is certainly a risk of martensite formation in the first two steels, especially near the root runs, due to the combination of short cooling times and the relatively long time taken for transformation to start. However, as seen from the TTT diagrams (Figure 6.6), the M_s temperature is higher in the lower carbon concentration steels. Any martensite formed then has a good chance of being autotempered during further cooling. Thus, near the root beads it is possible that there will be a martensitic microstructure, which is either untempered (for the normalized steel) or tempered (for the lower carbon concentration steels). For the filling passes, the cooling time is just above that needed to avoid martensite formation and no preheat is necessary. The microstructure will be of the lath type, mainly bainitic. The finer austenite grains in the titanium-alloyed steels give a finer packet size for the bainite.

The mechanical properties of the HAZ for these plate thicknesses are commonly measured both in the root and in the top. In the root region, the steels with autotempered martensite will have the best toughness. In the top region, the titanium-alloyed steel will probably have the best toughness due to the finer bainitic structure. The normalized steel will probably have the worst properties, because, first, the bainite will be quite coarse and, second, it will be hard due to the high carbon content. Toughness is, as noted previously, the most difficult property to assess. General conclusions such as those above can be drawn, but it is not possible to put more quantitative figures on the toughness. Data on toughness for procedures as above always show large scatter. However, most steels used in offshore structures, as well as the normalized steels used during the 1970s, show adequate toughness if the welding procedures were correctly designed. Occasional values of low toughness were connected to local brittle zones (LBZs) in the HAZ, a problem that still attracts interest. In the above procedures, the presence of LBZs has not been discussed, but toughness has mainly been assessed from the microstructure arising from a single pass. It must be strongly emphasized that, especially in the second welding procedure, the presence of many beads can significantly affect the toughness. If no LBZs appear, then multipass welding will generally improve the toughness.

The maximum hardness can be estimated with Suzuki's BL 70 formula. Using this (Table 6.12) it can be concluded that the requirement on 248 HV maximum hardness is very difficult to satisfy. To be able to meet this requirement, the welding procedure must be redesigned.

6.3.2.2. The Weld Metal

The microstructure and properties of the weld metal depend to some extent on the shielding gas used. Flux-cored wires having a rutile slag system are more sensitive to the choice of shielding gas than are wires with a basic slag system. For rutile-type wires, the type of shielding gas controls both the content of alloying elements (through the loss of elements) and the oxygen content, with CO_2 gas giving a higher oxygen content and larger losses of manganese and silicon. Metal-cored wires, having only a small amount of slag-forming elements in the filling, behave approximately as rutile-type wires.

To meet the strength requirement of the steels, a wire giving a weld metal yield strength of about 500 MPa should be used, because overmatching weld metal strength is required. This is commonly achieved with wires having a typical chemical composition of 0.07C-1.3Mn-0.6Si (wt%), welded with Ar/20%CO_2 gas. In basic wires, only manganese and silicon are used as deoxidizing elements, while in rutile wires there is about 0.015 wt% titanium. The aluminum level is as low as possible, about 0.002 wt%, coming mainly from the metal strip. In rutile wires alloyed with titanium and boron, the titanium concentration is around 0.04 wt%.

TABLE 6.12
Maximum Hardness Values Calculated According to Suzuki's BL 70 Formula

Steel	Root	Top
X-60	302	258
Normalized	384	341
TMCP	298	244

The composition of the weld metals in the welded joints will differ somewhat from the all-weld metal composition, due to the dilution with the base plate. In the root area, where the dilution is largest, higher contents of alloying elements are found. Because the content of the alloying elements manganese and silicon is quite similar between the plate and the weld metal, the dilution effect of these elements can be neglected. It is mainly the increased amounts of carbon that may be of concern, as this significantly influences the microstructure and hardness of the root beads. Also, the dilution of elements such as aluminum, titanium, vanadium, and niobium should be monitored.

The dilution in these types of welds is typically 25 to 50%, depending on the welding parameters. Because the welding is made semiautomatically, the welder's technique can influence the dilution. Assuming that the dilution is 40%, the root beads will have the chemical composition given in Table 6.13. As can be seen, the dilution from the base plate does not change the composition very much. The increased carbon content of the weld in the normalized steel will decrease the M_s temperature, but not affect the position of the noses in the CCT diagram. The oxygen content from a basic wire is around 450 ppm in an all-weld metal test. The aluminum diluted from the base plate will combine with about 100 ppm of oxygen. Although the oxygen content will also be diluted (to around 200 ppm), there will still be free oxygen to combine to either MnO, which can form galaxite, or to some titanium oxide. Thus, the condition for acicular ferrite formation seems fulfilled.

In the filling beads, away from the fusion boundary, the chemical composition of the weld metal is almost exactly the same as for the pure all-weld metal. The nucleation of acicular ferrite then must occur on manganese silicate particles, although these are generally believed to be less effective nuclei. It is possible that there are titanium oxides or nitrides formed as shells on these particles, aiding acicular ferrite formation, in spite of the low concentration of titanium.

The microstructure of all-weld metal basic-type wires contains appreciable amounts of acicular ferrite. It is difficult to directly compare with microstructures in weld metals from other processes, such as shielded metal arc welding (SMAW) or SAW, because the welding parameters may differ and thus the thermal conditions may vary. Even if the welding parameters were very similar,

TABLE 6.13
Chemical Composition of the Root Beads

Weld metal	C	Si	Mn	Ni	Nb	V	Al	Ti	Mo
X-60	0.07	0.40	1.37	0.15	0.006	0.002	0.011	0.002	0.048
Normalized	0.11	0.48	1.36	—	0.002	0.010	0.011	0.002	—
TMCP	0.08	0.48	1.28	—	0.010	0.002	0.002	0.008	—

the cooling conditions would still be different, because each process has its own thermal characteristics. The toughness of weld metals from flux-cored wires is determined mainly from the oxygen content. Basic-type wires, with about 450 ppm oxygen, typically have a toughness of 50 J (37 ft-lb) at –50°C (–58°F), when alloyed with 1 wt% nickel. This is somewhat lower than a weld metal from a similarly alloyed stick electrode. The difference mainly lies in the amount of oxygen, which is about 100 ppm lower in the stick electrode weld metal.

Basic wires have relatively poorer operating characteristics in positional welding than rutile wires. The rutile weld metals on the other hand have a higher oxygen content and thus lower toughness. To improve toughness, some newly developed rutile wires are alloyed with titanium and boron. The Ti-B alloying concept is common in Japanese consumables, in stick electrodes, cored wires, and in submerged arc fluxes. In other countries, this concept is rarer and is mainly used in cored wires and occasionally in SAW wires. The microstructure of such weld metals is shown in Figure 6.14, which illustrates the high proportion of acicular ferrite that is found in these weld metals. The toughness is also impressively high, about 100 J (75 ft-lb) at –40°C (–40°F), despite an oxygen content of about 600 ppm.

In these weld metals the nucleation of acicular ferrite relies on titanium oxides as nucleants. The aluminum content is kept low (below 0.002 wt%) and the nitrogen content is also very low (around 25 ppm). The chemical composition of the particles has not been investigated, but assuming that Ti_2O_3 is the effective particle and that the particles are stoichometric, 0.040 wt% titanium ties up about 400 ppm oxygen. Thus, the full effect is taken from the titanium content, but there is still a surplus of oxygen.

These wires have the disadvantage that the weld metals are sensitive to heat treatments, in that the toughness is lowered. They are therefore not recommended to be used in situations requiring stress-relieving heat treatment or hot-forming operations. Addition of nickel is frequently used to improve the toughness. Figure 6.15a shows the effect on the acicular ferrite content from the addition of nickel to a base composition of the weld metal of (wt%) 0.07C-1.3Mn-0.6Si. Figure 6.15b shows the effect of nickel on the yield strength. As can be seen, increasing nickel has a great effect on the acicular ferrite content. The toughness improvement obtained with addition of nickel thus has two

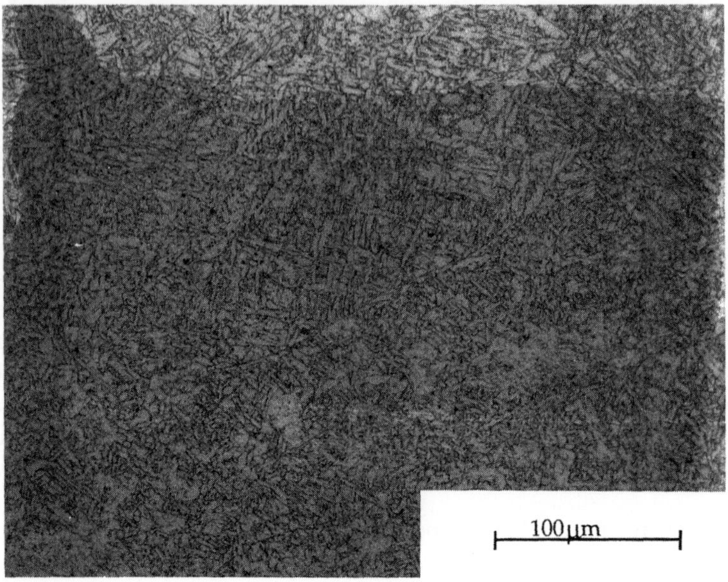

FIGURE 6.14. The microstructure of Ti-B-alloyed weld metals, consisting almost entirely of acicular ferrite.

sources: a refinement of the grain size and lowering of the stacking fault energy.

GMAW with cored wires is relatively common in the U.S. and Japan. In Europe, the use of the process is rapidly increasing. Much development is also taking place, resulting in new, better consumables. Another fascinating development in this process is the ability to closely control the drop detachment with the new synergic power sources. This will increase the possibilities of positional welding with basic-type wires, enabling improved weld metal properties.

6.4. CONTROLLED BEAD PLACEMENT

Based on the original ideas of Alberry and Jones,[9] Reed[10] developed a model to analyze the possibility of achieving complete reaustenization of underlying beads. As noted previously, reaustenitized structures usually have better mechanical properties than the as-deposited microstructure. The model was developed for SMAW. To predict the positions of the isotherms more precisely than is possible with the Rosenthal equations, Reed used the extension of the Rosenthal equations made by Ashby and Easterling.[11] They modified the equations by letting the power intensity of the heat source be distributed over a finite area and by deducting the latent heat of fusion from the arc power.

The size and shape of a bead-on-plate weld was calculated from these modified heat flow equations and from a knowledge of the volume of deposited

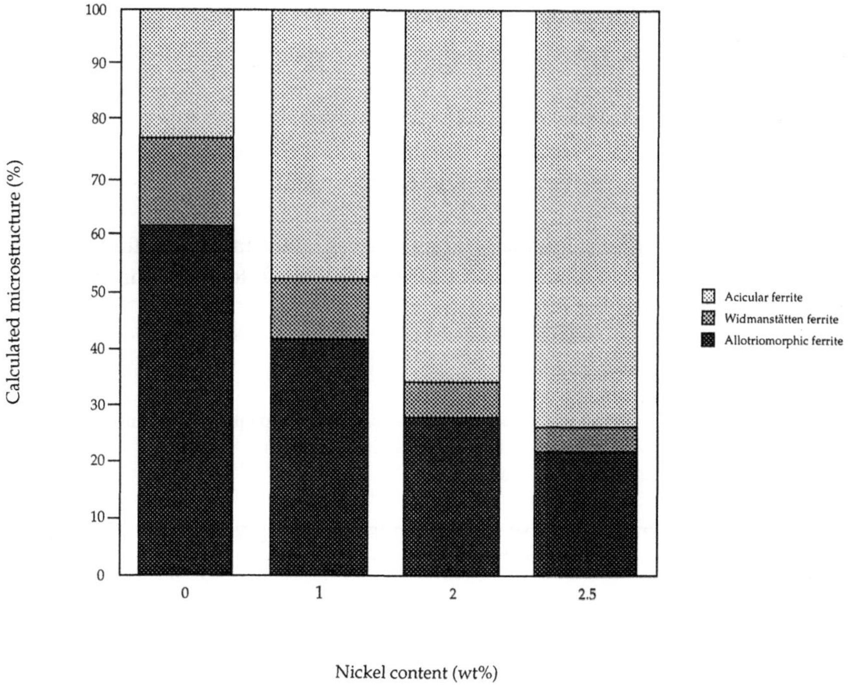

a

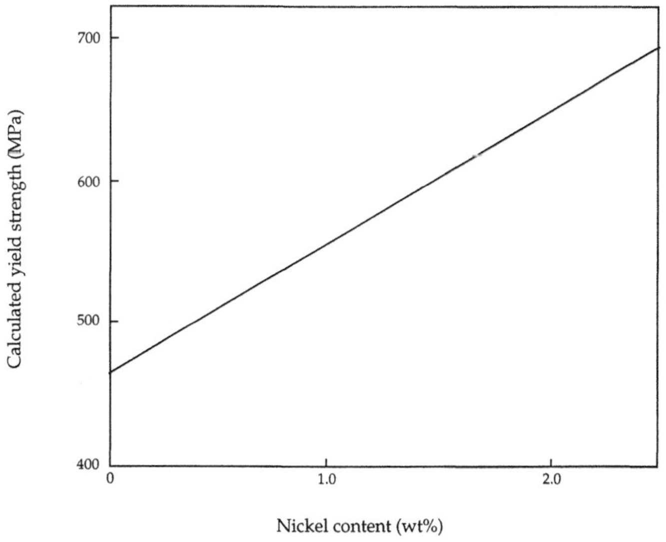

b

FIGURE 6.15. (a) The calculated changes in microstructure in flux-cored wire weld metals, from the alloying of nickel to a base composition of the weld metal of 0.07 C-1.3 Mn-0.6 Si. (b) The calculated effect of nickel on the yield strength of weld metals from flux-cored wires.

metal per unit length of weld. This volume is calculated from the electrode diameter, the efficiency, the feed speed of the electrode, and the welding speed by the relation

$$A_1 = [(\pi \text{ electrode diameter}^2)/4] \times \text{efficiency} \times (\text{feed speed})/(\text{welding speed}) \quad (6.4)$$

To determine the influence of the welding process on the microstructure of the HAZ (either in the weld metal or in the base plate), the following temperatures were used to describe the microstructure:

T_s	solidus temperature
T_{gc}	γ-grain-coarsening temperature
Ac_3	temperature where the α/γ transformation is completed on heating
Ac_1	temperature at which the α/γ begins on heating
T_t	tempering temperature

In a computer program, all these temperatures could be given different values, depending on steel type. The following parameters were analyzed by Reed:

- Electrode diameter
- Interpass temperature
- Arc current
- Feed speed
- Transformation temperature

It was previously noted by Clark[12] that the feed speed varied linearly with the arc current, as

$$\text{feed speed} = (4KI)/(\pi \rho d^2) \quad (6.5)$$

where K is a numerical constant (= 2.5 mg/As), I is the welding current, d is the diameter of the electrode, and ρ is the density of the electrode.

Plate 6* shows the effect of increasing the electrode diameter d from 3.25 mm to 6 mm, *keeping the current constant.* As expected, more beads are needed to fill the joint with a smaller rather than a larger diameter electrode. However, what is more interesting is what happens to the underlying material. With the model, the volume fraction of unreaustenitized (columnar) structure and coarse-grained structure can be calculated. Increasing the electrode diameter leads to a slight decrease in the volume fraction of the columnar structure, while the volume fraction of the coarse-grained zone remains virtually constant. In practice, higher currents are used with larger diameter electrodes, depositing larger beads, so that even fewer beads are needed to fill the joint.

* Plates 6 and 7 appear following page 84.

The effect of welding current, keeping all other variables constant, is shown in Plate 7.* Fewer weld beads are needed with higher currents, and the temperature field changes below the beads. This leads to an increase in the volume fraction of columnar structure and a decrease in the volume fraction of the coarse-grained zone. An increase in the interpass temperature moves the isotherms away from the weld bead, leading to a larger degree of reaustenitization, as shown in Plate 8.*

The computer model can now be used to find the optimum combination of variables in the welding procedure, so that as complete reaustenitization as possible is obtained. To obtain as high a proportion of reaustenitized material as possible, a low Ac_3 temperature is beneficial, as shown in Plate 9.* Depositing very thin beads by having a very low electrode feed speed (Plate 10)* also gives large amounts of reaustenitized material. However, it must be realized that this procedure will result in lower productivity if the welding cannot be done at very high speeds.

To summarize, it is possible to analyze with this method the influence of various variables on the weld metal and HAZ structure in multipass welds. However, these ideas are still in the beginning of their development and there is much additional research and correlations with actual welds that must be made to be able to fully utilize the method.

REFERENCES

1. **Bhadeshia, H. K. D. H.,** Thermodynamic analysis of isothermal transformation diagrams, *Met. Sci.,* 16, 159, 1982.
2. **Mills, A. R., Thewlis, G., and Whiteman, J. A.,** Nature of inclusions in steel weld metals and their influence on formation of acicular ferrite, *Mater. Sci. Technol.,* 3(December), 1051, 1987.
3. **Terashima, H. and Hart, P. H. M.,** Effect of aluminum on C-Mn steel submerged arc weld metal properties, *Weld. J.,* 63(June), 173 s, 1984.
4. **Bhadeshia, H. K. D. H., Svensson, L.-E., and Gretoft, B.,** A model for the development of microstructure in low-alloy steel (Fe-Mn-Si-C) weld deposits, *Acta Metall.,* 33, 1271, 1985.
5. **Svensson, L.-E., Gretoft, B., Sugden, A. A. B., and Bhadeshia, H. K. D. H.,** Computer-aided design of electrodes for arc welding processes. II., in *Proc. Int. Conf. Computer Technology in Welding II,* The Welding Institute, Abington, U.K., 1988, paper 24.
6. **Dolby, R. E.,** HAZ toughness of structural and pressure vessel steels — improvement and prediction, *Weld. J.,* 58(August), 225-s, 1979.
7. **Nevasmaa, P., Cederberg, M., and Vilpas, M.,** Weldability of Accelerated-Cooled (AcC) High Strength TMCP Steel HT50, VTT Res. Notes 1410, VTT, Espoo, Finland, 1992.
8. **Nevasmaa, P., Cederberg, M., and Vilpas, M.,** Weldability of Direct-Quenched and Tempered (DQT) High Strength Steel HT80, VTT Res. Notes 1406, VTT, Espoo, Finland, 1992.
9. **Alberry, P. J. and Jones, W. K. C.,** Computer model for prediction of heat-affected zone microstructures in multipass weldments, *Met. Technol.,* 9, 419, 1982.

* Plates 8 to 10 appear following page 84.

10. **Reed, R. C.,** The Characterisation and Modelling of Multipass Steel Weld Heat-Affected Zones, Ph.D. thesis, University of Cambridge, Cambridge, U.K., 1990, chap. 3.
11. **Ashby, M. F. and Easterling, K. E.,** The transformation hardening of steel surfaces by laser beams. I. Hypo-eutectoid steels, *Acta Metall.*, 32, 1935, 1984.
12. **Clark, J. N.,** Manual metal arc weld modelling. I. The effect of process parameters on dimensions of weld beads, *Mater. Sci. Technol.*, 1, 1069, 1985.

INDEX

C

D

H

I

J

K

L

W

Y

Z

For Product Safety Concerns and Information please contact our EU representative GPSR@taylorandfrancis.com Taylor & Francis Verlag GmbH, Kaufingerstraße 24, 80331 München, Germany

Printed and bound by CPI Group (UK) Ltd, Croydon, CR0 4YY
08/05/2025
01864491-0001